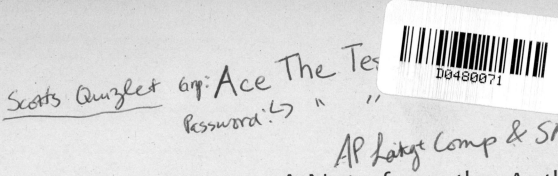

A Note from the Author

This book has been designed for you to use in preparation for the Advanced Placement English Language and Composition Exam. In it you will find information about the AP Exam, important test-preparation advice, strategies on approaching multiple-choice questions, advice and examples for dealing with the essay questions, and a comprehensive list of terminology typically used on the test. Finally, two practice exams are included for you to hone your skills. Responses are discussed, so that you can better understand why some responses are wrong, some are almost right, and others are the only possible correct responses.

Those of you who have completed an Advanced Placement course in English Language and Composition are to be congratulated. Not only have you conquered a challenging curriculum as well as completed many impressive reading and writing assignments, you have learned how to manage your time and assume demanding responsibility and self-discipline. Now you have only to prepare for the AP Exam. I hope that this book will help you with this last step in an arduous but rewarding adventure.

Best wishes,

Denise Pivarnik-Nova

RELATED TITLES

AP Biology

AP Calculus AB & BC

AP Chemistry

AP English Literature and Composition

AP Macroeconomics/Microeconomics

AP Physics B & C

AP Psychology

AP Statistics

AP U.S. History

AP U.S. Government & Politics

AP World History

SAT Subject Test: Biology

SAT Subject Test: Chemistry

SAT Subject Test: Literature

SAT Subject Test: Mathematics Level 1

SAT Subject Test: Mathematics Level 2

SAT Subject Test: Physics

SAT Subject Test: Spanish

SAT Subject Test: U.S. History

SAT Subject Test: World History

Test Prep and Admissions

AP® English Language & Composition

2006 Edition

Denise Pivarnik-Nova

Simon & Schuster

NEW YORK · LONDON · SYDNEY · TORONTO

Kaplan Publishing
Published by SIMON & SCHUSTER
Rockefeller Center
1230 Avenue of the Americas
New York, NY 10020

Material used in this book was adapted from the following:

"Libido for the Ugly," from *Prejudices* by H.L. Mencken. Copyright © 1927. Reprinted by permission of Ross & Perry, Inc.

Reprinted courtesy of SPORTS ILLUSTRATED: "Let Us Pray/Play" by Rick Reilly, April 26, 2004. Copyright © 2004. Time Inc. All rights reserved.

"Skin," from *Mortal Lessons: Notes on the Art of Surgery* by Richard Selzer. Copyright © 1974, 1975, 1976, 1987 by Richard Selzer. Reprinted by permission of Georges Borchardt, Inc. on behalf of the author.

"Letter of Sandy Kempner," from *Dear America: Letters Home from Vietnam*, ed. Bernard Edelman. Copyright © 1985 by The New York Vietnam Veterans Memorial Commission. Reprinted by permission.

Living Out Loud by Anna Quindlen. Copyright © 1988 by Anna Quindlen. Reprinted by permission of Random House.

"At the Dam," from *The White Album* by Joan Didion. Copyright © 1979 Joan Didion. Reprinted by permission of Farrar, Straus & Giroux, LLC.

"The Death of a Moth" from *The Death of a Moth and Other Essays* by Virginia Woolf. Copyright © 1927. Reprinted by permission of Harcourt, Brace & Company.

Contributing Editor: Jon Zeitlin
Editorial Director: Jennifer Farthing
Project Editor: Eileen McDonnell
Production Manager: Michael Shevlin
Content Manager: Patrick Kennedy
Page Layout: India Amos
Cover Design: Mark Weaver

Manufactured in the United States of America.
Published simultaneously in Canada.

10 9 8 7 6 5 4 3 2
January 2006

ISBN-13: 978-0-7432-6581-2
ISBN-10:   0-7432-6581-5

For information regarding special discounts for bulk purchases, please contact Simon & Schuster Special Sales at 1-800-456-6798 or business@simonandschuster.com.

Table of Contents

[Handwritten annotations: "H, Q, C" and "H, Q C*" beside Chapters 1 and 2; "SKIM & Return" beside Countdown to the Test; "TAKE This! By End of Break" beside Diagnostic Test; "Highlight, Question, Comment" at bottom of page]*

About the Author

Denise Pivarnik-Nova is an AP English Teacher and an independent consultant for the Midwest Office of the College Board in AP English and English Vertical Teams (pre-AP). She has been an AP English Exam reader for sixteen years, and has also taught freshman literature and composition at the college level. In addition to working on College Board publications and other AP prep materials, Denise is a teacher and College Advisor at Breck School in Golden Valley, Minnesota. Every summer she facilitates AP English teacher workshops throughout the Midwest.

KAPLAN
Test Prep and Admissions

TEACHERS AND STUDENTS—GO ONLINE!

FOR TEACHERS ONLY:
HOW TO USE THIS BOOK IN YOUR CLASSROOM

simonsaysteach.com

Visit our resource area for teachers. We've provided ideas about how this book can be used effectively in and outside of your AP classroom. Easy to implement, these tips are designed to complement your curriculum plans and help you create a classroom full of high-scoring students.

FOR STUDENTS AND TEACHERS

kaptest.com/publishing

The material in this book is up-to-date at the time of publication, but the College Board may have instituted changes in the test since that date. Be sure to carefully read the materials you receive when you register for the test. If there are any important late-breaking developments—or any changes or corrections to the Kaplan test preparation materials in this book—we will post that information online at kaptest.com/publishing.

FEEDBACK AND COMMENTS

kaplansurveys.com/books

If you have comments and suggestions about this book, we invite you to fill out our online survey form at kaplansurveys.com/books. Your feedback is extremely helpful as we continue to develop high-quality resources to meet your needs.

Kaplan Panel of AP Experts

Congratulations—you have chosen Kaplan to help you get a top score on your AP exam.

Kaplan understands your goals, and what you're up against—achieving college credit and conquering a tough test—while participating in everything else that high school has to offer.

You expect realistic practice, authoritative advice, and accurate, up-to-the-minute information on the test. And that's exactly what you'll find in this book, as well as every other in the AP series. To help you (and us!) reach these goals, we have sought out leaders in the AP community. Allow us to introduce our experts:

AP English Language & Composition Experts

NATALIE GOLDBERG recently retired from St. Ignatius College Prep in Chicago, IL, where she helped develop a program to prepare juniors for the AP English Language and Composition exam and taught AP English Literature. She was a reader for the AP English Language and Composition exam for 6 years, and has been a consultant with the Midwest Region of the College Board since 1997.

RONALD SUDOL has been a reader of AP English Language and Composition for 20 years and a workshop consultant for 12. He is Professor of Rhetoric at Oakland University in MI, where he is also Acting Dean of the College of Arts and Sciences.

AP Biology Experts

Larry Calabrese has taught biology for 36 years, and AP Biology for 19 years at Palos Verdes Peninsula High School in CA. He also teaches Anatomy and Physiology at Los Angeles Harbor College in Wilmington, CA. He has been an AP Biology reader since 1986, and a table leader since 1993. For the past 10 years, he has taught College Board workshops.

Cheryl G. Callahan has been teaching biology for over 20 years, first at the college level and now at the high school level at Savannah Country Day School, Savannah, GA. She has been an AP Biology reader and table leader since 1993. She also moderates the AP Biology Electronic Discussion Group.

AP Calculus Expert

William Fox has been teaching calculus at the university level for over 20 years. He has been at Francis Marion University in Florence, SC since 1998. He has been a reader and table leader for the AP Calculus AB and BC exams since 1992.

AP Chemistry Experts

Lenore Hoyt teaches chemistry at Idaho State University. She has done post-doctoral studies at Yale University, and holds a Ph.D. from University of Tennessee. She has been a reader for the AP Chemistry exam for 5 years.

Lisa Zuraw has been a professor in the Chemistry Department at The Citadel in Charleston, SC for 12 years. She has served as a faculty reader for the AP Chemistry exam as well as a member of the AP Chemistry Test Development Committee.

AP English Literature & Composition Experts

Mitchell S. Billings has taught for 35 years and began the AP program at Catholic High School in Baton Rouge, LA 12 years ago. He has been an Endorsed College Board Consultant for 12 years. He has also been a reader for the AP exam for 10 years, and for the Alternate AP exam for 2 years.

William H. Pell has taught AP English for the past 20 years, and chairs the Language Arts Department at Spartanburg High School in Spartanburg, SC. He has been an adjunct instructor of English at the University of South Carolina Upstate, and has been active in many programs for the College Board, including the reading, workshops, institutes, conferences, and vertical teams.

AP Macroeconomics/Microeconomics Experts

Linda M. Manning is a visiting professor and researcher in residence at the University of Ottawa in Ontario, Canada. She has worked with the AP Economics Program and the Educational Testing Service as a faculty consultant for almost 15 years, and served on the test development committee from 1997–2000.

Bill McCormick has been teaching AP Economics at Spring Valley High School and Richland Northeast High School in Columbia, SC for the past 26 years. He has served as a reader of AP Macroeconomics and Microeconomics exams for the past 8 years.

Peggy Pride has taught AP Economics at St. Louis University High School in St. Louis, MO for 15 years. She served for 5 years on the AP Economics Test Development Committee, and was the primary author for the new AP Economics Teacher's Guide published by College Board in the spring of 2005.

AP Physics B & C Experts

Jeff Funkhouser has taught high school physics since 1988, and since 2001 has taught AP Physics B and C at Northwest High School in Haslet, TX. He has been a reader and table leader for the AP Physics B & C exams for the past 3 years.

Martin Kirby has taught AP Physics B and tutored students for Physics C at Hart High School in Newhall, CA for the last 18 years. He has been a reader for the AP Physics B & C exams and a workshop presenter for the College Board for the past 10 years.

AP Psychology Experts

Ruth Ault has taught psychology for the past 26 years at Davidson College in Davidson, NC. She was a reader for the AP Psychology exam from 1998–2001 and has been a table leader since 2001.

Nancy Homb has taught AP Psychology for the past 7 years at Cypress Falls High School in Houston, TX. She has been a reader for the AP Psychology exam since 2000, and began consulting for the College Board in 2005.

AP Statistics Experts

Lee Kucera has been teaching Statistics at Capistrano Valley High School in Mission Viejo, CA for 12 years, where she has been a teacher for 26 years. Lee has also been a reader for the AP Statistics exam since its inception in 1997.

Mary Mortlock has been teaching statistics since 1996, beginning at Thomas Jefferson High School for Science & Technology in Alexandria, VA, and continuing on to her current position at Cal Poly State University, CA, where she has taught since 2001. Mary has also been a reader for the AP Statistics exam since 2000.

AP U.S. Government & Politics Expert

Chuck Brownson teaches AP U.S. Government & Politics and AP Economics at Stephen F. Austin High School in Sugar Land, TX. He is currently a graduate student working on his Master's Degree in Political Science at the University of Houston. He has been teaching AP U.S. Government & Politics and AP Economics classes for 2 years.

AP U.S. History Experts

Steven Mercado has taught AP U.S. History and AP European History at Chaffey High School in Ontario, CA for the past 12 years. He has also served as a reader for the AP U.S. History exam, and as a reader and table leader for the AP European History exam.

Diane Vecchio has taught in the History Department at Furman University in Greenville, SC since 1996. She has been Chief Faculty Consultant for the AP U.S. History exam for the past four years, and also served as a member of the AP U.S. History Test Development Committee.

AP World History Expert

Jay Harmon has taught world history for the past 22 years at Catholic High School in Baton Rouge, LA. He has been a table leader for the AP World History exam since 2002, and also serves on the test development committee.

| PART ONE |

The Basics

Chapter 1: Inside the AP English Language and Composition Exam

- An overview of the test structure
- How the exam is scored
- Getting your grades
- Registration and fees
- Additional resources and information

AN OVERVIEW OF THE TEST STRUCTURE

The Advanced Placement English Language and Composition exam is a three-hour exam, designed yearly by the AP Test Development Committee in English. The exam is an opportunity for you to demonstrate that you have mastered skills equivalent to those typically found in introductory college composition classes. There are two sections:

Section I	52–58 multiple-choice questions		1 hour
Section II	3 essay responses		2 hours
		Total Length	3 hours

In Section I, you will be presented with four or five passages—mostly from nonfiction, occasionally from fiction. Each piece will be followed by 12 to 15 questions. If the test has five passages, the pieces are shorter with fewer questions than those with only four passages.

The multiple-choice section contains skills questions that test your ability to analyze passages critically as well as rhetorically—for style, organization, purpose, and effect. There are also a few fact questions based upon the specific selection that is given. Generally, these questions increase in difficulty as you progress through each passage, but that is not an absolute.

Each multiple-choice question has five possible answers. These questions are scored by the Educational Testing Service (ETS) and standardized to national norms. There is a 25-percent penalty for wrong answers, to discourage blind guessing. You can find more information about the multiple-choice questions in Chapter 5.

Section II consists of three essay questions; some are prose analysis, others have to do with rhetoric and argumentation. The prose is generally, but not always, nonfiction. Sometimes there is a double passage, requiring you to compare and contrast two pieces based on their stylistic and rhetorical development. The argument prompt might be an opinion already written, and you must analyze it based on the tasks given in the prompt. However, you might also have to develop an argument of your own on a specific topic, often derived from a quotation. Recent tests have included an argumentative prompt that requires students to explain different sides of a concept, to synthesize information, and then to develop a stance of their own. The prompt or question for each essay will specify aspects of a passage that you are to explore. You can find more information about this section, including its evolution, in Chapter 6.

HOW THE EXAM IS SCORED

Essays are scored by AP Readers, who come together each June to assess the essay responses. The multiple-choice section makes up 45 percent of your final score, and 55 percent depends on your performance on the essays. All AP Exams are rated on a scale of 1 to 5, with 5 being the highest:

5 Extremely well qualified

4 Well qualified

3 Qualified

2 Possibly qualified

1 No recommendation

GETTING YOUR GRADES

You can obtain your AP grade report in July. When you take your exam you can designate which colleges you would like to receive your grade. If you are unsure at the time you take the exam, then you may contact AP Services and have them forward your grade when you are closer to making your college decision.

REGISTRATION AND FEES

Registration for taking the exam begins in March of the year you are taking it. If you are not sure, your AP teacher, AP Coordinator, and/or your school guidance counselor can help you. If your school does not administer the exam, you can contact AP services for a listing of schools in your area that do.

As of this printing, the fee for each AP exam is about $82.00. The College Board offers a $22.00 credit to students who qualify for free or reduced lunch. If you register and pay for an exam and then do not take it, only some of your money will be refunded. If an exam is ordered late, there is an additional $20.00 late fee. Your school or AP Services can give you this information. If you are fortunate, you may live in a state that partially or fully reimburses test fees to students. Again, your teacher, AP Coordinator, or Guidance Counselor should have this information.

ADDITIONAL RESOURCES

For more information on the AP Program and the English Language and Composition Exam, contact:

AP Services

P.O. Box 6671

Princeton, NJ 08541–6671

Phone: (609) 771–7300 or (877) 274–6474

Email: apexgrams@info.collegeboard.org

Website: www.collegeboard.com/student/testing/ap/about.html

Chapter 2: **Strategies for Success: It's Not Always How Much You Know**

- How to use this book
- What the test requires
- How to approach the multiple-choice questions
- How to approach the essay questions
- Take Control: How to Approach the Test as a Whole
- Handling Stress
- Countdown to the Test

HOW TO USE THIS BOOK

You should be proud of yourself for deciding to take the AP English Language and Composition Exam. If you took AP English Language and Composition in high school, or if you have a good foundation in rhetorical analysis, a broad reading background, and strong composition skills, taking the exam can help you earn college credit and/or placement into advanced coursework. Think of the money and time you can save! It can also improve your chances of acceptance to competitive schools, since colleges know that AP students are better prepared for the demands of college courses.

As you work your way through the chapters, you will discover precisely what knowledge and skills you'll need in order to do your very best on the AP English Language and Composition exam. You will learn the most effective way to tackle each type of question, and you'll reinforce your studies with lots of practice questions.

In the following pages you will find information about the format of the exam, test-taking strategies, and an extensive review of essential topics. Various sections include relevant review questions. These will help you to identify your strengths and weaknesses and help you to establish a plan for preparing for the exam. Also included are a full-length diagnostic test and two practice tests, with answers and explanations following each.

With Kaplan's proven test-taking strategies, dozens of practice questions, a review of rhetorical analysis and stylistic terms, and guidelines for writing your essay responses, you will be able to take the exam with confidence.

Cramming = Failure

months

If possible, work your way through this book bit by bit over the course of several weeks. Cramming the week before the test is NOT a good idea; you probably would absorb little information; that approach is bound to make you more anxious.

The first thing you need to do is find out what is on the AP English Language and Composition exam. In the next chapter of this book, the overall test structure and a brief overview of its scoring is presented. This book provides you with background information about the test, and it gives you the most effective test strategies to help you score your best.

VocAB helps
4x
— AP, SAT sub,
SAT, HS GPA,
College, Career,
Parties / Life

No doubt you have a lot more interesting things to do than go through this study guide. Nevertheless, make a commitment, just until the test, to give yourself every opportunity to improve your test score. This book will help you focus on language and composition. It provides the key terminology you need to understand both multiple-choice passages and essay prompts.

The different types of prose you might encounter on the exam are discussed in this book-as well as guidelines for successful multiple-choice testing and essay construction.

Don't fight what is here. Bite the bullet and move forward. It's not that much more time before your test date.

WHAT THE TEST REQUIRES

Although the AP Language and Composition exam is not a test that one passes or fails, generally a 3 or higher on the 5-point scale is necessary to receive advanced placement, credit, or both from the college of your choice. Many states such as Minnesota, Texas, and Wisconsin post online or offer in hard copy (usually from their Department of Education) the AP test score requirements for the various colleges and universities within their state. This will vary from state to state, just as score requirements vary from college to college.

The best way to find out what the test requires is to take the AP Diagnostic Exam. This includes detailed explanations for each question. There are sample student responses for each essay question and a commentary from an "AP Reader" who will tell you why the response received the score it did. Use the scoring guides provided and these commentaries to get a sense of your own strengths and weaknesses.

The best way to use the practice tests is to take them under test-like conditions. Don't just drop in and do a random question here and there. Use these tests to gain experience with the complete testing experience, including pacing and endurance. You may do these tests at any time. You do not necessarily have to save them all until after you have read the whole book. You should, however, try to reserve one of the practices until near time for the exam itself. That will give you the best experience simulating the actual exam and its time constraints.

Attitude = Success or Failure

If you have at least looked at the Diagnostic Test, you will see that the AP Language and Composition Exam is a unique test. It does not expect you to have memorized specific authors and their works. Instead, it tests your critical and analytical thinking skills; it asks you to understand the ways writers use language to provide both meaning and pleasure for their readers; it requires you to apply concepts and terms to any piece of writing presented, and most important, it necessitates your translating some of this information into multiple-choice selections and written responses. These multiple-choice questions and written responses ask you to make careful observations of textual detail, establish connections among their characteristics, and draw from your observations a series of associations and inferences that lead to a meaningful and interpretive conclusion about a passage of writing.

The more familiar you become with the test as a whole, the better (and more comfortably) you will perform. Your teacher has probably given you bits and pieces of the exam, but due to the usual constraints of a school day's time schedule, often students do not have the opportunity to sit down and take an entire exam. Use the Diagnostic and practice tests for practice. Go to the College Board AP website, or ask your AP English teacher for additional exposure to exams.

After you have experienced taking the entire exam in one sitting (with a 10- or 15-minute break between the multiple-choice and essay sections) you will have a better handle on the test. Use this book to study what types of questions may be on the exam, but also spend time studying the directions and format of the exam.

HOW TO APPROACH THE MULTIPLE-CHOICE SECTION

The following are must-know hints that will help you tackle the multiple-choice section. We will elaborate on them throughout the book.

Read Actively

You cannot be passive when reading the passages or the questions in the multiple-choice section. Read carefully but quickly, and mark any important words and points. Underline key words and phrases in the question. This will help you to focus on just what it is you are looking for in the passage. Be sure to read all the answer choices. Sometimes more than one response is correct, but only one will be the _best_ response.

Some people find it helpful to skim the questions before they read the passage. Although this takes more time, these people find that they are better able to focus when they read the passage. If this sounds do-able for you, try it as you are practicing before the test.

Specific Line or Word References

Occasionally a question will direct you to a particular line or even a specific word within the passage. Find the location, but be ready to read a few lines before and after the reference to understand the context. Rarely can you go right to a word and grasp the answer to the question.

Critical Words

Read the instructions carefully, paying particular attention to critical words such as *only*, *except*, *always*, *not*, *never*, *best*.

Students often find the most difficult multiple-choice questions to be the ones that ask for "all of the following EXCEPT." This is understandable, for you are used to looking for one correct response among other wrong answers. This is how most multiple-choice questions are set up. In EXCEPT questions, however, all but one of the responses are correct. Pay particular attention to these when you take the Diagnostic and practice tests.

Put Your Pride Aside

Easy questions are worth just as much as more difficult ones. To maximize your score, you need to answer as many questions correctly as possible. Generally speaking, the easier questions are at the beginning of a series of questions following a passage. However, what one person thinks is an easy question might really stump the next person. Do not get too concerned with order of difficulty. Just answer what you can and move on.

How Many Passages?

The 60-minute time limit includes reading and understanding four or five passages as well as answering the questions that follow. When you open the multiple-choice section, immediately check the number of passages. If it is four, estimate an average of about 15 minutes for each passage. If it contains five passages, estimate about 12 minutes. Also, with four passages the test will have more questions on each passage than it will with five passages.

Don't be too rigid about these timing rules. Some passages will be harder than others. This is often a very individual judgment. A lot of it has to do with interest in the topic or even the possibility of prior knowledge about the topic of the passage.

You can even read a passage out of order and answer its questions before returning to what you have skipped. This can get tricky, however, and you *must* be aware of the number of the question and where you are on the scoring grid.

Predict an Answer

Before you look at the possible responses, try to think of the answer on your own. That will help you narrow down your choice. It will also help you avoid the seductions of wrong answers that "seem" right at first glance, a favorite trap of the test makers.

To Guess or Not to Guess; Process of Elimination (POE)

Guess intelligently and with caution. Random guessing will not help your score, and it may very well hurt you. You lose a quarter of a point for each wrong answer, but no deduction is made for blank answers.

As your read through the possible responses, cross off the ones you know are wrong, being sure to read every possible answer before you make your selection. Once again, look out for words like EXCEPT or *never* in the question stem.

If you are able to eliminate at least one wrong answer, though make an educated guess. The more wrong answers you can eliminate the better. Remember, with the penalty for wrong answers, you want the odds to be one of three, or better yet, one of two. Only guess if you can narrow the "guess factor."

Grid Carefully and Cleanly

You will need a No. 2 pencil to fill in the answer sheet for the multiple-choice section of the exam. Bring several sharpened pencils. Your test site may not provide a pencil sharpener. Be sure to erase changes thoroughly and do not allow any stray marks to appear on your answer sheet.

Frequently check to make sure that the number of the question on your answer sheet corresponds to the number of the question in your exam booklet. It is easy to get out of sequence if you skip a question. Put a large, easy-to-see mark in your test booklet (not on your answer sheet) when you skip a question. If there is time left after you finish that section of questions, then you should return to any skipped questions and think about them again. Who knows, you may see things differently after you've been away for them for a few minutes.

Be Careful with the Answer Grid

We cannot stress this enough: 45 percent of your score is based on the multiple-choice answers you select on your answer grid. If you know the right answer but mis-grid, you'll receive a low score. So be careful! Don't disdain the process of filling in the "little bubbles" on the grid. Sure, it's mindless, but under time pressure it is easy to lose control and make mistakes.

Develop a disciplined strategy for filling in the answer grid. Some students find that it's smart to grid the answers in groups rather than one question at a time. As you figure out each question, circle your answer choice in the test booklet. Transfer those answers to the answer grid in groups of five or more (until you get close to the end of the section; then you must start gridding answers one by one). Gridding in groups cuts down on errors, because you can focus on this one task and do it correctly. It also saves time you'd otherwise spend moving papers around, finding your place, redirecting your mind. Answering AP questions takes deep, hard thinking. Filling out answer grids is easy, but you have to be careful, especially if you do a lot of skipping around. Shifting between "hard thinking" and "careful bookkeeping" takes time and effort.

This may not be how you are used to taking tests. If you are not sure of this batching of answers then try your way—probably recording your answer one at a time after each question. Practice both ways and choose what works best for you.

Don't Sweat It

Never agonize for too long over any one multiple-choice question. If you are not sure, circle the question clearly in the test booklet so that you can find it readily after you have completed the other questions. Be sure to leave that number unmarked on the answer sheet. You may very likely have time to return to the question before the 60 minutes are up.

HOW TO APPROACH THE ESSAY QUESTIONS

Here's what you need to know and do to succeed on the essay portion of the test.

What Does the Question Ask?

Before you begin writing, read and decode the essay prompt carefully. What is it asking? Is there more than one part to the question? Usually there is. Then read the passage and then reread the prompt to assure that that you respond to all tasks. In about 40-minutes (average for 3 essays in 2 hours), you should study the problem, identify the focus of the question, read the selection, reread the prompt, make a plan, and start writing within seven to ten minutes. If you are confused about how to start, restate the topic as it is addressed in the question and start writing.

Most AP essay questions ask you to analyze on a two-level system: what did the author do (in terms of main idea, central attitude, or basic response evoked from the reader) and how did he or she do it (examining such elements as imagery, figurative language, diction, syntax, structure, tone, style)? Brainstorm and plan quickly by jotting notes in the test booklet.

Read, Read, and Read Again

Read the prompt; read the passage; read the prompt again. Make sure you know what you are supposed to do. Often students will read the prompt and then the passage and jump right into the writing. This is a good way to overlook a particular angle of the prompt you might not have noticed upon the first reading. Read, read, and read again. If all of this sounds repetitive, it is. Repetition leads to remembering.

Choose the Easiest Question First

You do *not* have to answer the essays in the order in which they appear. When you open your essay test packet, quickly scan the three choices and begin responding to the question for which you seem to have the most ready response. Beginning with the "easiest" question will help give you confidence and reduce your stress. You are asked to put your responses on pages that are clearly marked with 1, 2, or 3 across the top of the answer booklet. Let's face it—if a reader cannot readily identify what question you are answering by what you have said, then you have a real problem.

Read Critically

When you read the prompt and the essay, do so with your pen in your hand, ready to underline, circle, and make notations. Mark the prompt carefully, identifying the task it presents and what it tells you to consider while fulfilling each task.

For instance, a prompt may ask you to identify the narrator's attitude through his or her use of stylistic devices and rhetorical structure. When you read the passage itself—whether it be a short piece requiring your reaction or a longer passage requiring analysis—annotate and make notes as you read, looking especially for support that is most relevant to the prompt. This becomes your prewriting.

Many prompts ask you to investigate the language in order to make an assessment of the writer/narrator's attitude. If this is the case, remember your main task is to explain that attitude with specific examples and support.

Organize Your Essay

In responding to the prose analysis questions, it is best to write one body paragraph for each major section of the passage. Generally, let your response flow chronologically with the passage.

If this doesn't work for you, then take the elements you are talking about and let each of them become a major paragraph in your response. Although this is not the recommended method for organizing your answer, it may be the most comfortable for you.

Keep Your Quotes Short

Integrate words and phrases from the passage within your response. A direct quote of more than one or two lines of the text is too much. You need not always write out the actual quotations; sometimes you can simply make a reference to a particular section by giving the line numbers.

Discuss and Explain, Don't Retell or List

When writing about a passage, direct your attention to the elements addressed in the prompt. You should be prepared to discuss tone, attitude, point of view, imagery, rhetoric and the effect of the passage. Avoid the trap of just rephrasing or retelling the passage with quotes. Avoid listing, but be sure to explain and show your thinking.

When responding to an argument be sure you follow the task(s) in the prompt precisely. Sometimes you are asked to evaluate the success of someone's argument without the opportunity of becoming involved in the topic of the argument. That is difficult to do.

When you are writing an argument, be sure you follow the dictates of the prompt. Make your statement and support it thoroughly, using examples from your experience, your reading or observations.

How Long?

The length of your answer is not a guarantee of quality; however, it takes more than a paragraph or two to merit an upper-half score (remember, essays are scored on a scale of 1–9). As a rule, five paragraphs—an introduction, three body paragraphs, and a good conclusion—make an adequate essay. This can vary, however, depending on the length of your paragraphs, your writing style, etc. Also, the cookie-cutter 5-paragraph structure may not be the best for developing your ideas or expressing your opinion. It is just a baseline, not an absolute. You will find more information about the essays in chapter 6.

Using Outside References

Use examples and support that make sense to the development of your thesis. These do not always have to be from profound resources. Sometimes, especially in the argument questions, more local and sometimes even personal examples are quite acceptable. Use examples with which you are familiar. Don't bring in some obscure piece of history unless it fits the issue and unless you truly know what you are talking about. If you do not, it will show.

What If I Make Mistakes?

Those who read and score AP essays are trained to reward students for what they do well, rather than look for little "missing pieces" or tiny errors. They recognize that essays are barely-revised first drafts.

If you have made an error that you wish to correct, don't hesitate to cross it out neatly and either write the correction between the lines if you can, or, if it is a lengthy change, use an asterisk and put the revised information at the end of your essay. You should be writing your essays in ink, so readers expect to see corrected errors within an essay.

Legibility Counts

Be sure to write your essays in blue or black ink. As mentioned above, cross-outs will not count against you. Avoid using a pen that may bleed through the paper; it is best to use a ballpoint. Bring at least two pens. If your handwriting is particularly small, make an effort to make it large enough to be read easily. If your penmanship is bad, do not hesitate to print. Some students find that well-cushioned pens help clarify difficult-to-read handwriting. Just remember that human eyes will be trying to read your response. Severe or numerous mechanical difficulties will reduce your score if they hamper communication. The test booklet has 16 pages—enough to make corrections and additions. Some students whose handwriting is not particularly large find they are most comfortable writing on one side of the page only.

TAKE CONTROL: HOW TO APPROACH THE TEST AS A WHOLE

The AP English Language and Composition exam requires a logical and creative mindset, not only in the subject matter you will be approaching, but also in your overall attitude towards the test. Remember the following three basic strategies as you prepare, as well as on test day.

Question Triage

In a hospital emergency room, the triage nurse evaluates each patient and decides which ones get attention first and which ones can be treated later. You should do the same thing on the AP English Language and Composition exam.

Practicing triage is one of the most important ways of controlling your test-taking experience. It's a fact that there are some multiple-choice questions on the test that most students could never answer correctly, no matter how much time or effort they spent on them. Do not let that alarm you.

The first time you look at a multiple-choice question, make a quick decision about how hard and time-consuming it looks. Then decide whether to answer it now or skip it and do it later.

- If the question looks comprehensible and reasonably do-able, do it right away.
- If the question looks tough and time-consuming but ultimately do-able, skip it, circle the question number in your test booklet and return to it later, after you have answered the other questions for that passage.
- If the question looks impossible, forget about it. Make a guess if you can narrow the choices; leave it blank if you have no clue. Then move on, never to return unless you have still have time after going through all the other passages and questions.

Develop a Plan of Attack

The best plan of attack is to do each passage as a block. First you must determine whether you have 15 minutes for each of four passages and their questions or 12 minutes for each of five passages and their questions. Then make a longish first pass through the questions (call it the "triage" pass), doing the easy ones, skipping the impossible ones, and reserving any that look like they might cause trouble. You should actually do this in the test booklet. Then, make a second pass (call it the "cleanup pass"), and do those questions you think you can answer with some thought. If you have to leave a couple of questions unanswered, do not become unduly upset.

Paraphrase

AP English Language questions are not always presented in the simplest, most helpful way. Sometimes the passages are confusing; other times the questions might not be readily understandable. If any of the material seems intimidating to you, reword it into a form you can better handle. Even if you are not sure of all the words that are being used, make your best guess based on the context.

Mark Up Your Test Booklet

This strategy should be employed on both the multiple-choice and essay sections. The secret is to put the passages into a form you can understand and use. Circle or underline the main idea, for starters. Then make a map of the passage, labeling each paragraph so you understand how it all fits together. This acts as a type of brainstorming/outlining to get you jump-started into answering multiple-choice questions or responding to an essay prompt.

Check Back

Don't hesitate to refer to the passage. Much of the information is too complex to remember accurately, and no one expects you to absorb it all after only one reading. Often, the wrong answers of the multiple-choice section will be "misplaced details"—details taken from different parts of the passage. They are things that don't answer the question properly but that might sound good to you if you aren't careful. By checking back in the passage, you can avoid choosing such devilishly clever wrong choices. And, by checking back to the passage and the prompt while you are responding to the essay questions, you will be more likely to write more coherent and accurate responses.

Answer the Right Question

This strategy is a natural extension of the last. The test makers often include among the wrong choices for a question the correct answer to a different question. Keep an eye out for those key words *not* and EXCEPT. Under time pressure, it's easy to fall for one of these red herrings, i.e., thinking that you know what's being asked for when really you don't.

If necessary check the question again before choosing your answer. Doing all the right work but then getting the wrong answer can be seriously depressing. So, make sure you are answering the right question.

Keep Track of Time

Pace yourself. Multiple-choice passages will be about 12–15 minutes each, depending on the number of passages you must read. Then read each one and respond to the questions following it. Essay questions should take about 40 minutes each. Remember, you can begin with your favorite or the easiest passage. Watch your time, no matter how much you have to say about it.

Reminders:

- Food and drinks are not allowed during the exam. Some locations may permit capped bottled water. Remember that this is a 3-hour test. You may want to eat a piece of fruit or an energy bar or have a juice drink during the short break between the multiple-choice and essay sections. Be sure to have a good breakfast before the test—nothing unusual or too greasy. And watch your caffeine intake. Test day is not the best time to give it up or to ingest in large quantities if your body is not used to it.

- Never count on there being a clock in your testing room. Even if one is available, it may not work, or it may be too difficult for you to see it easily. Bring our own watch, but you will not be permitted to use an alarm or timer settings.

- You may write and underline in your test booklet, but you may not use a highlighter.

STRESS MANAGEMENT

Imagine the countdown has begun. Your date with the test is looming on the horizon. Anxiety is on the rise. The butterflies in your stomach seem to have had too much caffeine. Perhaps you feel as if the last thing you ate has turned into a lead ball. Your thinking is getting cloudy. Maybe you think you won't be ready. Maybe you already know your stuff, but you're going into panic mode anyway. Worst of all, you're not sure of what to do about it.

Don't freak! It is possible to tame that anxiety and stress—before and during the test. The following pages will show you how. You won't believe how quickly and easily you can deal with that killer anxiety.

Lack of control is one of the prime causes of stress. A ton of research shows that if you don't have a sense of control over what's happening in your life, you can easily end up feeling helpless and hopeless. So, just having concrete things to do and to think about—taking control—will help reduce your stress. This section shows you how to take control during the days leading up to taking the test.

Identify the Sources of Stress

In the space provided, jot down anything you identify as a source of your test-related stress. The idea is to pin down that free-floating anxiety so that you can take control of it. Here are some common examples to get you started:

- I always freeze up on tests.
- I'm nervous about the essay (or the argument, or remembering synecdoche)
- I need a good/great score to go to Acme College.
- My older brother/ sister/ best friend did really well. I must match his/her score or do better.
- My parents, who are paying for school, will be really disappointed if I don't test well.
- I'm afraid of losing my focus and concentration half-way through the test.
- I know I'm not spending enough time preparing.
- I study like crazy, but nothing seems to stick in my mind.
- I always run out of time and get panicky.
- Right now I feel as though thinking is like wading through thick mud.

Now list your own.

Sources of Stress

_____ _____

_____ _____

_____ _____

_____ _____

Take a few minutes to think about the things you've just written down. Then rewrite them. List the statements you most associate with your stress and anxiety first, and put the least disturbing items last. Chances are, the top of the list is a fairly accurate description of exactly how you react to test anxiety, both physically and mentally.

The later items usually describe your fears (disappointing Mom and Dad, looking bad to your peers, etc.) As you write the list, you're forming a hierarchy of items so you can deal first with the anxiety provokers that bug you most. Very often, taking care of the major items from the top of the list goes a long way toward relieving overall testing anxiety. You probably won't have to bother with the things you placed last.

Your Strengths and Weaknesses

Take one minute to list the areas in AP Language and Composition where you have the most skill. They can be general ("prose analysis") or specific ("rhetorical devices"). Write down as many as you can think of, and if possible, time yourself. Write for the entire time. Don't stop writing until you have reached the one-minute stopping point.

Strong AP Language and Composition Skills

_____   _____

_____   _____

_____   _____

_____   _____

Next, take one minute to list areas of AP Language and Composition where you think you are weakest, just plain bad at, have failed at, or keep messing up. Again, keep it to one minute and continue writing until you reach the cutoff. Don't be afraid to identify and write down your weak spots! In all probability, as you do both lists, you will find you are strong in some areas and not so strong in others. Taking stock of your assets and liabilities lets you know the areas you don't have to worry about, and the ones that will demand extra attention and effort.

Weak AP Language and Composition Skills

_____   _____

_____   _____

_____   _____

_____   _____

Facing your weak spots gives you some distinct advantages. It helps a lot to find out where you need to spend extra effort. Increased exposure to tough material makes it more familiar and less intimidating. (After all, we mostly fear what we don't know and are probably afraid to face.) You will feel better about yourself because you're dealing directly with areas of the test that bring on your anxiety. You can't help feeling more confident when you know you're actively strengthening your chances of earning a higher overall test score.

Now, go back to the "good" list, and expand it for two minutes. Take the general items on that first list and make them more specific; then take the specific items and expand them into more general conclusions. Naturally, if anything new comes to mind, jot it down. Focus all of your attention and effort on your strengths. Don't underestimate yourself or your abilities. Give yourself full credit. At the same time, don't list strengths you really don't have; you'll only be fooling yourself.

Expanding from general to specific might go as follows. If you listed "argument" as a broad topic you feel strong in, you would then narrow your focus to include areas of this subject about which you are particularly knowledgeable. Perhaps you are a debater, and you understand the configuration of successful argumentation: thesis, concession, and presentation using support and detail.

Whatever you feel comfortable about goes on your "good" list. You get the idea—check the time and start writing for at least two minutes your expanded "good" list.

Strong AP Language and Composition Skills: An Expanded List

_____   _____

_____   _____

_____   _____

_____   _____

After you've stopped, check your time. Did you find yourself going beyond two minutes? Did you write down more things than you thought you knew? Is it possible you know more than you've been giving yourself credit for? That means you've probably found a number of areas in which you feel strong.

You just took an active step toward helping yourself. Notice any increased feelings of confidence? Has your stress level decreased, maybe a little bit? Good, enjoy this new confidence.

Here's another way to think about this little exercise. Every area of strength and confidence you can identify is much like having a reserve of solid gold at Fort Knox. You'll be able to draw on your reserves as you need them. You can use your reserves to solve difficult questions, maintain confidence, and keep test stress and anxiety at a distance. The encouraging thing is that every time you recognize another area of strength, succeed at coming up with a solution, or get a good score on a test, you increase your reserves. And there is absolutely no limit to how much self confidence you can have or how good you can feel about yourself.

Imagine Yourself Succeeding

The next little group of exercises is both physical and mental. It's a natural follow-up to what you've just accomplished with your lists.

First get yourself into a comfortable sitting position in a quiet setting. Wear loose clothes. If you wear glasses, take them off. Close your eyes and inhale a deep, satisfying breath of air. Really fill your lungs until your rib cage is fully expanded and you can't take in any more. Then, exhale the air completely. Imagine you are blowing out a candle with your last little puff of air. Do this two or three more times, filling your lungs to their maximum and emptying them totally. Keep your eyes closed, comfortably but not tightly. Let your body sink deeper into the chair as you become even more comfortable.

With your eyes shut you can notice something very interesting. You're no longer dealing with worrisome stuff going on in the world outside of you. Now you can concentrate on what happens inside you. The more you recognize your own physical reactions to stress and anxiety, the more you can do about them. You might not realize it, but you've begun to regain a sense of being in control.

Let images begin to form on the "viewing screens" on the back of your eyelids. You're experiencing visualizations from the place in your mind that makes pictures. Allow the images to come easily and naturally; don't force them. Imagine yourself in a relaxing situation. It might be in a special place you've visited before or one you've read about. It can be a fictional location that you create in your imagination, but a real-life memory of a place or situation you know is usually better. Make it as detailed as possible, and notice as much as you can.

Stay focused on the images as you sink farther back into your chair. Breathe easily and naturally. You might have the sensations of any stress or tension draining from your muscles and flowing downward, out your feet and away from you.

Take a moment to check how you're feeling. Notice how comfortable you've become. Imagine how much easier it would be if you could take the test feeling this relaxed and in this state of ease. You've combined the images of your special place with sensations of comfort and relaxation. You've also found a way to become relaxed simply by visualizing your own safe, special place.

Now, close your eyes and start remembering a real-life situation in which you did well on a test. If you can't come up with one, remember a situation in which you did something (academic or otherwise) that you were really proud of—a genuine accomplishment. Make the memory as detailed as possible. Think about the sights, the sounds, the smells, even the tastes associated with this remembered experience. Remember how confident you felt as you accomplished your goal. Now start thinking about the upcoming test. Keep your thoughts and feelings in line with that successful experience. Don't make comparisons between them. Just imagine taking the upcoming test with the same feelings of confidence and relaxed control.

This exercise is a great way to bring the test down to Earth. You should practice this exercise often, especially when the prospect of taking the exam starts to bum you out. The more you practice it, the more effective the exercise will be for you.

Exercise Frustrations Away   *YES!*

Whether it is jogging, walking, biking, mild aerobics, pushups, or a pickup basketball game, physical exercise is a very effective way to stimulate your mind and body and to improve your ability to think and concentrate. A surprising number of students get out of the habit of regular exercise, ironically because they are spending so much time prepping for exams. Also, sedentary people—this is a medical fact—get less oxygen to the blood and hence to the head than active people. You can live fine with a little less oxygen; you just can't think as well.

Any big test is a bit like a race. Thinking clearly at the end is just as important as having a quick mind early on. If you cannot sustain your energy level in the last sections of the exam, there's too good a chance you could blow it. You need a fit body that can weather the demands any big exam puts on you. Along with a good diet and adequate sleep, exercise is an important part of keeping yourself in fighting shape and thinking clearly for the long haul.

Another thing happens when students don't make exercise an integral part of their test preparation. Like any organism in nature, you operate best if all your "energy systems" are in balance. Studying uses a log of energy, but it's all mental energy. When you take a study break, do something active instead of raiding the fridge or vegging out in from t of the TV. Take a 5–10 minute activity break for every 50 or 60 minutes that you study. The dog will love you; take him around the block for a quick jog. The physical exertion gets your body into the act, which helps to keep your mind and body in sync. Then, when you finish studying for the night and hit the sack, you won't lie there, tense and unable to sleep because your head is overtired and your body wants to pump iron or run a marathon.

One warning about exercise, however: It's not a good idea to exercise vigorously right before you go to bed. This could easily cause sleep onset problems. For the same reason, it's also not recommended to study right up to bedtime. Make time for a "buffer period" before you go to bed: For 30–60 minutes, take a hot shower, meditate, or simply veg out.

Take a Deep Breath

Here's another natural route to relaxation and invigoration. It's a classic isometric exercise that you can do whenever you get stressed out—just before the test begins, even during the test. It's very simple and takes just a few minutes.

Close your eyes. Starting with your eyes and—without holding your breath—gradually tighten every muscle in your body (but not to the point of pain) in the following sequence:

- Close your eyes tightly.
- Squeeze your nose and mouth together so that your whole face is scrunched up. (If it makes you self-conscious to look like an apple doll in the test room, skip the face-scrunching part.)
- Pull your chin into your chest, and pull your shoulders together.
- Tighten your arms to your body; then clench your hands into tight fists.
- Pull in your stomach
- Squeeze your thighs and buttocks together, and tighten your calves.
- Stretch your feet, then curl your toes (watch out for cramping).

KAPLAN
Test Prep and Admissions

At this point, every muscle should be tightened. Now, relax your body, one part at a time, in reverse order, starting with your toes. Let the tension drop out of each muscle. The entire process might take five minutes from start to finish (maybe only two or three minutes during the test). This clenching and unclenching exercise should help you to feel very relaxed.

And Keep Breathing

Conscious attention to breathing is an excellent way of managing test stress (or any stress, for that matter). The majority of people who get into trouble during tests take shallow breaths. They breathe using only their upper chests and shoulder muscles, and may even hold their breath for long periods of time. Conversely, the test taker who by accident or design keeps breathing normally and rhythmically is likely to be more relaxed and in better control during the entire test experience.

So, now is the time to get into the habit of relaxed breathing. Do the next exercise to learn to breathe in a natural, easy rhythm. By the way, this is another technique you can use during the test to collect your thoughts and ward off excess stress. The entire exercise should take no more than three to five minutes.

With your eyes closed, breathe in slowly and deeply through your nose. Hold the breath for a bit, and then release it through your mouth. The key is to breathe slowly and deeply by using your diaphragm (the big band of muscle that spans your body just above your waist) to draw air in and out naturally and effortlessly. Breathing with your diaphragm encourages relaxation and helps minimize tension. Try it and notice how relaxed and comfortable you feel.

Quick Tips as You Prepare for the Exam

- Be sure you know the schedule for the AP exams ahead of time. Your teacher should have this year's testing schedule. If you are taking other AP exams in addition to AP English Language and Composition, you should know when, during the two-week exam period, these are going to be held so you can adjust your mental and physical energies accordingly.

- Make sure you adjust any lunch schedule to fit with your test schedule. You do *not* want to go into an afternoon exam without having had lunch. Also, if you usually eat during the first lunch, you will want to have that adjusted to accommodate any morning exams you may be taking.

- For the last several years, the AP English Language exam has been the first exam given on Monday morning of the two-week AP exam schedule.

- Whatever you do, try to get enough sleep the night before the test.

- If something serious interferes with any of the test times, be aware that each test does have an alternative test and date that you might be able to take under extreme extenuating circumstances. This is not a desirable option, but it is a possibility.

- No matter what else is going on at testing time, put it out of your mind. Your job, during the three hours of the exam, is to score your best.

Quick Tips for the Days Just Before the Exam

- The best test takers do less and less as the test approaches. Taper off your study schedule and take it easy on yourself. You want to be relaxed and ready on the day of the test. Give yourself time off, especially the evening before your exam. By then, if you've studied well, everything you need to know is firmly stored in your memory banks.

- Positive self-talk can be extremely liberating and invigorating, especially as the test looms closer. Tell yourself things such as, "I choose to take this test" rather than "I have to"; "I will do well" rather than "I hope things go well"; "I can" rather than "I cannot." Be aware of negative, self-defeating thoughts and images and immediately counter any you become aware of. Replace them with affirming statements that encourage your self-esteem and confidence. Create and practice visualizations that build on your positive statements.

- Get your act together sooner rather than later. Have everything (including choice of comfortable, layered clothing) laid out days in advance. Most important, know where the test will be held and the easiest, quickest way to get there. You will gain great peace of mind if you know that all the little details—gas in the car, directions to the room, etc.—are firmly in your control before the day of the test.

- Visit the test site a few days in advance. This is especially important if the site is unfamiliar to you.

- Forego any practice or study cram sessions on the day before the test. It is in your best interest to marshal your physical and psychological resources for 24 hours or so. Even race horses are kept in the paddock and treated like princes the day before a race. Try to keep worries about the test on the back burner of your mind. Go to a movie; take a pleasant hike, or just relax. Don't eat junk food or tons of sugar. And—of course—get plenty of rest the night before. However, you don't want to go to bed too early. The last thing you need is to lie in bed, unable to sleep, only to find yourself worrying about the test.

Handling Stress During the Test

The biggest stress monster will be the test itself. Fear not; there are methods for quelling your stress during the test.

- Keep moving forward instead of getting bogged down in by a difficult question. You don't have to get everything right to achieve a fine score. The best test takers skip difficult material temporarily in search of the easier stuff. They mark the questions that require extra time and thought. This strategy buys time and builds confidence so you can handle the tough stuff later.

- Don't be thrown if other test takers seem to be working more furiously than you are. It may be all showmanship. Continue to spend your time patiently thinking through your answers; it's going to lead to better results. Don't mistake the other people's sheer activity for signs of progress and higher scores.

- Keep breathing. Weak test takers tend to forget to breathe properly as the test proceeds. They start holding their breath without realizing it, or they breathe erratically. Improper breathing interferes with clear thinking.

- Some quick isometrics during the test—especially if your concentration is wandering or your energy is waning—can help. Try this: Put your palms together and press intensely for a few seconds. Concentrate on the tension you feel throughout your palms, wrists, forearms, and up into your biceps and shoulders. Then, quickly release the pressure. Feel the difference as you let go. Focus on the warm relaxation that floods through the muscles. Now you're ready to return to task.

- Here's one other isometric that will relieve tension in both your neck and eye muscles. Slowly rotate your head from side to side. Turning your head and eyes to look as far back over each shoulder as you can. Feel the muscles stretch on one side or your neck as they contract on the other. Repeat five times in each direction.

COUNTDOWN TO THE TEST

Is it starting to feel like your whole life is a build-up to the AP English Language test? As the test date gets closer, you may find your anxiety is on the rise. Try not to worry. After the preparation you have done, you are in good shape for the test.

To calm any very-last-minute, pretest jitters you may have, here is a sane schedule for the last week.

The Week before the Test

Review the chapters in this book and in your textbook and any notes you have made from this book and/or from your AP English class. Are there major holes in your preparation? If there are, choose a few of these areas to work on—but do not try to overload your mind.

Take a full length practice test. If you haven't done so already, take one or more of the practice tests in this book. These are a good practice for the real thing.

Two Days before the Test

Do your last studying—a few more passages, an essay outline, and/or a look through the Key Terminology chapter—and then call it quits.

The Night before the Test

- Don't study. Get together the following items:
- A watch or whatever timepiece you are used to using—turn all the sound off
- A few sharpened No. 2 pencils for the multiple-choice section, and a couple of reliable ball point pens (blue or black)
- Erasers
- Photo ID card (sometimes necessary in large testing situations where the proctor does not know you)

Know exactly where you are going and exactly how and when you will get there.

Relax the night before the test. Read a good book; take a warm bubble bath, watch TV. Get a good night's sleep. Go to bed at a reasonable hour and leave yourself a bit of extra time in the morning.

The Morning of the Test

Eat breakfast. Make it something substantial, but not anything too heavy or greasy. Don't drink a lot of coffee if you are not used to it. Bathroom breaks may or may not be allowed other than the normal break time between the multiple-choice and the essay section of the test. If they are allowed, they will cut into your testing time.

Dress in layers so that you can adjust to the temperature of the test room.

Read something. Warm up your brain with a newspaper or magazine or the cereal box. You should not let the test questions be the first thing you read that day.

Arrive at the test site in plenty of time.

During the Test

Don't be shaken. If you find your confidence slipping, remind yourself how well you have prepared. You know the structure of the test; you know the instructions; you have studied for every type of question.

Even if something goes really wrong, don't panic. If the test booklet is defective—two pages are stuck together or the ink has run—try to stay calm. Raise your hand; tell the proctor you need a new book. If you accidentally misgrid your answer page on the multiple-choice section, again don't panic. Raise your hand, tell the proctor. She might be able to arrange for you to regrid your test after it's over, when it won't cost you any time, or she herself might do it for you while everyone is writing their essays.

Food or drinks are not allowed during the exam. Some test sites may permit capped bottled water. Remember, however, that this is a three-hour test. You may want to eat a piece of fruit or have a juice drink or power bar during the short break between the multiple-choice and essay sections of the AP exam.

After the Test

Once the test is over, put it out of your mind. Feel free to start thinking about more interesting things than tests. If you have subsequent AP tests to take now you may start thinking about them.

Even if you walk out of the test room thinking that you blew it, you probably didn't. You tend to remember the questions that stumped you, not the many that you knew. We're positive that you will have performed well and scored your best on the exam because you followed the Kaplan strategies outlined in this section. Be confident in your preparation, and celebrate the fact that the AP test is soon to be a distant memory.

| PART TWO |

Diagnostic Test

Diagnostic Test Answer Grid

Before taking this Diagnostic test, find a quiet place where you can work uninterrupted for about three hours. Make sure you have a comfortable desk, several No. 2 pencils, and a few ballpoint pens.

The Diagnostic test includes a multiple-choice section and a free-response question. Use the answer grid to record your multiple-choice answers. Write the essays on the pages provided; use additional sheets if needed.

Once you start the test, don't stop until you've finished, except for a 10-minute break between the multiple-choice and essay sections. The answer key and explanations follow the test.

Good luck!

1. Ⓐ Ⓑ Ⓒ Ⓓ Ⓔ	19. Ⓐ Ⓑ Ⓒ Ⓓ Ⓔ	37. Ⓐ Ⓑ Ⓒ Ⓓ Ⓔ
2. Ⓐ Ⓑ Ⓒ Ⓓ Ⓔ	20. Ⓐ Ⓑ Ⓒ Ⓓ Ⓔ	38. Ⓐ Ⓑ Ⓒ Ⓓ Ⓔ
3. Ⓐ Ⓑ Ⓒ Ⓓ Ⓔ	21. Ⓐ Ⓑ Ⓒ Ⓓ Ⓔ	39. Ⓐ Ⓑ Ⓒ Ⓓ Ⓔ
4. Ⓐ Ⓑ Ⓒ Ⓓ Ⓔ	22. Ⓐ Ⓑ Ⓒ Ⓓ Ⓔ	40. Ⓐ Ⓑ Ⓒ Ⓓ Ⓔ
5. Ⓐ Ⓑ Ⓒ Ⓓ Ⓔ	23. Ⓐ Ⓑ Ⓒ Ⓓ Ⓔ	41. Ⓐ Ⓑ Ⓒ Ⓓ Ⓔ
6. Ⓐ Ⓑ Ⓒ Ⓓ Ⓔ	24. Ⓐ Ⓑ Ⓒ Ⓓ Ⓔ	42. Ⓐ Ⓑ Ⓒ Ⓓ Ⓔ
7. Ⓐ Ⓑ Ⓒ Ⓓ Ⓔ	25. Ⓐ Ⓑ Ⓒ Ⓓ Ⓔ	43. Ⓐ Ⓑ Ⓒ Ⓓ Ⓔ
8. Ⓐ Ⓑ Ⓒ Ⓓ Ⓔ	26. Ⓐ Ⓑ Ⓒ Ⓓ Ⓔ	44. Ⓐ Ⓑ Ⓒ Ⓓ Ⓔ
9. Ⓐ Ⓑ Ⓒ Ⓓ Ⓔ	27. Ⓐ Ⓑ Ⓒ Ⓓ Ⓔ	45. Ⓐ Ⓑ Ⓒ Ⓓ Ⓔ
10. Ⓐ Ⓑ Ⓒ Ⓓ Ⓔ	28. Ⓐ Ⓑ Ⓒ Ⓓ Ⓔ	46. Ⓐ Ⓑ Ⓒ Ⓓ Ⓔ
11. Ⓐ Ⓑ Ⓒ Ⓓ Ⓔ	29. Ⓐ Ⓑ Ⓒ Ⓓ Ⓔ	47. Ⓐ Ⓑ Ⓒ Ⓓ Ⓔ
12. Ⓐ Ⓑ Ⓒ Ⓓ Ⓔ	30. Ⓐ Ⓑ Ⓒ Ⓓ Ⓔ	48. Ⓐ Ⓑ Ⓒ Ⓓ Ⓔ
13. Ⓐ Ⓑ Ⓒ Ⓓ Ⓔ	31. Ⓐ Ⓑ Ⓒ Ⓓ Ⓔ	49. Ⓐ Ⓑ Ⓒ Ⓓ Ⓔ
14. Ⓐ Ⓑ Ⓒ Ⓓ Ⓔ	32. Ⓐ Ⓑ Ⓒ Ⓓ Ⓔ	50. Ⓐ Ⓑ Ⓒ Ⓓ Ⓔ
15. Ⓐ Ⓑ Ⓒ Ⓓ Ⓔ	33. Ⓐ Ⓑ Ⓒ Ⓓ Ⓔ	51. Ⓐ Ⓑ Ⓒ Ⓓ Ⓔ
16. Ⓐ Ⓑ Ⓒ Ⓓ Ⓔ	34. Ⓐ Ⓑ Ⓒ Ⓓ Ⓔ	52. Ⓐ Ⓑ Ⓒ Ⓓ Ⓔ
17. Ⓐ Ⓑ Ⓒ Ⓓ Ⓔ	35. Ⓐ Ⓑ Ⓒ Ⓓ Ⓔ	53. Ⓐ Ⓑ Ⓒ Ⓓ Ⓔ
18. Ⓐ Ⓑ Ⓒ Ⓓ Ⓔ	36. Ⓐ Ⓑ Ⓒ Ⓓ Ⓔ	

COMPUTING YOUR SCORE

There is no way to determine precisely what your AP grade will be because:

- The conditions under which you take the practice test will not exactly mirror real test conditions.
- While the multiple-choice questions are scored by computer, the free-response questions are graded manually by faculty consultants. You will not be able to accurately grade your own essays.

Section I: Multiple-Choice

Number Correct ☐ − (¼ × Number Wrong*) ☐ = ☐ × 1.296 = ☐ = Multiple-Choice Raw Score

*Do not include questions left blank.

Section II: Free-Response

Question 1: (out of 9 points possible) ☐ × 2.933 = ☐

Question 2: (out of 9 points possible) ☐ × 2.933 = ☐

Question 3: (out of 9 points possible) ☐ × 2.933 = ☐

Total Questions 1, 2, and 3 = ☐ = Free-Response Raw Score

Composite Score

Section I Multiple-Choice Score ☐ + Section II Free-Response Score ☐ = ☐ = Composite Score

CONVERSION CHART

Composite Score Range	AP Grade
114–144	5
88–113	4
67–87	3
40–66	2
0–39	1

Diagnostic Test

Section I: Multiple-Choice Questions

Time—1 hour
Number of questions—53
Percent of total grade—45%

<u>Directions</u>: This part consists of selections from prose works and questions on their content, form, and style. After reading each passage, choose the best answer to each question and completely fill in the corresponding oval on the answer sheet.

Questions 1–14. Read the following passage carefully before you choose your answers.

Although my early life tended to encourage my flirting propensities it did not make me the real heartless coquette, I afterwards became. The flir-
Line tations of school life were harmless, for there was
(5) no real love between myself and the parties concerned. When I left school I was just seventeen. Young, gay, rich, happy and thoughtless, without a wish ungratified. I had been accustomed to admiration all my life, and now I really deserved
(10) it. I was rather stylish in my personal appearance, so every one said. Every advantage, that money could give, had been given me, and I do not flatter myself, when I say I improved my talents. I rode well, danced well, played and sang well, con-
(15) versed well, and in truth everything I attempted I did well.

Among the first satellites that moved around my sphere, were two young gentlemen, both handsome, but very unlike in personal appearance
(20) and disposition. One was dark as a Spaniard, with eyes and hair as dark as night when the moon and stars have hid their beams under a canopy of cloud. He was very handsome and talented, yet I could not love the man, for I feared him. Still it
(25) amused me to lead him on, intending to tell him every time we met, that his love was vain; but I continued putting it off.

The other—God knows I loved him, if woman is capable of loving. He was fair, very fair, with dark
(30) eyes and light hair. His mouth was beautiful, but deceit lurked in each exquisite curve of his lips. An Adonis was not more perfect in form: and he knew it. He was young in years, yet old in sin. I now sometimes think that he, like Bulwer's Zanoni, had
(35) found the true secret of perpetual youth, and that he had lived for centuries, so well was he versed in the ways of the world, and in each phase of human nature. He often boasted of the many conquests he had made, and said that no woman he chose to
(40) captivate could escape loving him. I did not like this speech; but I loved him. He had certainly many rare traits of character. His generosity was proverbial; he was a warm friend and had the most perfect control over his very high temper. It was
(45) not long before we became engaged. He said that he loved me at first sight; and God knows that his love was more than returned. He called to see me each day, and every night escorted me to some place of amusement. He was very jealous, but I
(50) liked that. He was my sun during the day, and my moon at night. There was a cloud over all my happiness when he failed to come. He was young, ardent, fiery and passionate, and I—I was a fool! The passionate devotion of my heart was lavished
(55) upon a worthless object. I knew nothing of his former conduct or character, as he had come to Macon but recently. Knowing how particular my father was about such things, I employed a friend to visit the town he was from, and enquire into his
(60) past history. Now, friends, bear with pity my sad trial, and paint to your own imaginations how you would feel in such a case.

Within two weeks of marriage, with a man that you loved with your whole heart and soul, a
(65) perfect man, as you thought, imagine how you would feel to hear that he had (Oh God! how can I relate truth as I heard it! but I must or you will never hear with charity my flirtations,) that he had been compelled to leave the town in which he
(70) lived, on account of his base seduction of a most beautiful, but poor girl, under solemn promise of marriage. He lived as a husband with her for a few months, and then deserted her, leaving her to die alone, in ignominy, and the most abject poverty.
(75) On her death-bed she divulged her secret to her brother, who traced the seducer to the city and wounded him in a duel, and was fatally shot himself. A seducer and a double murderer, the man I thought free from guile as an angel in
(80) heaven! It was enough to drive one mad, and I am sure I was crazed for years.

He came to see me that night! How my hand trembles! I can scarcely write to describe our meeting. I was sitting alone, for I had refused to
(85) receive visitors that night, when he entered the room.

'Ah! darling,' said he, kissing me. 'Alone I see. I

GO ON TO THE NEXT PAGE

am very glad too, for I wanted to see you with no one near.' How handsome he looked, with his
(90) flushed cheeks, red from his ride in the wintry wind. 'What's the matter with my bird to-night? her voice is as sweet as ever, but it is too sad for me.' 'Ella do let me urge you to appoint our wedding day a week sooner, for you are so pretty
(95) and sweet, you will tempt me to'—he did not finish the sentence, but I understood his meaning but too well. It was the first time he had ever acted in such a singular manner, and I saw he was excited highly by spirituous liquors.
(100) 'Indeed sir,' I answered, 'If I have heard the truth I am not the first woman who proved too sweet and pretty for you, and in whose presence you could not control your passions.'

'Who told you that Ella?' he exclaimed, starting
(105) from his seat! 'By all that is sacred if I find out, he shall not live an hour!'

'You shall never know,' said I. 'Two murders are quite enough to doom your blackened soul, Dudley Earle!'
(110) How pale he looked, but not with penitence, it was anger only toward the person who had divulged his secret. He remained an hour trying to persuade me to revoke my decision, and then left me a heart-broken sad woman, without an object
(115) in life. And then and there I bent my knee, before the throne of God. (I know now it was blasphemy) but I was crazy then! and vowed to revenge myself upon the whole sex, for the misery one, I then supposed the type of the species, had wrought in
(120) my soul; and faithfully I kept that vow.

The Devil aids his own, and he surely helped me. Even unsought, men would lay their love at my feet, and their foibles, rendered harmless by my own self-control, became my playthings. Often,
(125) very often have I acted in such a way, that I knew would inflame an even unimpressable man, and then would send his love back ungratified, to corrode his very heart. Was that just or right? No indeed, it was not. It was dangerous to me, and
(130) outrageous to others. But dear reader in pity for my anguish, and for the long years of intense mental suffering, forgive me. Never! believe me, would I divulge this passage of my life to any one, did I not think that perhaps it may be a warning to

(135) the young, of both sexes.

Let the young gentlemen always think and know, that no matter how secret an evil act may be committed, it will always come to light, and at the very time you may wish it to be kept concealed. To
(140) the girls: No matter my dears, how handsome or fascinating a gentleman may appear, never allow your affections to become fixed on any human being, until you know that being worthy. Often times the veriest serpent wears a shining coat,
(145) most beautiful to look upon, but the poison of whose fangs will corrupt a young heart and mar its peace a whole life time.

From *Confessions of a Flirt* by Mrs. Edward Leigh (1859)

1. This passage can best be described as

    (A) a process narrative that provides the background of a flirtatious young woman

    (B) a personal narrative that shows the development of a flirtatious nature

    (C) a cause and effect essay that explains some unladylike behavior

    (D) an argument that justifies personal revenge

    (E) a comparison of two very handsome but very different young gentlemen

2. The narrator can best be described as

    (A) indulged but sensitive

    (B) revengeful but trustworthy

    (C) angry but personable

    (D) vindictive but personable

    (E) spoiled but generous spirited

GO ON TO THE NEXT PAGE

3. In the context of the entire essay, paragraph two provides which of the following?

    (A) It describes the naiveté of a young ingénue.

    (B) It discloses a heartlessness preparatory to her later behavior towards men.

    (C) It gives the reader a poetic description using astronomy.

    (D) It contrasts two very different young suitors and the narrator's behavior towards them.

    (E) It explains the narrator's naiveté in her early years of womanhood.

4. Paragraph three utilizes all of the following stylistic devices EXCEPT

    (A) allusion

    (B) antithesis

    (C) hyperbole

    (D) polysyndeton

    (E) anaphora

5. In paragraph three, the narrator primarily relies upon which of the following sentence structures?

    (A) Simple sentences

    (B) Compound sentences

    (C) Parenthetical sentences

    (D) Fragmented sentences

    (E) Periodic sentences

6. Based on the rest of the passage, the best description of the young man as depicted in paragraph three is

    (A) charming and thoughtful

    (B) sensitive and artistic

    (C) suave and experienced

    (D) brave and adventurous

    (E) modest and mannerly

7. The last two sentences of paragraph 4 (lines 78–81) employ which of the following two characteristics?

    (A) repetition and exaggeration

    (B) irony and hyperbole

    (C) explanation and sorrow

    (D) simile and metaphor

    (E) juxtaposition and understatement

8. The most likely meaning of the word "singular" (line 98) would be

    (A) remarkable

    (B) by oneself

    (C) earnest

    (D) deceitful

    (E) duplicitous

9. The pronoun "that" in line 63 refers to

    (A) his guilty conscience

    (B) his surprise at her anger

    (C) the despicable gentleman

    (D) the murder he committed

    (E) her sadness over his deceit

10. The phrase "The Devil aids his own" (line 121) can best be interpreted to mean

    (A) the narrator's prayers were directed to the Devil

    (B) the Devil only helps out other devils

    (C) the narrator's evil revenge on men was accomplished with the help from the Devil

    (D) the deceitful gentleman was like the Devil in his actions

    (E) without the Devil's help, the narrator might never have learned the truth

GO ON TO THE NEXT PAGE

11. Paragraph 11 (lines 121–135) utilizes all of the following rhetorical devices EXCEPT

    (A) alliteration

    (B) assonance

    (C) rhetorical question

    (D) zeugma

    (E) exclamation

12. The tone of the last paragraph can best be described as

    (A) sarcastic

    (B) melodramatic

    (C) angry

    (D) injured

    (E) didactic

13. The best alternative for the phrase "veriest serpent wears a shining coat," (line 144) is

    (A) wolf in sheep's clothing

    (B) coal in a holiday stocking

    (C) garbage wrapped in shiny paper

    (D) snake in the shiny wet grass

    (E) reptile clothed in jewels

14. This story, especially in light of its last paragraph, can best be summed up by the cliché

    (A) "Beware of Greeks bearing gifts"

    (B) "Don't judge a book by its cover"

    (C) "Beauty is only skin deep"

    (D) "Always walk a mile in another's moccasins"

    (E) "Don't look a gift horse in the mouth"

GO ON TO THE NEXT PAGE

<u>Questions 15–27.</u> Read the following passage carefully before you choose your answers.

The only purpose of being in politics is to strive for the values and ideals we believe in: freedom, justice, what we Europeans call solidarity but you
Line might call respect for and help for others. These
(5) are the decent democratic values we all avow. But alongside the values we know we need a hard-headed pragmatism—a *realpolitik*—required to give us any chance of translating those values into the practical world we live in.
(10) The same tension exists in the two views of international affairs. One is utilitarian: each nation maximizes its own self-interest. The other is Utopian: we try to create a better world. Today I want to suggest that more than ever before those
(15) two views are merging.

I advocate an enlightened self-interest that puts fighting for our values right at the heart of the policies necessary to protect our nations. Engagement in the world on the basis of these
(20) values, not isolationism from it is the hard-headed pragmatism for the 21st Century.

Why? In part it is because the countries and people of the world today are more inter-dependent than ever. In truth, it is very rare today
(25) that trouble in one part of the globe remains limited in its effect. Not just in security, but in trade and finance—witness the crisis of 1998 which began in Thailand and ended in Brazil—the world is interlocked.
(30) This is heightened by mass communications and technology. In Queen Victoria's time, reports of battles came back weeks or months after they were won or lost. Today we see them enacted live on the BBC, Sky or CNN. Their very visibility, immediate
(35) and in technicolour, inflame feelings that can spread worldwide across different ethnic, religious and cultural communities.

So today, more than ever, "their" problem becomes "our" problem. Instability is contagious
(40) and, again today, more than ever, nations, at least most of them crave stability. That's for a simple reason. Our people want it, because without it, they can't do business and prosper. What brings nations together—what brought them together

(45) post-September 11—is the international recognition that the world needs order. Disorder is the enemy of progress.

The struggle is for stability, for the security within which progress can be made. Of course,
(50) countries want to protect their territorial integrity but few are into empire-building. This is especially true of democracies whose people vote for higher living standards and punish governments who don't deliver them. For 2,000 years Europe fought
(55) over territory.

Today boundaries are virtually fixed. Govern-ments and people know that any territorial ambition threatens stability, and instability threatens prosperity.
(60) And of course the surest way to stability is through the very values of freedom, democracy and justice. Where these are strong, the people push for moderation and order. Where they are absent, regimes act unchecked by popular
(65) accountability and pose a threat; and the threat spreads.

So the promotion of these values becomes not just right in itself but part of our long-term security and prosperity. We can't intervene in every
(70) case. Not all the wrongs of the world can be put right, but where disorder threatens us all, we should act.

Like it or not, whether you are a utilitarian or a Utopian, the world is interdependent. One
(75) consequence of this is that foreign and domestic policy are ever more closely interwoven.

It was September 11 that brought these thoughts into sharper focus. Watching the horror unfold, imagining the almost unimaginable suffering of
(80) the thousands of innocent victims of the terror and carnage, the dominant emotion after the obvious feelings of revulsion, sympathy and anger, was determination.

The guts and spirit of the people of New York
(85) and America in the aftermath of that terrible day were not just admirable, they were awesome. They were the best riposte to the terrorists that humanity could give and you should be very proud of that. I want you to know too that the

GO ON TO THE NEXT PAGE

(90) British people were with you from the first
moment, and we will always be with you at times
like those. We are not half-hearted friends and we
never will be. But the determination must be not
just to pursue those responsible and bring them to
(95) justice but to learn from September 11. There is a
real danger we forget the lessons of September 11.
Human beings recover from tragedy and the
memory becomes less fraught. That is healthy part
of living. But we should learn from our experience.
(100) The most obvious lesson is indeed our
interdependence. For a time our world stood still.
Quite apart from our security, the shock impacted
on economic confidence, on business, on trade
and it is only now with the terrorist network on
(105) the run, that confidence is really returning. Every
nation in the world felt the reverberation of that
fateful day. And that has been well illustrated by
the role which the United Nations—under Kofi
Annan's excellent leadership—has played since
(110) September 11.
  So if we didn't know it before, we know now:
these events and our response to them shape the
fate not of one nation but of one world.
  For America, it has laid bare the reality.
(115) American power affects the world fundamentally.
It is there. It is real. It is never irrelevant. It can
affect the world for good, or for bad. Stand aside
or engage; it never fails to affect.
  You know I want it engaged. Under President
(120) Bush, I am confident it will be and for good. But if
that's what I and many others want, it comes at a
price for us too. It means we don't shirk our
responsibility. It means that when America is
fighting for those values, then, however tough, we
(125) fight with her. No grandstanding, no offering
implausible but impractical advice from the
comfort of the touchline, no wishing away the
hard not the easy choices, but working together,
side by side.
  Prime Minister Tony Blair to the American
citizens following 9/11/2001

15. In opening this speech, Prime Minister Blair
engages his audience by immediately

(A) talking about politics

(B) referring to ideals the masses believe in

(C) referring to the need for hard-headed
pragmatism

(D) translating values into the practical world we
live in

(E) directing attention to international affairs

16. The sentence that best expresses the essence of the
message of the speech is

(A) "Disorder is the enemy of progress." (lines
46–47)

(B) "In truth, it is very rare today that trouble in
one part of the globe remains limited in its
effect." (lines 24–26)

(C) "We are not half-hearted friends, and we
never will be." (lines 92–93)

(D) "American power affects the world
fundamentally." (line 115)

(E) "So if we didn't know it before, we know it
now: these events and our response to them
shape the fate not of one nation but of one
world." (lines 112–114)

17. In two parts of this speech, lines 56–59 and lines
112–114, the two-sentence and single-sentence
paragraphs are included to

(A) provide a break from the tension of longer
paragraphs

(B) show a reader the syntactical cleverness of the
speech writer

(C) provide syntactical transition to indicate
shifts in the focus of the speech

(D) give the speaker a moment to collect his
thoughts

(E) keep the audience attentive

GO ON TO THE NEXT PAGE

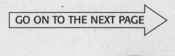

18. Throughout the speech, Prime Minister Blair includes all the following pairs of contrasting ideas EXCEPT

    (A) engagement not isolation

    (B) ours not theirs

    (C) interdependent not independent

    (D) utilitarian not utopian

    (E) stability not disorder

19. Blair's use of the words "guts" and "awesome" (lines 84 and 86) can best be described as

    (A) informal diction

    (B) an attempt to be humorous

    (C) a slip in his British stuffiness

    (D) a speech writer's error

    (E) a throwback to the speaker's common upbringing

20. The long sentence in lines 78–83 has its main clause appearing at the end of the sentence. This is known as what type of sentence?

    (A) loose

    (B) rhetorical

    (C) periodic

    (D) compound

    (E) complex

21. Paragraph 14 (lines 100–110) contains all of the following stylistic devices EXCEPT

    (A) parenthetical statement

    (B) hyperbole

    (C) metonymy

    (D) personification

    (E) assonance

22. The major effect of the syntactical structure, lines 116–118, makes this paragraph

    (A) pointedly powerful

    (B) boringly repetitions

    (C) unimaginatively simplistic

    (D) dramatically stressful

    (E) abruptly brief

23. In the final paragraph, Blair effectively makes his point by

    (A) explaining how England will work side by side with the US

    (B) appealing to responsibility and commitment

    (C) using a series of negatives followed by a positive

    (D) speaking directly to the audience by using the pronoun "you"

    (E) reminding the audience that everything comes with a price

24. The word "riposte" used in line 87 refers most specifically to

    (A) a meal

    (B) a request

    (C) a challenge

    (D) a retort

    (E) a retaliation

25. The sentence, "It can affect the world for good, or for bad" (lines 116–117) utilizes a literary device known as

    (A) contradiction

    (B) asyndeton

    (C) assonance

    (D) litote

    (E) zeugma

GO ON TO THE NEXT PAGE

26. From the last sentence of paragraph 5 (lines 34–37) we can infer that the speaker's attitude toward this point is

    (A) ambiguous
    (B) displeased
    (C) inflammatory
    (D) regretful
    (E) critical

27. In lines 116–117, the pronoun "it" refers to

    (A) September 11
    (B) international involvement
    (C) British solidarity
    (D) American power
    (E) American retaliation

GO ON TO THE NEXT PAGE

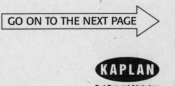

Questions 28–40. Read the following passage carefully before you choose your answers.

To a professional critic (I have been one myself) theatre-going is the curse of Adam. The play is the evil he is paid to endure in the sweat of his brow;
Line and the sooner it is over, the better. This would
(5) place him in irreconcilable opposition to the paying playgoer, from whose point of view the longer the play, the more entertainment he gets for his money. It does in fact so place him, especially in the provinces, where the playgoer goes to the
(10) theatre for the sake of the play solely, and insists so effectively on a certain number of hours' entertainment that touring managers are sometimes seriously embarrassed by the brevity of the London plays they have to deal in.
(15)   For in London the critics are reinforced by a considerable body of persons who go to the theatre as many others go to church, to display their best clothes and compare them with other people's; to be in the fashion, and to have
(20) something to talk about at dinner parties; to adore a pet performer; to pass the evening anywhere rather than home: in short, for any or every reason except interest in dramatic art as such. In fashionable centres the number of irreligious
(25) people who go to church, of unmusical people who go to concerts and operas, and of undramatic people who go to the theatre, is so prodigious that sermons have been cut down to ten minutes and plays to two hours; and, even at that,
(30) congregations sit longing for the benediction and audiences for the final curtain, so that they may get away to the lunch or supper they really crave for, after arriving as late as (or later than) the hour of beginning can possibly be made for them.
(35)   Thus from the stalls and in the Press an atmosphere of hypocrisy spreads. Nobody says straight out that genuine drama is a tedious nuisance, and that to ask people to endure more than two hours of it (with two long intervals of
(40) relief) is an intolerable imposition. Nobody says "I hate classical tragedy and comedy as I hate sermons and symphonies; but I like police news and divorce news and any kind of dancing or decoration that has an aphrodisiac effect on me or

(45) on my wife or husband. And whatever superior people may pretend, I cannot associate pleasure with any sort of intellectual activity; and I don't believe anyone else can either." Such things are not said; yet nine-tenths of what is offered as criticism
(50) of the drama in the metropolitan Press of Europe and America is nothing but a muddled paraphrase of it. If it does not mean that, it means nothing.
I do not complain of this, though it complains very unreasonably of me. But I can take no more
(55) notice of it than Einstein of the people who are incapable of mathematics. I write in the classical manner for those who pay for admission to a theatre because they like classical comedy or tragedy for its own sake, and like it so much when it is good
(60) of its kind and well done that they tear themselves away from it with reluctance to catch the very latest train or omnibus that will take them home. Far from arriving late from and eight or half-past eight o'clock dinner so as to escape at least the first half-
(65) hour of the performance, they stand in queues outside the theatre doors for hours beforehand in bitingly cold weather to secure a seat. In countries where a play lasts a week, they bring baskets of provisions and sit it out. These are the patrons on
(70) whom I depend for my bread. I do not give them performances twelve hours long, because circumstances do not at present make such entertainments feasible; but an all-night sitting in a theatre would be at least as enjoyable as an all-night
(75) sitting in the House of Commons, and much more useful.
Still I am sorry for the pseudo-critics and the fashionable people whose playgoing is a hypocrisy. They forget, however, that all men are not as they
(80) are. I cannot for their sakes undo my work and help the people who hate the theatre to drive out the people who love it, yet I may point out to them that they have several remedies in their own hands. They can escape the first part of the play by their usual
(85) practice of arriving late. They can escape the epilogue by not waiting for it. And if the irreducible

minimum thus attained is still too painful, they can stay away altogether. But I deprecate this extreme course, because it is good neither for my pocket nor
(90) for their own soul. Already a few of them, noticing that what matters is not the absolute length of time occupied by a play, but the speed with which that time passes, are discovering that the theatre, though purgatorial in its Aristotelian moments, is not
(95) necessarily always the dull place they have so often found it. What do its discomforts matter when the play makes us forget them?

George Bernard Shaw: "To the Critics, Lest They Should Feel Ignored" from *Saint Joan*

28. The writer's primary purpose in this passage is to

(A) explain why shorter plays need to be performed

(B) criticize the provincial playgoers' dramatic demands

(C) chastise the London public for their shallow-minded hypocrisy

(D) explain why his plays are so long

(E) berate the theater critics for their superficial reviews

29. The tone of this passage can best be described as

(A) complex and formal

(B) ambiguous and chastising

(C) direct and uncomplicated

(D) abstract and pedantic

(E) scathing and libelous

30. The dominant stylistic device used by the writer in the second paragraph is

(A) antithesis

(B) oxymoron

(C) metaphor

(D) analogy

(E) metonymy

31. The focus of the third paragraph is

(A) people's preferences of classical tragedy

(B) the publics preferences for entertainment

(C) the lack of originality in theater audiences

(D) society's general dislike of sermons and symphonies

(E) the hypocrisy of the Press and the public for not stating what they feel

32. Paragraph two is best summarized by which of the following?

(A) People often do the right thing for the wrong reason.

(B) In a busy world, churches and theaters have to accommodate the busy lifestyle of potential audiences.

(C) People will do just about anything to avoid returning home.

(D) Churches and theaters are experiencing a dramatic increase in their attendance.

(E) It is far more fashionable to attend a play than it is to attend church.

33. Lines 53 and 56 can best be understood as meaning which of the following?

(A) The author won't complain about things he cannot fix just as Einstein is unable to solve all problems.

(B) The author cannot worry about the London public's view of theater any more than Einstein can worry about the math-challenged people of the world.

(C) Einstein is more capable of helping people who dislike math than he is of helping people who dislike theater.

(D) Theater people and math people rarely belong to the same social circles.

(E) The author feels he has been unjustly criticized, just as Einstein has been unjustly misunderstood.

34. The main conclusion that one can draw from paragraph four (lines 53–76) is that

(A) the long lines (queues) of ticket buyers at some theaters have become a problem

(B) standing in long theater lines can be an unpleasant experience, especially in the winter cold

(C) twelve-hour-long performances are not unheard of

(D) week-long performances require theatergoers to bring their own food

(E) dedicated theater patrons are what make the author's efforts seem worthwhile

35. The repetition of infinitive phrases used in paragraph two is an example of the stylistic device

(A) anaphora

(B) apostrophe

(C) assonance

(D) ambiguity

(E) asyndeton

36. The author's reference to the House of Commons is most likely used to

(A) add credibility to the passage

(B) show that the author is politically correct

(C) indicate the author's probable disdain for the government

(D) demonstrate the author's intelligence

(E) provide an analogy to the point he is making

37. The phrase "irreducible minimum," lines 86–87, is a reference to

(A) the fewest number of plays the public needs to attend to be considered appropriately sociable

(B) the shortest time left after the beginning and end of an event have been eliminated

(C) the sum total of entertainment possibilities people have at their disposal

(D) that which remains after all the pseudo-critics have been eliminated

(E) the smallest price theaters can charge and still pay the playwright and make a prophet

38. When the author says in lines 89–90 that people avoiding the theater altogether is neither "good for [his] pocket nor for their own soul" he most likely means

(A) like church, the theater can be a religious experience

(B) hypocrisy is a sin, so people should avoid being guilty of it

(C) going to the theater will make audiences feel better

(D) inadvertently, people may actually learn something and possibly even come to appreciate the art of theater

(E) if people don't attend, they will be reducing the profits of the theaters and the income of the poor, starving playwrights

39. In lines 92–97, ". . .[They] are discovering that the theatre, though purgatorial in its Aristotelian moments, is not necessarily always the dull place they have so often found it," the author utilizes a rhetorical device known as

(A) ethical appeal

(B) historical reference

(C) analogy

(D) hyperbole

(E) allusion

GO ON TO THE NEXT PAGE

40. Overall, the conclusion of this passage is that

    (A) theater is boring and just an excuse to see and be seen

    (B) if given a chance, theater has more to offer than simply providing a social opportunity for Londoners

    (C) theater and church are closely aligned in their purpose and their audiences

    (D) shallow people are incapable of understanding the true artistic benefits of theater

    (E) attending a play is about as beneficial as attending a session of Parliament

GO ON TO THE NEXT PAGE

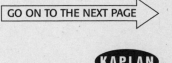

Questions 41–53. Read the following passage carefully before you choose your answers.

It is now many years ago, my children, when I was quite a young woman, and your father, Freddy, was less than you are at present, that we lived in a
Line village more than a hundred miles from here. It
(5) was a very pretty village, situated on the bank of a broad, beautiful stream, which added much to the fertility and loveliness of the whole country through which it passed. We had not always dwelt in so pretty a place; but your grandfather, thinking
(10) it would be better for his business, concluded to take up his abode there. About the time we removed, another family took a steerage passage in a vessel bound from Ireland to this country. There were seven of them altogether—the father, mother,
(15) and five children. Their home had hitherto been a cabin, with a mud floor. A Bible, an iron pot, and a few wooden stools constituted their furniture; while their fare consisted of the scanty supply of milk afforded by one ill-fed cow, with a few
(20) potatoes. Willing to labor, yet finding wages humbled so low that they were often obliged to go both weary and hungry to bed, they concluded, after many struggles, to leave kindred and friends and come to America. How often, when speaking
(25) of this unhappy country, is the sentence 'Why don't they emigrate?' uttered with the greatest indifference. But to a warm Irish heart, this is often a severe trial. They are taxed, we might almost say, for the very air they breathe; yet how fondly they
(30) still cling to the soil of that island home, where nature must smile in spite of oppression; where the dust of their kindred repose; where are more loving hearts and words of warmer greeting than are to be met with elsewhere. No wonder the
(35) Irishman loves his country, crushed, trampled upon as she is. Her soil is among the most fertile, her sons among the noblest, and the language of even her rudest children the most poetical of any on earth. Oh, Ireland, fair Ireland, would we might
(40) yet live to see thee take thy proper place among the nations to see the period approach when thy children will not be forced to seek in other

countries the bare sustenance denied them at home. The Nevilles, after many struggles to obtain
(45) means sufficient to defray the expenses of a passage, and after borrowing from several neighbors small sums, which they promised to repay with interest, found themselves in the steerage of a vessel on their way to this land of
(50) promise. I will pass over the first few weeks of their arrival—strangers on a strange soil. Suffice it to say, that some one directed them to our village as a place where they could likely find steady employment. And here, one evening in early
(55) spring, cold, hungry, and penniless, they arrived. My husband, contrary to his usual custom, chanced to be abroad on that evening; and, as he was a devout believer in that blessed word which teaches that we may sometimes entertain angels
(60) unawares, on hearing the landlord refuse to keep them on account of their inability to pay, he brought them all home with him. I confess, I was taken a good deal by surprise at this unusual act; but, as it was his pleasure, I bade them welcome;
(65) and the heartfelt blessing which the poor strangers asked over the meal we prepared for them went far towards prepossessing me in their favor. The man, his wife, and the two little girls we accommodated in the house, while the three boys found lodgings
(70) among the fragrant hay in the well-stored mow. These people, my children, were not particularly attractive as far as appearance was concerned; they all appeared healthy and good-humored, and the little ones seemed uncommonly well-mannered
(75) for children in their rank of life; but still I was in some way unaccountably interested in them; and I have since thought God permitted this feeling in order that I might bestir myself in behalf of those who were undoubtedly his followers. At any rate,
(80) we were willing to accommodate them a few days until something could be done for them; and, at the expiration of that time, a quiet-looking little cottage, with a willow tree before the door, standing just across the brook, was procured for
(85) them. I parted with several articles of furniture I could spare, in order to assist them in fitting out their new home; and my efforts among my

GO ON TO THE NEXT PAGE ⟶

neighbors procured them many other gifts of the same description. And now how happy was Mrs.
(90) Neville. Her husband had steady employment given him on a farm near by; her two eldest boys, of the ages of twelve and thirteen, both obtained good places; while the youngest boy, with the little girls, aged ten, eight, and six, were kept at home,
(95) where they were generally as busy as bees, for their mother held idleness to be the parent of all evil. I have often, on going in, been struck with the picture of neatness and humbled contentment their small kitchen presented.
(100)   The furniture was of the coarsest and most common description, yet scrupulously neat and clean. Here the family were generally found, pursuing their evening avocations, seated before the quiet blaze of their own fireside; and truly,
(105) where its comforts are properly appreciated, there is nothing gives the heart a finer or more touching idea of enjoyment than this same calm, domestic light. Evening, too, is the period of time which may truly be called the poor man's season of
(110) enjoyment; the implements of daily labor are laid aside, and it is then he may rest his wearied limbs and enjoy the prattle and playful wiles of his children, whose caresses sometimes lead him to forget the bitterness of his lot. The Nevilles were
(115) poor, very poor; the money they had borrowed from friends in Ireland, they had obligated themselves to return, and they were straining every nerve to accomplish this. It was ten months before they were able, by their united labor, with
(120) practicing the most rigid self-denial, to realize this amount. At length, however, the sum was raised; and a benevolent gentleman inclosed and forwarded it in such a manner as it would be sure to reach its destination. They had, however, barely
(125) felt their minds relieved in this particular, when Mr. Neville was laid upon a bed of sickness. He had, perhaps, overworked himself and taken cold. His disease was inflammatory rheumatism. He lingered for a month, oftentimes suffering greatly;
(130) and then, after commending his wife and little ones to the care of that God who is the protector of the widow and the fatherless, strong in the hope of a blissful immortality, he died. As I told you before, my children, the Nevilles were pious

(135) people; and I could not but notice, in their mode of expression, a degree of intellectual refinement peculiar to those who make the Holy Scriptures an habitual study.
    "You will observe, my children," said Mrs. Bruce,
(140) as she came to this portion of their discourse, "the unwavering faith which this poor woman possessed. She was a stranger in a strange land; there was no one upon whom she had any claim; yet I never heard her utter one repining word, or
(145) wonder how she was to get along without the assistance of her husband, there was so little selfishness in her grief. And although tears must flow at these sad sunderings of beloved ties, yet, when she did indulge in this outward exhibition of
(150) distress, she would almost immediately dry them, and give utterance to something which would discover how entire and unchanging was her trust in God. I was a great deal with her, and, I must say, after the last sad duties were performed, I was
(155) astonished to see how energetically she set to work in order to support herself and her children. Her husband had often told me that all the fortune his wife had brought him was her religion, her energy, and her steady habits of industry, and that these
(160) had proved the blessing of his life. Now, too, she found ample exercise for these estimable qualities, and it was surprising how she could turn her hand to anything that offered; and, indeed, with the assistance the children were able to afford her, they
(165) managed to live very comfortably."
    There, amid the far-stretching forests, on a farm which in Europe might be called a principality, a wife and mother, she is spending her days in the enjoyment of all that heart can desire. I have now
(170) done with the history of this family; yet I would have you observe how fearlessly Christian parents may repose upon the strength of the promises of Him who holds the hearts of all men in his hand. The skeptic may laugh and the worldling may
(175) sneer, but an appeal may confidently be made to those who have noted the dealings of Providence as to whether any who have trusted in him have been confounded.
    From *Godey's Lady's Book,* 1850

GO ON TO THE NEXT PAGE

KAPLAN
Test Prep and Admissions

41. In the lament expressed about Ireland and its people in lines 27–44, the narrator utilizes all of the following stylistic devices EXCEPT

    (A) apostrophe
    (B) paradox
    (C) anaphora
    (D) personification
    (E) litote

42. According to this passage, the Irish can best be described as

    (A) people who are anxious to leave their unpleasant living conditions
    (B) rude people whose children do not have any manners
    (C) indifferent folks whose apathy makes it easy for them to be tolerant
    (D) oppressed people who regret having to leave the land that they love
    (E) complacent folks who have learned to embrace their situation with understanding

43. Lines 1–36 utilizes all of the following types of sentences EXCEPT

    (A) compound-complex
    (B) imperative
    (C) rhetorical question
    (D) loose
    (E) periodic

44. Initially the Neville family can be characterized as

    (A) penurious and devout
    (B) weak and hopeless
    (C) fortunate but ungrateful
    (D) indifferent and idle
    (E) self-sufficient and apathetic

45. The narrator's attitude toward the Nevilles can be summed up as

    (A) taken aback by their forwardness
    (B) fascinated by their intrepid spirit
    (C) prepossessed in their favor
    (D) distraught by their presence in her house
    (E) apathetic towards their situation

46. Lines 89–99 encompass a long sentence with many independent clauses, without the aid of conjunctions. This is a syntactical device known as

    (A) periodic
    (B) an apostrophe
    (C) rhetorical question
    (D) a run-on
    (E) asyndeton

47. When the narrator states "They [the Irish] are taxed, we might say, for the very air they breathe" (lines 28–29), she is using a rhetorical exaggeration known as

    (A) juxtaposition
    (B) hyperbole
    (C) metonymy
    (D) parenthetical interruption
    (E) imperative declamation

GO ON TO THE NEXT PAGE

48. The phrase "uncommonly well-mannered for children in their rank of life" can be interpreted as meaning which of the following?

    (A) It is uncommon for children of rank to have manners.

    (B) Good manners were not commonly practiced during that historical time.

    (C) Poor people were not uncommon at that time nor were their children.

    (D) Children of the poor were often less well-mannered than those born to the more economically successful.

    (E) For their age, the children's manners can be well ranked compared to other children's manners.

49. The verb "to realize" in line 120, can be best defined as meaning

    (A) to amass

    (B) to recognize

    (C) to beg for

    (D) to squander

    (E) to return

50. The sentence beginning "And although tears must flow . . ." (lines 147–153) can best be interpreted as meaning

    (A) Mrs. Neville's love of God increases her sadness at her husband's death

    (B) Mrs. Neville's ties are reinforced by her beloved's tears and sundering

    (C) although Mrs. Neville inevitably cries due to her loss she finds strength in her faith

    (D) although Mrs. Neville's trust in God is unchanging, her life is not

    (E) tears come and they go just as beloved people come and go in our own lives

51. After the loss of her husband, Mrs. Neville can best be characterized as

    (A) irretrievably lost in grief

    (B) so remorseful that she was unable to go on

    (C) resourceful and plucky in her movement forward

    (D) caught up in her need to exercise her energy amply in order to live comfortably

    (E) so caught up in her own endeavors that she quickly forgot her grief

52. The word "repining," line 144, means

    (A) resting

    (B) depositing

    (C) distrustful

    (D) lamenting

    (E) complaining

53. The most significant message in this ladies' story is best summarized by which of the following?

    (A) Hard work and a good marriage are what bring you a successful life.

    (B) Sometimes we must leave our beloved home country in order to live comfortably and prosper.

    (C) No matter what difficulties one might encounter, a strong faith in Providence will help you through life.

    (D) A hard-working woman is always the center of a happy family.

    (E) Friendship and generosity are attributes worth having; they will bring you new and good-hearted friends.

IF YOU FINISH BEFORE TIME IS CALLED, YOU MAY CHECK YOUR WORK ON THIS SECTION ONLY. DO NOT TURN TO ANY OTHER SECTION IN THE TEST.

STOP

Section II

Total time—2 hours
Number of questions—3
Percent of total grade—55%

Directions: This section contains three essay questions. Answer all three questions, budgeting your time carefully. Each essay counts as one-third of your total essay score.

QUESTION ONE

(Suggested time—40 minutes)

In his description of springtime at Walden Pond, Henry David Thoreau shares his ideas about Nature with us. After reading the passage closely, discuss Thoreau's attitudes toward nature and its importance to us. Be sure to discuss his uses of the resources of language to convey his feelings to the reader.

On the 29th of April, as I was fishing from the bank of the river near the Nine-Acre Corner bridge, standing on the quaking grass and willow roots, where the muskrats lurk, I heard a singular rattling sound, somewhat like that of the sticks which boys play with their
Line fingers, when, looking up, I observed a very slight and graceful hawk, like a nighthawk,
(5) alternately soaring like a ripple and tumbling a rod or two over and over, showing the under side of its wings, which gleamed like a satin ribbon in the sun, or like the pearly inside of a shell. This sight reminded me of falconry and what nobleness and poetry are associated with that sport. The Merlin it seemed to me it might be called: but I care not for its name. It was the most ethereal flight I had ever witnessed. It did not simply flutter like a
(10) butterfly, nor soar like the larger hawks, but it sported with proud reliance in the fields of air; mounting again and again with its strange chuckle, it repeated its free and beautiful fall, turning over and over like a kite, and then recovering from its lofty tumbling, as if it had never set its foot on *terra firma*. It appeared to have no companion in the universe— sporting there alone—and to need none but the morning and the ether with which it
(15) played. It was not lonely, but made all the earth lonely beneath it. Where was the parent, which hatched it, its kindred, and its father in the heavens? The tenant of the air, it seemed related to the earth but by an egg hatched some time in the crevice of a crag;—or was its native nest made in the angle of a cloud, woven of the rainbow's trimmings and the sunset sky, and lined with some soft midsummer haze caught up from earth? Its eyry[1] now some
(20) cliffy cloud.
    Beside this I got a rare mess of golden and silver and bright cupreous fishes, which looked like a string of jewels. Ah! I have penetrated to those meadows on the morning of many a first spring day, jumping from hummock to hummock[2], from willow root to willow root, when the wild river valley and the woods were bathed in so pure and bright a
(25) light as would have waked the dead, if they had been slumbering in their graves, as some suppose. There needs no stronger proof of immortality. All things must live in such a light. O Death, where was thy sting? O Grave, where was thy victory, then?
    Our village life would stagnate if it were not for the unexplored forests and meadows which surround it. We need the tonic of wildness—to wade sometimes in marshes where
(30) the bittern and the meadow-hen lurk, and hear the booming of the snipe; to smell the whispering sedge where only some wilder and more solitary fowl builds her nest, and the mink crawls with its belly close to the ground. At the same time that we are earnest to explore and learn all things, we require that all things be mysterious and unexplorable, that land and sea be infinitely wild, unsurveyed and unfathomed by us because
(35) unfathomable. We can never have enough of nature. We must be refreshed by the sight of inexhaustible vigor, vast and titanic features, the sea-coast with its wrecks, the wilderness

1. *eyry*—home for birds
2. *hummock*—a hill or a rise in the land

GO ON TO THE NEXT PAGE

with its living and its decaying trees, the thunder-cloud, and the rain which lasts three weeks and produces freshets. We need to witness our own limits transgressed, and some life pasturing freely where we never wander. We are cheered when we observe the vulture
(40) feeding on the carrion which disgusts and disheartens us, and deriving health and strength from the repast. There was a dead horse in the hollow by the path to my house, which compelled me sometimes to go out of my way, especially in the night when the air was heavy, but the assurance it gave me of the strong appetite and inviolable health of Nature was my compensation for this. I love to see that Nature is so rife with life that myriads can
(45) be afforded to be sacrificed and suffered to prey on one another; that tender organizations can be so serenely squashed out of existence like pulp—tadpoles which herons gobble up, and tortoises and toads run over in the road; and that sometimes it has rained flesh and blood! With the liability to accident, we must see how little account is to be made of it. The impression made on a wise man is that of universal innocence. Poison is not
(50) poisonous after all, nor are any wounds fatal. Compassion is a very untenable ground. It must be expeditious. Its pleadings will not bear to be stereotyped.

GO ON TO THE NEXT PAGE

Write Your Essay Here

QUESTION TWO
(Suggested time—40 minutes)

Read the following selection by Annie Dillard carefully, and consider the attitude of the
narrator in the passage. Then, in a well-organized essay, identify this attitude and how the
author's choice of diction, syntax, tone, and rhetorical devices helps demonstrate this attitude
within the passage.

    Here, on the obstetrical ward, is a double sink in a little room—a chrome faucet, two
basins and drains, just like any kitchen sink. There is a counter on the left, and a counter
on the right. Overhead, a long heat lamp lights and warms the two counters and the sink.
Line   This is where they wash the newborns like dishes. A nurse, one or another, spends most
(5) of an eight-hour shift standing here at the sink.
    Different nurses bring in newborns, one after another, and line them down the counter
to the sink's left. The newborns wear flannel blankets. Knit hats the size of teacups keep
sliding up their wet heads. Their faces run the spectrum from lavender through purple
and red to pink and beige.
(10)   Nurse Pat Eisberg wears her curly blond hair short in back; her thin neck bends out of a
blue collarless scrub as she leans left for the next bundle. The newborn's face is red.
    "Now you," she says to it in a warm voice, unsmiling. She slides it along the counter
toward her, plucks off its cap, unwraps its body and leaves the blanket underneath. This
baby is red all over. His tadpole belly is red; his scrotum, the size of a plum, is fiercely red,
(15) and looks as if it might explode. The top of his head looks like a dunce cap; he is a
conehead. He gazes up attentively from the nurse's arms. The bright heat lamp does not
seem to bother his eyes, nor do the silver nitrate eyedrops, which prevent gonorrhea. His
plastic ID bracelet, an inch wide, covers a full third of his forearm. Someone has taped his
blue umbilical cord—the inch or so left of it—upward on his belly. A black clamp grips
(20) the cord's end, so it looks like a jumper cable.
    The nurse washes this boy; she dips a thin washcloth again and again in warm water.
She cleans his head and face, careful to wash every fold of his ears. She wipes white lines of
crumbled vernix from folds in his groin and under his arms. She holds one wormy arm
and one wormy leg to turn him over; then she cleans his dorsal side, and ends with his
(25) anus. She has washed and rinsed every bit of his red skin. The heat lamp has dried him
already. The Qur'an says Allah created man from a clot. The red baby is a ball of blood
Allah wetted and into which he blew. So does a clown inflate a few thin balloons and twist
them lickety-split into a rabbit, a dog, a giraffe.
    Nurse Pat Eisberg drains the sink. She drops the newborn's old blanket and hat into an
(30) open hamper, peels a new blanket and hat from the pile on the right and sticks the red
baby on the right-hand counter. She diapers him. She swaddles him: she folds the right
corner of the blanket over him and rolls him back to tuck it under him; she brings up the
bottom blanket corner over his chest: she wraps the left corner around and around, and
his weight holds it tight as he lies on his back. Now he is tidy and compact, the size of a
(35) one-quart Thermos. She caps his conehead, and gives the bundle a push to slide it down
the counter to the end of the line with the others she has just washed.

GO ON TO THE NEXT PAGE ⟹

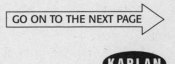

The red newborn looks up and studies his surroundings, alert, seemingly pleased, and preternaturally calm, as if enchanted. Every few minutes another nurse comes in to pick up whichever washed baby has reached the head of the line. The nurse returns the parcel
(40) to its mother. When the red boy's number is up, I follow.

The mother is propped on a clean hospital bed she looks a bit wan. The mother is white as the sheets, in her thirties, puffy, pretty, and completely stunned. She looks like the cartoon Road Runner who has just had a steamroller drive over it.

The nurse has put the baby on his back in a basinet cart. Americans place infants on
(45) their backs now—never on their stomachs, lest they smother in their sleep and die. Ten years ago, Americans placed infants on their stomachs—never on their backs, lest they choke in their sleep and die.

A nurse unwraps him. He does not like it; he hates being unwrapped. He is still red. His fingernail slivers are red, as if someone had painted nail polish on them. His toenails are
(50) red. The nurse shows the father how to swaddle him.

"... and then you wrap the last corner tight around the whole works, the nurse says. As she finishes binding him into his proper Thermos shape, the baby closes his mouth, opens his eyes, and peers about like a sibyl. He looks into our faces. When he meets our eyes in turn, his father and I each say "Hi," involuntarily. In the nurses, this impulse has perhaps
(55) worn out.

GO ON TO THE NEXT PAGE ⟹

Write Your Essay Here

QUESTION THREE
(Suggested time—40 minutes)

Think carefully about the challenging ideas presented in the following quotations:

"Stubborn and ardent clinging to one's opinion is the best proof of stupidity."
(Montaigne)

"Time has a way of demonstrating that the most stubborn are the most intelligent."
(Yevtushenko)

On first look, the above quotations seem somewhat contradictory. What is your opinion
concerning stubbornness: Is it proof of stupidity or the sign of intelligence? In a well-organized
essay, briefly explain the two positions; then defend the one position you believe is stronger.
Support your explanation using details and citing examples taken from your readings,
experiences, or observations.

GO ON TO THE NEXT PAGE

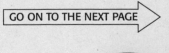

Write Your Essay Here

Diagnostic Test: **Answer Key**

1. A	19. A	37. B
2. D	20. C	38. D
3. B	21. E	39. E
4. E	22. A	40. B
5. B	23. D	41. E
6. C	24. D	42. D
7. B	25. E	43. B
8. A	26. A	44. A
9. C	27. D	45. B
10. C	28. C	46. E
11. D	29. B	47. B
12. E	30. D	48. D
13. A	31. E	49. A
14. B	32. A	50. C
15. B	33. B	51. C
16. E	34. F	52. E
17. C	35. A	53. C
18. D	36. C	

ANSWERS AND EXPLANATIONS

Questions 1–14

Although my early life tended to encourage my flirting propensities it did not make me the real heartless coquette, I afterwards became. The flir-
Line tations of school life were harmless, for there was
(5) no real love between myself and the parties concerned. When I left school I was just seventeen. Young, gay, rich, happy and thoughtless, without a wish ungratified. I had been accustomed to admiration all my life, and now I really deserved
(10) it. I was rather stylish in my personal appearance, so every one said. Every advantage, that money could give, had been given me, and I do not flatter myself, when I say I improved my talents. I rode well, danced well, played and sang well, con-
(15) versed well, and in truth everything I attempted I did well.

Among the first satellites that moved around my sphere, were two young gentlemen, both handsome, but very unlike in personal appearance
(20) and disposition. One was dark as a Spaniard, with eyes and hair as dark as night when the moon and stars have hid their beams under a canopy of cloud. He was very handsome and talented, yet I could not love the man, for I feared him. Still it
(25) amused me to lead him on, intending to tell him every time we met, that his love was vain; but I continued putting it off.

The other—God knows I loved him, if woman is capable of loving. He was fair, very fair, with dark
(30) eyes and light hair. His mouth was beautiful, but deceit lurked in each exquisite curve of his lips. An Adonis was not more perfect in form: and he knew it. He was young in years, yet old in sin. I now sometimes think that he, like Bulwer's Zanoni, had
(35) found the true secret of perpetual youth, and that he had lived for centuries, so well was he versed in the ways of the world, and in each phase of human nature. He often boasted of the many conquests he had made, and said that no woman he chose to
(40) captivate could escape loving him. I did not like this speech; but I loved him. He had certainly many rare traits of character. His generosity was

proverbial; he was a warm friend and had the most perfect control over his very high temper. It was
(45) not long before we became engaged. He said that he loved me at first sight; and God knows that his love was more than returned. He called to see me each day, and every night escorted me to some place of amusement. He was very jealous, but I
(50) liked that. He was my sun during the day, and my moon at night. There was a cloud over all my happiness when he failed to come. He was young, ardent, fiery and passionate, and I—I was a fool! The passionate devotion of my heart was lavished
(55) upon a worthless object. I knew nothing of his former conduct or character, as he had come to Macon but recently. Knowing how particular my father was about such things, I employed a friend to visit the town he was from, and enquire into his
(60) past history. Now, friends, bear with pity my sad trial, and paint to your own imaginations how you would feel in such a case.

Within two weeks of marriage, with a man that you loved with your whole heart and soul, a
(65) perfect man, as you thought, imagine how you would feel to hear that he had (Oh God! how can I relate truth as I heard it! but I must or you will never hear with charity my flirtations,) that he had been compelled to leave the town in which he
(70) lived, on account of his base seduction of a most beautiful, but poor girl, under solemn promise of marriage. He lived as a husband with her for a few months, and then deserted her, leaving her to die alone, in ignominy, and the most abject poverty.
(75) On her death-bed she divulged her secret to her brother, who traced the seducer to the city and wounded him in a duel, and was fatally shot himself. A seducer and a double murderer, the man I thought free from guile as an angel in
(80) heaven! It was enough to drive one mad, and I am sure I was crazed for years.

He came to see me that night! How my hand trembles! I can scarcely write to describe our meeting. I was sitting alone, for I had refused to
(85) receive visitors that night, when he entered the room.

'Ah! darling,' said he, kissing me. 'Alone I see. I am very glad too, for I wanted to see you with no one near.' How handsome he looked, with his

(90) flushed cheeks, red from his ride in the wintry
wind. 'What's the matter with my bird to-night?
her voice is as sweet as ever, but it is too sad for
me.' 'Ella do let me urge you to appoint our
wedding day a week sooner, for you are so pretty

(95) and sweet, you will tempt me to'—he did not
finish the sentence, but I understood his meaning
but too well. It was the first time he had ever acted
in such a singular manner, and I saw he was
excited highly by spirituous liquors.

(100)   'Indeed sir,' I answered, 'If I have heard the truth
I am not the first woman who proved too sweet
and pretty for you, and in whose presence you
could not control your passions.'

   'Who told you that Ella?' he exclaimed, starting
(105) from his seat! 'By all that is sacred if I find out, he
shall not live an hour!'

   'You shall never know,' said I. 'Two murders are
quite enough to doom your blackened soul,
Dudley Earle!'

(110)   How pale he looked, but not with penitence, it
was anger only toward the person who had
divulged his secret. He remained an hour trying to
persuade me to revoke my decision, and then left
me a heart-broken sad woman, without an object

(115) in life. And then and there I bent my knee, before
the throne of God. (I know now it was blasphemy)
but I was crazy then! and vowed to revenge myself
upon the whole sex, for the misery one, I then
supposed the type of the species, had wrought in

(120) my soul; and faithfully I kept that vow.

   The Devil aids his own, and he surely helped
me. Even unsought, men would lay their love at
my feet, and their foibles, rendered harmless by my
own self-control, became my playthings. Often,

(125) very often have I acted in such a way, that I knew
would inflame an even unimpressable man, and
then would send his love back ungratified, to
corrode his very heart. Was that just or right? No
indeed, it was not. It was dangerous to me, and

(130) outrageous to others. But dear reader in pity for
my anguish, and for the long years of intense
mental suffering, forgive me. Never! believe me,
would I divulge this passage of my life to any one,
did I not think that perhaps it may be a warning to

(135) the young, of both sexes.

   Let the young gentlemen always think and know,
that no matter how secret an evil act may be
committed, it will always come to light, and at the
very time you may wish it to be kept concealed. To
(140) the girls: No matter my dears, how handsome or
fascinating a gentleman may appear, never allow
your affections to become fixed on any human
being, until you know that being worthy. Often
times the veriest serpent wears a shining coat,
(145) most beautiful to look upon, but the poison of
whose fangs will corrupt a young heart and mar its
peace a whole life time.

   Selection from *Confessions of a Flirt* by Mrs.
Edward Leigh (1859)

1. A

This first question is identifying the mode of discourse of
the passage. The young lady is telling us about her own
story. Although there is some justification of behavior going
on (cause and effect), the dominant mode of discourse is
a simple personal narrative, making (A) the correct
response.

2. D

It is not unusual for the AP exam to ask you to make a
judgment about the probable attitude or characteristics of
the narrator. In this case, we have a young woman who is
definitely out for revenge. However, she is so up-front and
likeable, that (D) is the best response to this question.

3. B

Basically, paragraph two is a foreshadowing of the young
lady's later behavior. She talks about how she dallied with
suitors and mercilessly kept stringing one man along. This
early behavior is a precursor to her later vindication against
men. Therefore, (B) is the correct response.

4. E

Paragraph three uses a couple of *allusions*, including a reference to mythology. In addition, line 26 shows *antithesis*; exaggeration, *hyperbole*, is evident in several places, in particular in her lavish description of the young gentleman; the narrator also presents a series of clauses, almost every one of them connected by conjunctions, *polysyndeton*. Nowhere, however, is there a repetition of wording in a series of phrases or clauses, making (E) the correct answer.

5. B

In conjunction with the previous question, paragraph three has numerous independent clauses (connected by appropriate conjunctions). The syntactical structure of this paragraph is primarily compound sentences, (B).

6. C

Remember, you are being asked for the *best* description of the young man. Although several of the responses describe his character, the *best* response is (C)—he is smooth and a man with a history.

7. B

"A seducer and a double murderer, the man I thought free from guile as an angel in heaven! It was enough to drive one mad, and I am sure I was crazed for years." These lines definitely display *irony*, contrast between the expected and the actual, as well as *hyperbole*, exaggeration. Response (B) is the correct answer to this question.

8. A

"It was the first time he had ever acted in such a singular manner . . ." The narrator is surprised and taken aback by this young man's unusual behavior. Although several of the responses readily describe this young man, (A), "remarkable," is the most accurate synonym in this case for singular.

9. C

This question is actually one of basic grammar. It asks you to identify the antecedent (word being replaced by the pronoun). Although all of the responses are present somewhere in the passage, the antecedent of "that" is the despicable gentleman, (C).

10. C

This question actually is a bit of a confession on the part of the narrator. She admits she is part devil, and therefore it apparently takes a devil to know and aid a fellow devil. Her successful revenge on all men was aided by the devil, (C).

11. D

Paragraph eleven (lines 121–135) demonstrates several rhetorical devices: although not abundant, alliteration, repetition of initial consonant sounds, is present; assonance, repetition of similar internal vowel sounds, is also present. In addition, a rhetorical question is asked in line 128, exclamation in line 132. Nowhere is zeugma present, that is, grammatically correct linkage of one subject with two or more verbs or a verb with two or more objects. Therefore, (D) is the correct response.

12. E

The last paragraph is very moralistic and almost preachy. Given the response choices, didactic, (E) is the best.

13. A

The *best* alternative for "veriest serpent wears a shining coat," means that even the lowliest snake can pass itself off as something glamorous. This makes (A) the best cliché to echo the meaning of this phrase.

14. B

Overall, the story is a lesson to young women everywhere to beware of men who seem more than they are. This can best be stated by the cliché in (B), not to judge a book by its cover.

Questions 15–27

The only purpose of being in politics is to strive for the values and ideals we believe in: freedom, justice, what we Europeans call solidarity but you Line might call respect for and help for others. These
(5) are the decent democratic values we all avow. But alongside the values we know we need a hard-headed pragmatism—a *realpolitik*—required to give us any chance of translating those values into the practical world we live in.
(10) The same tension exists in the two views of international affairs. One is utilitarian: each nation maximizes its own self-interest. The other is Utopian: we try to create a better world. Today I want to suggest that more than ever before those
(15) two views are merging.

I advocate an enlightened self-interest that puts fighting for our values right at the heart of the policies necessary to protect our nations. Engagement in the world on the basis of these
(20) values, not isolationism from it, is the hard-headed pragmatism for the 21st Century.

Why? In part it is because the countries and people of the world today are more inter-dependent than ever. In truth, it is very rare today
(25) that trouble in one part of the globe remains limited in its effect. Not just in security, but in trade and finance—witness the crisis of 1998 which began in Thailand and ended in Brazil—the world is interlocked.
(30) This is heightened by mass communications and technology. In Queen Victoria's time, reports of battles came back weeks or months after they were won or lost. Today we see them enacted live on the BBC, Sky or CNN. Their very visibility, immediate
(35) and in technicolour, inflame feelings that can spread worldwide across different ethnic, religious and cultural communities.

So today, more than ever, "their" problem becomes "our" problem. Instability is contagious
(40) and, again today, more than ever, nations, at least most of them crave stability. That's for a simple reason. Our people want it, because without it, they can't do business and prosper. What brings nations together—what brought them together
(45) post-September 11—is the international recognition that the world needs order. Disorder is

the enemy of progress.

The struggle is for stability, for the security within which progress can be made. Of course,
(50) countries want to protect their territorial integrity but few are into empire-building. This is especially true of democracies whose people vote for higher living standards and punish governments who don't deliver them. For 2,000 years Europe fought
(55) over territory.

Today boundaries are virtually fixed. Govern-ments and people know that any territorial ambition threatens stability, and instability threatens prosperity.
(60) And of course the surest way to stability is through the very values of freedom, democracy and justice. Where these are strong, the people push for moderation and order. Where they are absent, regimes act unchecked by popular
(65) accountability and pose a threat; and the threat spreads.

So the promotion of these values becomes not just right in itself but part of our long-term security and prosperity. We can't intervene in every
(70) case. Not all the wrongs of the world can be put right, but where disorder threatens us all, we should act.

Like it or not, whether you are a utilitarian or a Utopian, the world is interdependent. One
(75) consequence of this is that foreign and domestic policy are ever more closely interwoven.

It was September 11 that brought these thoughts into sharper focus. Watching the horror unfold, imagining the almost unimaginable suffering of
(80) the thousands of innocent victims of the terror and carnage, the dominant emotion after the obvious feelings of revulsion, sympathy and anger, was determination.

The guts and spirit of the people of New York
(85) and America in the aftermath of that terrible day were not just admirable, they were awesome. They were the best riposte to the terrorists that humanity could give and you should be very proud of that. I want you to know too that the
(90) British people were with you from the first moment, and we will always be with you at times like those. We are not half-hearted friends and we never will be. But the determination must be not just to pursue those responsible and bring them to

(95) justice but to learn from September 11. There is a
real danger we forget the lessons of September 11.
Human beings recover from tragedy and the
memory becomes less fraught. That is healthy part
of living. But we should learn from our experience.

(100)   The most obvious lesson is indeed our
interdependence. For a time our world stood still.
Quite apart from our security, the shock impacted
on economic confidence, on business, on trade
and it is only now with the terrorist network on

(105) the run, that confidence is really returning. Every
nation in the world felt the reverberation of that
fateful day. And that has been well illustrated by
the role which the United Nations—under Kofi
Annan's excellent leadership—has played since

(110) September 11.

So if we didn't know it before, we know now:
these events and our response to them shape the
fate not of one nation but of one world.

For America, it has laid bare the reality.

(115) American power affects the world fundamentally.
It is there. It is real. It is never irrelevant. It can
affect the world for good, or for bad. Stand aside
or engage; it never fails to affect.

You know I want it engaged. Under President

(120) Bush, I am confident it will be and for good. But if
that's what I and many others want, it comes at a
price for us too. It means we don't shirk our
responsibility. It means that when America is
fighting for those values, then, however tough, we

(125) fight with her. No grandstanding, no offering
implausible but impractical advice from the
comfort of the touchline, no wishing away the
hard not the easy choices, but working together,
side by side.

Prime Minister Tony Blair to the American
citizens following 9/11/2001

15. B

The best way for the speaker to get his audience on his
side and listening to him is to appeal to those ideas with
which the majority of the audience will agree. This is exactly
what Tony Blair has done in this speech. Therefore, (B) is
the correct response.

16. E

To answer this questions correctly, you must go through a
process of elimination. Although almost every choice has
some validity, the focus of Prime Minister Blair's speech is
that we can no longer be independent nations, but as John
Donne reminded us many years ago, "No man is an
island." Blair extends this sentiment by implying that each
"island" is a part of the whole, making (E) the correct
response to this question.

17. C

Common sense and your composition skills should lead
you to the correct response, (C). Each time a short one-
sentence paragraph is injected into Blair's speech, it
indicates a transition to the next point he intends to make.

18. D

Lines 74–75 assure us that utilitarian and Utopian are not
necessarily contrasting ideas, but philosophies that can co-
exist. Choice (D) is correct.

19. A

Although you might be tempted to respond with one of the
other answers to this question, the inclusion of "guts" and
"awesome" are examples of informal diction—an unusual
inclusion in a British politician's vocabulary (A).

20. C

When the main, independent clause follows a series of
introductory phrases and clauses, the syntactical structure is
known as (C), periodic sentence.

21. E

In paragraph 14, parenthetical statement (A) is found
between the dashes. Hyperbole, exaggeration for effect (B)
is present throughout the paragraph. Metonymy—figure of
speech that uses the name of one thing to name or
designate something else—is present in the reference to
"terrorist network" and United Nations. Personification is
present in that nations, per se cannot really "feel"
reverberations, a human feeling. Therefore, the correct
response is (E), assonance. There is no repetition of similar
vowel sounds in close proximity within this paragraph.

22. A

Because of Blair's well-crafted appeal to the majority of his audience, embracing of the United States in times of trauma and consequential girding of strength, repetition of key points, all manipulated by the syntactical structure of short and long sentences as well as short, terse paragraphs, (A), pointedly powerful best describes the major effect of his speech.

23. D

In the finale of this speech, Prime Minister Blair returns to his appeal to the audience. He shifts to the pronoun "you" and intones the camaraderie between Britain and the United States. He appeals to the audience directly, making (D) the correct response.

24. D

"They were the best <u>riposte</u> to the terrorists that humanity could give" indicates a response, or in this case a retort (strong response), making (D) the correct response

25. E

A zeugma, (E), is when two or more parts of a sentence utilize another part that is only stated once. In other words, these lines really say "It can affect the world for good, *or it can affect the world* for bad." In other words, the phrase "it can affect the world" is assumed but not stated. None of the other devices are present in this paragraph.

26. A

It is difficult to tell exactly how Blair feels about what he says in these lines. Although we might think it is just a statement, the word "inflame" indicates a possible negative inference, but this is not clear. Therefore, (A), ambiguous is correct.

27. D

This last question is basically just a grammar question. The job of pronouns is to replace or rename a noun somewhere else in the sentence. In this case, the antecedent for the pronoun "it" is American power, (D).

Questions 28–40

To a professional critic (I have been one myself) theatre-going is the curse of Adam. The play is the evil he is paid to endure in the sweat of his brow;
Line and the sooner it is over, the better. This would
(5) place him in irreconcilable opposition to the paying playgoer, from whose point of view the longer the play, the more entertainment he gets for his money. It does in fact so place him, especially in the provinces, where the playgoer goes to the
(10) theatre for the sake of the play solely, and insists so effectively on a certain number of hours' entertainment that touring managers are sometimes seriously embarrassed by the brevity of the London plays they have to deal in.
(15) For in London the critics are reinforced by a considerable body of persons who go to the theatre as many others go to church, to display their best clothes and compare them with other people's; to be in the fashion, and to have
(20) something to talk about at dinner parties; to adore a pet performer; to pass the evening anywhere rather than home: in short, for any or every reason except interest in dramatic art as such. In fashionable centres the number of irreligious
(25) people who go to church, of unmusical people who go to concerts and operas, and of undramatic people who go to the theatre, is so prodigious that sermons have been cut down to ten minutes and plays to two hours; and, even at that,
(30) congregations sit longing for the benediction and audiences for the final curtain, so that they may get away to the lunch or supper they really crave for, after arriving as late as (or later than) the hour of beginning can possibly be made for them.
(35) Thus from the stalls and in the Press an atmosphere of hypocrisy spreads. Nobody says straight out that genuine drama is a tedious nuisance, and that to ask people to endure more than two hours of it (with two long intervals of
(40) relief) is an intolerable imposition. Nobody says "I hate classical tragedy and comedy as I hate sermons and symphonies; but I like police news and divorce news and any kind of dancing or decoration that has an aphrodisiac effect on me or
(45) on my wife or husband. And whatever superior people may pretend, I cannot associate pleasure

with any sort of intellectual activity; and I don't believe anyone else can either." Such things are not said; yet nine-tenths of what is offered as criticism
(50) of the drama in the metropolitan Press of Europe and America is nothing but a muddled paraphrase of it. If it does not mean that, it means nothing.

I do not complain of this, though it complains very unreasonably of me. But I can take no more
(55) notice of it than Einstein of the people who are incapable of mathematics. I write in the classical manner for those who pay for admission to a theatre because they like classical comedy or tragedy for its own sake, and like it so much when
(60) it is good of its kind and well done that they tear themselves away from it with reluctance to catch the very latest train or omnibus that will take them home. Far from arriving late from and eight or half-past eight o'clock dinner so as to escape at
(65) least the first half-hour of the performance, they stand in queues outside the theatre doors for hours beforehand in bitingly cold weather to secure a seat. In countries where a play lasts a week, they bring baskets of provisions and sit it out. These are
(70) the patrons on whom I depend for my bread. I do not give them performances twelve hours long, because circumstances do not at present make such entertainments feasible; but an all-night sitting in a theatre would be at least as enjoyable as an all-
(75) night sitting in the House of Commons, and much more useful.

Still I am sorry for the pseudo-critics and the fashionable people whose playgoing is a hypocrisy. They forget, however, that all men are not as they
(80) are. I cannot for their sakes undo my work and help the people who hate the theatre to drive out the people who love it, yet I may point out to them that they have several remedies in their own hands. They can escape the first part of the play by their usual
(85) practice of arriving late. They can escape the epilogue by not waiting for it. And if the irreducible minimum thus attained is still too painful, they can stay away altogether. But I deprecate this extreme course, because it is good neither for my pocket nor
(90) for their own soul. Already a few of them, noticing that what matters is not the absolute length of time occupied by a play, but the speed with which that time passes, are discovering that the theatre, though purgatorial in its Aristotelian moments, is not

(95) necessarily always the dull place they have so often found it. What do its discomforts matter when the play makes us forget them?

George Bernard Shaw: "To the Critics, Lest They Should Feel Ignored" from *Saint Joan*

28. C

Although all the answers are mentioned in the passage, the *overall* message comes across as (C), a chastisement of the London public for their lack of imagination or artistic appreciation.

29. B

Shaw's tone is not always clear. Often he chastises, but overall his messages are mixed, making them somewhat ambiguous, (B).

30. D

Antithesis is contradiction—although there is a bit of that, it does not dominate paragraph two. There are no examples of oxymoron, metaphor, or metonymy in this paragraph. However, the comparison between dramatic presentation and church services, particularly the sermon, is definitely an analogy, (D).

31. E

Reading paragraph three, you can find several of the responses present; however, the focus of the paragraph is his criticism of the public audiences "from the stalls" and the Press for not coming out and saying what they really feel. This is the point of the topic sentence and is supported within the paragraph, making (E) the correct choice.

32. A

Since Shaw seems to be most concerned with the idea that the public only comes to the theater in droves so they can see and be seen. In reality, the public is bored by theater and finds it tedious; nevertheless, they continue to attend so they can be seen in public. This fact makes (A) the correct answer for this question.

33. B

These lines are "I do not complain of this, though it complains very unreasonably of me. But I can take no more notice of it than Einstein of the people who are incapable of mathematics." The best interpretation of these sentences is that Shaw cannot do anything about the attitude of the public and their ignorance any more than Einstein can worry that math-challenged people will be unable to grasp the depth of his theories, (B).

34. E

Paragraph four basically says that despite all the fools who come to the theater, there are still a few theatergoers who make Shaw's work worth doing. This makes choice (E) the best response for this question.

35. A

Anaphora (A) is the correct answer—it is a series of phrases or clauses that begin with parallel openings. *Apostrophe* is an address to an inanimate object; *assonance* is the repetition of vowel sounds, usually in close proximity. Ambiguity has the ideas of multiple interpretations, and *asyndeton* is a series of phrases or clauses in succession without being connected by conjunctions.

36. C

Shaw says that sitting all night in the theater cannot be worse than sitting all night in the House of Commons. This indicates that Shaw does not have much admiration or affection towards the government and its institutions. That makes (C) correct.

37. B

Shaw's use of the phrase "irreducible minimum" is preceded by "They can appreciate the first part of the play by their usual practice of arriving late. They can escape the epilogue by not waiting for it." In other words, audiences need only spend the shortest time possible while attending a play. This makes (B) the best choice.

38. D

If people avoid the theater altogether, Shaw will lose money and the audience will lose the opportunity to view plays. Actually, all the responses are correct. Nevertheless, (D) is the *best* response for the question.

39. E

References to *purgatory* and *Aristotle* are references to religion and to ancient philosophy. References to history, mythology, religion, etc are all *allusions*. Therefore (E) is correct.

40. B

Considering the passage as a whole, what Shaw is trying to say is that those who shun the theater, or those who attend it just for the social interaction, are missing something special. If given the opportunity, they might find theater worthwhile and actually rewarding. This makes (B) the correct response.

Questions 41–53

It is now many years ago, my children, when I was quite a young woman, and your father, Freddy, was less than you are at present, that we lived in a
Line village more than a hundred miles from here. It
(5) was a very pretty village, situated on the bank of a broad, beautiful stream, which added much to the fertility and loveliness of the whole country through which it passed. We had not always dwelt in so pretty a place; but your grandfather, thinking
(10) it would be better for his business, concluded to take up his abode there. About the time we removed, another family took a steerage passage in a vessel bound from Ireland to this country. There were seven of them altogether—the father, mother,
(15) and five children. Their home had hitherto been a cabin, with a mud floor. A Bible, an iron pot, and a few wooden stools constituted their furniture; while their fare consisted of the scanty supply of milk afforded by one ill-fed cow, with a few
(20) potatoes. Willing to labor, yet finding wages humbled so low that they were often obliged to go both weary and hungry to bed, they concluded, after many struggles, to leave kindred and friends and come to America. How often, when speaking
(25) of this unhappy country, is the sentence 'Why don't they emigrate?' uttered with the greatest indifference. But to a warm Irish heart, this is often a severe trial. They are taxed, we might almost say, for the very air they breathe; yet how fondly they
(30) still cling to the soil of that island home, where nature must smile in spite of oppression; where

the dust of their kindred repose; where are more loving hearts and words of warmer greeting than are to be met with elsewhere. No wonder the (35) Irishman loves his country, crushed, trampled upon as she is. Her soil is among the most fertile, her sons among the noblest, and the language of even her rudest children the most poetical of any on earth. Oh, Ireland, fair Ireland, would we might (40) yet live to see thee take thy proper place among the nations to see the period approach when thy children will not be forced to seek in other countries the bare sustenance denied them at home. The Nevilles, after many struggles to obtain (45) means sufficient to defray the expenses of a passage, and after borrowing from several neighbors small sums, which they promised to repay with interest, found themselves in the steerage of a vessel on their way to this land of (50) promise. I will pass over the first few weeks of their arrival—strangers on a strange soil. Suffice it to say, that some one directed them to our village as a place where they could likely find steady employment. And here, one evening in early (55) spring, cold, hungry, and penniless, they arrived. My husband, contrary to his usual custom, chanced to be abroad on that evening; and, as he was a devout believer in that blessed word which teaches that we may sometimes entertain angels (60) unawares, on hearing the landlord refuse to keep them on account of their inability to pay, he brought them all home with him. I confess, I was taken a good deal by surprise at this unusual act; but, as it was his pleasure, I bade them welcome; (65) and the heartfelt blessing which the poor strangers asked over the meal we prepared for them went far towards prepossessing me in their favor. The man, his wife, and the two little girls we accommodated in the house, while the three boys found lodgings (70) among the fragrant hay in the well-stored mow. These people, my children, were not particularly attractive as far as appearance was concerned; they all appeared healthy and good-humored, and the little ones seemed uncommonly well-mannered (75) for children in their rank of life; but still I was in some way unaccountably interested in them; and I have since thought God permitted this feeling in order that I might bestir myself in behalf of those

who were undoubtedly his followers. At any rate, (80) we were willing to accommodate them a few days until something could be done for them; and, at the expiration of that time, a quiet-looking little cottage, with a willow tree before the door, standing just across the brook, was procured for (85) them. I parted with several articles of furniture I could spare, in order to assist them in fitting out their new home; and my efforts among my neighbors procured them many other gifts of the same description. And now how happy was Mrs. (90) Neville. Her husband had steady employment given him on a farm near by; her two eldest boys, of the ages of twelve and thirteen, both obtained good places; while the youngest boy, with the little girls, aged ten, eight, and six, were kept at home, (95) where they were generally as busy as bees, for their mother held idleness to be the parent of all evil. I have often, on going in, been struck with the picture of neatness and humbled contentment their small kitchen presented.

(100) The furniture was of the coarsest and most common description, yet scrupulously neat and clean. Here the family were generally found, pursuing their evening avocations, seated before the quiet blaze of their own fireside; and truly, (105) where its comforts are properly appreciated, there is nothing gives the heart a finer or more touching idea of enjoyment than this same calm, domestic light. Evening, too, is the period of time which may truly be called the poor man's season of (110) enjoyment; the implements of daily labor are laid aside, and it is then he may rest his wearied limbs and enjoy the prattle and playful wiles of his children, whose caresses sometimes lead him to forget the bitterness of his lot. The Nevilles were (115) poor, very poor; the money they had borrowed from friends in Ireland, they had obligated themselves to return, and they were straining every nerve to accomplish this. It was ten months before they were able, by their united labor, with (120) practicing the most rigid self-denial, to realize this amount. At length, however, the sum was raised; and a benevolent gentleman inclosed and forwarded it in such a manner as it would be sure to reach its destination. They had, however, barely (125) felt their minds relieved in this particular, when

Mr. Neville was laid upon a bed of sickness. He
had, perhaps, overworked himself and taken cold.
His disease was inflammatory rheumatism. He
lingered for a month, oftentimes suffering greatly;
(130) and then, after commending his wife and little
ones to the care of that God who is the protector
of the widow and the fatherless, strong in the hope
of a blissful immortality, he died. As I told you
before, my children, the Nevilles were pious
(135) people; and I could not but notice, in their mode
of expression, a degree of intellectual refinement
peculiar to those who make the Holy Scriptures an
habitual study.

"You will observe, my children," said Mrs. Bruce,
(140) as she came to this portion of their discourse, "the
unwavering faith which this poor woman
possessed. She was a stranger in a strange land;
there was no one upon whom she had any claim;
yet I never heard her utter one repining word, or
(145) wonder how she was to get along without the
assistance of her husband, there was so little
selfishness in her grief. And although tears must
flow at these sad sunderings of beloved ties, yet,
when she did indulge in this outward exhibition of
(150) distress, she would almost immediately dry them,
and give utterance to something which would
discover how entire and unchanging was her trust
in God. I was a great deal with her, and, I must say,
after the last sad duties were performed, I was
(155) astonished to see how energetically she set to work
in order to support herself and her children. Her
husband had often told me that all the fortune his
wife had brought him was her religion, her energy,
and her steady habits of industry, and that these
(160) had proved the blessing of his life. Now, too, she
found ample exercise for these estimable qualities,
and it was surprising how she could turn her hand
to anything that offered; and, indeed, with the
assistance the children were able to afford her, they
(165) managed to live very comfortably."

There, amid the far-stretching forests, on a farm
which in Europe might be called a principality, a
wife and mother, she is spending her days in the
enjoyment of all that heart can desire. I have now
(170) done with the history of this family; yet I would
have you observe how fearlessly Christian parents
may repose upon the strength of the promises of

Him who holds the hearts of all men in his hand.
The skeptic may laugh and the worldling may
(175) sneer, but an appeal may confidently be made to
those who have noted the dealings of Providence
as to whether any who have trusted in him have
been confounded.

From *Godey's Lady's Book*, 1850

41 F

If you look at these lines, you will find that it includes an
address to Ireland, an *apostrophe*; a contradiction in that
people who love their land still have to leave it; an
anaphora, repetition of opening phrases or clauses; and
personification of the home country. Therefore, litote, (E),
understatement, is the correct answer.

42. D

Since the passage talks about how the Irish are so torn
about leaving the land they love and the land that has
brought them heartache, (D) is the correct response to this
question.

43. B

The first part of this passage contains all of the different
kinds of sentences except the imperative—that is, a
command or a directive, (B). Nowhere is there such a
sentence within these lines.

44. A

The important word here is "initially." You are to consider
the very first impressions of the Neville family. No doubt
they are devout in their religion/faith. In addition, after
reading the description of their situation, it is easy to see
they are penurious, that is destitute. This makes (A) the
correct response to this question.

45. B

The Nevilles are easy to understand. The narrator finds
them fascinating, and despite her initial surprise at their
presence in their house, she is impressed by their strong
character. This makes (B) the correct response.

46. E

Phrases and clauses in a series that do not use any conjunctions are asyndeton, that is, without "syn" (together) conjunctions. These lines do not present any of the other choices, so (E) is the correct response to this question.

47. B

Although it may seem like it to many people, air is yet to be taxed by any country. Therefore this is an exaggeration. Hyperbole, (B), is an exaggeration used for stylistic effect. None of the other choices is appropriate for this question.

48. D

Rank in this situation has to do with socio-economic level. Therefore, (D), the children of the poor were expected to be less well mannered than those of more economically successful parents.

49. A

"To realize" comes from the sentence before that talks about how poor the Nevilles were; nevertheless, the family was able to strain and practice self-denial, they were able to *realize* the amount that the family owed back home. Therefore, (A). to amass (collect/save) is the correct response.

50. C

The key to this entire section has to do with the word "although." Basically, Mrs. Neville is saddened by her husband's death, but her faith in Providence keeps her strong. This makes (C) the correct choice for this question.

51. C

Mrs. Neville is easily characterized as being able to pick up and move forward. This makes (C) to be the best response for this question.

52. E

"Repining" in this case means to comment in a negative way. Therefore, (E) is the correct response for this question.

53. C

The reader must be aware of the concept of a "ladies' book" written in the mid-1800s. Most of you will realize that this was an era in which women always knew their place. Therefore, the message of this piece is bound to be somewhat moralistic. After considering all of the choices, (C) is the correct response to this question.

Essay Question One: Thoreau

Analysis of Essay Question One

This passage is, of course from Thoreau's *Walden*. It is readily accessible, although some find it less than exciting to read and "get into." However, those who give it a chance will find that Thoreau's wonderful language and rich imagery offers an easy passage on which to respond.

Scoring Guide for Question One

9 Essays meet all of the criteria for 8 papers, and in addition, are especially full or apt in their analysis or demonstrate particularly impressive composition skills.

8 Essays successfully analyze the rhetorical and stylistic strategies Thoreau employs to convey his attitude about Nature and the onset of spring. They refer to the passage directly or indirectly and explain convincingly how specific strategies such as imagery, tone, and figurative language contribute to an understanding of the writer's attitude. Their prose controls a wide range of effective writing but is not flawless.

7 Essays fit the description of 6 essays but employ more complete analysis or demonstrate a more mature prose style.

6 Essays adequately analyze how the stylistic devices Thoreau employs in his passage reveal his attitude about Nature and springtime. They refer to the passage directly or indirectly, and they recognize the narrator's attitude and how he conveys it by utilizing strategies such as choice of detail, tone, or figurative language. A few lapses in diction or syntax may be present, but generally the prose of 6 essays is clear.

5 Essays analyze Thoreau's rhetorical techniques, but the development of those techniques of the understanding of Thoreau's attitude is limited or too simplistic. These essays may treat techniques superficially or develop ideas about the narrator's attitude inconsistently. A few lapses in diction or syntax may appear, but the prose in these essays usually conveys the writers' ideas adequately.

4 Essays inadequately respond to the task of the prompt. They may misrepresent Thoreau's attitude or analyze rhetorical strategies inaccurately or with little understanding of how strategies reveal his attitude. Often the prose of these essays suggests immature control over organization, diction, or syntax.

3 Essays meet the criteria for the score of 4 but are less perceptive about how rhetorical strategies convey attitude or are less consistent in controlling the elements of writing.

2 Essays are unsuccessful in analyzing how stylistic strategies convey Thoreau's attitude about Spring. These essays tend to pay little or cursory attention the specific features, and they may generalize, or simplify attitude and tone. They may simply paraphrase or comment on the passage without analyzing technique. The prose of 2 papers often reveals consistent weaknesses in writing, such as a lack of development or organization, grammatical problems, or a lack of control.

1 Essays meet the criteria for the score of 2 but are especially simplistic in their discussion or weak in controlling elements of language.

Student Response A to Question One

Thoreau uses devices such as imagery, diction and anaphora to convey his awe of nature and his happy and contented attitude.

The speaker in this passage is euphoric at the dawn of springtime. He sees a "graceful" and "beautiful hawk soar through the air and he feels that everything in the world is connected. He asks, "or was its native nest made in the angle of a cloud...from the earth?" (lines 17–19). All at once the speaker feels like Nature's kindred spirit and he begins to feel, see and understand the true beauty of nature. He sees "a rare mess of golden and silver and bright cupreous fishes." (line 21) He notices that Nature is life and death, and in that way all things are immortal. He realizes that Poison is not poisonous after all, nor are any wounds fatal." (lines 49–50). Suddenly it all falls into place for the narrator: Nature is important to us because it is us, and we are nature.

Thoreau expresses his journey to this realization with a succession of images. He uses similes and metaphors to help the reader see what he sees. The hawk "sported" in the "fields of air," "turning over and over like a kite." The reader has a clear image of this playful hawk, as well as the fishes "which looked like a strand of jewels." Likewise, the reader can see "tadpoles which herons gobble up, and tortoises and toads run over in the road, and [it seems] that sometimes it has rained flesh and blood." But the death is as much a part of nature as the beautiful life. All is one, and the narrator challenges: "death where is thy victory now?"

The reader is able to feel these effects through the pace of the passage as well. As the speaker becomes more engrossed in the actions of the hawk, his tone becomes more animated and the narrator starts to use word in pairs, as if to emphasize the glory he sees and the excitement he feels. The hawk mounts the air "again and again" and turns "over and over." At the climax of the passage, the speaker jumps 'from hummock to hummock, from willow root to willow root," and the author feels the energy and the warmth of the bright sunlight. The pace slows when the speaker contemplates death's role in nature. However, this is not because of sadness or regret but to emphasize to us that because we are one with nature, we have nothing to fear.

The author successfully conveys his blissful tone and opinions of nature to the reader through vivid imagery, very connotative diction and other stylistic devices. He "refreshes" the reader with his account of the "inexhaustible vigor" of nature."

Student Response B to Question One

Thoreau uses various methods express his awe with nature. His tone is somewhat poetic in the middle of the passage. He describes the Merlin's (hawk's) wings as "satin ribbons in the sun" and "the pearly inside of a shell." He also states that he does not care about the name of the animal. He is so awestruck by simply how it looks and flies through the air that nothing else matters. He even describes how, thought the bird is alone, it is not lonely, but the world is lonely beneath it. He implies that the hawk is so divine that without its presence the earth is incomplete.

In the second paragraph Thoreau begins by describing a school of fish in a river. When he sees the meadow beyond the river, he tells of how the sunlight on it "would have waked the dead." He says that anything in such a light has to be immortal, and he challenges death with hypothetical question: "Oh Death where was thy sting? O grave, where was thy victory then?" He is completely enveloped in the greatness of nature and describes it again (like the bird in paragraph one) as if it is completely above his world. In nature's cycle things constantly die and are reborn, so in reality there is no death.

In the final paragraph the author brings forth the point that people need nature to be beyond their realm of thinking. Finally completing his description, he describes it as though nature were not as it is, the world would cease to spin on its axis! People need to see the beauty of nature in order to live.

Thoreau brings the passage to a close by telling about the beauty of the cycle of the environment. He is overjoyed to see that the carcasses of dead animals still fuel the whole of nature and sustain life, which sets the readers up for his ending statement: "Poison is not Poison after all. . . ." He is completely fulfilled to see that the death of great beasts is never a waste in such an environment.

Commentary on Student Response A

This essay is very well executed. Not only does it demonstrate all the characteristics of a strong writer, it also demonstrates an excellent understanding of both the task of the prompt and the passage being analyzed.

The introduction is brief and to the point. It shows no special insight, but nevertheless it permits the writer to move right to her points. In fact, the first body paragraph is the controlling point of the entire passage: the epiphany of the narrator understanding man and nature are one, and that there is hope to be had in this—although not everything is alive and vibrant, that even death is a part of the vibrancy.

In her next paragraph, she explores the animated imagery of the passage. The essay provides numerous examples of these images, explaining them where necessary. The following paragraph discusses the syntax of the passage. The writer has cleverly connected the syntax with the nearly effervescent tone of the passage. There is no doubt that Thoreau is deliriously excited by the coming of spring; this student has captured the essence of this with her mention of specific details and pace, and she brings good examples in for support.

Finally, the conclusion ties all together. If the introduction had been longer, the conclusion may have seemed like only an echo of the beginning. Here, however, the writer has managed to pull together all the ideas developed the passage. Readers no doubt would award this essay a score of 8.

Commentary on Student Response B

This student has some great ideas and insights. Although many of the comments are very accurate, this writer does not go into specific detail about any of the specific stylistic devices that the writer uses.

Many of the references to style are implied; however, the specific examples are quite apt and numerous. The student no doubt has a good grasp on the significance of the passage and the task of the prompt. This is one of those responses that needs a rewrite (obviously an impossibility under timed AP testing conditions.)

Too much is told about without being shown directly through examples. Unfortunately, however, such an opportunity is not a privilege of this AP Exam. Therefore, the inconsistency of this response—being on target for the understanding of the passage, but being less than successful on the presentation—qualifies this response for about a 5 score.

This student clearly has a handle on the task at hand. Unfortunately, he was unable to pull enough together to earn an upper-half score. Because of the limited development of specific ideas and scarcity of examples, this essay would most likely earn the score of 5

Essay Question Two: Obstetrics

Analysis of Essay Question Two

This is a very interesting and challenging passage from *For the Time Being* by Annie Dillard. It is intriguing because Dillard's description and reactions to the obstetrics ward seem almost blasphemous to the reader. The passage offers stimulating imagery and interesting word choice. If you are faced with a passage such as this, just take it for what is in front of you. Do not get upset or critical of the narrator's stance. You have been asked to deal with what is on the page—no more.

Student response to this passage is always interesting and varied. You will see that the two student samples, albeit overlapping in a couple ideas, are also quite different.

Scoring Guide for Question Two

9 Essays meet all of the criteria for 8 papers, and in addition, are especially full or apt in their analysis or demonstrate particularly impressive composition skills.

8 Essays successfully analyze the rhetorical and stylistic strategies Annie Dillard employs to convey her attitude about newborns and the obstetrics ward. They refer to the passage directly or indirectly and explain convincingly how specific strategies such as imagery, tone, and figurative language contribute to an understanding of the writer's attitude. Their prose controls a wide range of effective writing but is not flawless.

7   Essays fit the description of 6 essays but employ more complete analysis or demonstrate a more mature prose style.

6   Essays adequately analyze how the stylistic devices Dillard employs in his passage reveal his attitude about the obstetrics ward and the newborns. They refer to the passage directly or indirectly, and they recognize the narrator's attitude and how he conveys it by utilizing strategies such as choice of detail, tone, and figurative language. A few lapses in diction or syntax may be present, but generally the prose of 6 essays is clear.

5   Essays analyze Dillard's rhetorical techniques, but the development of those techniques of the understanding of Dillard's attitude is limited or too simplistic. These essays may treat techniques superficially or develop ideas about the narrator's attitude inconsistently. A few lapses in diction or syntax may appear, but the prose in these essays usually conveys the writers' ideas adequately.

4   Essays inadequately respond to the task of the prompt. They may misrepresent Dillard's attitude or analyze rhetorical strategies inaccurately or with little understanding of how strategies reveal his attitude. Often the prose of these essays suggests immature control over organization, diction, or syntax.

3   Essays meet the criteria for the score of 4 but are less perceptive about how rhetorical strategies convey attitude or are less consistent in controlling the elements of writing.

2   Essays are unsuccessful in analyzing how stylistic strategies convey Dillards's attitude about the obstetrics ward and the newborns. These essays tend to pay little or cursory attention the specific features, and they may generalize, or simplify attitude and tone. They may simply paraphrase or comment on the passage without analyzing technique. The prose of 2 papers often reveals consistent weaknesses in writing, such as a lack of development or organization, grammatical problems, or a lack of control.

1   Essays meet the criteria for the score of 2 but are especially simplistic in their discussion or weak in controlling elements of language.

Student Response A to Question Two

Childbirth and newborns have always been perceived as the miracle of life and a joy and privilege to every parent. Annie Dillard uses nurse Pat Eisberg and her job to show how all the joy of such a wonderful event is vanishing. Dillard uses a deliberate word choice to develop her tone to relate how childbirth and the immediate events following have become so efficient as to become an assembly line. Her attitude is one of regret. She laments our society's loss of wonder for the phenomenon of bringing new life into the world.

At the very beginning of the passage she sets the tone by comparing the babies to dishes. By saying that a nurse spends most of the eight-hour shift at the sink, she involves images of a factory worker mindlessly working at the cleaning station of an assembly line. In all that nurse Eisberg does, she demonstrates no emotion. Only a comment in a warm voice. "Now you" expresses her reaction to what she is doing. If anything it expresses the boredom and monotony of one who is stuck doing the same thing hour after hour, day after day. Dillard likens the boy's limbs to worms, implying that there is no tenderness or joy in this job. The nurse grabs one arm and deliberately turns him over. Again, no tenderness. The chosen method of turning him over is similar to the description one might use to describe handling a small dog or a large baby doll, or a newly caught fish with a dorsal fin.

In the sixth paragraph, she changes tactics a bit. She mentions Allah and the Qur'an. Here she mentions the creation of man from near nothing. The spiritual wonder of such a feat is soon canceled in the following sentence when she introduces the image of a clown twisting a few skinny balloons into a dog, a giraffe (or a child?) This seems to be Dillard's main tactic in this passage: just when she suggests the "miracle" she cancels it with an antithesis of the clown. By mentioning the clown and his balloons she belittles the creation— Allah's sacred breath becomes "lickety-split". Nothing is sacred on this obstetrics ward. It's just another job in another type of factory. After Eisberg finishes washing the babies, they are left on the counter until someone comes to collect them, one at a time. The coldness of this assembly line process reminds me of the clinical, matter-of-fact tone of <u>Brave New World.</u>

Even in wrapping the babies there is standardization. Do it correctly and the child is restrained and kept warm. Throughout the piece, the wrapped child is compared to a Thermos. The comparison emphasizes the idea of mass production of an object, with most feelings gone. Even with the parents, their reaction seems automatic, not heartfelt. They "involuntarily" say "hi!" It seems an impulse, not an act of love.

Throughout the piece, Annie Dillard's use of diction and the nurse Pat Eiseberg's (iceberg's?) actions show that the production of children and their subsequent care have lost the tenderness, and possibly the love we would expect in exchange for the cold, mass-produced assembly line. The magic of the process has been replaced by the tedium of the job.

Student Response B to Question Two

In this passage, Annie Dillard conveys a slightly disturbed attitude towards her experience in an obstetrical ward. She sees the process of cleaning the newly-born children as almost industrial, and uses diction, antithesis and imagery to effectively convey her opinions.

When describing the process of washing the infant, Dillard opts for cold, scientific words regarding the baby's anatomy Words such as dorsal and anus are most certainly not what one would expect to describe the fragility and innocence of infants. Dillard also compares the child's newly severed umbilical cord to a jumper cable. This in addition to her previously mentioned word choices, creates a factory-like atmosphere. This creation of a "birthing factory" very clearly conveys Dillard's view of American obstetrics as cold and uncaring.

Dillard's view of Americans is also conveyed in the ninth paragraph through her use of antithesis. She states "Americans place infants on their backs now. . . lest they choke and die." Dillard, throughout the passage, seems to view the events as not only an observer, but an outsider. Through this statement we can infer that some of her sense of isolation may come from the fact that she is possibly a foreigner. Through her use of antithesis, one can examine her confusion over American practices and their swiftly changing nature.

Much of the mood in this passage is set up by the visuals Dillard creates. In the first sentence of the first paragraph, a sterile metal sink is described as the common kitchen variety. These cold images are carried throughout the passage. Examples include the reference to the jumper cable in paragraph 4 and the "wormy" limbs in paragraph 5. Even the reference to Allah and humankind's divine origins is quickly demeaned by something as trite as a clown's balloon animals. The final image in the passage, one of a blasé nurse, brings about the realization that the sterility seen in the sinks and equipment has transcended to the people who work with the infants.

Dillard's view of this event as an outsider definitely increased her awareness of the situation, and through this she effectively conveys her views through her word choice, rhetorical devices and imagery.

Commentary on Student Response A

Without a doubt, this student has successfully understood the prompt, read and understood the passage, and written a strong composition. This writer has a good vocabulary and he uses it well. In addition, the examples from the passage he has chosen to include are ample and apt.

The focus of this response is actually the antithesis of Allah and the clown. This is the crux of the problem, as this student rightly sees it. Birth is no longer something special. It's just another day of work in the obstetrics factory—wormy limbs, dorsal fins, clowns and all.

He has identified the iceberg nurse accurately, and it is her attitude that seems to pervade the entire nursery. The reference to *Brave New World* is apt, and with more time, this might have been an interesting analogy to pursue.

This is a very well-written essay. Errors are minimal. Yes it is 5-paragraphs, but nowhere do you have the feeling of an essay written on an assembly line. The ideas flow between the paragraphs, and excellent composition skills are demonstrated.

No doubt this response will receive many 8s from readers. Perhaps some may think it needs a bit more bulk and give it a 7. However, given the limited time and the tightness of the essay, this is a very successful response to a challenging essay.

Commentary on Student Response B

This is an adequate analysis of Annie Dillard's passage. This student cites many different aspects of the essay in support of what she says. However, it is not as successful as Student Response A, and this is a good pair for you to look at.

Response B includes many of the same concepts mentioned in A, such as the lack of emotion, factory-like nature, mechanical handling of the newborns and others. However, it is easy to see that the first response is better written. There is a tightness to the composition that B lacks.

You would not necessarily be graded down because of the misconception of Annie Dillard's being an outsider or perhaps a foreigner. The misunderstanding of the comments about whether babies should be placed on their back or on their stomachs is included mostly to remind us how the "rules" that govern child rearing are constantly changing. This student is not too sure about the meaning of this. Notice, however, Response A doesn't mention it at all. Such a minor misunderstanding won't gravely affect one's grade, but to have made such a point of this paragraph, and then done so incorrectly, is going to affect the score somewhat.

Overall this is an acceptable response to the Annie Dillard question. It would be scored a 6. A few readers might be disturbed enough about the multiple inaccuracies found in paragraph 3 that they might award this response a 5.

No doubt, however, this student understands the task of the prompt and most of the passage and has responded with an adequate composition.

Essay Question Three: Stubbornness

Analysis of Question Three

These two quotations are very accessible and present an outstanding writing opportunity. Usually, argumentation, or developing a stand on an issue, is something with which most teenagers are successful. In addition, this particular topic, on stubbornness, is probably a great topic that most of you have something to say about.

At first glance these quotations seem to cancel each other out. The first says that stubbornness proves stupidity; the second says the most stubborn are the most intelligent. However, notice that Montaigne's quote indicates stubborn and ardent clinging to one's opinion, while Yevtushenko's implies that stubbornness is more akin to dogged determination rather than simple opinion such as "I'm right" and "you are wrong." In such a case, then, stubbornness is not necessarily all bad.

Not everyone will be able to recognize the nuances of the concept "stubborn" in these quotations. Nevertheless, you should be able to embrace one and demonstrate sound argumentation in its favor. Or you may take from each and acknowledge that often the circumstances of the stubbornness can dictate the stubbornness or the stupidity of the situation.

Scoring Guide for Essay Question Three

9 Essays meet all the criteria for papers that earn a score of 8 and, in addition, are particularly persuasive or carefully reasoned, or demonstrate unusual insights or impressive stylistic and argumentative skills.

8 Essays persuasively defend one or the other of the two quotations. In addition, they may demonstrate an insightful interpretation of the two and show how each is right or wrong depending upon circumstances. These essays present cohesive and carefully reasoned arguments using appropriate evidence from their reading, knowledge, or observation. Support and detail are apt and adequate. The prose of these essays demonstrates the student's ability to control a wide range of the elements of effective writing, but they need not be flawless.

7 Essays fit the description of essays that receive 6 points but are distinguished by a fuller or more purposeful argument, or stronger prose style.

6 Essays adequately defend, or challenge one or a combination of the presentations of stubbornness. These essays will present arguments that are generally sound and that use appropriate evidence from students' reading, experience, or observations. They are generally less fully developed than those found earning higher scores. A few lapses in diction or syntax may be present, but for the most part the purpose of these essays conveys the writers' ideas clearly.

5 Essays clearly understand the task of the prompt and make assertions that defend one of the quotations or parts of both. Their arguments are generally clear, but they may use more superficial or limited evidence, or exhibit uneven or inconsistent development. Some lapses in diction or syntax may be evident, but for the most part the prose of these essays conveys the writers' ideas clearly.

4 Essays inadequately respond to the tasks of the prompt. They may misunderstand, misrepresent, or oversimplify the challenge of the prompt or the quotations themselves. The prose of these essays usually conveys the writers' ideas, but may suggest inconsistent control over such elements of writing as organization, diction, and syntax.

3 Essays are described by the criteria for the score of 4, but are less persuasive in their attempts to develop their position, or are less consistent in their ability to control the elements of writing.

2 Essays demonstrate little or no success in developing their position or argument. They may seriously misread the task of the prompt or one or both of the quotations, or even substitute a simpler task, by merely summarizing the quotations or writing responses only remotely related to the prompt. The prose of these essays often reveals consistent weaknesses in their control of elements of writing, such as organization, grammar, or diction.

1 Essays are less qualified than those fulfilling the criteria for a score of 2, but are particularly simplistic in their response to the prompt or the quotations, or weak in their control of language.

Student Response A to Question Three

Each of these quotations portrays stubbornness in its own way. The quote by Montaigne states that stubbornness is proof of stupidity, whereas Yevtushenko's quote states that stubbornness is a sign of intelligence. I think that Yevtushenko's quotation is more accurate than Montaigne's quote because stubbornness is not necessarily a bad thing.

Most people think negatively when they hear or see the word *stubborn*. Personally, I believe stubbornness has good and bad characteristics. Stubbornness is a sign of intelligence because intelligence is staying by what we believe. If an intelligent person were to argue with someone about any topic, he would stand by what he believes in and he won't be affected by the other person's argument. The person is being stubborn because he is not changing his mind, but he is intelligent because of that.

Also, another reason why stubbornness is a sign of intelligence is because stubbornness is like being wise. A "wise man" is often stubborn because he knows what he is saying. He is so wise that he must be stubborn, so that others will side with him and understand what he is talking about. Since he is stubborn, it shows that he is intelligent because he knew what he was saying was correct.

The reason most people believe that stubbornness is such a bad thing is because ever since we were children, we have been taught that stubbornness was a bad thing. Nowadays, when someone is called stubborn, it is an insult rather than a compliment. We need to redefine stubbornness so that the real meaning of stubbornness is shown. I think that stubbornness means that someone is standing by what he believes in, and does not take other opinions into effect.

Another way to look at the quotation is that intelligent people are stubborn people. This is true because if the most intelligent person in the world was told that what he/she believes in is all wrong because of the following reasons, and then he will probably never take it to heart because he knows what he says is right. He is stubborn because of his knowledge or intelligence.

Stubbornness is not proof of stupidity because if someone is stupid, and another person convinces him to believe in something else, the stupid person will let himself become affected by it. He may be stubborn at first, but because he is stupid, he will not stand by what he believes.

In the end, although stubbornness is associated with stupidity since it is supposedly "a stupid action" it does not mean that a stubborn person is a stupid person. Stubbornness is, in fact, an intelligent act because it is intelligent to stand by what one believes. We are taught to resist peer pressure and not to follow the crowd, and in order to do so, we must be stubborn. So, in the end, we are intelligent for being stubborn.

Student Response B to Question Three

After reading the two quotations pertaining to stubbornness, there is a noticeable contradiction between the two. Montaigne's quote is stating that if a person doesn't have her own opinion and is stubborn; it is evidence that she is stupid. On the other hand, Yevtushenko's quote that says that if a person is stubborn for an extended period of time, she is proven the most intelligent. I agree with Montaigne's quotation because I disagree that a person should depend on one's opinion, which therefore makes her "stupid."

When I think of the word stubborn, the word I think of is unaccepting. These are the people who won't accept help or money from anyone. They also prefer to complete and handle everyday activities on their own.

I had a neighbor named Dorothy, and the one word to describe her was stubborn. My family, especially my parents, always offered to help her out since she was older and in a nursing home. She would often not call us because she felt like it was an imposition to our lives. So when we did take her grocery shopping, she would always try to give my parents money, showing that she felt bad, and probably embarrassed to be at their mercy. The truth is, we didn't feel bad at all: we wanted to help her out as much as possible. Sometimes behavior this can make people seem very stupid because they just don't understand that there are people like my family out there. People who are willing to help them out. People who understand when a person needs help, no matter how hard they try to cover it up. My feeling is that Dorothy tried to mask the fact that she needed help. I also don't know why she would be afraid to ask us, especially since we were the ones who offered to help her. This brought out the "stupid" stubbornness in her because she seemed oblivious to the fact that our goal was to help her in any way possible.

Also, clinging to one's opinion, shows that she isn't confident enough to think for herself. Making a decision can be difficult, but if she doesn't stick up for herself, she'll become involved with activities against her morals. Dorothy's "stupidity" shows because she couldn't express her true opinion to us. She held back, and in a way she probably suffered because she didn't get the help that she truly deserved.

In conclusion, Montaigne's quote tells us that stupidity is shown through stubbornness. I agree with it because people need to make their own choices and not be afraid to ask people for help when they truly need it. There are willing people out there.

Commentary on Student Response A

This first essay is successful. The writer is not satisfied with the either/or definitions of stubborn equaling stupidity or intelligence. Instead she chooses to qualify situations and make sure that one does not confuse the stupidity of an action with stupidity of the person.

This response is in the 7 to low-7 range. It is not outstanding, but the writer has demonstrated insight into the prompt and the quotations, as well as fine composition style. The biggest shortcoming is that, although the argument explains the statement that the author makes, no specific examples are cited. Nevertheless, the reference to societal expectations ("since childhood we are taught that stubbornness...") and the writer's obvious success in looking at both sides of the issue keep the essay strong. She does this confidently, relaying no sense of uncertainty in her response.

The essay fulfills the requirements of an 8, but will receive some 7s due to the lack of specific references. Nevertheless, this is a good response.

Commentary on Student Response B

In contrast to the first essay's broad outlook on stubbornness, this response is much narrower. This student has chosen a particular circumstance and has centered her essay upon it. This is also a successful response, albeit a bit less revealing about the writer's interpretation of the quotations and the prompt.

The task of the prompt is fulfilled. Perhaps the strength of this essay might also be its weakness—the focus upon the lady-in-need Dorothy is certainly apt and well developed. The writer gives us several angles of Dorothy's "stupidity" as a result of her stubbornness. On the other hand, this narrow focus tends to pigeonhole the woman as stupid, just because she might be proud. Senior citizens often are reluctant to ask for and/or accept help for many reasons, none of them having to do with stupidity.

Although this example works well for this response, it could be improved by offering the idea that stubbornness might be the result of numerous causes, and perhaps stupidity is not one of them at all.

Nevertheless, this paper shows a good handle on composition skills and it develops its central idea well. This is a good response to this question, and would garner no less than a 6 and possibly a few 7s from readers.

HOW TO MAKE THIS BOOK WORK FOR YOU BASED ON THE RESULTS OF YOUR DIAGNOSTIC

Your score on the Diagnostic will go a long way toward helping you perform well by helping you identify areas in which you need further study. The answer explanations for questions you got wrong can steer you to specific chapters of this book that you should focus on or to specific areas of literature in which you show weakness. To score well on the AP exam, you'll need to do your homework. Don't just skim over what you read; try to apply it to other contexts and to connect it to what you already know.

PART THREE

The AP English Language and Composition Exam

Chapter 3: **Key Terminology**

- Key terminology definitions and usage examples
- Applying key terminology

KEY TERMINOLOGY

Every academic subject has a vocabulary that describes and identifies its inherent substance. You will be expected to apply that vocabulary to any piece of writing presented in the English Language exam.

On the following pages are the most common terms you have to face on the English Language Exam. You should be able to use some of this terminology—correctly of course!—as you describe the writing within the passages that you must read and write about on the essay questions.

Review unfamiliar terms. Notice how many language terms are also used to describe aspects of literature. That's because they have to do with an author's writing style. In addition, Language and Composition has terminology that is specific to rhetoric and argument.

As you begin to see some of these terms appear, especially in multiple-choice questions, do not hesitate to refer to this list for clarification. The more you use it, the more familiar the terms will become. Many examples are given within the definitions to help you commit the term to memory.

Allegory—a narrative in which the characters, behavior, and even the setting demonstrate multiple levels of meaning and significance. Often allegory is a universal symbol or personified abstraction, such as Cupid portrayed as a chubby angel with a bow and arrows.

Alliteration—the sequential repetition of a similar initial sound, usually applied to consonants, usually in closely proximate stressed syllables. For instance, "She sells sea shells by the sea shore."

Allusion—a literary, historical, religious, or mythological reference. For example, one might contrast the life and tribulations of Frederick Douglass to the trials of Job.

Anaphora—the regular repetition of the same words or phrases at the beginning of successive phrases of clauses. The following is an example: "To raise a happy, healthful, and hopeful child, it takes a family; it takes teachers; it takes clergy; it takes business people; it takes community leaders; it takes those who protect our health and safety; it takes all of us." (Hillary Clinton, National Convention Address, 1996)

Antithesis—the juxtaposition of sharply contrasting ideas in balanced or parallel words, phrases grammatical structure, or ideas. For example, Alexander Pope reminds us that "To err is human, to forgive divine."

Aphorism—a concise statement designed to make a point or illustrate a commonly held belief. For example, "Spare the rod and spoil the child" is an aphorism.

Apostrophe—an address or invocation to something inanimate—such as when the slave Frederick Douglass exclaims as he looks upon the ships in the Chesapeake Bay: "I would pour out my soul's complaint, in my rude way, with an *apostrophe* to the moving multitude of ships."

Appeals to . . . authority, emotion, or logic—rhetorical arguments in which the speaker claims to be an authority or expert in a field, or attempts to play upon the emotions, or appeals to the use of reason. Classically trained rhetoricians identify these appeals with their Greek names: *ethos* is authority, *logos* is logic, and *pathos* is emotion.

Assonance—the repetition of identical or similar vowel sounds, usually in successive or proximate words. The alliteration example also demonstrates assonance: "She sells sea shells by the sea shore."

Asyndeton—a syntactical structure in which conjunctions are omitted in a series, usually producing more rapid prose. For example: "*Veni, vidi, vici* (I came, I saw, I conquered)," supposedly said by Julius Caesar.

Attitude—the sense expressed by the tone of voice or the mood of a piece of writing; the author's feelings toward his or her subject, characters, events, or theme. It might even be his or her feelings for the reader. AP English Exam essay prompts often require students to respond to some aspect of the attitude of the writer, speaker, or narrator.

Begging the question—an argumentative ploy where the arguer sidesteps the question or the conflict, evades or ignores the real question.

Cannon—that which has been accepted as authentic, such as in cannon law, or the "Cannon according to the Theories of Einstein."

Chiasmus—a figure of speech and generally a syntactical structure wherein the order of the terms in the first half of a parallel clause is reversed in the second. For example "He thinks I am but a fool. A fool, perhaps I am."

Claim—in argumentation, an assertion of something as fact.

Colloquial—a term identifying the diction of the common, ordinary folks, especially in a specific region or area. For instance, most people expect Southerners to use the colloquial expression, "y'all" to engage the attention of a group of people. In some parts of the United States, a Coke® is a product of the Coca-Cola Company. In some parts of the country, coke means any type of carbonated beverage. Other people refer to Coke as "pop" or "soda pop." These are all colloquial terms for the drink.

Comparison and contrast—a mode of discourse in which two or more things are compared, contrasted, or both. On the 1993 English Language exam, students were asked to contrast two marriage proposals taken from literature, analyzed for the use the narrators made of rhetorical devices and their argumentative success.

Connotation—the implied, suggested, or underlying meaning of a word or phrase. It is opposite of **denotation** which is the "dictionary definition" of the word.

Conceit—a comparison of two unlikely things that is drawn out within a piece of literature, in particular an extended metaphor within a poem. However, conceits can also be used in non-fiction and prose. For instance, Richard Selzer's passage "The Knife" compares the preparation and actions of surgery to preparing for and conducting a religious service or a sacred ritual.

Consonance—the repetition of two or more consonants with a change in the intervening vowels, such as pitter-patter, splish-splash, and click-clack.

Convention—An accepted manner, model, or tradition. For instance, Aristotle's conventions of tragedy.

Critique—an assessment or analysis of something, such as a passage of writing, for the purpose of determining what it is, what its limitations are, and how it conforms to the standard of the genre.

Deductive reasoning (deduction)—the method of argument in which specific statements and conclusions are drawn from general principals: movement from the general to the specific, in contrast to Inductive reasoning (induction).

Dialect—the language and speech idiosyncrasies of a specific area, region, or group. For example, Minnesotans say "you betcha" when they agree with you. Southerners refer to the gathering of folks as "y'all." Although dialect is most often found in fiction, sometimes it is evident in speeches from a different era or from a different culture.

Diction—the specific word choice an author uses to persuade or convey tone, purpose, or effect. The 1982 English Language exam included Adlai Stevenson's famous "Cat Bill" veto addressed to the Illinois State Senate. Cats roaming without leashes were "feline delinquency," and irritated citizen reactions were referred to as "small game hunts by zealous citizens." On the AP exam you must relate how a writer's diction, combined with syntax, figurative language, literary devices, etc., all come together to become the author's style.

Didactic—(from the Greek, meaning "good teaching") writing or speech is didactic when it has an instructive purpose or a lesson. It is often associated with a dry, pompous presentation, regardless of its innate value to the reader/listener. Some of Aesop's fables are didactic in that they maintain an underlying moral or social message.

Elegy—a poem or prose work that laments, or meditates upon the death of, a person or persons. Sometimes an elegy will end with words of consolation. Many public elegies were presented in the aftermath of 9/11.

Epistrophe—in rhetoric, the repetition of a phrase at the end of successive sentences. For example: "If women are healthy and educated, their families will flourish. If women are free from violence, their families will flourish. If women have a chance to work . . . their families will flourish." (Hillary Clinton, October 1, 1995)

Epitaph—writing in praise of a dead person, most often inscribed upon a headstone.

Ethos—in rhetoric, the appeal of a text to the credibility and character of the speaker, writer, or narrator. (Who is this person saying what, and what makes him able to say so?)

Euphemism—an indirect, kinder, or less harsh or hurtful way of expressing unpleasant information. For instance, it is much nicer for a person who has just been given a pink slip to hear that she has been made redundant, rather than she has hereby been terminated.

Exposition—the interpretation or analysis of a text.

Eulogy—a speech or written passage in praise of a person; an oration in honor of a deceased person. Elegy laments; eulogy praises. Many eulogies were spoken in honor of the brave New York Fire Fighters who heroically lost their lives on 9/11.

Extended metaphor—a series of comparisons within a piece of writing. If they are consistently one concept, this is also known as a conceit.

Figurative language/Figure of speech—figurative (in contrast to literal) language has levels of meaning expressed through figures of speech such as personification, metaphor, hyperbole, irony, oxymoron, litote, and others.

Flashback—(also known as retrospection) an earlier event is inserted into the normal chronology of the narration.

Genre—a type or class of literature, such as epic, narrative, poetry, biography, history.

Homily—a sermon, but more contemporary uses include any serious talk, speech, or lecture involving moral or spiritual life. John Donne was known for his homilies, among other things.

Hyperbole—overstatement characterized by exaggerated language, usually to make a point or draw attention. If in a state of exhaustion you say "I'm really beat," that is hyperbole.

Imagery—broadly defined, any sensory detail or evocation in a work; more narrowly, the use of figurative language to evoke a feeling, to call to mind an idea, or to describe an object. Basically, imagery involves any or all of the five senses. A writer generally uses imagery in conjunction with other figures of speech, such as simile and metaphor. "Her cheeks were rosy and so was my love— bursting with fragrance and softness." Here metaphor is used, with the images of rosy cheeks (the visual color) and the smell and feel of roses.

Inductive reasoning (induction)—the method of reasoning or argument in which general statements and conclusions are drawn from specific principals: movement from the specific to the general. In other words, a general supposition is made after investigating specific instances, a common logic used in scientific study. See Deductive reasoning.

Inference—a conclusion or proposition arrived at by considering facts, observations, or some other specific data. It is through inference—looking at the clues, learning the facts—that Sherlock Holmes was able to solve the crimes. It was elementary.

Irony (ironic)—the contrast between what is stated explicitly and what is really meant. The intended meaning is often the opposite of what is stated, often suggesting light sarcasm. The most famous classical ironist is Jonathan Swift in his "Modest Proposal." Irony is used for many reasons, often to create poignancy or humor. There are three major types of irony:

> *Verbal irony*—what the author/narrator says is actually the opposite of what is meant.
>
> *Situational irony*—when events end up the opposite of what is expected.
>
> *Dramatic irony*—in drama and fiction, facts or situations are known to the reader or audience but not to the characters.

Isocolon—parallel structure in which the parallel elements are similar not only in grammatical structure, but also in length. For example: the Biblical admonition: "Many are called, but few are chosen" is an isocolon.

Jargon—specialized or technical language of a trade, profession, or similar group. The computer industry, for example, has introduced much jargon into our vocabulary, such as *geek, crash, interface, down, delete, virus,* and *bug.*

Juxtaposition—the location of one thing adjacent to or juxtaposed with another to create an effect, reveal an attitude, or accomplish some other purpose.

Litote—a figure of speech that emphasizes its subject by conscious understatement—for instance, the understated "not bad" as a comment about something especially well done. George Orwell wrote, "Last week I saw a woman flayed and you would hardly believe how much it altered her person for the worse."

Loose sentence—(a term from syntax) a long sentence that starts with its main clause, which is followed by several dependent clauses and modifying phrases. For example. "The child ran, frenzied and ignoring all hazards, as if being chased by demons."

Metaphor—one thing pictured as if it were something else, suggesting a likeness or analogy. Metaphor is an implicit comparison or identification of one thing with another, without the use of a verbal signal such as *like* or *as*. Shakespeare's Romeo says, "It is the east and Juliet is the sun," directly comparing Juliet to the sun. Sometimes the term *metaphor* is used as a general term for any figure of speech.

Metonymy—a figure of speech in which an attribute or commonly associated feature is used to name or designate something, as in "Buckingham Palace announced today . . . "

Mode of discourse—the way in which information is presented in written or spoken form. The Greeks believed there were only four modes of discourse: narration, description, exposition (cause and effect, process analysis, comparison/contrast), and argumentation. Contemporary thought often includes other modes, such as personal observation and narrative reflection.

Mood—a feeling or ambience resulting from the tone of a piece as well as the writer/narrator's attitude and point of view. It is a "feeling" that establishes the atmosphere in a work of literature or other discourse.

Narrative—a mode of discourse that tells a story of some sort and it is based on sequences of connected events, usually presented in a straightforward, chronological framework.

Onomatopoeia—a word capturing or approximating the sound of what it describes; "buzz" is a good example. The purpose of these words is to make a passage more effective for the reader or listener. For example, "Becca *whacked* the ball over the fence and took her time walking the bases."

Oxymoron—a figure of speech that combines two apparently contradictory elements as in "wise fool," "baggy tights," or "deafening silence."

Paradox—a statement that seems contradictory but may probably be true. A popular paradox from the 1960's was that war protesters would "fight for peace."

Parallel structure—the use of similar forms in writing for nouns, verbs, phrases, or thoughts, for example, "Jane enjoys reading, writing, and skiing." In prose, parallel, recurrent syntactical similarity where several parts of a sentence or several sentences are expressed alike to show that their ideas are equal in importance. *A Tale of Two Cities* opens with "It was the best of times, it was the worst of times, it was the age of wisdom, it was the age of foolishness . . ."

Pathos—that element in literature that stimulates pity or sorrow. In argument or persuasion it tends to be the evocation of pity from the reader/listener. Think of it as the "poor starving children" approach to convincing you.

Periodic sentence—a long sentence in which the main clause is not completed until the end. For example, "Looking as if she were being chased by demons, ignoring all hazards, the child ran." "The child, who looked as if she were being chased by demons, frenzied and ignoring all hazards, ran."

Personification—treating an abstraction or nonhuman object as if it were a person by endowing it with human features or qualities. William Wordsworth speaks of the stars "Tossing their heads in sprightly dance." Or, looking at a prose speech: "Once again the heart of America is heavy. The spirit of America weeps for a tragedy that denies the very meaning of our land." (Lyndon B. Johnson)

Point of View—the relation in which a narrator/author stands to a subject of discourse. Point of view in nonfiction requires the reader to establish the historical perspective of what is being said.

Prose—the ordinary form of written language without metrical structure in contrast to verse and poetry.

Realism—attempting to describe nature and life without idealization and with attention to detail. Mark Twain is an author of this school. Thoreau, with his romantic outlook toward nature is not.

Rebuttal/refutation—an argument technique wherein opposing arguments are anticipated and countered.

Rhetoric—the art of using words to persuade in writing or speaking. All types of writing may seek to persuade and rhetoricians study these genres for their persuasive qualities.

Rhetorical question—a question that is asked simply for the sake of stylistic effect and is not expected to be answered.

Sarcasm—a form of verbal irony in which apparent praise is actually critical. Sarcasm can be light, and gently poke fun at something, or it can be harsh, caustic, and mean.

Satire—a literary work that holds up human failings to ridicule and censure. Jonathan Swift and George Orwell were masters of satire. Several years ago, the English Language exam included a satirical piece by columnist Ellen Goodman, "The Company Man," a satire attacking the struggle for corporate survival by the little man. Arthur Miller exposed the same subject several decades ago in his tragic play, *Death of a Salesman.*

Simile—a direct, explicit comparison of one thing to another, usually using the words *like* or *as* to draw the connection. For instance, Charles Dickens wrote: "There was a steamy mist in all the hollows, and it had roared in its forlornness up the hill <u>like</u> an evil spirit."

Style—the manner in which a writer combines and arranges words, shapes ideas, and utilizes syntax and structure. It is the distinctive manner of expression that represents that author's typical writing style. This is often queried on the English Language test. In particular, when two passages on the same topic are presented, you must pay the most attention to their styles.

Symbolism—use of a person, place, thing, event, or pattern that figuratively represents or "stands for" something else. Often the thing or idea represented is more abstract or general than the symbol, which is concrete. Everyone recognizes the symbol of the Golden Arches representing McDonald's™ restaurants.

Synecdoche—a figure of speech in which a part signifies the whole, such as "fifty <u>masts</u>" representing fifty ships or "100 <u>head</u> of steer had to be moved to their grazing land."

Syntax—the way words are put together to form phrases, clauses, and sentences. Syntax is sentence structure and how it influences the way the reader receives a particular piece of writing. It is important in establishing the tone of a piece and the attitude of the author/narrator. See Loose sentence, Parallel structure, and Periodic sentence.

Theme—the central or dominant idea or focus of a work. The statement a passage makes about its subject.

Tone—the attitude the narrator/writer takes toward a subject and theme; the tenor of a piece of writing based on particular stylistic devices employed by the writer. Tone reflects the narrator/author's attitude.

Voice—the acknowledged or unacknowledged source of the words of the story; the speaker's or narrator's particular "take" on an idea based on a particular passage and how all the elements of the style of the piece come together to express his or her feelings.

Zeugma—a grammatically correct construction in which a word, usually a verb or adjective, is applied to two or more nouns without being repeated. Often used to comic effect ("the thief <u>took</u> <u>my wallet</u> and the Fifth Avenue <u>bus</u>").

APPLYING KEY TERMINOLOGY

The following passage is followed by several questions not unlike those in the multiple-choice section of the English Language exam.

The following passage was written (on the last night of 1849) by Florence Nightingale. She was not only the premier mover in the profession of nursing, but also one of the first European women to travel into Egypt (1849–50) and keep a detailed journal of her letters and reflections of her journey.

> My Dear People,
> Yes, I think your imagination has hardly followed me through the place where I have
> been spending the last night of the old year. Did you listen to it passing away and think of
Line me? Where do you think I heard it sigh out its soul? In the dim unearthly colonnades of
(5) Karnak, which stood and watched it, motionless, silent, and awful, as they had done for
> thousands of years, to whom, no doubt, thousands of years seem but as a day. Would that I
> could call up Karnak before your eyes for one moment, but it "is beyond expression."
> No one could trust themselves with their imagination alone there. Gigantic shadows
> spring upon every side; "the dead are stirred up for thee to meet thee at thy coming, even
(10) the chief ones of the earth", and they look out from among the columns, and you feel as
> terror-stricken to be there, miserable intruder, among these mighty dead, as if you had
> awakened the angel of the Last Day. Imagine six columns on either side, of which the last
> is almost out of sight, though they stand very near each other, while you look up to the
> stars from between them, as you would from a deep narrow gorge in the Alps, and then,
(15) passing through 160 of these, ranged in eight aisles on either side, the end choked up with
> heaps of rubbish, this rubbish consisting of stones twenty and thirty fee long, so that it
> looks like a mountain fallen to ruin, not a temple. How art thou fallen from heaven, oh
> Lucifer, son of the morning! He did exalt his throne above the stars of God; for I looked
> through a colonnade, and under the roof saw the deep blue sky and star shining brightly;
(20) and as you look upon these mighty ruins, a voice seems continually saying to you, And
> seekest though good things for thyself? Seek them not, for it there ought like this ruin?
> One wonders that people come back from Egypt and live lives as they did before.

Yet Karnak by starlight is not to me painful: we had seen Luxor in the sunshine. I had expected the temples of Thebes to be solemn, but Luxor was fearful. Rows of painted
(25) columns, propylae, colossi, and—built up in the Holy Place—mud (not even huts, but) unroofed enclosures chalked out, or rather mudded out, for families, with their one oven and broken earthen vessel; and, squatting on the ground among the painted hieroglyphs, creatures with large nose-rings, the children's eyes streaming with matter, on which the mothers let the flies rest, because "it is good for them", without an attempt to drive them
(30) off; tattooed men on the ground, with camels feeding out of their laps, and nothing but a few doura stalks strewed for their beds;—I cannot describe the impression it makes: it is as if one were steering towards the sun, the glorious Eastern sun, arrayed in its golden clouds, and were to fine, on nearing it, that it were full—instead of glorified beings as one expected—of a race of dwarf cannibals, stained with blood and dressed in bones. The
(35) contrast could not be more terrible than the savages of the Present in the temples of the Past at Luxor.

But Karnak by starlight is peace; not peace and joy, but peace—solemn peace. You feel like spirits revisiting your former world, strange and fallen to ruins; but it has done its work, and there is nothing agonizing about it. Egypt should have no sun and no day, no
(40) human beings. It should always be seen in solitude and by night; one eternal night it should have, like Job's, and let the stars of the twilight be its lamps; neither let it see the dawning of the day.

1. The mode of discourse that best describes this passage is

    (A) exposition

    (B) description

    (C) argumentation

    (D) comparison/ contrast

    (E) personal reflection and narration

Answer (B)

Although there are certain elements of exposition and personal reflection, the predominant mode of discourse of this passage is that of description. Ms. Nightingale is telling her readers, the recipients of her letter, what she has seen and felt.

2. Because this is a letter sent to far-away recipients, the questions posed in the first paragraph can be described as

    (A) useless

    (B) imperative

    (C) interrogative

    (D) rhetorical

    (E) redundant

Answer (D)

Rhetorical questions are those asked by a speaker or writer that are used strictly for stylistic purposes—often bringing focus or emphasis to a particular idea. The writer/speaker does not expect such questions to be answered. They are included strictly as a stylistic device.

3. This passage relies upon the writer's appeal to the reader's reaction to

   (A) logic
   (B) authority
   (C) emotion
   (D) humor
   (E) sarcasm

Answer (C)

The writer of this letter, Florence Nightingale, is appealing to her readers reacting emotionally to her vivid descriptions.

4. In the second paragraph, references to the angel of the Last Day, line 12, and to Lucifer, line 18, is a stylistic device known as

   (A) oxymoron
   (B) onomatopoeia
   (C) metaphor
   (D) exaggeration
   (E) allusion

Answer (E)

An allusion is a reference to a literary, historical, religious, or mythological reference. In this case, the reference is to Judgment Day and to the fallen archangel Lucifer.

5. The six columns on either side mentioned by the writer are described using a comparison that is known as

   (A) contrast
   (B) simile
   (C) metaphor
   (D) antithesis
   (E) juxtaposition

Answer (B)

The columns are compared to the Alps, and the phrase "as you would from. . " indicate that this is a simile, a comparison using like or as.

6. The writer describes Karnak awaiting the dawning of a new year by using the stylistic device of

   (A) metaphor
   (B) simile
   (C) personification
   (D) imagery
   (E) diction

Answer (C)

Although you might argue that metaphor and imagery would work for this response, the AP exam is always looking for the most exact response. Consequently, (C) Personification is the most accurate response. Karnak seems to come alive as it stands motionless and silent, waiting for the advent of a new year.

7. The fact that the writer is more comfortable "seeing" Karnak in the dark is an example of

   (A) situational irony
   (B) verbal irony
   (C) dramatic irony
   (D) juxtaposition
   (E) antithesis

Answer (A)

Situational irony is a contrast between what is expected and what really happens. In this case, it is truly ironic that the writer is most comfortable "seeing" a place in the dark in contrast to the bright light of day.

8. "...ranged in eight aisles on either side, the end choked up with heaps of rubbish," lines 15–16, utilizes the stylistic device

   (A) allusion
   (B) onomatopoeia
   (C) anaphora
   (D) alliteration
   (E) assonance

Answer (E)

Assonance is the repetition of identical or similar vowel sounds, usually in successive or proximate words. You can hear the assonance: "eight aisles on either side the end choked up with. . . ."

9. The second paragraph (lines 8–22) contains all of the following stylistic devices EXCEPT

   (A) simile
   (B) apostrophe
   (C) allusion
   (D) rhetorical question
   (E) hyperbole

Answer (B)

This paragraph contains a couple of similes, comparisons using like or as. It has an allusion to the Old Testament with the mention of Lucifer, and it uses a couple questions used for stylistic effect. Finally, although the ruins are gargantuan, it is an exaggeration to compare it to a fallen mountain.

10. Ms Nightingale contrasts her reaction to the beauties of Karnak with the horrors of

   (A) London streets at night
   (B) alleys of Cairo at midnight
   (C) horrors of Luxor in the daylight
   (D) Egypt by moonlight
   (E) the Last Day of judgment

Answer (C)

Lines 23–36 describe the horrors that Ms Nightingale had experienced during an earlier, daytime trip to Luxor.

Multiple-choice sections that accompany reading passages rarely have this many questions asking about specific key terminology. Nevertheless, this should give you an idea of the types of questions you might be asked among the 50–55 questions found on your AP exam.

IF YOU LEARNED ONLY ONE THING IN THIS CHAPTER . . . .

Learn the key terminology and use it in your Free-Response essays.

Chapter 4: **Reading for Understanding**

- Reading critically
- The How–What approach
- Applying the How–What approach
- Sample annotations

Much of your exam score—for both the multiple-choice passages and the free response (essay) passages—will be earned through your ability as a reader. You will find information specific to reading passages for multiple-choice questions and for essays in chapters 5 and 6. This chapter is an overview of reading for understanding

You will see in chapters 5 and 6 how the multiple-choice questions and essay prompts not only expect you to understand what is being said in a passage, but they will require you to understand the author's purpose, tone, attitude, style, use of structure, and many other things. In other words, successful reading on the AP test requires you to decode everything that goes into a piece of writing and subsequently synthesize them as required for an essay.

READING CRITICALLY

Careful, close reading of a text is the first stage in writing an essay that responds to or builds upon the ideas in the original. Sometimes this is referred to as "reader response" writing. This reading goes beyond merely extracting facts from the original text. It prepares you to analyze it critically through your own writing.

Such a close reading process involves the following steps:

1. Annotate as you read

With a pencil or pen in hand, read through the text quickly, but do not just skim it. Highlight key words, phrases, or ideas that strike you as unusual or important. Note how the writer goes about providing details and significant information.

2. Read for Topic, Scope, Purpose, and Main Idea

After reading the text, consider the author's position. What do you interpret as the main points of the passage, and how does the author arrive at a conclusion? If the passage is an argument, follow the logic to ensure that you are correctly interpreting what the author is saying, and be sure that the passage is indeed logical.

3. Evaluate the author's effectiveness

Having deciphered the author's meaning, do you agree or disagree? What questions do you still have? Go back to the passage and see if the answers are still there to be discovered. What about the passage is convincing or not convincing? Have you begun to establish an internal dialogue about the passage as you engage the text more closely?

4. Organize

Now that you have examined the text, and extracted what you can from it, you should be ready to organize and present your interpretation and/or evaluation of it. Go to your notes and any annotations you have made. Review the information and details that you found particularly engaging. If you agree with the author's argument, how can you extend and, perhaps, relate it to more global issues. If you disagree, be sure you have sound reasons and details to support your position. You might even consider how the author could have improved his/her stance within the passage. Double check to make sure you are not misrepresenting the author's intention or manipulating information to fit your interpretation. Remember you are responding, not summarizing the original.

5. Select

Unless you have unlimited time, you probably have to pick and choose things to write about. Under timed conditions, it is rare to cover everything. Be discerning; be ready to synthesize ideas, and do not be afraid to think outside the box.

Needless to say, mastering this level of reading does not come easily to most people. It is a painstaking process that needs to start slowly and long before the day of the exam. Remember that nothing in a well-written passage happens by accident.

THE HOW–WHAT APPROACH

When reading a passage that you must quickly respond to, in particular with a written response of your own, a good strategy is the How–What Approach.

How   does the author or narrator indicate his/her attitude, purpose, intent? Is there a slant or a bias that you can discover? Are things obvious or implied? Is this passage purely meant to entertain, or inform, or persuade?

What   is the main idea? Can you summarize it in a couple sentences? Can you identify an underlying thesis or the purpose of the passage? When you aren't pressed for time, it is helpful actually to write this purpose or focus down in a couple of sentences.

What   underlying structure does this passage rely on? What is presented first, or last? Might this be significant? Does the passage use repetition or other stylistic or rhetorical devices that are a part of the underlying structure of the piece?

How   does the author or narrator create an effect on the reader? Is there a difference between the intended effect and the actual effect? Is this disparity important to the passage?

What   are the author's qualifications on the topic of the passage? Is this important to the passage or not?

How   can you best recognize/identify the necessary information?

The first thing you generally do when you read a passage is to consider the opening. How is it that the author, or what is it in the opening, that catches your attention or directs you to read further? Can you make a judgment from the opening about the tone or attitude of the writer/narrator? What major points are you immediately aware of from reading the opening?

When you read the body of a passage, pay particular attention to the connotations of words and nuances of the tone words the author has chosen and how they are presented. Is the author/narrator's attitude detectable from his/her diction or tone? Mark Twain said of word choice that the best word was akin to lightning while a good word was like a lightning bug—a very distinct difference!

In addition to words, as you read you also want to be aware of individual sentences, groups of sentences, and paragraphs. Just how is the passage put together? What makes it work (or not work, as the case may be)? Consider the sorts of transitions used by the writer to link ideas together.

Within the sentences and paragraphs, you should be aware of any particular stylistic devices the author has employed to make a point. Is the passage rife with images, for instance, or does it offer a cold, clinical presentation? These are all things you must become aware of as you read the multiple-choice or essay passages on the AP Language and Composition Exam.

KAPLAN
Test Prep and Admissions

Finally, you must not overlook the conclusion of a passage. Sometimes most of what you need to know can be gleaned from the last paragraph or last several sentences of a passage. Successful writing tends to have a summarizing quality at the end of a passage. It is this quality that evokes satisfaction from the reader. However, rarely will a well-written passage merely reiterate what has already been said. Instead, a successful writer will give the reader a bit extra. That's what makes a piece meaningful. Often successful closings will not hold up out of context. They need the entire piece to provide them with significance.

Take a look at the following passage, a reproduction of Abraham Lincoln's "Second Inaugural Address," given one month before the end of the Civil War. It is the shortest presidential inaugural address ever given. This address appeared as a passage in one of the essays on the 2002 AP Language and Composition Language Exam.

At this second appearing to take the oath of the Presidential office there is less occasion for an extended address than there was at the first. Then, a statement somewhat in detail of a course to be pursued seemed fitting and proper. Now, at the expiration of four years, during which public declarations have been constantly called forth on every point and phase of the great contest which still absorbs the attention and engrosses the energies of the nation, little that is new would be presented. The progress of our arms, upon which all else chiefly depends, is as well known to the public as to myself, and it is, I trust, reasonably satisfactory and encouraging to all. With high hope for the future, no prediction in regard to it is ventured.

On the occasion corresponding to this, four years ago all thoughts were anxiously directed to an impending civil war. All dreaded it, all sought to avert it. While the inaugural address was being delivered from this place, devoted altogether to saving the Union without war, insurgent agents were in the city seeking to destroy it without war, seeking to dissolve the Union and divide effects by negotiation. Both parties deprecated war, but one of them would make war rather than let the nation survive, and the other would accept war rather than let it perish, and the war came.

One-eighth of the whole population were colored slaves, not distributed generally over the Union, but localized in the southern part of it. These slaves constituted a peculiar and powerful interest. All knew that this interest was somehow the cause of the war. To strengthen, perpetuate, and extend this interest was the object for which the insurgents would rend the Union, even by war; while the Government claimed no right to do more than to restrict the territorial enlargement of it. Neither party expected for the war the magnitude or the duration which it has already attained. Neither anticipated that the cause of the conflict might cease with, or even before the conflict itself should cease. Each looked for an easier triumph, and a result less fundamental and astounding. Both read the same Bible and pray to the same God, and each invoked His aid against the other. It may seem strange that any men should dare to ask a just God's assistance in wringing their bread from the sweat of other men's faces, but lest us judge not, that we be not judged. The prayers of both could not be answered. That of neither has been answered fully. The Almighty has His own purposes. "Woe unto the world because of offenses; for it must needs be that offenses come, but woe to that man by whom offense cometh." If we shall suppose that American slavery is one of those offenses which, in the providence of God, must needs come, but which, having continued through His appointed time. He now wills to remove, and that He gives to both North and South this terrible war as the woe due to those by whom the offense came, shall we discern therein any departure from those divine attributes which the believers in a living God always ascribe to Him? Fondly do we hope, fervently do we pray, that this mighty scourge of war may speedily pass away. Yet, if God wills that it continue until all the wealth piled by the bondsman's two hundred and fifty years of unrequited toil shall be sunk, and until every drop of blood drawn with the lash shall be paid by another drawn with the sword, as was said three thousand years ago, so still it must be said "the judgments of the Lord are true and righteous altogether."

With malice toward none, with charity for all, with firmness in the right as God gives us to see the right let us strive on to finish the work we are in, to bind up the nation's wounds, to care for him who shall have borne the battle and for his widow and his orphan, to do all which may achieve and cherish a just and lasting peace among ourselves and with all nations. *(March 4, 1865)*

APPLYING THE HOW–WHAT APPROACH

Go through the questions methodically, and mark the passage to help you keep track of your answers

What is Lincoln's main idea?

That they must bind up the nation's wounds and as a union work together to make amends and move forward with a minimum of recrimination from either side.

How does he do it?

He appeals to the common decency of both sides. He assures them that neither shall be held at fault, and the nation cannot move forward without each other.

What is the underlying structure?

He begins by recalling his inauguration of four years ago and the imminence of disaster that loomed. The North and the South, each believing it had justice on its side, consequently moved forward. Lincoln highlights a few things in the middle of his speech, including the subject of slavery, but notice how he always returns to the commonality of both sides—for instance, both sides reading the same bible and believing in the same God, both suffering losses, both leaving loved ones behind. He builds up to his brilliant conclusion, his fervent appeal to all: "With malice toward none and charity for all."

How does the narrator create an effect?

Mostly Lincoln appeals to mankind and his common feelings of doing the right thing and wanting the horror and waste to be over. Without dwelling on particular details, Lincoln refers to the horrors of the war and the damage—the numbers lost and the morale destroyed, both for those fighting and for the bereft back home. He reminds us that both sides read the same bible and believed in what they were doing. He takes special pains to not point the finger of blame at anyone. All listeners would have felt cared about as a result of hearing this speech. Not only does it persuade listeners to go along with him, but it lauds them for all that they have done or endured.

What are his qualifications?

Not all answers are this easy. This was the onset of a second term for this president. Not only has he been deemed an outstanding leader, he was an intelligent person who had studied much and seemed to know some basic psychology of the masses.

How can you best identify pertinent information?

Lucky for us, Lincoln was a good statesman. He knew how to appeal to the people's better conscience by appealing to the common man in us all. He is straightforward with his words, and he pulls no punches. The challenge is to uncover within the simplicity of his lines and his words the great depth and richness of what he says.

SAMPLE ANNOTATION

Observe the following annotations; yours should look fairly similar. Critics and historians have spent decades studying every nuance of this speech. Nevertheless, some of the most obvious points have been noted. Hopefully you found these and others as well.

> At this second appearing to take the oath of the Presidential office
> ~~tells us it will be short~~ there is less occasion for an extended address than there was at the first. That was then,
> Then, a statement somewhat in detail of a course to be pursued seemed   this is now
> fitting and proper. Now, at the expiration of four years, during which
> public declarations have been constantly called forth on every point

euphemism/ understatement

nice phrase

and phase of the <u>great contest</u> which still absorbs the attention and <u>engrosses the energies</u> of the nation, little that is new would be presented. The progress of our arms, upon which all else chiefly depends, is as well known to the public as to myself, and it is, I trust, reasonably satisfactory and encouraging to all. With high hope for the

inevitable end

future, no prediction in regard to it is ventured.

1st inaugural

On <u>the occasion corresponding to this</u>, four years ago all thoughts were anxiously directed to an impending civil war. <u>All dreaded it, all</u> <u>sought to avert it.</u> While the inaugural address was being delivered from this place, devoted altogether to saving the Union without war, insurgent agents were in the city seeking to destroy it without war, seeking to dissolve the Union and divide effects by negotiation. Both parties deprecated war, but one of them would make war rather than let the nation survive, and the other would accept war rather than let it perish, and the war came.

parallelism

Everyone dreaded it; no one wanted it, but one side would make war

clanky-sounding

One-eighth of the whole population were colored slaves, not distributed generally over the Union, but localized in the southern part of it. <u>These slaves constituted a peculiar and powerful interest.</u> All knew that this interest was somehow the cause of the war. To strengthen, perpetuate, and extend this interest was the object for which the insurgents would rend the Union, even by war; while the Government claimed <u>no right to do more than to restrict the territorial enlargement</u> of it. (Neither) party expected for the war the magnitude or the duration which it has already attained. (Neither) anticipated that the cause of the conflict might cease with, or even before the conflict itself should cease. (Each) looked for an easier triumph, and a result less fundamental and astounding. (Both) read the same Bible and pray to the same God, and each invoked His aid against the other. It may seem strange that any men should dare to ask a just God's assistance in wringing their bread from the sweat of other men's faces, but lest us judge not, that we be not judged. <u>The prayers of both could not be answered. That of neither</u> <u>has been answered fully.</u> The Almighty has His own purposes. "(Woe) unto the world because of offenses; for it must (needs be) that offenses come, but woe to that man by whom offense (cometh)." If we shall suppose that American slavery is one of those offenses which, in the providence of God, must needs come, but which, having continued through His appointed time. He now wills to remove, and that He gives to both North and South this terrible war as the woe due to those by whom the offense came, shall we discern therein any departure from those divine attributes which the believers in a living God always ascribe to Him? Fondly do we hope, fervently do we pray, that this mighty scourge of war may speedily pass away. Yet, if God wills that it continue until all the wealth piled by the bondsman's two hundred and fifty years of unrequited toil shall be sunk, and until every drop of blood drawn with the lash shall be paid by another drawn with the sword, as was said three thousand years ago, so still it must be said "the <u>judgments of the Lord</u> are true and righteous altogether."

separate

together

archaic language

this will pass— nation move forward together

much use of religious reference. compare Bush's inaugural?

KAPLAN
Test Prep and Admissions

parallel—anaphora?

With malice toward none, with charity for all, with firmness in the right as God gives us to see the right let us strive on to finish the work we are in, to bind up the nation's wounds, to care for him who shall have borne the battle and for his widow and his orphan, to do all which

similar sounds

may achieve and cherish a just and lasting peace among ourselves and with all nations.   *(March 4, 1865)*

Most of the notation has to do with the What of the passage—some of the marks and comments relate to the How of the passage.

Some quick conclusions are obvious: Lincoln used a lot of parallelism—yes, it makes good copy, but more importantly, he is trying to align two antagonistic parts of the country. How better than to use parallelism in his speech as well. A very strong religious sense pervades this speech. Perhaps today's audiences would object to such a thing, but Lincoln held strong religious beliefs in common with the vast majority of the nation's citizens. Of course the United States at the time of the Civil War was a much different country from what it is today. God and religion were strong influences on our forefathers and the shaping of the Nation, and to understand what they were saying and doing, we have to be mindful of the context in which they spoke and acted.

This should give you an idea of the things you need to be seeing and thinking about as you read. What you see here is the beginning of a "dialogue" between you and the passage. As mentioned before—close reading skills are not developed overnight. This is something you must work on long before your AP Test is imminent.

IF YOU LEARNED ONLY THREE THINGS IN THIS CHAPTER . . . .

1. Read critically.
2. Apply the How–What approach.
3. Annotate as you go.

Chapter 5: **The Multiple-Choice Section**

- Reading the questions
- The types of questions
- Applying the strategies
- Practice Sets

The multiple-choice section of the AP English Language exam consists of four or five passages followed by a set of questions. On this exam the passages will be prose of some sort—perhaps fiction, but most likely from essays, letters, journals, diaries, biographies, speeches, or government documents. Several might be persuasive or argumentative.

You will not have time to do an in-depth analysis of a passage on the multiple-choice section. Remember, you have 12 to 15 minutes per passage and question set. On the multiple-choice section of the test, you will have to read for meaning and use your close analysis and annotation habits, circling, underlining, and evaluating as you read. Then you will need to attack the questions, returning to the passage for the information you need to answer each one.

If you are unsure of an answer, mark your book and return to that question (if you have time) before you start reading the next passage. If you have no idea of the answer; you are totally clueless; skip that one entirely and move on. Only at the very end of the section should you bother returning to the "clueless" questions. Work with what you know and what you think you know. You are *not* expected to know all the answers.

The best strategy for preparing for this section is to have *a specific reading plan* for the questions and passages and to familiarize yourself with the *categories and types of questions* you will face.

READING THE QUESTIONS

Chapter 4 gave you a look at "Reading for Understanding." Now let's apply that information specifically to test Section I, the multiple-choice questions.

Questions or Passage First

Many debate the comparative wisdom of skimming the questions before reading the passage or of quickly reading the passage first and then tackling the questions. That is something that you will have to decide for yourself.

If you are a slow reader, you may not have enough time to look at the questions first. You may have to eliminate that first step. On the other hand, some students find that skimming the questions really helps them to focus better when they read, so their reading time is actually shorter. While you practice the multiple-choice section in this book or look at passages and questions online at AP Central, try it both ways and decide what works best for you.

Read Critically

Whether you read the passage first or second, read actively and critically—that is, by marking key words and ideas.

Know What the Question Asks

Read the question carefully. Sometimes it helps to mark that as well, to help you to decide just what it is you are being asked.

Predict an Answer

Try to formulate the answer in your mind before you look at the choices given.

Read Every Answer Choice

Next, read every answer choice, even if the correct response jumps out at you right away. It is not unusual to have more than one acceptable answer but only one *best* answer.

Don't Waste Time on Hard Questions

If you have no clue about a question, skip it and move on to the next one. If you just need a bit of time to "work it out," mark it in the book and move on. Return to any you have marked before going on to the next passage. If you are pushing the time limit (an average of 12 minutes per passage for 5 passages; 15 minutes per passage for 4 passages), go on to the next passage and return at the end of the multiple-choice section if you have any time.

Read the Explanations and Look for Patterns

On practice sets, review your performance. Can you detect a pattern to your errors? If so, what do you need to do? What types of questions are you missing? Try to refurbish those shaky areas.

Think Like the Test Maker

In the following pages you will find a discussion of the types and characteristics of questions with some template sentences to give you an idea of how such categories might be expressed on the test. You may be tempted to skip this part. However, one very valuable activity you can undertake in preparation for the AP English Language and Composition Exam is to create your own multiple-choice questions based on passages you may have in your textbook or from other sources. This is even more helpful—not to mention more interesting—if you can create these questions with some study cohorts from your AP English class. Perhaps you might want to work in partners and then have the partners swap their questions with each other to test your skills.

THE TYPES OF QUESTIONS

AP English Language and Composition test questions are surprisingly predictable. They fall into only a few categories, with a variety of approaches within each category. Once you are familiar with the basic types of questions, you will find your confidence growing and your response speed increasing. Since the multiple-choice section of the exam makes up 45 percent of your AP test score, conquering multiple-choice questions is essential for your success.

The categories are:

- the main idea/theme/attitude
- the author's meaning and purpose (Why did the writer. . .)
- the language of rhetoric (syntax, diction, figurative language, tone, etc.)
- the speaker or narrator
- the attitude (of the narrator or of the author)
- word choice and selection of details (connotation)
- sentence structure (syntax)
- rhetorical reasoning
- inferences
- general conclusions
- organization and structure (is their contrast, deduction, spatial description, etc.)
- rhetorical modes (narration, description, argumentation, etc.)

Main Idea

These are very common questions on the exam. Often the first or last questions of a series have to do with main idea. What is the author saying? Can you restate it? That's what you need to do, at least in your mind. You might have to make a few marginal notes or you may find the main idea stated in one or two lines that you can underline. You will want to mark this somehow. Work on developing an annotation code that works for you.

The main idea is tested using a variety of question stems:

The author would most likely agree with which of the following?

The narrator's/writer's/author's/speaker's attitude can be described as . . .

The author would most/least likely agree that . . .

The writer has presented all of the following ideas EXCEPT

We can infer that the author values the quality of . . .

The attitude of the narrator helps the writer create a mood of . . .

In context lines "_____" most likely refer to . . .

Rhetoric

Questions about rhetoric dominate the AP English exam. How does the language work in a passage? What are the point of view or the syntax and diction; how does the author express his tone; what is the narrator's attitude? These are not words just to be thrown around recklessly. You need to understand how all or the elements synthesize together to make the entire passage. How does each "rhetorical device" affect the whole?

Rhetoric questions appear in a variety of different forms:

A shift in point of view is demonstrated by . . .

The repetitive syntax of lines "____" serves to . . .

"_____" can best be said to represent

The second sentence is unified by the writer's use of _____ rhetorical device?

The word "___" is the antecedent for. . .

The style of the passage can best be characterized as . . .

The author employs "_____" sentence structure to establish . . .

The tone of the passage changes when the writer . . .

Meaning and Purpose

This is a common question in the multiple-choice questions. What is the purpose of the passage? How does it fit a meaning? Why was it written? Since so many of the passages on this exam are taken from nonfiction—speeches, letters, autobiographies, essays—usually the author had a very strong reason for writing. Usually you can discover meaning by looking at the connotations of the author's words.

You will have to determine how or why the specific word choice demonstrates the author's thematic intention(s).

These questions also take a variety of forms:

"_____" can best be defined as . . .

The purpose of lines "____" can best be interpreted as . . .

The writer clarifies "____" by . . .

The writer emphasizes "____" in order to . . .

By saying "____", the author intends for us to understand that . . .

By "_____" the author most likely means . . .

The purpose of the sentence/paragraph/passage can best be summarized as . . .

The passage can be interpreted as meaning all of the following EXCEPT

Structure and Organization

How has the author organized his or her passage? Is there a consistency or a planned inconsistency that should be noted? Is this an argument? If so, is it deductive or inductive? Is this a personal observation? How is the information presented? Although there are not a lot of organization and structure questions in the multiple-choice section of the exam, you need to know what to expect when you are faced with one.

Some sample forms for structure and organization questions are:

The shift from "___" to "____" is seen by the author's use of . . .

In presenting the author's point the passage utilizes all of the following EXCEPT

The speaker has included "____" in her argument in order to . . .

The type of argument employed by the author is most similar to which of the following?

The passage can be said to move from "___" to "____".

The "___" paragraph can be said to be ___ in relation to "___".

The structure of this passage is primarily one of . . .

Rhetorical Modes

Only a few questions about modes are on the test. A mode (rhetorical mode, mode of discourse) simply means what type of writing has the author used? Is it description, narration, argumentation, comparison and contrast, etc? Sometimes understanding the author's choice of mode helps us to understand the author's purpose in writing.

These questions may appear in such forms as:

- All of the following modes can be found within the passage EXCEPT
- The rhetorical mode that best describes this passage is . . .
- The author's uses cause and effect in order to . . .
- Which of the following best describes the author's method of presenting the information?
- The author combines retrospection with which other rhetorical mode within this passage?

Miscellaneous

The question types listed in this chapter do not constitute a complete list. You will most likely encounter questions that don't seem to fit into a category. It is important, however, to become familiar with the more common types of questions you will encounter. Just don't be so set on every question having to fit into a particular category that you get flustered when faced with one that does not.

One thing you can always count on is that just when you think you have an AP test completely figured out, they will surprise you with something you never anticipated.

APPLYING THE STRATEGIES

You must practice applying the strategies as you work, in order to make them second nature by test day.

Read the following passages and answer the questions that follow. Each represents a category or type of multiple-choice question that correspond to those typically found in the multiple-choice section of the AP English Language exam. Don't forget to practice the methods and strategies discussed in this chapter about reading the multiple-choice questions.

<u>Directions:</u> The following excerpt is from the *Narrative of the Life of Frederick Douglass, an American Slave*. After reading the passage, answer the questions that follow.

His mistress had been severely reprimanded by her husband for helping Frederick Douglass learn to read. After all, the husband admonished, giving a
Line *slave the knowledge to read was like giving the slave*
(5) *access to thinking he or she was human. If you give the slaves an inch, they will take the ell.*

My mistress was, as I have said, a kind and tender-hearted woman; and in the simplicity of her soul she commenced, when I first went to live with
(10) her, to treat me as she supposed one human being ought to treat another. In entertaining upon the duties of a slaveholder, she did not seem to perceive that I sustained to her the relation of a mere chattel, and that for her to treat me as a
(15) human being was not only wrong, but dangerously so. Slavery proved as injurious to her as it did to me. When I went there, she was pious, warm, and tender-hearted woman. There was no sorrow or suffering for which she had not a tear. She had
(20) bread for the hungry, clothes for the naked, and comfort for every mourner that came within her reach. Slavery soon proved its ability to divest her of these heavenly qualities. Under its influence, the tender heart became stone, and the lamblike
(25) disposition gave way to one of tiger-like fierceness. The first step in her downward course was in her ceasing to instruct me. She now commenced to practice her husband's precepts. She finally became even more violent in her opposition [to my
(30) learning to read] than her husband himself. She was not satisfied with simply doing as well as he had commanded; she seemed anxious to do better. Nothing seemed to make her more angry than to see me with a newspaper. She seemed to think that
(35) here lay the danger. I have had her rush at me with a face made all up of fury, and snatch from me a newspaper, in a manner that fully revealed her apprehension. She was an apt woman; and a little experience soon demonstrated, to her satisfaction,
(40) that education and slavery were incompatible with each other.

From this time I was most narrowly watched. If I was in a separate room any considerable length of time, I was sure to be suspected of having a book,
(45) and was at once called to give an account of myself. All this, however, was too late. The first step had been taken. Mistress, in teaching me the alphabet, had given me the *inch*, and no precaution could prevent me from taking the *ell*.
(50) The plan which I adopted, and the one by which I was most successful, was that of making friends of all the little white boys whom I met in the street. As many of these as I could, I converted into teachers. With their kindly aid, obtained at
(55) different times and in different places, I finally succeeded in learning to read. When I was sent on errands, I always took my book with me, and by going one part of my errand quickly, I found time to get a lesson before my return. I used also to
(60) carry bread with me, enough of which was always in the house, and to which I was always welcome, for I was much better off in this regard than many of the poor white children in our neighborhood. This bread I used to bestow upon the hungry little
(65) urchins, who, in return, would give me that more valuable bread of knowledge. I am strongly tempted to give the names of two or three of those little boys, as a testimonial of the gratitude and affection I bear them; but prudence forbids;—not
(70) that it would injure me, but it might embarrass them; for it is almost a unpardonable offence to teach slaves to read in this Christian country. I used to talk this matter of slavery over with them. I would sometimes say to them, I wished I could be
(75) as free as they would be when they got to be men. This used to trouble them; they would express for me the liveliest sympathy, and console me with the hope that something would occur by which I might be free.

1. The narrator's attitude toward his mistress can best be described as

   (A) compassion and understanding

   (B) hatred and vengeance

   (C) ridicule and dismissal

   (D) disgust and disappointment

   (E) regret and thankfulness

The narrator regrets that his mistress turned against him so vehemently, but he nevertheless is thankful that she gave him the rudiments of reading and awakened in him the desire to learn as much as he can. This question would fit under the *main idea* category of questions. When you are presented with descriptors in pairs or in threes, remember that all must apply correctly to the question. (E) is the correct choice.

2. The narrator would most likely adhere to the concept that

   (A) all's well that ends well

   (B) some people's piety is only skin deep

   (C) take advantage of that which is close at hand

   (D) sometimes things don't work out the way you want them to

   (E) white people are not to be trusted

This narrator is going places; he will take any advantage he can in pursuing his goals. This is also a *main idea* question. Although Frederick Douglass might agree with one or two of the other choices, (C) is certainly the most accurate.

3. The short second paragraph concludes with the author's clever use of

   (A) a sentence

   (B) a version of an aphorism

   (C) an alliteration

   (D) a trite expression

   (E) a metaphor

Give an inch and take an ell (mile) is what is known as an aphorism. Ben Franklin was full of such aphorisms, about early birds getting worms, and mending something before the tear gets worse. If you know what an aphorism is, then this was an easy question for you; choice (B) is correct. If not, at least you do now. Sayings, aphorisms, allusions to things past—these are all a part of *rhetoric*.

4. The repetition of the opening word "She" in the sentences starting in lines 19, 27, 28, 30, 34, and 38 is an example of the specific rhetorical device known as

   (A) repetition

   (B) alliteration

   (C) rhetorical statement

   (D) anaphora

   (E) allusion

If you look in the key terminology section of this book, anaphora (D) is a repetition that occurs in opening words of phrases or clauses in a series. This is a *rhetoric question*—that is, it is a question that is asked about a term of rhetorical language. You will possibly find a number of these questions in the multiple-choice section of the AP English Language and Composition exam.

5. In line 72, the words "Christian country" are most specifically chosen to

   (A) express an irony

   (B) demonstrate alliteration

   (C) show the religious element of the passage

   (D) express the spiritual feelings of the writer

   (E) present an allusion

This response shows that you recognize that Frederick Douglass did indeed have a bit of an attitude when he wrote this passage, and that the juxtaposition of the treatment of slaves and the phrase "Christian country" demonstrates Douglass's deeper understanding of the vagaries of humankind and the double-standard by which many white people lived at this time. So (A) is correct. None of the alternative responses makes sense as an answer. This question assumes you understand the *meaning and purpose* of this passage.

6. The purpose of this passage can be interpreted as all of the following EXCEPT

   (A) to relate a Negro slave's struggle to learn to read

   (B) to explain the impetus of a slave to seek freedom

   (C) to expose the hypocrisy of the Christian slave owners

   (D) to reveal the determination of one man to seek freedom

   (E) to show the innate meanness of the slave's mistress

You might say that several of the choices given to answer this question might work. However, there is only one, (B), that truly responds to the questions asked. This is another *meaning/purpose* question.

7. Paragraph 3, in contrast to paragraphs 1 and 2 can best be described as

(A) the narrator's shift from being passive to pro-active

(B) the difference in what went on inside versus outside the house

(C) a discussion of children's behavior versus adult behavior

(D) a movement from the metaphoric to the concrete

(E) a solution to a problem

This question requires you to take a look at the *structure* of the passage. However, not only do you need to recognize structure, but you need to understand any shifts or changes in attitude or point of view of the narrator. (A) is correct.

8. The passage uses all of the following elements to tell his story EXCEPT

(A) retrospective story telling

(B) personal perspective

(C) movement from the personal to the general

(D) movement from the narrator's childhood to his adulthood

(E) reference to specific people to a more general population

Another *structure/organization* question. This question expects you to get a "feel" for the narrator's perspective. What you need to realize is that the earlier part of this essay has nothing to do with the narrator's childhood. This narrator is an adult—older when he writes, but still a young adult when he recalls himself learning to read. (D) is correct.

9. The rhetorical mode that best describes the characteristics of this passage is one of

(A) comparison and contrast

(B) argumentation

(C) personal reflection

(D) description

(E) cause and effect

This is a question having to do with *rhetorical mode* or mode of discourse. Actually, there is only one response—this is a reminiscence piece. In other words, this is a personal reflection, (C).

10. One could characterize the narrator of this passage as

(A) an angry young man

(B) a despairing slave

(C) one who had it better than most of his peers

(D) a frustrated author who knew he could write

(E) a young man determined to succeed

In this case, the narrator is a young man determined to succeed, (E). This is a miscellaneous type of question. It doesn't quite fit any of the other categories, but it is not unlike other multiple-choice questions you might face.

IF YOU LEARNED ONLY FOUR THINGS IN THIS CHAPTER . . . .

1. Read the questions carefully.
2. Answer the easy questions first.
3. Predict an answer before looking at the choices.
4. Know what types of question you can expect and the best strategies for handling them.

PRACTICE SETS

Practice Set 1

A child was standing on a street-corner. He leaned with one shoulder against a high board-fence and swayed the other to and fro, the while *Line* kicking carelessly at the gravel.

(5) Sunshine beat upon the cobbles, and the lazy summer wind raised yellow dust which trailed in clouds down the avenue. Clattering trucks moved with indistinctness through it. The child stood dreamily gazing.

(10) After a time, a little dark-brown dog came trotting with an intent air down the sidewalk. A short rope was dragging from his neck. Occasionally he trod upon the end of it and stumbled.

(15) He stopped opposite the child, and the two regarded each other. The dog hesitated for a moment, but presently he made some little advances with his tail. The child put out his hand and called him. In an apologetic manner the dog

(20) came close, and the two had an interchange of friendly pattings and waggles. The dog became more enthusiastic with each moment of the interview, until with his gleeful caperings he threatened to overturn the child. Whereupon the

(25) child lifted his hand and struck the dog a blow upon the head.

This thing seemed to overpower and astonish the little dark-brown dog, and wounded him to the heart. He sank down in despair at the child's

(30) feet. When the blow was repeated, together with an admonition in childish sentences, he turned over upon his back, and held his paws in a peculiar manner. At the same time with his ears and his eyes he offered a small prayer to the child.

(35) He looked so comical on his back, and holding his paws peculiarly, that the child was greatly amused and gave him little taps repeatedly, to keep him so. But the little dark-brown dog took this chastisement in the most serious way, and no

(40) doubt considered that he had committed some grave crime, for he wriggled contritely and showed his repentance in every way that was in his power.

He pleaded with the child and petitioned him, and offered more prayers.

(45) At last the child grew weary of this amusement and turned toward home. The dog was praying at the time. He lay on his back and turned his eyes upon the retreating form.

Presently he struggled to his feet and stared after

(50) the child. The latter wandered in a perfunctory way toward his home, stopping at times to investigate various matters. During one of these pauses he discovered the little dark-brown dog who was following him with the air of a footpad.

(55) The child beat his pursuer with a small stick he had found. The dog lay down and prayed until the child had finished, and resumed his journey. Then he scrambled erect and took up the pursuit again.

On the way to his home the child turned many

(60) times and beat the dog, proclaiming with childish gestures that he held him in contempt as an unimportant dog, with no value save for a moment. For being this quality of animal the dog apologized and eloquently expressed regret, but he

(65) continued stealthily to follow the child. His manner grew so very guilty that he slunk like an assassin.

When the child reached his door step, the dog was industriously ambling a few yards in the rear.

(70) He became so agitated with shame when he again confronted the child that he forgot the dragging rope. He tripped upon it and fell forward.

The child sat down on the step and the two had another interview. During it the dog greatly

(75) exerted himself to please the child. He performed a few gambols with such abandon that the child suddenly saw him to be a valuable thing. He made a swift, avaricious charge and seized the rope.

He dragged his captive into a hall and up many

(80) long stairways in a dark tenement. The dog made willing efforts, but he could not hobble very skillfully up the stairs because he was very small and soft, and the last pace of the engrossed child grew so energetic that the dog became

(85) panic-stricken. In his mind he was being dragged
toward a grim unknown. His eyes grew wild with
the terror of it. He began to wiggle his head
frantically and to brace his legs.

   The child redoubled his exertions. They had a
(90) battle on the stairs. The child was victorious
because he was completely absorbed in his
purpose, and because the dog was very small. He
dragged his acquirement to the door of his home,
and finally with triumph across the threshold.

(95)   No one was in. The child sat down on the floor
and made overtures to the dog. These the dog
instantly accepted. He beamed with affection upon
his new friend. In a short time they were firm and
abiding comrades.

(100)   When the child's family appeared, they made a
great row. The dog was examined and commented
upon and called names. Scorn was leveled at him
from all eyes, so that he became much
embarrassed and drooped like a scorched plant.

(105) But the child went sturdily to the center of the
floor, and, at the top of his voice, championed the
dog. It happened that he was roaring protestations,
with his arms clasped about the dog's neck, when
the father of the family came in from work.

(110)   The parent demanded to know what the blazes
they were making the kid howl for. It was
explained in many words that the infernal kid
wanted to introduce a disreputable dog into the
family.

(115)   A family council was held. On this depended the
dog's fate, but he in no way heeded, being busily
engaged in chewing the end of the child's shoe.

   The affair was quickly ended. The father of the
family, it appears, was in a particularly savage
(120) temper that evening, and when he perceived that it
would amaze and anger everybody if such a dog
were allowed to remain, he decided that it should
be so. The child, crying softly, took his friend off to
a retired part of the room to hobnob with him,
(125) while the father quelled a fierce rebellion of his
wife. So it came to pass that the dog was a member
of the household.

1. The rhetorical mode that best describes this
    passage is

    (A) description
    (B) cause and effect
    (C) personal observation
    (D) process
    (E) narration

2. The dominant structural characteristic of this
    passage is the use of

    (A) a preponderance of compound sentences
    (B) rhetorical questions
    (C) an abundance of short paragraphs
    (D) a variety of parallel structure
    (E) numerous complex sentences

3. The following best describes the author's method
    of presenting the information

    (A) use of much flashback and foreshadowing
    (B) a sequential, naturally evolving manner
    (C) a deductive manner in which the answer
        appears near the end
    (D) a series of sad reminiscences
    (E) the liberal employment of humor

4. Lines 24–26 are most significant because they

    (A) indicate an abrupt mood shift in the passage
    (B) demonstrate a positive action on the part of
        the main character
    (C) display the submissive attitude of the dog
    (D) exhibit a change in the action
    (E) show the pettiness of the main character

5. The writer has presented all of the following ideas EXCEPT

(A) children can be cruel

(B) animals are often more human than humans

(C) a strong bond is easily established between boy and dog

(D) mothers always make the decision on whether or not a stray can become a pet

(E) boys often display an innate, unexplainable cruelty

6. Paragraphs 2–4, lines 5–26, contain all of the following stylistic devices EXCEPT

(A) personification

(B) onomatopoeia

(C) synecdoche

(D) imagery

(E) oxymoron

7. The word "row" in line 101 most likely means

(A) a line of people in the family standing at the door

(B) a commotion

(C) an objection to the dog

(D) a criticism of the poor pooch

(E) a reaction of praise and admiration for the fine animal

8. Lines 30–44 can best be compared to

(A) a supplicant at the feet of his master

(B) a silly animal playing tricks

(C) a stray dog who is demonstrating an unusual behavior

(D) a common animal who seems to have a religious leaning

(E) a human being trying to get his own way with someone who disagrees with him

9. In line 96, the term "overtures" most likely means

(A) symphonic movements

(B) extensions beyond the norm

(C) gambit toward conciliation

(D) hyperbolic exaggeration

(E) a movement leading to the next step

10. The irony that concludes this passage can best be summed up as

(A) the little boy hurts the dog that wants to be his friend

(B) the dog is too stupid to realize he is not wanted

(C) the family thinks the dog is beneath them

(D) the little boy really does not want the dog

(E) the father's ill-humor is what establishes the dog as a part of the family

Practice Set 2

From Mark Twain, "Taming the Bicycle"

I thought the matter over, and concluded I could do it. So I went down and bought a barrel of Pond's Extract and a bicycle. The Expert came
Line home with me to instruct me. We chose the back
(5) yard, for the sake of privacy, and went to work.

Mine was not a full-grown bicycle, but only a colt—a fifty-inch, with pedals shortened up to forty-eight—and skittish, like any other colt. The Expert explained the thing's points briefly, then he
(10) got on its back and rode around a little, to show me how easy it was to do. He said that the dismounting was perhaps the hardest thing to learn, and so we would leave that to the last. But he was in error there. He found, to his surprise and
(15) joy, that all that he needed to do was to get me on to the machine and stand out of the way; I could get off, myself. Although I was wholly inexperienced, I dismounted in the best time on record. He was on that side, shoving up the
(20) machine; we all came down with a crash, he at the bottom, I next, and the machine on top.

We examined the machine, but it was not in the least injured. This was hardly believable. Yet the Expert assured me that it was true; in fact, the
(25) examination proved it. I was partly to realize, then, how admirably these things are constructed. We applied some Pond's Extract, and resumed. The expert got on the other side to shove up this time, but I dismounted on that side; so the result was as
(30) before.

The machine was not hurt. We oiled ourselves up again, and resumed. This time the Expert took up a sheltered position behind, but somehow or other we landed on him again.
(35) He was full of surprised admiration; said it was abnormal. She was all right, not a scratch on her, not a timber started anywhere. I said it was wonderful, while we were greasing up, but he said that when I came to know these steel spider-webs I
(40) would realize that nothing by dynamite could cripple them. Then he limped out to position, and we resumed once more. This time the Expert took up the position of a short-stop, and got a man to

shove up behind. We got up a handsome speed,
(45) and presently traversed a brick, and I went out over the top of the tiller and landed, head down, on the instructor's back, and saw the machine fluttering in the air between me and the sun. It was well it came down on us, for that broke the fall,
(50) and it was not injured.

Five days later I got out and was carried down to the hospital, and found the Expert doing pretty fairly. In a few more days I was quite sound. I attribute this to my prudence in always
(55) dismounting on something soft. Some recommend a feather bed, but I think an Expert is better.

The Expert got out at last, brought four assistants with him. It was a good idea. These four held the graceful cobweb upright while I climbed
(60) into the saddle; then they formed in column and marched on either side of me while the Expert pushed behind; all hands assisted at the dismount.

The bicycle had what is called the "wabbles," and had them very badly. In order to keep my position,
(65) a good many things were required of me, and in every instance the thing required was against nature. Against nature, but not against the laws of nature. That is to say, that whatever the needed thing might be, my nature, habit, and breeding
(70) moved me to attempt it in one way, while some immutable and unsuspected law of physics required that it be done in just the other way. I perceived by this how radically and grotesquely wrong had been the life-long education of my
(75) body and members. They were steeped in ignorance; they know nothing—nothing which it could profit them to know. For instance, if I found myself falling to the right, I put the tiller hard down the other way, by a quite natural impulse,
(80) and so violated a law, and kept on going down. The law required the opposite thing—the big wheel must be turned in the direction in which you are falling. It is hard to believe this, when you are told it. And not merely hard to believe it, but
(85) impossible; it is opposed to all your notions. And it is just as hard to do it, after you do come to believe

it. Believing it, and knowing by the most convincing proof that it is true, does not help it; you can't any more do it than you could before; *(90)* you can neither force nor persuade yourself to do it at first. The intellect has to come to the front, now. It has to teach the limbs to discard their old education and adopt the new.

When you have reached the point in bicycling *(95)* where you can balance the machine tolerably fairly and propel it and steer it, then comes your next task—how to mount it. You do it in this way: you hop along behind it on your right foot, resting the other on the mounting-peg, and grasping the tiller *(100)* with your hands. At the word, you rise on the peg, stiffen your left leg, hang your other one around in the air in a general and indefinite way, lean your stomach against the rear of the saddle, and then fall off, maybe on one side, maybe on the other; *(105)* but you fall off. You get up and do it again; and once more; and then several times.

By this time you have learned to keep your balance; and also to steer without wrenching the tiller out by the roots (I say tiller because it is a *(110)* tiller; "handle-bar" is a lamely descriptive phrase). So you steer along, straight ahead, a little while, then you rise forward, and with a steady strain, bringing your right leg, and then your body into the saddle, catch your breath, fetch a violent hitch *(115)* this way and then that, and down you go again.

But you have ceased to mind the going down by this time; you are getting to light on one foot or the other with considerable certainty. Six or seven more attempts and six more falls make you perfect. *(120)* You land in the saddle comfortable, next time, and stay there—that is, if you can be content to let your legs dangle, and leave the pedals alone awhile; but if you grab at once for the pedals, you are gone again. You soon learn to wait a little and perfect your *(125)* balance before reaching for the pedals; then the mounting art is acquired, is complete, and a little practice will make it simple and easy to you, though spectators ought to keep off a rod or two to one side, along at first, if you have.

(130) And now you come to the voluntary dismount; you learned the other kind first of all. It is quite easy to tell one how to do the voluntary dismount; the words are few, the requirements simple, and apparently undifficult; let your left pedal go down *(135)* till your left leg is nearly straight, turn your wheel to the left, and get off as you would from a horse. It certainly does sound exceedingly easy; but it isn't. I don't know why it isn't, but it isn't. Try as you may, you don't get down as you would from a *(140)* horse, you get down as you would from a house afire. You make a spectacle of yourself every time.

1. The mode of discourse of this passage can be best described as

    (A) narration and description

    (B) cause and effect

    (C) classification and division

    (D) exposition and description

    (E) process analysis and narration

2. The central idea of this passage can best be described as a/an

    (A) a demonstration of the narrator's determination and stamina

    (B) a treatise on the early bicycle

    (C) an example of one man's stupidity

    (D) a pathetic endeavor by the narrator to amuse his audience

    (E) a description of a funny experience

3. The word "Expert" is most likely capitalized because

    (A) Twain admired the man who helped him with the bicycle

    (B) that is what name he uses

    (C) Twain was being ironic

    (D) Twain respected this man's expertise

    (E) Twain did not care for this person at all

4. In this passage, Twain refers to the bicycle by all of the following terms EXCEPT

    (A) steel spider webs
    (B) graceful cobweb
    (C) infernal beast
    (D) the machine
    (E) a colt

5. Paragraph eight, lines 63–93 contains all of the following rhetorical devices EXCEPT

    (A) oxymoron
    (B) personification
    (C) antithesis
    (D) irony
    (E) alliteration

6. The narrator likens the handlebars of the bicycle to

    (A) chest depressors
    (B) unreliable motion directors
    (C) recalcitrant rudders
    (D) a tiller
    (E) the sail on a boat

7. In lines 100–104, the verbs that go with the subject "you" include

    (A) stiffen
    (B) lean
    (C) hang
    (D) fall off
    (E) all of the above

8. The main point established in lines 116–129 is

    (A) the term "handle-bar" does not do that part of the bicycle justice
    (B) Twain is totally discouraged by his lack of progress
    (C) Twain's continued description of falling down
    (D) Twain's quiet triumph in having mastered the mount
    (E) the mortification that he underwent as he tried to get on the bicycle

9. The author/narrator would most likely agree that

    (A) things are rarely as simple as they seem
    (B) the bicycle is a ridiculous machine
    (C) public humiliation is good for the soul
    (D) triumph comes at a high price
    (E) one can become used to falling from grace

10. In the last paragraph, lines 130–141 the author utilizes all of the following rhetorical devices EXCEPT

    (A) personification
    (B) litote
    (C) metaphor
    (D) hyperbole
    (E) asyndeton

ANSWERS AND EXPLANATIONS

Set 1

1. E

This is a rhetorical *mode question*. This passage is actually a story by Stephen Crane, author of the novel, *The Red Badge of Courage*. A narrative is basically a story, and this passage is a story. None of the other choices fits this passage.

2. C

Questions about *structure* can cover a number of things. In this case, a quick glance at the passage reveals that it contains a lot of very short paragraphs. The passage contains no rhetorical questions, very few compound sentences, no parallelism, and a small number of complex sentences.

3. B

Presentation of information actually falls under the category of structure. In this case, the passage begins with the first meeting of child and dog and ends with the dog as a pet. Therefore, (B)—sequential and naturally evolving—is the best response to this question.

4. A

These lines demonstrate a change in the behavior of the young boy. "Whereupon the child lifted his hand and struck the dog a blow upon the head" is definitely a shift in the direction of this passage. Until now, the child seems to be entranced by the dog and really likes it.

5. D

This is a *main idea* question. In this case four of the choices are possible, but choice D is an exception. The mother's part in the establishment of this dog into the family seems to have no bearing. The young boy brings the dog home and the father seems to have a perverse streak that causes him to OK the dog's presence in their family.

6. E

Oxymoron is the one rhetorical term that cannot be found in these lines. *Personification* is present in the phrase, "Sunshine beat against the cobbles." *Onomatopoeia* can be found in the words "pattings and waggles." The expression about the dog "making advances with his tail," is *synecdoche*, and *imagery*, appeals to the senses, is strong within these lines.

7. B

This question is simply clarifying the definition of a word based upon the context in which it is used. We generally think of the word "row" as something in a straight line, or that which you do with a small boat or dinghy. In this case, however, the word has a different pronunciation. It is pronounced more like "raow," with the "a" sound blending into a long "o" sound.

8. A

These lines have to do with an image. In this case it is the image of the little dark brown dog, on his back, with his paws together and his ears splayed out. This is the picture of a pooch in prayer mode. He wants the boy to stop hitting him, but more importantly, he is importuning the narrator to take pity on him and take him home.

9. C

This question falls under the miscellaneous category. Although it is not especially common on the English AP exams for vocabulary to appear, that is what we have here. Some of this you can gather from the connotation of the sentence. The rest requires you to know the definitions of "gambit" and "conciliation." A *gambit* is a movement forward (a term often used in the game of chess). *Conciliation* means becoming friends. The dark brown dog is trying to forge a relationship with the narrator.

10. D

Irony is a turn of affairs unlike what is expected. Based on the child's seeming cruelty toward the stray dog as well as his family's overwhelming criticism of the creature, the reader could easily expect a bad ending to this narrative. Instead, the boy's father returns home from a seemingly bad day at work in the middle of the chaos of his family and the non-acceptance of the stray dog. By this time the young boy/narrator wants to keep the animal, if only to contradict the wishes of his siblings and mother. In a perverse action, the father sees the dog's remaining as contra-indicatory of most of his family. Therefore, he decrees the dog will stay. Therein lies the irony.

Set 2

1. E

Obviously, this question is asking you to identify what mode of discourse has been utilized in presenting this passage. Twain is recalling an incident, supposedly from his life. That makes the passage *narration*. In addition, he does give us "how to" instructions, albeit very dated. Wouldn't he be amazed at today's titanium bicycles. Anyhow, this passage also gives us some "how to" advice, which also makes it *process*.

2. A

This question is asking for your evaluation of the overall meaning or significance of the passage. Although several of the responses might be argued, choice A is the most accurate. Above all else, Twain shows us his diligence and definitely his stamina in this passage.

3. C

Expert becomes the instructor's name. However, the more we read, the more we realize that bicycle riding is something that one has to learn for oneself, and no Expert can really do it for us. Therefore, there is an ironic twist to his use of the capital E in Expert.

4. C

Although I am sure Twain thought that the bicycle was an "infernal beast," his words only mention the other choices.

5. A

This is a question having to do with rhetorical/stylistic terminology. You must decide what specific devices Twain does (and does not) employ in this passage. All of the others are present except for oxymoron, a contradiction in terms such as jumbo shrimp. Although you might think that since there is an antithesis present, natural instinct versus reality, oxymoron is still not present.

6. D

The narrator has a lot to say about the bicycle and the handlebars, among other things such as falling off the machine at an alarming rate. If you peruse the passage, however, her refers to the handlebars as the "tiller." Apparently "handlebars" just does not do this part of the bicycle justice. And it is true: the handlebars *do* steer the bike as a tiller steers a boat.

7. E

Were you waiting for this one? Rarely does the AP Exam include a question like this. However, you must be ready for anything. Actually, you do need to look at these lines and note how the subject pronoun "you" has a stream of verbs attached to it. You—rise, stiffen, hang, lean, fall off.

8. D

These lines direct us to a very significant part of this passage. It refers to the entire second-to-last paragraph. The answer, however, is not blatant. What we have to pick up on is the subtle tone of pride that Twain, thought trying to hide it, seems to have developed. He *has* conquered the dismount, at least most of the time.

9. A

This is an overview question. Sometimes these are placed at the beginning of a question sequence; sometimes near the end. You are actually being asked to put yourself in Twain's shoes (or head) for a time. What *is* the point/purpose of all that he has told us? Based on the choices given, the only logical response is (A)—he is admitting that what he thought would be a lark as turned into a turkey.

10. B

The last paragraph is full. Twain's finale utilizes a number of stylistic (rhetorical) devices in this paragraph. However, litote, understatement for stylistic effect, is not among them and therefore the correct response.

Chapter 6: **Writing the Essays**

- A brief review
- The scoring guide
- The types of prompts
- The 3-D approach
- Applying the 3-D approach
- Practice set

A BRIEF REVIEW

Before we start, let's recall the highlights of the discussion in Chapter 2 on *How to Approach the Essay Questions*:

- Be sure you understand what the question (the prompt) is asking
- Read the prompt; read the passage; read the prompt again
- Choose the easiest question (for you) to start with
- Read critically and mark the text as you read
- Organize your essay before you start to write
- Quote from the passage judiciously; discuss and explain, don't retell or list
- Make your response long enough to get the job done
- Use suitable outside references
- Be sure your writing is legible

Now let's take a closer look at the Section II Essay Questions.

First and foremost (excuse the trite expression), you need to go to the AP Central website: www.collegeboard.com/ap/students/english, where you will find past Essay questions as well as some student responses and scoring guides used to assess these responses. It is imperative that you check these out. The prompts on the AP English Language and Composition exam are more involved and complex than those on other writing tests you may have taken. Before you even begin to practice writing responses to the essay questions, spend time analyzing the prompts themselves. Analyze the accompanying passage in light of the task in the prompt.

THE SCORING GUIDE

When you view past AP English essays on AP Central, and when you look at the samples found in the following pages, pay particular attention to the scores given to the student responses *as well as* to the scoring guides. The scoring guides (sometimes referred to as *rubrics*) are extremely important to understanding the assessment of the AP English Essay responses.

Although every question has a scoring guide that is unique to the prompt, overall the scoring guides have some basic norms to which they adhere. The scoring guide is a 9-point rubric (which we'll examine in more detail in connection with the types of essay prompts). However, if you break this down to the even scores: 8—6—4—2 we find the following breakdown.

- An 8 is a *successful* response to the prompt.
- A 6 is an *adequate* response to the prompt.
- A 4 is an *inadequate* response to the prompt.
- A 2 is an *inadequate* response.

If you keep this in mind, you can better understand the idea of upper half and lower half papers. For those of you who are Trekkies, think of Spock's hand when he separates two fingers from two fingers. What you want to write is an upper half paper: a 6–9 assessment. What you want to avoid is a lower-half paper, a 4–1 assessment.

Now you are wondering whatever happened to number 5. It is still there. Usually it distinguishes those responses that are erratic and/or inconsistent. You are better off aiming for a 6 or above. As you read the student responses to some of the essay prompts, you may want to take notes on what you see as the successful and unsuccessful parts of the essay. Then, read any commentary that might be available, and pay particular attention to the scoring guide.

In particular, note what the successful responses (scores of 7, 8, or 9) have in common, as well as what is lacking in the unsuccessful responses (scores of 3, 2, 1). After that, study the less-successful-to-middle score responses (4, 5, 6). What are their characteristics? How could you improve upon these responses? Establish a mantra for yourself: "6 and higher; 6 and higher; 6 and higher."

Successful Writing

The College Board's *AP Course Description in English* makes an excellent statement about writing successfully. The following are the skills that are expected of a successful AP English student:

- A wide-ranging vocabulary used appropriately and effectively
- A variety of sentence structures, including appropriate use of subordination and coordination
- A logical organization, enhanced by specific techniques to increase coherence, such as judicious repetition, strong transitions, and appropriate emphasis
- A balance of generalization and specific illustrative detail
- An effective use of rhetoric, including controlling tone, establishing and maintaining voice, and achieving appropriate emphasis through diction and sentence structure

Admittedly, this is a tall order. Nevertheless, there is no reason why you cannot be successful in all of these areas.

While the test makers assume you have basic standard English writing skills, we can all benefit from periodic re-evaluation of our performance and review of basic rules. With that in mind, we've provided a Grammar Reference Guide and a Guide to Usage and Style at the back of the book.

THE TYPES OF PROMPTS

At this time, the AP English Language and Composition exam consists of three types of essay prompts.

1. Prose Analysis

This is the essay prompt that is most similar to the questions on the AP Literature and Composition Exam. In fact, years ago when the Language exam first "broke away" from the Literature exam, between the two exams there were only five essay questions. For a couple of years one prose analysis question was common to both of the exams. Soon after, the exams separated completely.

In these essays, students are asked to identify the central idea of a passage or to consider the attitude of the writer toward the subject and how rhetorical devices were used to express this attitude. In some cases, the attitude is identified for the students, such as, "discuss the writer's conflicted attitudes toward nature." Often, however, students must figure out the attitude for themselves. In the past, sometimes a so-called "laundry list" of rhetorical or stylistic devices would be mentioned in the prompt. In other cases, students had to identify which devices were the best to discuss based on the passage.

The AP Language and Composition Exam tests your skills at reading an analyzing prose—some fiction, but mostly nonfiction. Some of the recent prose analysis questions have included passages by George Eliot, Annie Dillard, Jamaica Kincaid, Richard Rodriguez, Mary Oliver, Joan Didion, Frederick Douglass, Meena Alexander, Charles Lamb, and Abraham Lincoln. Currently, selections have been nonfiction prose, although college composition textbooks include fiction for the study of rhetoric and the same questions asked about a narrative from an autobiography can be asked about a short story.

These prompts might be similar to any of the following:

- Carefully read the following passage by _____. Then, paying particular attention to the changing tone within the passage, write an essay in which you analyze the techniques the author has used to express his attitude toward _____.

- The passage below is from _____ by ____. Read the entire passage carefully. Then write an essay analyzing the rhetorical strategies the author employs to convey her attitude toward_____.

- Read the following two passages about _____ carefully. Then write an essay in which you analyze how the distinctive style of each passage reveals the purpose of its writer.

- Read the passage carefully. Then write an essay in which you define the attitude toward __ that the author would like his readers to adopt, and analyze the rhetorical strategies the author employs to promote that attitude.

- The following paragraphs are from the essay _____ by _____. Read them carefully. Then write an essay in which you characterize the author's view of _____ and analyze how the author conveys this view. Your analysis might consider such stylistic elements as diction, imagery, syntax, structure, tone, and selection of detail.

- In the following excerpt from the memoirs of _____, the author reflects upon ____. Read the passage carefully. Then write an essay in which you analyze how the author uses language to convey the significance of these moments from her past. (or . . . to convey the significance of these past moments on the development of the author's _____ today.)

Whatever the case, you will need to be tuned into stylistic devices such as diction, images, details, and nuances of connotation, tone, mood, or attitude.

Usually the passages of the essay questions are not too lengthy, for the test's Development Committee realizes that you only have two hours in which to read, synthesize, and respond to the essays. The committee takes all these things into consideration as they choose the passages and prompts that best go together on each exam. Nevertheless, a passage might be as lengthy as a page. Only occasionally are they longer. If they are longer, then the other two question passages are predictably shorter.

2. Argumentation/Persuasion

Argument and persuasion has been a part of the AP Language and Composition Exam since its beginning. This essay can assume a number of guises.

- You might be given a controversial quotation and asked to defend, challenge, or qualify what has been stated.

- You may be presented with an argument and asked to analyze it. In this case, you are expected to look at the logic of the argument, but not necessarily to offer your own opinion on the subject.

- You may be presented with two different views on an idea or belief, and then asked to explain each side of the argument and develop your own opinion.

All of these argument questions require you to have a basic understanding of rhetorical argument and presentation of *pro* and *con* information to support your response. Some of the issues may be contemporary—such as the question about entertainment leading to our ruination. Others may be more universal—such as the notion that the rich can get away with things that the poor cannot, or that some things in life are private and should remain that way.

The common argumentation question is a short passage or quotation by someone with the prompt asking the student to read it carefully, consider the topic discussed, and then write an essay to defend, challenge, or qualify the writer's position. Over the years, some of the controversial topics have included:

- discussion about the relationship between the artist and society
- that your language and how you speak is your "key to identity"
- Neil Postman's view that the ideas in Huxley's *Brave New World* are more relevant than those found in *1984*
- John Ruskin's claim that precedence should be given to the soldier over the merchant or manufacturer
- Lewis Lapham's observations about the attitudes of Americans toward wealth;
- Sophocles' declaration that man's only crime is his pride
- King Lear's comments on the relationship between justice and wealth
- Neal Gabler stating that entertainment will be our ruin

These are just a few examples from many years of argument topics. Argument passages have included writings by Neil Postman, George Orwell, William Shakespeare, James Baldwin, Milan Kundera, Neil Gabler, Susan Sontag, and many others.

Variations and Recent Evolution

Although not very common, occasionally the prose analysis of two passages also has an underlying persuasive message. In 1984, for instance, two short pieces—one by Percy Shelley and one by John Milton, both defining freedom. The prompt asked that the student discuss the concept as it is presented in each passage and draw some conclusions. This is prompt has only the suggestion of persuasion.

In 1993 the two passages were two marriage proposals: one from *Pride and Prejudice* and the other from a novel by Charles Dickens. Students were asked to compare rhetorical strategies in each, and the possible effect each might have on the listener. Again, this isn't strong argumentation, but since the subject of each was supposedly a persuasive speech by a man asking a woman to marry him, an element of persuasion was certainly present.

This pattern changed a bit on the 2004 exam. Students were asked to explain both sides of an issue and then formulate their own persuasive response supporting one side or the other, supplemented with the students' own background, reading, and observations.

In 2005, the Language and Composition Exam actually had two Argument prompts.

- The first question asks students to read a passage from "Training for Statesmanship" an article written by George F. Kennan. Students are then asked to select what they think are Kennan's most compelling observations and write and essay that discusses the extent to which these observations hold true for the U. S. or any other country.

- The second "argument essay" is based on a quotation by Peter Singer who suggests that whatever money one spends above the necessity level should be given away. Students are asked to evaluate the pros and cons of Singer's argument and using appropriate evidence and support, they are supposed to develop an essay based on whichever position they find more persuasive.

As you can see, the test is beginning to evolve. Students are being asked to consider more than one point of view before they respond. This is good, and probably much more realistic and pragmatic for all that students have to consider in their college classes.

One other argumentative essay might be an analysis of an argument already written. This is a challenging essay to write. One such question appeared in 2000 when George Orwell actually wrote a persuasive essay criticizing Gandhi for believing in such strict adherence to his beliefs that he would let his own family die rather than feed them life-sustaining chicken broth. If you are confronted with such a challenge, follow the directives of the prompt. If you are *not* invited to partake in the subject of the argument, but only told to analyze the argument according to_____, then do *only* that. Only if you are asked for your opinion should you offer it.

A similar question appeared in 1981, the veto of a bill by the one-time Governor of Illinois, Adlai Stevenson. This argument question asked students to analyze the strategies or rhetorical devices that make the argument effective for the audience. Over the years this has affectionately been called the "Cat Bill" question because the governor effectively and humorously stopped all attempts to pass leash laws for cats. Nevertheless, students were not asked their opinion of the topic. They were only to analyze the passage as an argument, and substantiate their responses with specific examples from the text.

This third type of argumentative essay is less common, but not to be overlooked. The key to the entire thing is *read the prompt*. Decipher the task it asks you to perform. Do that well; don't get involved in arguing when you haven't been asked to do so.

3. Comparison/Contrast

For these questions you will be given two shorter passages on a similar topic by different writers. You will be asked to analyze the essays for certain specified aspects or qualities.

Usually, the essays are two different interpretations of the same topic, and you might be expected to compare tone, diction, structure, language, style, or other rhetorical or stylistic devices. In recent years comparison/contrast prompts have dealt with descriptions of the Galapagos Islands (by Melville and Darwin), two marriage proposals (by Charles Dickens and Jane Austen), and descriptions of the Okefenokee Swamp in Florida (from a chamber of commerce pamphlet and an encyclopedia). Often, one comparison/contrast passage is a romanticized, imagistic passage and the other is factual—even tediously detailed.

Prose Analysis and Compare-and-Contrast prompts are really more alike than different. The main thing to remember when you are given two passages to consider, is that you will do a prose analysis of each passage, similarities and differences.

You can either analyze one and then the other, or, better yet, analyze both of them as you develop the focus points of your essay. Below are examples of double passage prompts from AP English Language and Composition exams over the last dozen years or so.

- Read the following two passages carefully. Then write an essay in which you analyze how the distinctive style of each passage reveals the purpose of its writer.

- The two passages below begin essays dealing with the same historical event. The writers approach their subject and audiences very differently. Write an essay in which you analyze the specific stylistic and rhetorical differences between these introductory passages.

- In the following passages, two Native American writers describe similar landscapes. Read the passages carefully. Then, in a well-organized essay, explain how the passages reveal the differences in the authors' purposes. Consider such features as diction, syntax, imagery, and tone.

- Both passages below, written in the nineteenth century, describe the same place. Read the passages carefully. Then, in a well-organized essay, analyze the specific stylistic and rhetorical differences between the two descriptions.

- Each of the two passages below offers a definition of freedom. In a well-written essay, describe the concept of freedom embodied in each and discuss the differences between the two.

- The excerpts below represent early and later drafts of prose passages that records the writer's thoughts on how the experience of war affected his attitude toward language. Write a well-organized essay in which you discuss the probable reasons for the writer's additions and deletions and the ways in which those revisions change the effect of the paragraph.

Looking Ahead

Beginning with the AP English Language and Composition Exam of 2007, the essay section will have a different look to it. Most prose analysis will disappear. Notice that I said *most*. One thing about AP Exams is that one should never say never. ETS and the Development Committee in English do not want this test ever to become too predictable.

More information about this change will be forthcoming. AP Central is the best place to find the latest information.

Nevertheless, what we do know at this time is that a Synthesis Essay will emerge. The best way to describe it is that it will be like a small-scale Document Based Question of the type found on the AP History Exams. It will contain several documents (brief paragraphs, pictures, replicas of posters or socio-political cartoons, snatches of documents, etc.), most likely on a controversial topic. Students will be asked to respond to the questions (no prior knowledge required) based on at least some of these resources as well as the student's own knowledge of the topic. More will be available regarding these changes during the 2005–2006 school year.

The Scoring Guide and the Prompts

We've discussed the scoring rubric generally; now consider how it is affected by the type of prompt you are given.

9-point Scoring Guide for Prose Analysis and Compare-and-Contrast:

9 Essays meet all of the criteria for 8 papers, and in addition are especially full or apt in their analysis or demonstrate particularly impressive composition skills.

8 Essays successfully analyze the rhetorical and stylistic strategies the writer employs to convey her attitude. They refer to the passage directly or indirectly and explain convincingly how specific strategies such as imagery, tone, and figurative language contribute to an understanding of the writer's attitude. Their prose controls a wide range of effective writing but is not flawless.

7 Essays fit the description of 6 essays but employ more complete analysis or demonstrate a more mature prose style.

6 Essays adequately analyze how the stylistic devices that the author employs in his passage reveal his attitude. They refer to the passage directly or indirectly, and they recognize the narrator's attitude and how he conveys it by utilizing strategies such as choice of detail, tone, or figurative language. A few lapses in diction or syntax may be present, but generally the prose of 6 essays is clear.

5 Essays analyze the author's rhetorical techniques, but the development of those techniques and how they reveal the writer's attitude is limited or too simplistic. These essays may treat techniques superficially or develop ideas about the narrator's attitude inconsistently. A few lapses in diction or syntax may appear, but the prose in these essays usually conveys the writers' ideas adequately.

4 Essays inadequately respond to the task of the prompt. They may misrepresent the author's attitude or analyze rhetorical strategies inaccurately or with little understanding of how strategies reveal his attitude. Sometimes these writers will paraphrase and/or summarize more than analyze. Often the prose of these essays suggests immature control over organization, diction, or syntax.

3 Essays meet the criteria for the score of 4 but are less perceptive about how rhetorical strategies convey attitude or are less consistent in controlling the elements of writing.

2 Essays are unsuccessful in analyzing how stylistic strategies convey the writer's attitude. These essays tend to pay little or cursory attention the specific features, and they may generalize, or simplify attitude and tone. They may simply paraphrase or comment on the passage without analyzing technique. The prose of 2 papers often reveals consistent weaknesses in writing, such as a lack of development or organization, grammatical problems, or a lack of control.

1 Essays meet the criteria for the score of 2 but are especially simplistic in their discussion or weak in controlling elements of language.

9-point Scoring Guide for Argument questions

9 Essays meet all of the criteria for 8 papers, and in addition are especially full or apt in their analysis or demonstrate particularly impressive composition skills.

8 Essays successfully analyze the various ideas presented. These essays discuss the significance and effect of these ideas. They refer to the quotations directly or indirectly and explain convincingly how specific quotations support their argument. Their prose controls a wide range of effective writing but is not flawless.

7 Essays fit the description of 6 essays but employ more complete analysis or demonstrate a more mature prose style.

6 Essays adequately analyze the ideas presented. They refer to the passage directly or indirectly, and they talk about the significance and effect of those ideas. Few lapses in diction or syntax may be present, but generally the prose of 6 essays is clear and adequately written.

5 Essays analyze the ideas, but the development of this analysis is limited or too simplistic. These essays may treat some of the ideas superficially or develop ideas, for their argument inconsistently. A few lapses in diction or syntax may appear, but the prose in these essays usually conveys the writers' ideas adequately.

4 Essays inadequately respond to the task of the prompt. They may misrepresent the ideas presented by the quotations, or generalize the concepts therein. Sometimes these essays use the quotations in lieu of original synthesis and development. The arguments of these papers are often trite and/or the prose of these essays suggests immature control over organization, diction, or syntax.

3 Essays meet the criteria for the score of 4 but are less perceptive about the ideas presented and/or less successful in developing an original argument, or less consistent in controlling the elements of writing.

2 Essays are unsuccessful in analyzing concepts conveyed in the prompt. These essays tend to pay little or cursory attention the specific quotes, and their argument may be very general, trite and/or oversimplified. The prose of 2 papers often reveals consistent weaknesses in writing, such as a lack of development or organization, grammatical problems, or a lack of control.

1 Essays meet the criteria for the score of 2 but are especially simplistic in their discussion or weak in controlling elements of language.

THE 3-D APPROACH

Not all suggestions work for all students. However, some find that the 3-D approach to the essay passages is helpful: **Discover, Define, and Develop.**

Discover meaning as directed by the focus of the prompt: attitude, purpose, effect, assertion, challenge.

Discover what rhetorical devices are used by the author to create meaning: diction, imagery, tone, allusion, syntax, selection of detail, syntax and structure, pacing, contrast, repetition, figurative language.

Discover broader implications in meaning through reading, re-reading, and thinking.

Define the connection between how the language used by the author reveals more subtle meaning such as through connotation, shifts in tone, conflicted attitudes, or patterns of ideas.

Develop a connection throughout the essay beginning with a thesis (focus) statement and maintaining this controlling idea throughout each paragraph to the conclusion. Add information if it is relevant and supportive.

Discover new ideas and insights as you develop your response.

Develop the conclusion based on all the evidence. The final product must be a coherent explanation of the writer's multiple insights into the text-based prompt.

Discover errors and polish the essay into its final form. Cross outs are OK and will not detract from the quality of the essay. Always keep your eye on the time.

APPLYING THE 3-D APPROACH

Let's look at how this would work with the following speech by Helen Keller at Mount Airy, a school for the hearing- and sight-disabled.

In the following speech, Helen Keller, deaf and blind since soon after her birth, tells her audience about the joy of speaking. Read the speech carefully, then write an essay in which you analyze how Ms Keller presents herself in this speech. In addition to what she says about her struggle, consider the attitude she conveys concerning her limitations. You should consider such rhetorical features as tone, word choice, and rhetorical structure.

> If you knew all the joy I feel in being able to speak to you to-day, I think you would have some idea of the value of speech to the deaf, and you would understand why I want every little deaf child in all this great world to have an opportunity to learn to speak. I know that much has been said and written on this subject, and that there is a wide difference of opinion among teachers of the deaf in regard to oral instruction. It seems very strange to me that there should be this difference of opinion; I cannot understand how any one interested in our education can fail to appreciate the satisfaction we feel in being able to express our thoughts in living words. Why I use speech constantly, and I cannot begin to tell you how much pleasure it gives me to do so. Of course I know that it is not always easy for strangers to understand me, but it will be by and by; and in the meantime I have the unspeakable happiness of knowing that my family and friends rejoice in my ability to speak. My little sister and baby brother love to have me tell them stories in the long summer evenings when I am at home; and my mother and teacher often ask me to read to them from my favourite books. I also discuss the political

situation with my dear father, and we decide the most perplexing questions quite as satisfactorily to ourselves as if I could see and hear. So you see what a blessing speech is to me. It brings me into closer and tenderer relationship with those I love, and makes in possible for me to enjoy the sweet companionship of a great many persons from whom I should be entirely cut off if I could not talk.

I can remember the time before I learned to speak, and how I used to struggle to express my thoughts by means of the manual alphabet— how my thoughts used to beat against my finger tips like little birds striving to gain their freedom, until one day Miss Fuller opened wide the prison-door and let them escape. I wonder if she remembers how eagerly and gladly they spread their wings and flew away. Of course, it was not easy at first to fly. The speech-wings were weak and broken, and had lost all the grace and beauty that had once been theirs; indeed, nothing was left save the impulse to fly, but that was something. One can never consent to creep when one feels an impulse to soar. But, nevertheless, it seemed to me sometimes that I could never use my speech wings as God intended I should use them; there were so many difficulties in the way, so many discouragements; but I kept on trying, knowing that patience and perseverance would win in the end. And while I worked, I built the most beautiful air-castles, and dreamed dreams, the pleasantest of which was of the time when I should talk like other people; and the thought of the pleasure it would give my mother to hear my voice once more, sweetened every effort and made every failure an incentive to try harder the next time. So I want to say to those who are trying to learn to speak and those who are teaching them: Be of good cheer. Do not think of to-day's failures, but of the success that may come to-morrow. You have set yourselves a difficult task, but you will succeed if you persevere; and you will find a joy in overcoming obstacles—a delight in climbing rugged paths, which you would perhaps never know if you did not sometime slip backward—if the road was always smooth and pleasant. Remember, no effort that we make to attain something beautiful is ever lost. Sometime, somewhere, somehow we shall find that which we seek. We shall speak, yes, and sing, too, as God intended we should speak and sing.

Helen Keller speaking at Mt. Airy

OK—so now you have read a passage and prompt not unlike what you might face on the AP English Language and Composition Exam. Read the prompt one more time. Now let's look at the passage again with some editorial comments to the side, which should simulate the thoughts and ideas you might consider as you read the passage.

If you knew all the (joy) I feel in being able to speak to you to-day, I think you would have some idea of the value of speech to the deaf, and you would understand why I want every little deaf child in all this great world to have an opportunity to learn to speak. I know that much has been said and written on this subject, and that there is a wide difference of opinion among teachers of the deaf in regard to oral instruction. It seems very strange to me that there should be this difference of opinion;

Appeal to the audience, pathos

She questions the experts on the controversy re: teaching deaf to speak— her great satisfaction

Admits she is hard to understand—how does she know this?

Blessing, closeness to others, companionship from those she might never have known

Metaphor—prison door (silence)

Speech=impulse to fly

Incredible perseverance

Recurring sentiments= pleasure in the power of speech, feeling blessed and optimistic

I cannot understand how any one interested in our education can fail to appreciate the satisfaction we feel in being able to express our thoughts in living words. Why I use speech constantly, and I cannot begin to tell you how much pleasure it gives me to do so. Of course I know that it is not always easy for strangers to understand me, but it will be by and by; and in the meantime I have the unspeakable happiness of knowing that my family and friends rejoice in my ability to speak. My little sister and baby brother love to have me tell them stories in the long summer evenings when I am at home; and my mother and teacher often ask me to read to them from my favourite books. I also discuss the political situation with my dear father, and we decide the most perplexing questions quite as satisfactorily to ourselves as if I could see and hear. So you see what a blessing speech is to me. It brings me into closer and tenderer relationship with those I love, and makes in possible for me to enjoy the sweet companionship of a great many persons from whom I should be entirely cut off if I could not talk.

I can remember the time before I learned to speak, and how I used to struggle to express my thoughts by means of the manual alphabet— how my thoughts used to beat against my finger tips like little birds striving to gain their freedom, until one day Miss Fuller opened wide the prison-door and let them escape. I wonder if she remembers how eagerly and gladly they spread their wings and flew away. Of course, it was not easy at first to fly. The speech-wings were weak and broken, and had lost all the grace and beauty that had once been theirs; indeed, nothing was left save the impulse to fly, but that was something. One can never consent to creep when one feels an impulse to soar. But, nevertheless, it seemed to me sometimes that I could never use my speech wings as God intended I should use them; there were so many difficulties in the way, so many discouragements; but I kept on trying, knowing that patience and perseverance would win in the end. And while I worked, I built the most beautiful air-castles and dreamed dreams, the pleasantest of which was of the time when I should talk like other people; and the thought of the pleasure it would give my mother to hear my voice once more, sweetened every effort and made every failure an incentive to try harder the next time. So I want to say to those who are trying to learn to speak and those who are teaching them: Be of good cheer. Do not think of to-day's failures, but of the success that may come to-morrow. You have set yourselves a difficult task, but you will succeed if you persevere; and you will find a joy in overcoming obstacles—a delight in climbing rugged paths, which you would perhaps never know if you did not sometime slip backward—if the road was always smooth and pleasant. Remember, no effort that we make to attain something beautiful is ever lost. Sometime, somewhere, somehow we shall find that which we seek. We shall speak, yes, and sing, too, as God intended we should speak and sing.

Helen Keller speaking at Mt. Airy

Irony/antithesis—loves to speak but has unspeakable happiness

Talking, reading, discussing—make her more complete

What it was like before

Metaphor—manual alphabet=birds

Can't creep/must soar

Air castles= dreams of speaking

Incredible optimism

Discussion

With this in mind, let us consider Helen Keller's speech at Mount Airy. One assumption is that the AP reader would be at least vaguely familiar with who Helen Keller was. Helen was born in the late 1800's to a hardworking family in northern Alabama. When she was nineteen months old, she suffered a life-threatening illness, identified at that time as "brain fever," which left her both deaf and blind. It was through the remarkable perseverance of her teacher, Anne Sullivan, that Helen learned the meaning of language. By using a hand spelling technique, Helen was able to understand that the "spellings" in her hand actually represented words that stood for different things. It was not until some time later that she was able to speak. Her speech, however, always remained difficult for all but those closest to her to understand. Nevertheless, she did learn to speak, and it is in her address at Mount Airy that she shares her feelings about this conquest.

Are you expected to know all of this about Helen Keller? No, not all of it, but it would be expected that anyone taking an AP class and/or the exam would have at least some knowledge of who Helen Keller was and why she is significant.

Rhetoric

Rhetoric can be defined as the art of using words to persuade in writing or speaking. *All* modes of discourse—nonfiction, fiction, drama, and poetry—can be persuasive. It is up to the reader or listener—us as novice rhetoricians—to study language for its persuasive qualities. For the AP Language and Composition Exam, rhetoric is how speakers and writers use language, and how listeners and readers process this language.

Generally speaking rhetoric has three basic components: the *speaker or writer*, the *audience*, and the *subject*. In reality, however, these three components rely very heavily on several other factors: 1) *context*, 2) *purpose or intention*, and 3) *genre*, that is, the type of text that is used to deliver the message. Without getting too philosophical, just think about this. It is not possible to grasp and analyze any passage of writing or speech without considering the problem or the need that prompted the piece to be written or spoken. And, depending upon the writer/speaker's goal, one method of delivery may be preferable to another. Ask yourself why and how a particular passage was written or spoken to its audience.

The first three components of rhetoric are:

speaker	= Helen Keller
audience	= those at Mount Airy listening to the speech (presumably school officials and others connected with the world of educating the deaf)
subject	= Helen's feelings about learning to speak.

Of the next components we have:

context	= Helen has triumphed; she cannot stress enough how important speech is to her and should be for other deaf people, even if this is contradictory to some opposing philosophies;
purpose/intention	= this seems to be threefold—first to celebrate her joy in learning to speak; then to urge others to give deaf people a similar experience, despite some contrary beliefs; and finally, a motivational testament to optimism and perseverance.

All of these pieces come together to form the rhetoric of this speech.

The prompt gives us a bit of background about Helen Keller. Then the prompt gives you some tasks: analyze how Ms Keller presents herself during her struggle to learn; consider the attitude she conveys concerning her limitations.

It doesn't sound too bad, does it? In fact, if you think about the tasks given in the prompt in light of the passage, fulfilling one task should lead you to the next. The prompt also reminds you to consider rhetorical features—*tone* (can you hear her speaking, how do you think she is coming across?); *diction* (pay attention to connotation of words; are any words used more consistently than others?); *attitude* (how does she feel? How do you, the audience/reader feel? Is there a difference, and it that significant? How can she get away with such an I-centered speech? How is it that we find her inspiring rather than a braggart?) Consider the *structure* (starts with her joy, reflects on her struggles, returns in triumph); consider *imagery* (spelling out words with her fingers in the manual alphabet, her fingers are struggling, caged birds, beating to soar loose, to not be "silent" any more).

You are probably wondering how you can possibly take this much time with three different questions and write three decent essays in two hours. You can't. That's why you need to take some time to work through this thinking while you have the time. Then later, when the clock is ticking, much of this thinking process will be subconscious; you'll be able to do much of it in just one quick reading. Let us look at some student responses to this AP question.

Student Sample A

Helen Keller expresses her love of speaking in her speech about the joys in overcoming the tribulations when initially learning to speak. She describes this joy by metaphorically comparing speech to freedom, and by empathising with those who are struggling to learn how to speak.

Keller's attitude towards speech is conveyed in the very beginning of the passage. "If you knew all the joy I feel in being able to speak to you to-day. . .," describes this theme of excitement and triumph she has in conquering the struggles of learning to speak. Although she is deaf and blind, Keller never expects pity for her condition or dwell on the immense limitations she was born with. She describes the struggle, by comparing her thoughts to "little birds striving to gain their freedom." The whole process is described by the Ms Keller as an extended metaphor for young birds learning to fly and experiencing freedom. Throughout the entire piece, she is positive, evident in her choice of words. Although she reflects on the difficulties, the positive words emphasize the persistence and determination that she talks about, ". . .but I kept on trying, knowing that patience and perseverance would win in the end."

Not only does Keller talk about her initial experience of learning to speak, but she also reaches out to those with similar difficulties. She states "You have set yourselves a difficult task, but you will succeed if you persevere." Besides the fact that she wishes to help others, this phrase further demonstrates Ms Keller's unflagging resolve to conquer speech. Keller is a woman of conviction, ready to make the best of the situation that has been handed to her. She shares her images of "beautiful air-castles, and dreams" to those who are trying to follow her footsteps. Her attitude is one of sheer joy of being able to live, speak loud and reach out to others. Her message is simple: "Be of good cheer."

Unlike some who might blame God for their handicapped condition, Helen Keller accepts what has been dealt her. She does not see her self as not as good as others, but she embraces her differences. Overcoming obstacles becomes a part of who she is. In her final statement, she reaches the height of her message, "we shall speak, yes, and sing, too, as God intended we should speak and sing."

Think of the scoring guide:

9 Essays meet all of the criteria for 8 papers, and in addition, are especially full or apt in their analysis or demonstrate particularly impressive composition skills.

8 Essays successfully analyze the rhetorical and stylistic strategies the writer employs to convey her attitude. They refer to the passage directly or indirectly and explain convincingly how specific strategies such as imagery, tone and figurative language contribute to an understanding of the writer's attitude. Their prose controls a wide range of effective writing but is not flawless.

7 Essays fit the description of 6 essays but employ more complete analysis or demonstrate a more mature prose style.

6 Essays adequately analyze how the stylistic devices that the author employs in his passage reveal his attitude. They refer to the passage directly or indirectly, and they recognize the narrator's attitude and how he conveys it by utilizing strategies such as choice of detail, tone, figurative language. A few lapses in diction or syntax may be present, but generally the prose of 6 essays is clear.

5 Essays analyze the author's rhetorical techniques, but the development of those techniques and how they reveal the writer's attitude is limited or too simplistic. These essays may treat techniques superficially or develop ideas about the narrator's attitude inconsistently. A few lapses in diction or syntax may appear, but the prose in these essays usually conveys the writers' ideas adequately.

4 Essays inadequately respond to the task of the prompt. They may misrepresent the author's attitude or analyze rhetorical strategies inaccurately or with little understanding of how strategies reveal his attitude. Sometimes these writers will paraphrase and/or summarize more than analyze. Often the prose of these essays suggests immature control over organization, diction, or syntax.

3 Essays meet the criteria for the score of 4 but are less perceptive about how rhetorical strategies convey attitude or are less consistent in controlling the elements of writing.

2 Essays are unsuccessful in analyzing how stylistic strategies convey the writer's attitude. These essays tend to pay little or cursory attention the specific features, and they may generalize, or simplify attitude and tone. They may simply paraphrase or comment on the passage without analyzing technique. The prose of 2 papers often reveals consistent weaknesses in writing, such as a lack of development or organization, grammatical problems, or a lack of control.

1 Essays meet the criteria for the score of 2 but are especially simplistic in their discussion or weak in controlling elements of language.

Comments on Student Sample A

This response seems good on the surface. The student has made no egregious errors, and seems to understand Keller's two-fold purpose—to sing praise of being able to speak and to encourage others to persevere.

However, that is just about all this response does. It does not take any one thing far enough. If you look at the description of a 5 response on the scoring guide, it says: "Essays earning a score of 5 analyze the author's rhetorical techniques, but the development of those techniques and how they reveal the writer's attitude is limited or too simplistic. These essays may treat techniques superficially or develop ideas about the narrator's attitude inconsistently."

Student Sample A is more superficial than inconsistent. She gives little space to discussion of rhetorical techniques. In fact, only the "fingers as frustrated birds" is mentioned. She does, however, recognize Keller's unflagging optimism. Nowhere is pity sought, only admiration. As this young writer says, Keller embraces her differences and conquering her limitations has made her what she is.

This is not a bad response, and could easily be considered a high 5 by some readers. This writer has good language control. She uses apt transitions that give coherence and unity to the response. The essay does, however, lack the depth and breadth that is required of an upper-half response.

Student Sample B

Can anyone really imagine what living as a deaf and blind person would be like? One can try, but the full extent of the isolations would be impossible to imagine. Helen Keller does not attempt to describe what being deaf and blind is like, but instead she expounds upon the beauty of speech, the ability that "opened wide the prison-door" and allowed her to communicate with the world.

Keller begins her speech by expressing the joy that being able to speak gives her. She knows that able people cannot fully comprehend the "value of speech to the deaf," but she expresses much happiness and wishes that "every little deaf child is all this great world" be given the opportunity to learn to speak. Keller's optimism even in the face of the many obstacles in her life shines through in her choice of words. While "great" can be interpreted to mean "large" as well as "wonderful," Keller's love for the word and its many meanings in relationship to her ability to speak, are evident.

Moreover, Keller finds the idea that some teachers do not think the deaf should be given a chance to learn to speak. That makes little sense. The "satisfaction" and "unspeakable happiness" she finds in being able to use "living words" emphasizes her point that speech is a blessing. I wonder what she would think about the debate over the surgical implants for deaf people? As a hearing person, I find that difficult to understand. Why wouldn't a deaf person want to hear and, like Helen Keller, to speak as well?

Besides the obvious irony in her choice of the term "unspeakable" as a descriptor of her joy, Keller infuses the passage with an even more intense feeling of awe and gratitude at being able to speak when she describes spoken words as "living," as if her unspoken words—manual spelling, the written word or unspoken thoughts—were dead, useless in a world of speech. The unexpressed contrast between the spoken living words and unspoken dead words makes Keller appear to be all the more optimistic, despite her plight. Now she, too, has mastered the living word.

Further in her speech, Keller talks about the shared joy her family finds in being able to communicate with her, how speech makes the relationship between disabled Helen and the rest of the family "closer and tenderer." Speech also allows Keller the pleasure of the "sweet companionship" of many people with whom she would never have been able to communicate due to her inability to speak. To emphasize that she is exceedingly happy to be speaking, Keller describes her ability to discuss issues "as if [she] could see and hear." She feels that her life has definitely improved and become more pleasant and complete because of speaking.

Following her declarations of happy contentment, Keller describes the struggle she had gone through in attempting to communicate with the manual alphabet. She creates a metaphor of how her thoughts, transmitted through her clumsy fingers, were like birds prisoned in a cage. She expands this comparison when she compares learning to speak to [the birds=her thoughts] escaping to freedom. Now the birds and her thoughts can fly and soar. This creative metaphor reveals the struggle Keller experienced in first learning to speak, how her "speech-wings" were "weak and broken," and they needed to be trained and nursed back to health. Many times she felt discouraged, but she "kept on trying," because she knew that "patience and perseverance should win in the end," and any world is better when one is not isolated.

Keller ends her speech with an encouragement. First she describes the motivating thoughts at the joy her family would have in hearing her voice, then addresses "those who are trying to learn to speak and those who are teaching them" with a reassurance that optimism is rewarded. As a further emphasis of the positive attitude Ms Keller has demonstrated throughout this speech, she says: "When one does not think of present failures but only of the future successes." Speech is <u>beautiful</u>, Keller states, despite not having actually seen anything, and therefore being unable to know what a traditionally beautiful thing is. Nevertheless, her use of the word is effective and quite appropriate, when one considers the overwhelming joy a deaf person must feel in being able to communicate with other people.

Finally, her optimism reveals itself again as she finishes her speech with the emotionally-loaded statement, "We shall speak, yes, and sing, too, as God intended we should speak and sing." To Helen Keller, her disabilities are not great inconveniences, but only obstacles in her experience of the world, obstacles that she has overcome, and thus obstacles that have made her who she is.

Comments on Student Sample B

Of course, the most obvious difference between these two responses is length. This student response is eight rather well developed paragraphs versus Sample A's four paragraphs. Does length guarantee a higher score? Absolutely not! Many AP Readers will roll their eyes and tell you about four-page responses that merited only a 3 or 4 based on the scoring guide. On the other hand, use your common sense: a longer paper does give a writer more opportunity to develop ideas. That is the case here. Student Sample B not only has written a longer response, but it is a very good and complete response. It would most likely garner a score of 8 or 9 from a reader.

Looking at the guide and considering this response, it is apparent that this student has successfully analyzed the strategies the author used to convey her attitude. In addition, in response to the prompt, this student has a good understanding of just how Helen Keller presents herself—totally optimistic. Specific strategies are discussed and analyzed. This student also speculates about Ms Keller's probable response to present-day controversies concerning the deaf in light of her dismissal of those "experts" of her time who thought it was not judicious to teach the deaf to speak. This comment makes it clear that the student has a good handle on the character of Helen Keller.

Finally, in addition to demonstrating a wide range of composition skills, this response successfully discusses the irony of Ms Keller's choice of the words "unspeakable happiness." Many less successful essays mention this particular phrase, but they fail to go anywhere with the concept. This essay, however, insightfully continues the discussion of irony with the phrase "living words" as ironic as well.

Review the prompt and the essay. Then look at the scoring guide and these two sample papers. You should be able to see the differences, as well as understand the justification for their scores.

IF YOU LEARNED ONLY FOUR THINGS IN THIS CHAPTER . . . .

1. Each exam includes three essays based on a passage (or two passages) that may require prose analysis or argumentation. (Prose analysis will eventually be phased out, but not until 2007.)

2. Argument essays may ask students to respond to one side of an idea or to consider several points of view.

3. Essays are scored by readers who use a 9-point scoring guide (or rubric).

4. To write a successful essay, read the prompt, the passage, and the prompt again. Always complete the tasks the prompt requires. Use passage references for development and support, not just as filler. Analyze and explain, don't just paraphrase and summarize. Analyze wisely, trying to see beyond the obvious. Consider all sides of an argument, even if you are developing only one side.

PRACTICE SET

Practice on your own with the following Argument prompt. As the test evolves over the coming years, we may see some other changes to the argument question that we have not yet anticipated. Looking ahead to the time when students will be asked to consider more than one or two sides of an issue, the following essay prompt asks you to consider several angles of an issue before drawing your own conclusions about the topic.

Consider the ideas presented in the following quotations. In a well-organized essay, discuss the concept of whether or not clothes reflect who we are, or whether we are influenced by what we wear. How significant is our clothing, aside from keeping us covered? Incorporate at least three of the quotations below, as well as your experiences, observations, or reading to support your argument.

"Those who make their dress a principal part of themselves, will, in general, become of no more value than their dress." (William Hazlitt, 1810)

"Nothing that belongs to me is any measure of me. Certainly clothes don't express me, and heaven forbid they should!" (Henry James, 1881)

"There's no way I set out to be a certain kind of symbol—the way I dress is the way I am, the way I live my life." (Pamela Anderson, contemporary)

"Know first, who you are; and then adorn yourself accordingly." (Epictetus, 100 AD)

"Costly thy habit as thy purse can buy, but not expressed in fancy; rich not gaudy; for the apparel oft proclaims the man." (Shakespeare, 1600)

"Our clothes are too much a part of us for most of us ever to be entirely indifferent to their condition: it is as though the fabric were indeed a natural extension of the body, or even of the soul." (Quentin Bell, 1950)

The first purpose of clothes . . . was not warmth or decency, but ornamental. . . . Among wild people, we find tattooing and painting even prior to clothes. The first spiritual want of a barbarous man is decoration; as indeed we still see among the barbarous classes in civilized countries." (Thomas Carlyle, 1795–1881)

Write Your Essay Here

Analysis

You may wonder at the number of quotations that are in this prompt. However, the students are asked only to use three in their response.

This essay has a sense of the slow evolution that is taking place with this exam. Students have a variety of resources to consider and from which to draw their own argument and conclusions. The topic, clothing, is one that is something most every student will have some thoughts about.

Consider this 9-point Scoring Guide for this question:

9   Essays meet all of the criteria for 8 papers, and in addition, are especially full or apt in their analysis or demonstrate particularly impressive composition skills.

8   Essays successfully analyze the various ideas presented by the quotations on clothing. These essays discuss the significance of clothing and its effect on our character. They refer to the quotations directly or indirectly and explain convincingly how specific quotations support their argument. Their prose controls a wide range of effective writing but is not flawless.

7   Essays fit the description of 6 essays but employ more complete analysis or demonstrate a more mature prose style.

6   Essays adequately analyze the ideas presented by the quotations on clothing. They refer to the passage directly or indirectly, and they talk about the significance of clothing and its effect on our character. Few lapses in diction or syntax may be present, but generally the prose of 6 essays is clear and adequately written.

5   Essays analyze the ideas about clothing, but the development of this analysis is limited or too simplistic. These essays may treat some of the ideas superficially or develop ideas their argument inconsistently. A few lapses in diction or syntax may appear, but the prose in these essays usually conveys the writers' ideas adequately.

4   Essays inadequately respond to the task of the prompt. They may misrepresent the ideas presented by the quotations, or generalize the concepts therein. Sometimes these essays use the quotations in lieu of original synthesis and development. The arguments of these papers are often trite and/or the prose of these essays suggests immature control over organization, diction, or syntax.

3   Essays meet the criteria for the score of 4 but are less perceptive about the ideas of the quotations and/or less successful in developing an original argument, or less consistent in controlling the elements of writing.

2   Essays are unsuccessful in analyzing concepts conveyed by the quotation. These essays tend to pay little or cursory attention the specific quotes, and their argument may be very general, trite and/or oversimplified. The prose of 2 papers often reveals consistent weaknesses in writing, such as a lack of development or organization, grammatical problems, or a lack of control.

1   Essays meet the criteria for the score of 2 but are especially simplistic in their discussion or weak in controlling elements of language.

Student Sample A

The debate over whether or not the "clothes make the man" is one with a long history. . The majority of the given statements seem to have the belief that clothes may not decide who you are, but they are used to express the individual. Even Adam and Eve made a statement both with and without their clothes on.

Shakespeare said, "The apparel oft proclaims the man." In this he is correct. Walk into just about any high school in the nation and the various cliques and groups become evident very quickly. The goth/punk kids hang around in dark colors, typically black with chains or collars and piercings. The skaters wear a certain kind of shoes and jeans with a certain degree of bagginess. You can usually find a knit cap in their back pack. The jocks typically wear t-shirts with torn sleeves and jeans that aren't quite so baggy. In colder weather they usually wear sweatshirts naming their sport or a particular event, and some still wear the traditional letter jacket. Also the new kid in school is judged or tried by his dress. If he is dressed well in designer clothes it is a safe bet that he used to be one of the popular, preppy kids in his old school.

Epictetus said, "know first, who you are; then adorn yourself accordingly." In high school or even sometimes in colleges, the casual observer can get to know a little about someone by what they wear. Generally, an observer can tell if a person has a lot of money, what school a person has attended, or a relative might have attended by the t-shirt and sweatshirt logos he or she wears. In high school, it is easy to see who has been in what sport or activity. It is easy because the person has a shirt or sweatshirt proclaiming to the world, "Yes, I was in soccer or tennis or baseball, and I'm proud of it."

Thomas Carlyle states that "the first purpose of clothes. . .was not warmth or decency, but ornamental." In the inner city especially, but also elsewhere, this is obvious. People wear shirts that cost $50 or $60 just because of the brand or designer. No offense to those who are deprived, but in the poorest areas of the city one can see many people, barely able to pay rent, walking around in clothes that cost hundreds of dollars. They adorn themselves with clothes from Tommy or Billabong, and expect people to be impressed at their greatness or wealth of this man. In this, Qentin Bell's is right when he said, "It is as though the fabric were indeed a natural extension of . . . the soul." Christianity says that while the soul is desired by God, but it is a selfish thing born into sin and wrongdoing. People's desire to have attention focused on them, while being a natural and understandable desire, is a selfish desire. People's pride and longing to be someone who is rich and important drive them to purchase outrageously priced clothes to put forward an important or rich front to the rest of the world. What they should be concentrating on is their inner self. What sort of person are they? That's what they should be worried about.

To sum up, clothes do not make the man but simply express him and his desire for attention and respect.

Comments on Student Sample A

This essay would probably earn a score of 6. The introduction and second paragraph are good. Paragraph two, in particular, offers some good examples to support what the writer is saying. Paragraph 3 is OK, but somewhat repetitious of the second paragraph. Paragraph 4, although it has some really good insights, seems to be somewhat disconnected from the other two body paragraphs. The final, very brief statement is actually the main point that the entire essay is making.

The essay is adequate, no more. It doesn't flow really well because it seems not to have a central idea. It is implied, but the reader has to work too hard to find it. The examples and support for statements are well chosen and easily identifiable. Although some of the references may seem a bit trite, this writer has developed his ideas enough that one is not bored.

This is one of those papers that could be an 8 or a 9 with a little bit of rewrite work. However, that is a luxury this exam doesn't allow time for. Some might wonder why it is not a 5, but the strength of the writing, the fullness of the examples make this a bit better than a 5. It may not be the strongest 6 ever written, but it is truly an adequate response to the prompt.

Student Sample B

Clothes are something we all wear and we are all familiar with them. Some people see clothes as a way of staying covered; others look further and say it reflects who we are. Personally, I think that others identify us by our clothes, but clothes do not accurately describe how a person is. Our personality may cause us to wear a certain style of clothing, but it does not identify who we are. Overall, I think that who we are is reflected in what we wear.

"Nothing that belongs to me is any measure of me. Certainly clothes do not express me, and heaven forbid they should!" (Henry James) This quotation shows that clothes do not express a person. An example of this is that a poor person could have about the same personality of a rich person, but the poor person's clothes are a lot frumpier, and usually made of a cheaper fabric that those of the rich. Clothes do not identify us, what we do, and how we react to things is what identifies us. What belongs to us does not measure who we are, rather it shows others how fortunate we are. Usually a rich man's things are a lot more costly than those of a poor man even if they both have the same kind of personality.

"Those who make their dress a principal part of themselves, will, in general, become of no more value than their dress." (Hazlitt) This quote explains how clothes are just material possessions. If we allow ourselves to become obsessive in the way we dress, we will be worth no more than the value of the clothes themselves. This is very true in our society. The rich and popular worry about their clothes and spend hundreds of dollars on one outfit, and they are seen as materialistic.

They do not look past these clothes because they make their clothes more salient than their own personalities. Therefore, they are seen as materialistic or superficial as the clothes they wear.

"There is no way I set out to be a certain kind of symbol—the way I dress is the way I am, the way I live my life." (Pamela Anderson) People do not want to be seen as symbols. They want t be looked at more deeply—past their clothes and into their personality. ". . . The way I dress is the way I am. . ." I do not fully agree with this part of the quote because the way anyone dresses does not, or at least should not truly represent that person. We can all look elegant at a fancy restaurant and we can all look frumpy when cleaning the house. We should not identify ourselves with some material possessions; instead we should judge and be judged by the way we carry ourselves—by our manners, actions, and personality characteristics.

"Know first, who you are; and then adorn yourself accordingly." (Epictetus) We should worry about ourselves before we worry about the way we dress. If we have strong personalities and are confident in ourselves, we do not need clothes to identify us. We should not hide behind material things. Clothes are not significant, and we should not make them significant. We should dress properly for each event in our lives, but other than that, we should not use clothes as a means of identification. People do judge others on the way they dress, but they shouldn't. We must get to know people before judging them. Finally, we all need to understand what kind of person <u>we</u> are, and then worry about what to wear. We must not let clothes identify us; we must identify the clothes.

Comments on Student Sample B

This student response would garner a score of 8. This student has let the quotations guide each paragraph she develops and creates the rhythm of her essay through this development. She has successfully responded to the prompt and very aptly included relevant quotations.

Paragraph 3 is the essay's weak spot. Although it is clear what the student is trying to say, she fumbles a bit with the ideas. Otherwise, each paragraph progressively builds on her ideas; each paragraph grows out of one of the quotations. The introduction presents the controlling idea: Clothing is a reflection of who we are; it does not and should not identify who we are. Although there is no separate concluding paragraph, it is not necessary, since the last paragraph brings everything to a nice conclusion.

If you look at the description of an 8 paper from the scoring guide, this essay successfully analyzes the various ideas presented by the selected quotations. This essay discusses the significance of clothing and its effect on our character, or in the case of this essay, how the significance of our character affects our clothing. She explains convincingly how specific quotations support her argument aptly.

Student Sample C

I think what we wear depends on our moods. The exception to this is people with professions...

For example, high school students, administrators, teachers, custodians and co-workers all dress differently. Students can wear whatever they want; they are not expected to dress professionally. But administrators have to wear suits because they are expected to dress that way, and they want to dress that way to get people's respect for them. I'm sure when they are not in school they will wear more comfy clothing. Teachers are different because some teachers want respect, while others want to be friends with the student that they will dress the new age. Like mentioned before, people will wear clothes depending upon their profession.

On the other hand, custodians have a dress policy, like a uniform. They all have a blue shirt. That way we can tell who they are. That doesn't influence who they are, it's just part of their job.

For me, my mood definitely affects what I wear. During some days of the month, my body just doesn't want to dress up. I just wear sweatpants or something comfortable. Other days I feel more preppy, and I find myself reaching for my Dockers in the morning. One time I missed my old home, India, and I wore my Sari to school that day.

Overall, different types of people have different ways of dressing. People with professions are expected to have standards, so they will wear what will make them look the best. Others, without real professions, will wear whatever they want and that makes them look good—not. Certainly clothes do reflect who we are, and who we are influence what we wear.

Comments on Student Sample C

This student has made a major error. She has failed to respond to the tasks of the essay prompt. Yes, she does create a rather shallow argument about clothing being a result of one's mood, with the exception of those who must wear a certain type of clothing because of their profession. There is nothing wrong with her ideas, but she doesn't go very far with her discussion.

However, this essay fails to include any mention of the quotations. Of course reference to them is implied. Nevertheless, implication is not enough. Because of this, this essay is a lower half response—somewhere between a 3 and a 4. The lack of quotations keeps it in the 3 range. Her decent development of ideas within the paragraphs would probably push it into the 4 range. Obviously, this student has a good grasp of composition skills. However, the essay falls short of expectations because it fails to include any reference to the quotations.

PART FOUR

Practice Tests

COMPUTING YOUR SCORES

Remember not to take any score on the practice test too literally. There is no way to determine precisely what your AP grade will be because:

- The conditions under which you take the practice test will not exactly mirror real test conditions.
- While the multiple-choice questions are scored by computer, the free-response questions are graded manually by faculty consultants. You will not be able to accurately grade your own essays.

Section I: Multiple-Choice

Number Correct ☐ − (¼ × Number Wrong*) ☐ = ☐ × 1.296 = ☐ = Multiple-Choice Raw Score

*Do not include questions left blank.

Section II: Free-Response

Question 1: (out of 9 points possible) ☐ × 2.933 = ☐

Question 2: (out of 9 points possible) ☐ × 2.933 = ☐

Question 3: (out of 9 points possible) ☐ × 2.933 = ☐

Total Questions 1, 2, and 3 = ☐ = Free-Response Raw Score

Composite Score

Section I Multiple-Choice Score ☐ + Section II Free-Response Score ☐ = ☐ = Composite Score

CONVERSION CHART

Composite Score Range	AP Grade
114–144	5
88–113	4
67–87	3
40–66	2
0–39	1

Practice Test 1 Answer Grid

Before taking this practice test, find a quiet place where you can work uninterrupted for about three hours. Make sure you have a comfortable desk, several No. 2 pencils, and a few ballpoint pens.

The practice test includes a multiple-choice section and a free-response question. Use the answer grid to record your multiple-choice answers. Write the essays on the pages provided; use additional sheets if needed.

Once you start the test, don't stop until you've finished, except for a 10-minute break between the multiple-choice and essay sections. The answer key and explanations follow the test.

Good luck!

1. Ⓐ Ⓑ Ⓒ Ⓓ Ⓔ	19. Ⓐ Ⓑ Ⓒ Ⓓ Ⓔ	37. Ⓐ Ⓑ Ⓒ Ⓓ Ⓔ
2. Ⓐ Ⓑ Ⓒ Ⓓ Ⓔ	20. Ⓐ Ⓑ Ⓒ Ⓓ Ⓔ	38. Ⓐ Ⓑ Ⓒ Ⓓ Ⓔ
3. Ⓐ Ⓑ Ⓒ Ⓓ Ⓔ	21. Ⓐ Ⓑ Ⓒ Ⓓ Ⓔ	39. Ⓐ Ⓑ Ⓒ Ⓓ Ⓔ
4. Ⓐ Ⓑ Ⓒ Ⓓ Ⓔ	22. Ⓐ Ⓑ Ⓒ Ⓓ Ⓔ	40. Ⓐ Ⓑ Ⓒ Ⓓ Ⓔ
5. Ⓐ Ⓑ Ⓒ Ⓓ Ⓔ	23. Ⓐ Ⓑ Ⓒ Ⓓ Ⓔ	41. Ⓐ Ⓑ Ⓒ Ⓓ Ⓔ
6. Ⓐ Ⓑ Ⓒ Ⓓ Ⓔ	24. Ⓐ Ⓑ Ⓒ Ⓓ Ⓔ	42. Ⓐ Ⓑ Ⓒ Ⓓ Ⓔ
7. Ⓐ Ⓑ Ⓒ Ⓓ Ⓔ	25. Ⓐ Ⓑ Ⓒ Ⓓ Ⓔ	43. Ⓐ Ⓑ Ⓒ Ⓓ Ⓔ
8. Ⓐ Ⓑ Ⓒ Ⓓ Ⓔ	26. Ⓐ Ⓑ Ⓒ Ⓓ Ⓔ	44. Ⓐ Ⓑ Ⓒ Ⓓ Ⓔ
9. Ⓐ Ⓑ Ⓒ Ⓓ Ⓔ	27. Ⓐ Ⓑ Ⓒ Ⓓ Ⓔ	45. Ⓐ Ⓑ Ⓒ Ⓓ Ⓔ
10. Ⓐ Ⓑ Ⓒ Ⓓ Ⓔ	28. Ⓐ Ⓑ Ⓒ Ⓓ Ⓔ	46. Ⓐ Ⓑ Ⓒ Ⓓ Ⓔ
11. Ⓐ Ⓑ Ⓒ Ⓓ Ⓔ	29. Ⓐ Ⓑ Ⓒ Ⓓ Ⓔ	47. Ⓐ Ⓑ Ⓒ Ⓓ Ⓔ
12. Ⓐ Ⓑ Ⓒ Ⓓ Ⓔ	30. Ⓐ Ⓑ Ⓒ Ⓓ Ⓔ	48. Ⓐ Ⓑ Ⓒ Ⓓ Ⓔ
13. Ⓐ Ⓑ Ⓒ Ⓓ Ⓔ	31. Ⓐ Ⓑ Ⓒ Ⓓ Ⓔ	49. Ⓐ Ⓑ Ⓒ Ⓓ Ⓔ
14. Ⓐ Ⓑ Ⓒ Ⓓ Ⓔ	32. Ⓐ Ⓑ Ⓒ Ⓓ Ⓔ	50. Ⓐ Ⓑ Ⓒ Ⓓ Ⓔ
15. Ⓐ Ⓑ Ⓒ Ⓓ Ⓔ	33. Ⓐ Ⓑ Ⓒ Ⓓ Ⓔ	51. Ⓐ Ⓑ Ⓒ Ⓓ Ⓔ
16. Ⓐ Ⓑ Ⓒ Ⓓ Ⓔ	34. Ⓐ Ⓑ Ⓒ Ⓓ Ⓔ	52. Ⓐ Ⓑ Ⓒ Ⓓ Ⓔ
17. Ⓐ Ⓑ Ⓒ Ⓓ Ⓔ	35. Ⓐ Ⓑ Ⓒ Ⓓ Ⓔ	
18. Ⓐ Ⓑ Ⓒ Ⓓ Ⓔ	36. Ⓐ Ⓑ Ⓒ Ⓓ Ⓔ	

Practice Test 1

Section I: Multiple-Choice Questions

Time—1 hour
Number of questions—52
Percent of total grade—45%

<u>Directions:</u> This section contains selections from prose works with questions on their content, style, form, structure, and purpose. Read each selection. Then read each question, choosing the best of the five responses that follow. Fill in each oval with the correct answer, checking to be sure the number of the question corresponds to the number on the answer sheet.

Questions 1–13. Read the following essay carefully before responding to the questions.

On 7 June 1966, Robert Kennedy, then Senator of New York, addressed the National Union of South African Students' Day of Affirmation, in Cape Town, South Africa.

We stand here in the name of freedom.

At the heart of that Western freedom and democracy is the belief that the individual man,
Line the child of God, is the touchstone of value and all
(5) society, groups. The state exists for his benefit. Therefore the enlargement of liberty for individual human beings must be the supreme goal and the abiding practice of any Western society.

The first element of this individual liberty is the
(10) freedom of speech.

The right to express and communicate ideas, to set oneself apart from the dumb beasts of field and forest; to recall governments to their duties and obligations; above all, the right to affirm one's
(15) membership and allegiance to the body politic— to society—to the men with whom we share our land, our heritage and our children's future.

Hand in hand with freedom of speech goes the power to be heard—to share the decisions of
(20) government which shape men's lives. Everything that makes life worthwhile—family, work, education, a place to rear one's children and a place to rest one's head—all this rests on decisions of government; all can be swept away by a
(25) government which does not heed the demands of its people. Therefore, the essential humanity of men can be protected and preserved only where government must answer—not just to those of a particular religion, or a particular race; but to all
(30) its people.

And even government by the consent of the governed, as in our own Constitution, must be limited in its power to act against its people: so that there may be no interference with the right to
(35) worship, or with the security of the home; no arbitrary imposition of pains or penalties by officials high or low; no restrictions on the freedom of men to seek education or work or

opportunity of any kind so that each man may
(40) become all he is capable of becoming.

These are the sacred rights of Western society. These are the essential differences between us and Nazi Germany, as they were between Athens and Persia.
(45) They are the essence of our difference with Communism today. I am inalterably opposed to Communism because it exalts the state over the individual and the family, and because of the lack of freedom of speech, of protest, or religion and of the
(50) press, which is characteristic of totalitarian states.

The way of opposition to Communism is not to imitate its dictatorship, but to enlarge individual human freedom—in our own countries and all over the globe. There are those in every land who would
(55) label as "Communist" every threat to their privilege. But as I have seen on my travels in all sections of the world, reform is not Communism. And the denial of freedom, in whatever name, only strengthens the very Communism it claims to oppose.
(60) For two centuries, my own country has struggled to overcome the self-imposed handicap of prejudice and discrimination based on nationality, social class or race—discrimination profoundly repugnant to the theory and command
(65) of our Constitution. Even as my father grew up in Boston, signs told him that "No Irish need apply."

Two generations later President Kennedy became the first Catholic to head the nation but how many men of ability had, before 1961, been
(70) denied the opportunity to contribute to the nation's progress because they were Catholic, or of Irish extraction.

In the last five years, the winds of change have blown as fiercely in the United Sates as anywhere in
(75) the world. But they will not—they cannot—abate.

For there are millions of Negroes untrained for the simplest jobs, and thousands every day denied their full equal rights under the law; and the violence of the disinherited, the insulated the
(80) injured, looms over the streets of Harlem and Watts and South Chicago.

GO ON TO THE NEXT PAGE ⟩

But a Negro American trains as an astronaut, one of mankind's first explorers into outer space; another is the chief barrister of the United States
(85) Government, and dozens sit on the benches of court; and another, Dr. Martin Luther King, is the second man of African descent to win the Nobel Peace Prize for his nonviolent efforts for social justice between the races.

(90) We must recognize the full human equality of all our people before God, before the law, and in the councils of government. We must do this not because it is economically advantageous, although it is; not because the laws of God and man
(95) command it, although they do command it; not because people in other lands wish it so. We must do it for the single and fundamental reason that it is the right thing to do.

And this must be our commitment outside our
(100) borders as well as within.

It is your job, the task of the young people of this world to strip the last remnants of that ancient, cruel belief from the civilization of man.

Each nation has different obstacles and different
(105) goals, shadowed by the vagaries of history and experience. Yet as I talk to you and people around the world I am impressed not by diversity but by the closeness of their goals, their desires and concerns and hopes for the future. There is
(110) discrimination in New York, apartheid in South Africa and serfdom in the mountains of Peru. People stagnate in the streets of India; intellectuals go to jail in Russia; thousands are slaughtered in Indonesia; wealth is lavished on armaments
(115) everywhere. These are differing evils. But they are common works of man.

And therefore they call upon common qualities of conscience and of indignation, a shared determination to wipe away the unnecessary
(120) sufferings of our fellow human beings at home and particularly around the world.

In the world we would like to build, South Africa could play an outstanding role, and a role of leadership in that effort. This country is without
(125) question a preeminent repository of the wealth and the knowledge and the skill of the continent. Here are the greater part of Africa's research scientists and steel production, most of it

reservoirs of coal and of electric power. Many
(130) South Africans have made major contributions to African technical development and world science; the names of some are known wherever men seek to eliminate the ravages of tropical disease and of pestilence. In your faculties and councils, here in
(135) this very audience, are hundreds and thousands of men and women who could transform the lives of millions for all time to come.

So we part, I to my country and you to remain. We are—if a man of forty can claim the privilege—
(140) fellow members of the world's largest younger generation. Each of us has our own work to do. I know at times you must feel very alone with your problems and with your difficulties. But I want to say how impressed I am with what you stand for
(145) and for the effort you are making; and I say this not just for myself, but men and women all over the world. And I hope you will often take heart from the knowledge that you are joined with your fellow young people in every land, they struggling with
(150) their problems and you with yours, but all joined in a common purpose; that, like the young people of my own country and of every country that I have visited, you are all in many ways more closely united to the brothers of your time than to the
(155) older generation in any of these nations; you are determined to build a better future.

1. Which of the following best states the main idea of this address?

(A) It is the job of everyone to recognize the laws of God and of our land.

(B) Undemocratic governments can destroy one's family, one's work, one's education, and the place to rear one's children.

(C) Even government by the consent of the governed must be limited in its power against its people.

(D) The freedom of speech is the most important freedom if one is to have true individual liberty.

(E) The enlargement of liberty for all must be the supreme goal and abiding practice of any Western society.

GO ON TO THE NEXT PAGE

2. All of the following characteristics are present in paragraph 4, lines 11–17, EXCEPT

    (A) compound-complex sentence structure

    (B) asyndeton

    (C) parenthetical appositive

    (D) anaphora

    (E) items in a series

3. The main focus of paragraph 5, lines 18–30, is the

    (A) freedom of speech

    (B) power to be heard

    (C) liberty to raise one's children

    (D) decisions of the government

    (E) essential humanity of man

4. Kennedy most strongly emphasizes that a government by the consent of the governed must be limited in its power to act against its people so that man

    (A) can worship wherever he wishes

    (B) can attain an education of his choice

    (C) can become all that he is capable of

    (D) feels secure within his home

    (E) is able to pursue the work of his choice

5. Kennedy refers to the admonition "No Irish need apply" in order to

    (A) show a personal cultural bias

    (B) imply that the business is owned by the British

    (C) emphasize the weakness of the American Constitution

    (D) exemplify historical discrimination in the U.S.

    (E) win over his audience by reminding them of his heritage

6. The sentence, "But they will not—they cannot—abate" line 75 demonstrates all of the following EXCEPT

    (A) parenthetical emphasis

    (B) pronoun reference to "winds of change"

    (C) a type of anaphora

    (D) imperative tone

    (E) a sentence fragment

7. Kennedy maintains that Communism is

    (A) exalting the state over the individual

    (B) about to be extinguished from the globe

    (C) a threat to personal privilege

    (D) any sort of major reform

    (E) all denials of freedom

8. Paragraph 6 strings together a series of alternatives, several connected by the conjunction "or." This is a syntactical structure known as

    (A) polyparallelism

    (B) polysyndeton

    (C) hyperbole

    (D) onomatopoeia

    (E) zeugma

9. The end of this passage is most directly addressed to

    (A) people of the world

    (B) citizens of South Africa

    (C) the youth of the world

    (D) people in the many countries Kennedy had visited

    (E) the blacks of South Africa as well as those in America

GO ON TO THE NEXT PAGE

10. Within the context of this address, "moral courage" can best be described as

    (A) a rare commodity
    (B) bravery in battle
    (C) great intelligence
    (D) changing one's beliefs for the general good
    (E) maintaining one's ideals and goals in life

11. As Kennedy closes the speech he makes a special effort to

    (A) drive home the poignancy of his argument
    (B) appeal to the older generation who has suffered so much
    (C) ingratiate himself with the people of South Africa
    (D) identify himself as one of the world's largest younger generation
    (E) embrace the Chinese as well by quoting a Chinese proverb

12. At the time this speech was given in 1966, we can infer that South Africa was not known as a great repository of

    (A) wealth and knowledge
    (B) steel production
    (C) scientific research
    (D) power sources
    (E) unique racial tolerance

13. Robert Kennedy would most likely agree that the hope for the world's future relies upon its

    (A) wisdom
    (B) toleration
    (C) determination
    (D) youth
    (E) moral conscience

GO ON TO THE NEXT PAGE ▷

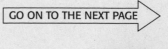

Questions 14–26. read the following essay carefully before responding to the questions.

On a winter day some years ago, coming out of Pittsburgh on one of the expresses of the Pennsylvania Railroad, I rolled eastward for an
Line hour through the coal and steel towns of
(5) Westmoreland county. It was familiar ground; boy and man, I had been through it often before. But somehow I had never quite sensed its appalling desolation. Here was the very heart of industrial America, the center of its most lucrative and
(10) characteristic activity, the boast and pride of the richest and grandest nation ever seen on earth—and here was a scene so dreadfully hideous, so intolerably bleak and forlorn that it reduced the whole aspiration of man to a macabre and
(15) depressing joke. Here was wealth beyond computation, almost beyond imagination—and here were human habitations so abominable that they would have disgraced a race of alley cats.

I am not speaking of mere filth. One expects
(20) steel towns to be dirty. What I allude to is the unbroken and agonizing ugliness, the sheer revolting monstrousness, of every house in sight. From East Liberty to Greensburg, a distance of twenty-five miles, there was not one in sight from
(25) the train that did not insult and lacerate the eye. Some were so bad, and they were among the most pretentious—churches, stores, warehouses, and the like—that they were downright startling; one blinked before them as one blinks before a man
(30) with his face shot away. A few linger in memory, horrible even there: a crazy little church just west of Jeannette, set like a dormer-window on the side of a bare, leprous hill; the headquarters of the Veterans of Foreign Wars at another forlorn town,
(35) a steel stadium like a huge rat-trap somewhere further down the line. But most of all I recall the general effect—of hideousness without a break. There was not a single decent house within eye range from the Pittsburgh suburbs to the
(40) Greensburg yards. There was not one that was not misshapen, and there was not one that was not shabby.

The country itself is not uncomely, despite the grime of the endless mills. It is, in form, a narrow
(45) river valley, with deep gullies running up into the hills. It is thickly settled, but not noticeably overcrowded. There is still plenty of room for building, even in the larger towns, and there are very few solid blocks. Nearly every house, big and
(50) little, has space on all four sides. Obviously, if there were architects of any professional sense or dignity in the region, they would have perfected a chalet to hug the hillsides—a chalet with a high-pitched roof to throw off the heavy winter snows, but still
(55) essentially a low and clinging building, wider than it was tall. But what have they done? They have taken as their model a brick set on end. This they have converted into a thing of dingy clapboards, with a narrow, low-pitched roof. And the whole
(60) they have set upon thin, preposterous brick piers. By the hundreds and thousands these abominable houses cover the bare hillsides, like gravestones in some gigantic and decaying cemetery on their deep sides they are three, four and even five stories high;
(65) on their low sides they bury themselves swinishly in the mud. Not a fifth of them are perpendicular. They lean this way and that, hanging on to their bases precariously. And one and all they are streaked in grime, with dead and eczematous
(70) patches of paint peeping through the streaks.

Now and then there is a house of brick. But what brick! When it is new it is the color of a fried egg. When it has taken on the patina of the mills it is the color of an egg long past all hope or caring.
(75) Was it necessary to adopt that shocking color? No more than it was necessary to set all of the houses on end. Red brick, even in a steel town, ages with some dignity. Let it become downright black, and it is still sightly, especially if its trimmings are of
(80) white stone, with soot in the depths and the high spots washed by the rain. But in Westmoreland they prefer that uremic yellow, and so they have the most loathsome towns and villages ever seen by mortal eye.

GO ON TO THE NEXT PAGE ⟹

(85)   I award this championship only after laborious research and incessant prayer. I have seen, I believe, all of the most unlovely towns of the world; they are all to be found in the United States. I have seen the mill towns of decomposing New

(90) England and the desert towns of Utah, Arizona and Texas. I am familiar with the back streets of Newark, Brooklyn and Chicago, and have made scientific explorations to Camden, N.J. and Newport News, Va. Safe in a Pullman, I have

(95) whirled through the gloomy, God-forsaken villages of Iowa and Kansas, and the malarious tide-water hamlets of Georgia. I have been to Bridgeport, Conn., and to Los Angeles. But nowhere on this earth, at home or abroad, have I seen anything to

(100) compare to the villages that huddle along the line of the Pennsylvania from the Pittsburgh yards to Greensburg. They are incomparable in color, and they are incomparable in design. It is as if some titanic and aberrant genius, uncompromisingly

(105) inimical to man, had devoted all the ingenuity of Hell to the making of them. They show grotesqueries of ugliness that, in retrospect, become almost diabolical. One cannot imagine mere human beings concocting such dreadful

(110) things, and one can scarcely imagine human beings bearing life in them.

    Are they so frightful because the valley is full of foreigners—dull, insensate brutes, with no love of beauty in them? Then why didn't these foreigners

(115) set up similar abominations in the countries that they came from? You will, in fact, find nothing of the sort in Europe save perhaps in the more putrid parts of England. There is scarcely an ugly village on the whole Continent. The peasants, however

(120) poor, somehow manage to make themselves graceful and charming habitations, even in Spain. But in the American village and small town the pull is always toward ugliness, and in that Westmoreland valley it has been yielded to with an

(125) eagerness bordering upon passion. It is incredible that mere ignorance should have achieved such masterpieces of horror.

    On certain levels of the American race, indeed, there seems to be a positive libido for the ugly, as

(130) on other and less Christian levels there is a libido for the beautiful. It is impossible to put down the wallpaper that defaces the average American home of the lower middle class to mere inadvertence, or to the obscene humor of the manufacturers. Such

(135) ghastly designs, it must be obvious, give a genuine delight to a certain type of mind. They meet, in some unfathomable way, its obscure and unintelligible demands. They caress it as "The Palms" caresses it, or the art of the movie, or Jazz.

(140) The taste for them is as enigmatical and yet as common as the taste for dogmatic theology and the poetry of Edgar A. Guest.

    Thus I suspect (though confessedly without knowing) that the vast majority of the honest folk

(145) of Westmoreland county, and especially the 100% Americans among them, actually admire the houses they live in, and are proud of them. For the same money they could get vastly better ones, but they prefer what they have got. Certainly there was

(150) no pressure upon the Veterans of Foreign Wars to choose the dreadful edifice that bears their banner, for there are plenty of vacant buildings along the track-side, and some of them are appreciably better. They might, indeed, have built a better one

(155) of their own. But they chose that clapboarded horror with their eyes open, and having chosen it, they let it mellow into its present shocking depravity. They like it as it is: beside it, the Parthenon would no doubt offend them. In

(160) precisely the same way the authors of the rattrap stadium that I have mentioned made a deliberate choice. After painfully designing and erecting it, they made it perfect in their own sight by putting a completely impossible pent-house, painted a

(165) staring yellow, on top of it. The effect is that of a fat woman with a black eye. It is that of a Presbyterian grinning. But they like it.

    Here is something that the psychologists have so far neglected: the love of ugliness for its own sake,

(170) the lust to make the world intolerable. Its habitat is the United States. Out of the melting pot emerges a race which hates beauty as it hates truth. The etiology of this madness deserves a great deal more study than it has got. There must be causes behind

GO ON TO THE NEXT PAGE

(175) it; it arises and flourishes in obedience to biological laws, and not as a mere act of God. What, precisely, are the terms of those laws? And why do they run stronger in America than elsewhere? Let some honest *Privat Dozent* in *(180)* pathological sociology apply himself to the problem.

14. The primary focus of this passage is

 (A) a portrayal of ugliness found in parts of Pennsylvania

 (B) a discussion of idiosyncrasies common to immigrants

 (C) a commentary on America's lust to make the world intolerant

 (D) to explore how some people can hate both truth and beauty

 (E) to discuss architectural preferences in a particular area of Pennsylvania

15. In describing the unusual characteristics of the houses he sees, the writer does not utilize the analogy of

 (A) a brick set upright on its small end

 (B) diabolic ingenuity of an aberrant genius

 (C) a steel trap like one for used for a rat

 (D) swine buried in the mud

 (E) an egg long past all hope or caring

16. Which of the following best describes the rhetorical development of the passage as a whole?

 (A) Expansion from definition to description

 (B) Development from description to argumentation

 (C) Transition from personal narrative to description

 (D) Movement from description to psychological reflection

 (E) Progress from description to definition

17. Paragraph 3 shows irony when the narrator wonders

 (A) how beauty can live among such squalor

 (B) how such a decent countryside can spawn such ugliness

 (C) how foreigners coming from beautiful homelands can settle for ugliness

 (D) why the houses are taller than they are wide

 (E) why houses seem to lean precariously on the hillside

18. As emphasized in paragraph two, the narrator disdains the ugliness he sees by utilizing all of the following stylistic devices EXCEPT

 (A) harsh sounding words in succession

 (B) strong image-evoking adjectives

 (C) whimsical speculation as to possible reasons for the ugliness

 (D) harsh verbs that enhance the power of the ugliness

 (E) specific identification of the geographical location

19. It can be inferred from the sentence "I award this championship . . .prayer" (lines 85–86) that the narrator

 (A) has seen his share of ugly places

 (B) is in charge of an ugly location contest

 (C) possesses an unwarranted sense of superiority

 (D) is an architectural critic

 (E) is basically a snob

GO ON TO THE NEXT PAGE

20. In the fourth paragraph, the descriptive term "uremic yellow", line 82, emphasizes

    (A) a reference to a biological hue
    (B) the writer's dislike for the color of the brick houses
    (C) a critical analysis of the array of colors available to architects
    (D) a metaphor relating to physiological functions
    (E) a color alternative for traditional red brick

21. The writer has utilized what stylistic device within the sentence "The peasants . . . in Spain" (lines 119–121)?

    (A) Hyperbole
    (B) Metaphor
    (C) Alliteration
    (D) Rhetorical question
    (E) Direct address

22. The author refers to the Parthenon in line 159 in order to

    (A) demonstrate his advanced education
    (B) provide an anachronism
    (C) make an historic allusion
    (D) contest contemporary preferences for ugliness with traditional desire for beauty
    (E) show that the clapboard horrors are the preference of the inhabitants who own them

23. The narrator facetiously criticizes psychologists for not studying all of the following EXCEPT

    (A) a race that hates beauty
    (B) a race that hates truth
    (C) etiology of the madness for ugliness
    (D) the lust to make the world intolerably ugly
    (E) why America runs strongly toward pathological sociology

24. It can be inferred that "*Privat Dozent*" (line 179) is a reference to

    (A) a dozen experts
    (B) a field of higher education
    (C) the reason for preferring ugliness
    (D) a sociological condition
    (E) an expert of some sort, usually academic

25. The author of this passage would most likely agree that

    (A) some houses are unavoidably ugly
    (B) architecture isn't what it used to be
    (C) there's no accounting for taste
    (D) Europe also has its ugly areas
    (E) there's no explanation for pride of ownership

26. When the author says "Here was wealth beyond computation, almost beyond imagination—and here were human habitations so abominable that they would have disgraced a race of alley cats" (lines 15–18), he establishes his tone as one of

    (A) harsh disparagement
    (B) strong satire
    (C) critical technology
    (D) sociological exploration
    (E) unbelievable integrity

GO ON TO THE NEXT PAGE

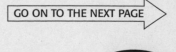

Questions 27–39. Read the following essay carefully before responding to the questions.

The struggle between Liberty and Authority is the most conspicuous feature in the portions of history with which we are familiar. By liberty, was
Line meant protection against the tyranny of the
(5) political rulers. The rulers were conceived (except in some of the popular governments of Greece) as in a necessarily antagonistic position to the people whom they ruled. They consisted of a governing One, or a governing tribe or caste, who derived
(10) their authority from inheritance or conquest, who, at all events, did not hold it at the pleasure of the governed, and whose supremacy men did not venture, perhaps did not desire, to contest, whatever precautions might be taken against its
(15) oppressive exercise. Their power was regarded as necessary, but also as highly dangerous; as a weapon which they would attempt to use against their subjects, no less than against external enemies. To prevent the weaker members of the
(20) community from being preyed on by innumerable vultures, it was needful that there should be an animal of prey stronger than the rest, commissioned to keep them down. But as the king of the vultures would be no less bent upon preying upon
(25) the flock than of the minor harpies, it was indispensable to be in a perpetual attitude of defence against his beak and claws. The aim, therefore, of patriots was to set limits to the power which the ruler should be suffered to exercise over
(30) the community; and this limitation was what they meant by liberty. It was attempted in two ways. First, by obtaining a recognition of certain immunities, called political liberties or rights, which it was to be regarded as a breach of duty in
(35) the ruler to infringe, and which, if he did infringe, specific resistance, or general rebellion, was held to be justifiable. A second, and generally a later expedient, was the establishment of constitutional checks, by which the consent of the community, or
(40) a body of some sort, supposed to represent its interests, was made a necessary condition to some of the more important acts of the governing power.

A time came, in the progress of human affairs, when men ceased to think it necessity of nature
(45) that their governors should be an independent power, opposed in interest to themselves. The notion, that the people have no need to limit their power over themselves, might seem axiomatic, when popular government was a thing only
(50) dreamed about, or read of as having existed at some distant period of the past. In time, however, a democratic republic came to occupy a large portion of the earth's surface, and made itself felt as one of the most powerful members of the
(55) community of nations; and elective and responsible government became subject to the observations and criticisms which wait upon a great existing fact. It was now perceived that such phrases as "self-government," and "the power of
(60) the people over themselves," do not express the true state of the case. The "people" who exercise the power are not always the same people with those over whom it is exercised; and the "self-government" spoken of is not the government of
(65) each by himself, but of each by all the rest. The will of the people, moreover, practically means the will of the most numerous or the most active *part* of the people; the majority, or those who succeed in making themselves accepted as the majority; the
(70) people, consequently, *may* desire to oppress a part of their number; and precautions are as much needed against this as against any other abuse of power. The limitation, therefore, of the power of government over individuals loses none of its
(75) importance when the holders of power are regularly accountable to the community, that is, to the strongest party therein. This view of things, recommending itself equally to the intelligence of thinkers and to the inclination of those important
(80) classes in European society to whose real or supposed interests democracy is adverse, has had no difficulty in establishing itself; and in political speculations "the tyranny of the majority" is now generally included among the evils against which
(85) society requires to be on its guard.

GO ON TO THE NEXT PAGE ⇒

Like other tyrannies, the tyranny of the majority was at first, and is still vulgarly, held in dread, chiefly as operating through the acts of the public authorities. But reflecting persons perceived that (90) when society is itself the tyrant—society collectively, over the separate individuals who compose it—its means of tyrannizing are not restricted to the acts which it may do by the hands of its political functionaries. Society can and does (95) execute its own mandates: and if it issues wrong mandates instead of right, or any mandates at all in things with which it ought not to meddle, it practices a social tyranny more formidable than many kinds of political oppression, since, though (100) not usually upheld by such extreme penalties, it leaves fewer means of escape, penetrating much more deeply into the details of life, and enslaving itself. Protection, therefore, against the tyranny of the magistrate is not enough: there needs to be (105) protection also against the tyranny of the prevailing opinion and feelings; against the tendency of society to impose, by other means than civil penalties, its own ideas and practices as rules of conduct on those whose dissent from (110) them; to fetter development, and, if possible, prevent the formation, of any individuality not in harmony with its ways, and compel all characters to fashion themselves upon the model of its own.

27. In the parenthetical phrase, lines 5–6, the word "popular" can best be defined as

(A) most congenial
(B) very famous
(C) publicly elected
(D) most notable
(E) unusually well known

28. The stylistic mode of discourse the writer has used in this essay can best be described as

(A) exposition
(B) narration
(C) argumentation
(D) compare/contrast
(E) cause and effect

29. In the first paragraph, outside foes to the community are referred to in all of the following ways EXCEPT

(A) innumerable vultures
(B) marauding hordes
(C) beak and claws
(D) animals of prey
(E) external enemies

30. The author of this passage defines "liberty" (line 31) as

(A) freedom to govern oneself
(B) supremacy of the populace
(C) freedom of the flock
(D) protection against tyranny of the governing One
(E) safety from enemy vultures

31. The term "axiomatic" (line 48) can best be defined as

(A) non-committal
(B) extra-sensory
(C) vaguely confusing
(D) reliably consistent
(E) self-evident

32. The irony expressed by the writer regarding governing by the people is best expressed by which of the following?

(A) The people are the ones who ought to be responsible for governing themselves.
(B) The people who are really in charge of governing are not always the same people who are being governed.
(C) Government by the people is really government by the powers who are in control.
(D) Power by the few cannot over-rule power by the many.
(E) Power by the majority is not really power at all.

GO ON TO THE NEXT PAGE

33. A significant conflict within this passage can be identified as

    (A) freedom vs. tyranny
    (B) the immune vs. the tainted
    (C) governing vs. the governed
    (D) resistance vs. compliance
    (E) elected vs. inherited

34. In the first paragraph, the author's use of the term "minor harpies" is a stylistic reference known as

    (A) a metaphor
    (B) personification
    (C) allusion
    (D) anachronism
    (E) hyperbole

35. Italics in paragraph 2 are used in order to

    (A) make sure the reader pays attention to what is being said
    (B) give some stylistic flair to this rather long paragraph
    (C) show the author is not sure of the veracity of what he is saying
    (D) provide a syntactical detail not found in the other paragraphs
    (E) show emphasis to the critical nuances of these words in relation to what is being said

36. In lines 94–103, the sentence beginning, "Society can . . . ," the pronoun "it" refers to the noun

    (A) mandates
    (B) social tyranny
    (C) extreme penalties
    (D) society
    (E) political oppression

37. The second paragraph focuses upon one of the main concerns of this passage. This can be identified as control by

    (A) tyranny
    (B) the governing One
    (C) selection of the majority
    (D) those accepted as the majority
    (E) those who abuse the power

38. In this passage, the narrator seems most concerned about the fact that

    (A) society executes its own mandates
    (B) society imposes civil penalties for rules that are disregarded
    (C) social tyranny is to be avoided at all costs
    (D) tyranny of the majority no longer exists
    (E) majority rule can result in abuses of power

39. The somewhat antithetical conclusion to this passage can be interpreted as

    (A) the governors often need to be governed
    (B) societies that rule themselves are always better
    (C) individual tyranny of the majority guarantees harmony
    (D) practices of social tyranny can often be more formidable than political oppression
    (E) some people were better off when they were oppressed than after they are liberated

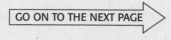

KAPLAN
Test Prep and Admissions

Questions 40–52. Read the following essay carefully before responding to the questions.

Moths that fly by day are not properly to be called moths; they do not excite that pleasant sense of dark autumn nights and ivy-blossom which the
Line commonest yellow-underwing asleep in the
(5) shadow of the curtain never fails to rouse in us. They are hybrid creatures, neither gay like butterflies nor sombre like their own species. Nevertheless the present specimen, with his narrow hay-coloured wings, fringed with a tassel
(10) of the same colour, seemed to be content with life. It was a pleasant morning, mid-September, mild, benignant, yet with a keener breath than that of the summer months. The plough was already scoring the field opposite the window, and where
(15) the share had been, the earth was pressed flat and gleamed with moisture. Such vigour came rolling in from the fields and the down beyond that it was difficult to keep the eyes strictly turned upon the book. The rooks too were keeping one of their
(20) annual festivities; soaring round the tree tops until it looked as if a vast net with thousands of black knots in it had been cast up into the air; which, after a few moments sank slowly down upon the trees until every twig seemed to have a knot at the
(25) end of it. Then, suddenly, the net would be thrown into the air again in a wider circle this time, with the utmost clamour and vociferation, as though to be thrown into the air and settle slowly down upon the tree tops were a tremendously exciting
(30) experience.

The same energy which inspired the rooks, the ploughmen, the horses, and even, it seemed, the lean bare-backed downs, sent the moth fluttering from side to side of his square of the window-pane.
(35) One could not help watching him. One was, indeed, conscious of a queer feeling of pity for him. The possibilities of pleasure seemed that morning so enormous and so various that to have only a moth's part in life, and a day moth's at that,
(40) appeared a hard fate, and his zest in enjoying his meagre opportunities to the full, pathetic. He flew vigorously to one corner of his compartment, and, after waiting there a second, flew across to the other. What remained for him but to fly to a third
(45) corner and then to a fourth? That was all he could do, in spite of the size of the downs, the width of the sky, the far-off smoke of houses, and the romantic voice, now and then, of a steamer out at sea. What he could do he did. Watching him, it
(50) seemed as if a fibre, very thin but pure, of the enormous energy of the world had been thrust into his frail and diminutive body. As often as he crossed the pane, I could fancy that a thread of vital light became visible. He was little or nothing but
(55) life.

Yet, because he was so small, and so simple a form of the energy that was rolling in at the open window and driving its way through so many narrow and intricate corridors in my own brain
(60) and in those of other human beings, there was something marvellous as well as pathetic about him. It was as if someone had taken a tiny bead of pure life and decking it as lightly as possible with down and feathers, had set it dancing and
(65) zigzagging to show us the true nature of life. Thus displayed one could not get over the strangeness of it. One is apt to forget all about life, seeing it humped and bossed and garnished and cumbered so that it has to move with the greatest circum-
(70) spection and dignity. Again, the thought of all that life might have been had he been born in any other shape caused one to view his simple activities with a kind of pity.

After a time, tired by his dancing apparently, he
(75) settled on the window ledge in the sun, and, the queer spectacle being at an end, I forgot about him. Then, looking up, my eye was caught by him. He was trying to resume his dancing, but seemed either so stiff or so awkward that he could only
(80) flutter to the bottom of the window-pane; and when he tried to fly across it he failed. Being intent on other matters I watched these futile attempts for a time without thinking, unconsciously waiting for him to resume his flight, as one waits for a
(85) machine, that has stopped momentarily, to start again without considering the reason of its failure.

GO ON TO THE NEXT PAGE

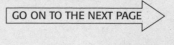

After perhaps a seventh attempt he slipped from the wooden ledge and fell, fluttering his wings, on to his back on the window sill. The helplessness of (90) his attitude roused me. It flashed upon me that he was in difficulties; he could no longer raise himself; his legs struggled vainly. But, as I stretched out a pencil, meaning to help him to right himself, it came over me that the failure and awkwardness (95) were the approach of death. I laid the pencil down again.

The legs agitated themselves once more. I looked as if for the enemy against which he struggled. I looked out of doors. What had happened there? (100) Presumably it was midday, and work in the fields had stopped. Stillness and quiet had replaced the previous animation. The birds had taken themselves off to feed in the brooks. The horses stood still. Yet the power was there all the same, (105) massed outside indifferent, impersonal, not attending to anything in particular. Somehow it was opposed to the little hay-coloured moth. It was useless to try to do anything. One could only watch the extraordinary efforts made by those tiny (110) legs against an oncoming doom which could, had it chosen, have submerged an entire city, not merely a city, but masses of human beings; nothing, I knew, had any chance against death. Nevertheless after a pause of exhaustion the legs (115) fluttered again. It was superb this last protest, and so frantic that he succeeded at last in righting himself. One's sympathies, of course, were all on the side of life. Also, when there was nobody to care or to know, this gigantic effort on the part of (120) an insignificant little moth, against a power of such magnitude, to retain what no one else valued or desired to keep, moved one strangely. Again, somehow, one saw life, a pure bead. I lifted the pencil again, useless though I knew it to be. But (125) even as I did so, the unmistakable tokens of death showed themselves. The body relaxed, and instantly grew stiff. The struggle was over. The insignificant little creature now knew death. As I looked at the dead moth, this minute wayside (130) triumph of so great a force over so mean an antagonist filled me with wonder. Just as life had been strange a few minutes before, so death was

now as strange. The moth having righted himself now lay most decently and uncomplainingly (135) composed. O yes, he seemed to say, death is stronger than I am.

40. This passage opens with a contradiction that states

(A) moths are not as beautiful as butterflies
(B) moths only fly around at night
(C) butterflies cannot be seen at night
(D) moths that fly in the daytime are not proper moths
(E) moths can be more beautiful than butterflies

41. The narrator calls daytime moths *hybrid* (line 6) because they

(A) are present in the daylight
(B) are not as beautiful as butterflies, but not as drab as moths
(C) are active not only at night but in the daytime too
(D) are in competition with butterflies
(E) don't know whether they should be coming or going

42. This passage can best be described as

(A) rhetorical argument
(B) personal reflection
(C) definition
(D) pure description
(E) technical writing

43. Identification of the season of the year is accomplished by all of the following EXCEPT

(A) keener breath
(B) rook activity
(C) scored fields
(D) ripe pumpkins
(E) moth's activity

GO ON TO THE NEXT PAGE

44. In lines 49–65, "Watching him . . .show us the true nature of life," the narrator identifies the moth as

    (A) a pathetic creature
    (B) a diminuitive body
    (C) the embodiment of life itself
    (D) energy gone amok
    (E) a dancing, zigagging insect

45. The description of the rooks as a vast, stylistic net rising and falling, employs the stylistic device of

    (A) anaphora
    (B) alliteration
    (C) analogy
    (D) aphorism
    (E) apostrophe

46. Lines 36–44 utilize sounds that make these lines both

    (A) hyperbolic and stressful
    (B) parallel and consonant
    (C) tedious and boring
    (D) consonant and onomatopoeic
    (E) assonant and alliterative

47. In lines 62–65, the narrator acknowledges the moth as

    (A) an apathetic creature
    (B) demonstrating the true nature of life
    (C) made of feathers and down
    (D) a dignified creature
    (E) something strange and awesome

48. "It flashed . . .vainly," lines 90–92, is a sentence of several clauses connected with no conjunctions, demonstrating the syntactical structure known as

    (A) a run on sentence
    (B) a periodical sentence
    (C) asyndeton
    (D) anaphora
    (E) parallelism

49. In paragraph four, the narrator most likely lays down her pencil because

    (A) she is tired of studying
    (B) her hand is cramped from writing
    (C) she used it to flick the moth away
    (D) she recognizes that the moth cannot be revived
    (E) the moth has died and she is sad.

50. The tone of the last paragraph of this passage can best be identified as

    (A) overwhelming and sad
    (B) resignedly fatalistic
    (C) spitefully satisfied
    (D) humanly superior
    (E) regretful and awed

51. The narrator of this passage would most likely agree with all EXCEPT which of the following comments?

    (A) Despite a creature's most valiant efforts, death is inevitable.
    (B) In nature the moth is but an insignificant creature.
    (C) The moth is to be admired for its valiant, albeit futile struggle.
    (D) Death is stronger than any opponent.
    (E) Even in death the moth displayed a courageous dignity.

GO ON TO THE NEXT PAGE

52. Within the context of the entire passage, the
    narrator's feelings can best be described as

    (A) empowered by her sense of strength
    (B) energized by the beauty of the fall morning
    (C) entranced by the moth's plight
    (D) sadness regarding the onset of a new season
    (E) unexplainable pity for the creature's
        limitations

IF YOU FINISH BEFORE TIME IS CALLED, YOU MAY CHECK YOUR WORK ON
THIS SECTION ONLY. DO NOT TURN TO ANY OTHER SECTION IN THE TEST.   STOP

KAPLAN
Test Prep and Admissions

Section II

Total Time—2 hours
Number of questions—3
Percent of total grade—55%

Directions: This section contains three essay questions. Answer all three questions, budgeting your time carefully. Each essay counts as one-third of your total essay score.

QUESTION I

(Suggested time—40 minutes)

The following letter was written by Sandy Kempner to his family while he was fighting in Vietnam. Read the letter carefully, analyzing the particular stylistic and rhetorical techniques Sandy uses to convey his attitude toward war. Be sure to consider whether or not this letter is a successful example of anti-war sentiment.

2 September 1966

Dear Mom, Dad, Shrub, the Egg and Peach:

Sorry to be so long in writing, but I have just come back from an abortion called
Line Operation Jackson. I spent a three-day "walk in the sun" (and paddies and fields and
(5) mountains and impenetrable jungle and saw grass and ants, and screwed-up radios and no word, and deaf radio operators, and no chow, and too many C-rations, and blisters and torn trousers and jungle rot, and wet socks and sprained ankles and no heels , and, and, and) for a battalion that walked on roads and dikes the whole way and a regiment that didn't even know where the battalion was, finished off by a 14,000-meter forced march on
(10) a hard road.

My God the epic poems I could write to that ambrosia of Marine Corps cuisine— peanut butter and/or hot coffee after three days of that! The only person in the whole battalion to see a VC was, of course, me. I was walking along a trail doing a village sweep all alone, and here comes Charlie, rifle in hand, with not a care in the world until he sees
(15) me, and then it's a race to see if he can get off the road before I can draw my .45 and get off an accurate shot (he won). Of course there was an incident when four snipers took on the battalion, which promptly, more to release the weight of all that unexpended ammunition than anything else, threw everything at them but the Missouri, and that would have been there too, except it could not get up the Sang Tra Bong [River]. So goes
(20) about $50,000 worth of ammo. They probably played it up as a second Iwo Jima at home, but it wasn't.

Then, two days after we got back, we played Indian Scout, and my platoon splashed its way through a rice paddy at 3:30 in the morning in a rainstorm to surround a hamlet which we managed to do somehow without alerting everyone in the district, which is
(25) surprising as we made enough noise to wake up a Marine sentry. It was "very successful" since we managed to kill a few probably innocent civilians, found a few caves and burned a few houses, all in a driving rainstorm. There's nothing more, I'm afraid.

Love,

Sandy

On 11 November 1966, Marion Lee (Sandy) Kempner was killed by shrapnel from a mine explosion. He was 24 years old.

Write Your Essay Here

QUESTION II
(Suggested time—40 minutes.)

Read the following two passages about human skin carefully. Then write an essay in which you analyze how the distinctive stylistic and rhetorical differences of each passage reveal the purpose of its writer.

Passage 1

I sing of skin, layered fine as baklava, whose colors shame the dawn, at once the scabbard upon which we are thrilled, protected and kept constant
Line in our natural place. Here is each man bagged and
(5) trussed in perfect amiability. See how it upholsters the bone and muscle underneath, now accenting the point of an elbow, now rolling over the pectorals to hollow the grotto of an armpit. Nippled and umbilicated, and perforated by the
(10) most diverse and marvelous openings, each with its singular rim and curtain.

What is it, then, this seamless body-stocking some two yards square, this our casing, our façade, that flushes pales, and pains us all our days, at once
(15) keeper of the organs within and sensitive probe adventurer to the world outside?

Two layers compose the skin—the superficial epidermis and, deeper, the dermis. Between is a plan of pure energy where the life force is in full
(20) gallop. Identical cells spring full-grown here, each as tall and columnar as its brother, to form an unbroken line over the body. No sooner are these cells formed than they move toward the surface, whether drawn to the open air by some proto-
(25) plasmic hunger or pushed outward by the birth of still newer cells behind. In migration the skin cells flatten, first to cubes, then plates. Twenty-six days later the plates are no more than attenuated wisps of keratin meshed together to guard against forces
(30) that would damage the skin by shearing or compression. Here they lie, having lost all semblance of living cellularity, until they are shed from the body in a continuous dismal rain. Thus into the valley of death this number marches in
(35) well-stepped soldiery, gallant, summoned to a sacrifice beyond its ken. But . . . let the skin be cut or burned, and the brigade breaks into a charge,

Passage 2

Human skin is the body's largest organ. An adult's skin comprises between 15 and 20 percent of the total body weight. Each square centimeter
Line has 6 million cells, 5,000 sensory points, 100 sweat
(5) glands and 15 sebaceous glands. The outer layer, the epidermis, consists of rows of cells about 12 to 15 deep, and is between .07 and .12 millimeters thick (the thickness of a piece of paper). This top layer is mainly composed of dead cells, and these
(10) are constantly being replaced by newer cells. One square inch of skin contains up to 4.5 m of blood vessels which have as one of their functions the regulation of body temperature. The skin varies in thickness from .5mm on the eyelids to 4mm or
(15) more on the palms and the soles.

The skin forms a protective barrier against the action of physical, chemical, and bacterial agents on the deeper tissues and contains the special nerve organs for the various sensations commonly
(20) grouped as the sense of touch. The body replaces its skin every month, and because the skin constitutes the first line of defense against dehydration, infection, injuries and temperature, the skin detoxifies harmful substance with many of the
(25) same enzymatic processes the liver uses.

Skin is constantly being regenerated. A cell is born in the lower layer of the skin called the dermis, which is supplied with blood vessels and nerve endings. For the next two weeks the cell
(30) migrates upward until it reaches the bottom portion epidermis, which is the epidermis. The cell then flattens out and continues moving toward the surface until it dies and is shed.

The most important property of the skin is that
(35) it contains our sense of touch. All other senses have a definite key organ which can be studied, but the skin is spread over the entire body and cannot be as

GO ON TO THE NEXT PAGE

fanning out laterally across the wound, racing to seal off the defect. The margins are shored up;
(40) healing earthworks are raised, and guerilla squads of invading bacteria are isolated and mopped up. The reserves too are called to the colors and the rate of mitosis increases throughout the injured area. Hurrah for stratified squamous epithelium!

(45)   Beneath the epidermis lies the dermis, a resilient pad of elastic tissue in which glands, hair follicles, nerves and blood vessels are arranged in an infinitely variable mosaic. The three million sweat glands are helpmates to the kidney as they labor to
(50) keep the body cleansed and comfortable.

easily studied. Receptors located at the ends of nerve fibers are used to detect stimuli and convert
(40) them into neural impulses to be sent to the brain through the peripheral and central nervous systems. The sense of touch is actually recorded in the dermis (skin) and passed on to the central nervous system.

(45)   The most important job of the skin is that it protects the inside of the body; it acts like a "shock absorber." If a body falls, the skin protects all of the internal organs. When the skin is broken, it has its own defense system that immediately goes into
(50) repair mode. It also acts as a thermostat to balance body temperature.

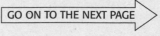
GO ON TO THE NEXT PAGE

Write Your Essay Here

QUESTION III
(Suggested time—40 minutes)

The following passage is from journalist Anna Quidlen's commencement address delivered to
Mt. Holyoke College, May, 1999. Carefully read the following passage from this address. Then
write an essay in which you define the central argument of the passage and evaluate the validity
of Quindlen's argument.

    Trying to be perfect may be inevitable for people like us, who are smart and ambitious
and interested in the world and in its good opinion. But at one level it's too hard, and at
another, it's too cheap and easy. Because it really requires you mainly to read the zeitgeist*
Line of wherever and whenever you happen to be, and to assume the masks necessary to be the
(5) best of whatever the zeitgeist dictates, or requires. Those requirements shape and shift,
sure, but when you're clever you can read them, and do the imitation required. But
nothing important, or meaningful, or beautiful, or interesting, or great ever came out of
imitations.
    The thing that is really hard, and really amazing, is giving up on being perfect and
(10) beginning the work of becoming yourself. More difficult, because there is no zeitgeist to
read, no template to follow, no masks to wear. Set aside what your friends expect, what
your parents demand, what your acquaintances require. Set aside the messages this culture
sends, through its advertising, its entertainment, its disdain and its disapproval, about how
you should behave. Set aside the old traditional notion of female as nurturer and male as
(15) leader; set aside, too, the new traditional notions of female as superwoman and male as
oppressor. Begin with that most terrifying of all things, a clean slate. And then look, every
day, at the choices you are making and when you ask yourself why you are making them,
find this answer: for me, for me. Because they are who and what I am, and mean to be.
    This is the hard work of your life in the world, to make it all up as you go along, to
(20) acknowledge the introvert, the clown, the artist, the reserved, the distraught, the goofball,
the thinker. You will have to bend all your will not to march to the music that all of those
great "theys" out there pipe on their flutes. They want you to go to professional school, to
wear khakis, to pierce your navel, to bare your soul. These are the fashionable ways. The
music is tinny, if you listen close enough. Look inside. That way lays dancing to the
(25) melodies spun out by your own heart. This is a symphony. All the rest are jingles.
    Look at your fingers. Hold them in front of your face. Each one is crowned by an abstract
design that is completely different than those of anyone in this crowd, in this country, in
this world. They are a metaphor for you. Each of you is as different as your fingerprints.
Why in the world should you march to any lockstep? The lockstep is easier, but here is why
(30) you cannot march to it. Because nothing great or even good ever came of it.
    George Eliot wrote, "It is never too late to be what you might have been." It is never too
early, either. And it will make all the difference in the world.
    * *The spirit of the time; the general intellectual and moral state or temper characteristic of
any period of time.*

Write Your Essay Here

Practice Test 1: **Answer Key**

PASSAGE 1	PASSAGE 2	PASSAGE 3	PASSAGE 4
1. E	14. A	27. C	40. D
2. A	15. C	28. A	41. B
3. B	16. D	29. B	42. B
4. C	17. B	30. D	43. D
5. D	18. E	31. E	44. C
6. E	19. A	32. B	45. C
7. A	20. B	33. C	46. E
8. B	21. C	34. C	47. B
9. C	22. D	35. E	48. C
10. A	23. E	36. D	49. D
11. D	24. E	37. D	50. E
12. E	25. C	38. E	51. B
13. D	26. A	39. A	52. E

ANSWERS AND EXPLANATIONS

Section I: Multiple Choice

On 7 June 1966, Robert Kennedy, then Senator of New York, addressed the National Union of South African Students' Day of Affirmation, in Cape Town, South Africa.

We stand here in the name of freedom.
At the heart of that Western freedom and democracy is the belief that the individual man,
Line the child of God, is the touchstone of value and all
(5) society, groups. The state exists for his benefit.
Therefore the enlargement of liberty for individual human beings must be the supreme goal and the abiding practice of any Western society.
The first element of this individual liberty is the
(10) freedom of speech.
The right to express and communicate ideas, to set oneself apart from the dumb beasts of field and forest; to recall governments to their duties and obligations; above all, the right to affirm one's
(15) membership and allegiance to the body politic—
to society—to the men with whom we share our land, our heritage and our children's future.
Hand in hand with freedom of speech goes the power to be heard—to share the decisions of
(20) government which shape men's lives. Everything that makes life worthwhile—family, work, education, a place to rear one's children and a place to rest one's head—all this rests on decisions of government; all can be swept away by a
(25) government which does not heed the demands of its people. Therefore, the essential humanity of men can be protected and preserved only where government must answer—not just to those of a particular religion, or a particular race; but to all
(30) its people.
And even government by the consent of the governed, as in our own Constitution, must be limited in its power to act against its people: so that there may be no interference with the right to
(35) worship, or with the security of the home; no arbitrary imposition of pains or penalties by officials high or low; no restrictions on the

freedom of men to seek education or work or opportunity of any kind so that each man may
(40) become all he is capable of becoming.
These are the sacred rights of Western society. These are the essential differences between us and Nazi Germany, as they were between Athens and Persia.
(45) They are the essence of our difference with Communism today. I am inalterably opposed to Communism because it exalts the state over the individual and the family, and because of the lack of freedom of speech, of protest, or religion and of the
(50) press, which is characteristic of totalitarian states.
The way of opposition to Communism is not to imitate its dictatorship, but to enlarge individual human freedom—in our own countries and all over the globe. There are those in every land who would
(55) label as "Communist" every threat to their privilege. But as I have seen on my travels in all sections of the world, reform is not Communism. And the denial of freedom, in whatever name, only strengthens the very Communism it claims to oppose.
(60) For two centuries, my own country has struggled to overcome the self-imposed handicap of prejudice and discrimination based on nationality, social class or race—discrimination profoundly repugnant to the theory and command
(65) of our Constitution. Even as my father grew up in Boston, signs told him that "No Irish need apply."
Two generations later President Kennedy became the first Catholic to head the nation but how many men of ability had, before 1961, been
(70) denied the opportunity to contribute to the nation's progress because they were Catholic, or of Irish extraction.
In the last five years, the winds of change have blown as fiercely in the United Sates as anywhere in
(75) the world. But they will not—they cannot—abate.
For there are millions of Negroes untrained for the simplest jobs, and thousands every day denied their full equal rights under the law; and the violence of the disinherited, the insulated the
(80) injured, looms over the streets of Harlem and Watts and South Chicago.
But a Negro American trains as an astronaut, one of mankind's first explorers into outer space; another is the chief barrister of the United States

(85) Government, and dozens sit on the benches of
court; and another, Dr. Martin Luther King, is the
second man of African descent to win the Nobel
Peace Prize for his nonviolent efforts for social
justice between the races.

(90) We must recognize the full human equality of all
our people before God, before the law, and in the
councils of government. We must do this not
because it is economically advantageous, although
it is; not because the laws of God and man

(95) command it, although they do command it; not
because people in other lands wish it so. We must
do it for the single and fundamental reason that it
is the right thing to do.

And this must be our commitment outside our

(100) borders as well as within.

It is your job, the task of the young people of
this world to strip the last remnants of that
ancient, cruel belief from the civilization of man.

Each nation has different obstacles and different

(105) goals, shadowed by the vagaries of history and
experience. Yet as I talk to you and people around
the world I am impressed not by diversity but by
the closeness of their goals, their desires and
concerns and hopes for the future. There is

(110) discrimination in New York, apartheid in South
Africa and serfdom in the mountains of Peru.
People stagnate in the streets of India; intellectuals
go to jail in Russia; thousands are slaughtered in
Indonesia; wealth is lavished on armaments

(115) everywhere. These are differing evils. But they are
common works of man.

And therefore they call upon common qualities
of conscience and of indignation, a shared
determination to wipe away the unnecessary

(120) sufferings of our fellow human beings at home
and particularly around the world.

In the world we would like to build, South Africa
could play an outstanding role, and a role of
leadership in that effort. This country is without

(125) question a preeminent repository of the wealth
and the knowledge and the skill of the continent.
Here are the greater part of Africa's research
scientists and steel production, most of it
reservoirs of coal and of electric power. Many

(130) South Africans have made major contributions to
African technical development and world science;

the names of some are known wherever men seek
to eliminate the ravages of tropical disease and of
pestilence. In your faculties and councils, here in

(135) this very audience, are hundreds and thousands of
men and women who could transform the lives of
millions for all time to come.

So we part, I to my country and you to remain.
We are—if a man of forty can claim the privilege—

(140) fellow members of the world's largest younger
generation. Each of us has our own work to do. I
know at times you must feel very alone with your
problems and with your difficulties. But I want to
say how impressed I am with what you stand for

(145) and for the effort you are making; and I say this not
just for myself, but men and women all over the
world. And I hope you will often take heart from
the knowledge that you are joined with your fellow
young people in every land, they struggling with

(150) their problems and you with yours, but all joined
in a common purpose; that, like the young people
of my own country and of every country that I
have visited, you are all in many ways more closely
united to the brothers of your time than to the

(155) older generation in any of these nations; you are
determined to build a better future.

1. E

This main idea is actually expressed in paragraph 2,
"Therefore the enlargement of liberty for individaul human
beings must be the supreme goal and the abiding practice
of any Western society." Robert Kennedy then proceeds to
elaborate on this point in the remainder of his speech.

2. A

It is not unusual for the multiple choice questions to move
from an idea question such as question one to a stylistic
question such as this one. If you take a close look at
paragraph 4, you will find everything but compound-complex
sentence structure. Paragraph 4 is actually one very long
fragment. It does, however, have items in a series without
conjunctions, (A); a parenthetical appositive, (C); "to society",
which renames or defines what is meant by the "body
politic"; anaphora, (D); or phrases starting with the same
infinitive opening; and it certainly has many items in a
series, (E).

3. B

It is common for the main idea of a paragraph to appear in the topic sentence, and that is exactly what we have here. However, a lot of other very important things are mentioned in this as well, but they are all supportive of this idea of "hearing" the common voice of man.

4. C

You can find the answer to this questions at the end of paragraph 6. The main point that Kennedy is making is that governments must allow people to have as much freedom as is reasonably possible. Man has certain unalienable rights, and it is through these rights that he or she can become the person he or she is meant to be.

5. D

Kennedy is attempting to establish common ground with his audience. When he gave this speech in South Africa, apartheid was rampant. He wants his listeners to understand that they are not alone in suffering discrimination. Of course, by his generation, most of the anti-Irish sentiments in the United States had dissipated.

6. E

The sentence, "But they will not—they cannot—abate" demonstrates parenthetical emphasis (A) with the use of the dashes. The pronoun "they" is a reference to "winds of change" in the first sentence of the paragraph. The near repetition of the phrasing "they will not" and "they cannot" is a loose form of anaphora (C). And there is no mistaking the imperative, almost imperious tone of the sentence, (D).

7. A

Kennedy makes several references to Communism, but the main point he makes is that Communism sacrifices the individual for the common good, and that is unacceptable.

8. B

When a series of words or phrases is strung together without the use of conjunctions it is referred to as asyndeton, without conjunctions. When this series uses conjunctions between the parts of the series, then it is polysyndeton (many conjunctions).

9. C

Although Kennedy is addressing the entire audience in South Africa, as well as knowing that he would be heard and read by the people of the world, the presentation was given at a Students' Day Affirmation, and as he draws his speech to a close, he particularly addresses the youth in his audience.

10. A

Basically, Kennedy is expressing the need for people around the world to stand up for what is right; to have the courage of their convictions—to be like a Martin Luther King and say and do what is right for all mankind, regardless of opposition or the ease in just accepting what is happening, and not becoming involved. This can best be seen in lines 120–124.

11. D

As Kennedy closes his speech, he attempts to do many things, but most of all he appeals to the younger generation, identifying with them (in the last paragraph) in the burden that they must shoulder to make the world a better place in which all people may live.

12. E

In lines 125–140, Kennedy highlights the strengths that South Africa has. He commends them for their advancements and hopes that they will participate more with the rest of the world. All of the responses are covered in this paragraph except racial tolerance, which, of course, was the significant focus of this speech.

13. D

This response makes the most sense since the speech was addressed to the National Union of South African Students' Day of Affirmation. As he concludes the speech, he calls upon the youth of South Africa to join with the youth from around the world in creating a better world for all of their futures.

On a winter day some years ago, coming out of
Pittsburgh on one of the expresses of the
Pennsylvania Railroad, I rolled eastward for an
Line hour through the coal and steel towns of
(5) Westmoreland county. It was familiar ground; boy
and man, I had been through it often before. But
somehow I had never quite sensed its appalling
desolation. Here was the very heart of industrial
America, the center of its most lucrative and
(10) characteristic activity, the boast and pride of the
richest and grandest nation ever seen on earth—
and here was a scene so dreadfully hideous, so
intolerably bleak and forlorn that it reduced the
whole aspiration of man to a macabre and
(15) depressing joke. Here was wealth beyond
computation, almost beyond imagination—and
here were human habitations so abominable that
they would have disgraced a race of alley cats.

I am not speaking of mere filth. One expects
(20) steel towns to be dirty. What I allude to is the
unbroken and agonizing ugliness, the sheer
revolting monstrousness, of every house in sight.
From East Liberty to Greensburg, a distance of
twenty-five miles, there was not one in sight from
(25) the train that did not insult and lacerate the eye.
Some were so bad, and they were among the most
pretentious—churches, stores, warehouses, and the
like—that they were downright startling; one
blinked before them as one blinks before a man
(30) with his face shot away. A few linger in memory,
horrible even there: a crazy little church just west
of Jeannette, set like a dormer-window on the side
of a bare, leprous hill; the headquarters of the
Veterans of Foreign Wars at another forlorn town,
(35) a steel stadium like a huge rat-trap somewhere
further down the line. But most of all I recall the
general effect—of hideousness without a break.
There was not a single decent house within eye
range from the Pittsburgh suburbs to the
(40) Greensburg yards. There was not one that was not
misshapen, and there was not one that was not
shabby.

The country itself is not uncomely, despite the
grime of the endless mills. It is, in form, a narrow
(45) river valley, with deep gullies running up into the
hills. It is thickly settled, but not noticeably
overcrowded. There is still plenty of room for

building, even in the larger towns, and there are
very few solid blocks. Nearly every house, big and
(50) little, has space on all four sides. Obviously, if there
were architects of any professional sense or dignity
in the region, they would have perfected a chalet to
hug the hillsides—a chalet with a high-pitched roof
to throw off the heavy winter snows, but still
(55) essentially a low and clinging building, wider than
it was tall. But what have they done? They have
taken as their model a brick set on end. This they
have converted into a thing of dingy clapboards,
with a narrow, low-pitched roof. And the whole
(60) they have set upon thin, preposterous brick piers.
By the hundreds and thousands these abominable
houses cover the bare hillsides, like gravestones in
some gigantic and decaying cemetery on their deep
sides they are three, four and even five stories high;
(65) on their low sides they bury themselves swinishly
in the mud. Not a fifth of them are perpendicular.
They lean this way and that, hanging on to their
bases precariously. And one and all they are
streaked in grime, with dead and eczematous
(70) patches of paint peeping through the streaks.

Now and then there is a house of brick. But
what brick! When it is new it is the color of a fried
egg. When it has taken on the patina of the mills it
is the color of an egg long past all hope or caring.
(75) Was it necessary to adopt that shocking color? No
more than it was necessary to set all of the houses
on end. Red brick, even in a steel town, ages with
some dignity. Let it become downright black, and
it is still sightly, especially if its trimmings are of
(80) white stone, with soot in the depths and the high
spots washed by the rain. But in Westmoreland
they prefer that uremic yellow, and so they have
the most loathsome towns and villages ever seen
by mortal eye.

(85) I award this championship only after laborious
research and incessant prayer. I have seen, I
believe, all of the most unlovely towns of the
world; they are all to be found in the United States.
I have seen the mill towns of decomposing New
(90) England and the desert towns of Utah, Arizona
and Texas. I am familiar with the back streets of
Newark, Brooklyn and Chicago, and have made
scientific explorations to Camden, N.J. and
Newport News, Va. Safe in a Pullman, I have

(95) whirled through the gloomy, God-forsaken villages of Iowa and Kansas, and the malarious tide-water hamlets of Georgia. I have been to Bridgeport, Conn., and to Los Angeles. But nowhere on this earth, at home or abroad, have I seen anything to
(100) compare to the villages that huddle along the line of the Pennsylvania from the Pittsburgh yards to Greensburg. They are incomparable in color, and they are incomparable in design. It is as if some titanic and aberrant genius, uncompromisingly
(105) inimical to man, had devoted all the ingenuity of Hell to the making of them. They show grotesqueries of ugliness that, in retrospect, become almost diabolical. One cannot imagine mere human beings concocting such dreadful
(110) things, and one can scarcely imagine human beings bearing life in them.

Are they so frightful because the valley is full of foreigners—dull, insensate brutes, with no love of beauty in them? Then why didn't these foreigners
(115) set up similar abominations in the countries that they came from? You will, in fact, find nothing of the sort in Europe save perhaps in the more putrid parts of England. There is scarcely an ugly village on the whole Continent. The peasants, however
(120) poor, somehow manage to make themselves graceful and charming habitations, even in Spain. But in the American village and small town the pull is always toward ugliness, and in that Westmoreland valley it has been yielded to with an
(125) eagerness bordering upon passion. It is incredible that mere ignorance should have achieved such masterpieces of horror.

On certain levels of the American race, indeed, there seems to be a positive libido for the ugly, as
(130) on other and less Christian levels there is a libido for the beautiful. It is impossible to put down the wallpaper that defaces the average American home of the lower middle class to mere inadvertence, or to the obscene humor of the manufacturers. Such
(135) ghastly designs, it must be obvious, give a genuine delight to a certain type of mind. They meet, in some unfathomable way, its obscure and unintelligible demands. They caress it as "The Palms" caresses it, or the art of the movie, or jazz.
(140) The taste for them is as enigmatical and yet as common as the taste for dogmatic theology and the poetry of Edgar A. Guest.

Thus I suspect (though confessedly without knowing) that the vast majority of the honest folk
(145) of Westmoreland county, and especially the 100% Americans among them, actually admire the houses they live in, and are proud of them. For the same money they could get vastly better ones, but they prefer what they have got. Certainly there was
(150) no pressure upon the Veterans of Foreign Wars to choose the dreadful edifice that bears their banner, for there are plenty of vacant buildings along the track-side, and some of them are appreciably better. They might, indeed, have built a better one
(155) of their own. But they chose that clapboarded horror with their eyes open, and having chosen it, they let it mellow into its present shocking depravity. They like it as it is: beside it, the Parthenon would no doubt offend them. In
(160) precisely the same way the authors of the rattrap stadium that I have mentioned made a deliberate choice. After painfully designing and erecting it, they made it perfect in their own sight by putting a completely impossible pent-house, painted a
(165) staring yellow, on top of it. The effect is that of a fat woman with a black eye. It is that of a Presbyterian grinning. But they like it.

Here is something that the psychologists have so far neglected: the love of ugliness for its own sake,
(170) the lust to make the world intolerable. Its habitat is the United States. Out of the melting pot emerges a race which hates beauty as it hates truth. The etiology of this madness deserves a great deal more study than it has got. There must be causes behind
(175) it; it arises and flourishes in obedience to biological laws, and not as a mere act of God. What, precisely, are the terms of those laws? And why do they run stronger in America than elsewhere? Let some honest *Privat Dozent* in
(180) pathological sociology apply himself to the problem.

14. A

The narrator of this passage has a mission, and that mission is to describe to us the extreme ugliness of this section of Pennsylvania. Although some of the other choices may be found within the passage, the primary focus is on ugliness.

15. C

All of the choices except this one are used to describe the houses. The reference to a rat trap is used to describe a steel stadium.

16. D

At first the narrator describes what he sees and depicts its ugliness. As the passage continues, howeve, he begins musing over just why humanity would tolerate and even choose to surround itself with such incredible ugliness.

17. B

The narrator says in paragraph 3 that "the country itself is not uncomely, despite the grime of the endless mills. It is in form, a narrow river valley, with deep gullies running up into the hills. It is thickly settled, but not noticeably overcrowded," and so on. What he just cannot understand is how such ugliness could be built upon a landscape that seemingly deserves much better.

18. E

The second paragraph has much in it that demonstrates the author's disdain of the horrors he views. Howeyer, the specific identification of the geographical location is not one of those characteristics. Perhaps it could be, by connotation, for some, but it is not specifically a device used to express the ugliness.

19. A

The author's words make it sound like he is holding an ugliness contest. In order to have such a contest, it can be assumed that the narrator has seen several, perhaps many, other displeasing places that have offended his eye. Nevertheless, the one he talks about in this passage is the worst.

20. B

The descriptor "uremic yellow," a phrase that the writer seems to have coined, is simply more proof of his total disdain for the ugliness of the houses he is viewing.

21. C

The phrase "peasants however poor" is nicely alliterative, giving the sentence a stylistic ring.

22. D

In the eighth paragraph the narrator says "They like it [the ugliness of their houses] as it is: beside it, the Parthenon would no doubt offend them." Again the narrator is flabbergasted by the inhabitants' preference for the ugly. Their tastes are so skewed that the Parthenon—traditionally and historically considered a building of great beauty—would be found offensive by these people who prefer ugliness.

23. E

The narrator thinks that the ugliness of the archtecture and the people who seem to prefer it would all make great psychological studies. Nowhere, however, does he mention pathological sociology.

24. E

"Privat Dozent" actually refers to someone who is an expert. You would not be expected to know this term, but from context, you should be able to gather that this would be some kind of specialist who might want to study such aberrations of ugliness.

25. C

Responses (A), (B) and (E) might work as responses, but the author would be *most likely* to agree that sometimes there is just no explanation for bad taste.

26. A

Looking at this sentence, you should be able to pick up on how the narrator feels about the situation. In addition, you are being asked to strain your knowledge of vocabulary to do some elimination. The most accurate description of tone is that of harsh disparagement (disgust).

The struggle between Liberty and Authority is the most conspicuous feature in the portions of history with which we are familiar. By liberty, was meant protection against the tyranny of the (5) political rulers. The rulers were conceived (except in some of the popular governments of Greece) as in a necessarily antagonistic position to the people whom they ruled. They consisted of a governing One, or a governing tribe or caste, who derived (10) their authority from inheritance or conquest, who, at all events, did not hold it at the pleasure of the governed, and whose supremacy men did not venture, perhaps did not desire, to contest, whatever precautions might be taken against its (15) oppressive exercise. Their power was regarded as necessary, but also as highly dangerous; as a weapon which they would attempt to use against their subjects, no less than against external enemies. To prevent the weaker members of the (20) community from being preyed on by innumerable vultures, it was needful that there should be an animal of prey stronger than the rest, commissioned to keep them down. But as the king of the vultures would be no less bent upon preying upon (25) the flock than of the minor harpies, it was indispensable to be in a perpetual attitude of defence against his beak and claws. The aim, therefore, of patriots was to set limits to the power which the ruler should be suffered to exercise over (30) the community; and this limitation was what they meant by liberty. It was attempted in two ways. First, by obtaining a recognition of certain immunities, called political liberties or rights, which it was to be regarded as a breach of duty in (35) the ruler to infringe, and which, if he did infringe, specific resistance, or general rebellion, was held to be justifiable. A second, and generally a later expedient, was the establishment of constitutional checks, by which the consent of the community, or (40) a body of some sort, supposed to represent its interests, was made a necessary condition to some of the more important acts of the governing power.

A time came, in the progress of human affairs, when men ceased to think it necessity of nature (45) that their governors should be an independent power, opposed in interest to themselves. The notion, that the people have no need to limit their power over themselves, might seem axiomatic, when popular government was a thing only (50) dreamed about, or read of as having existed at some distant period of the past. In time, however, a democratic republic came to occupy a large portion of the earth's surface, and made itself felt as one of the most powerful members of the (55) community of nations; and elective and responsible government became subject to the observations and criticisms which wait upon a great existing fact. It was now perceived that such phrases as "self-government," and "the power of (60) the people over themselves," do not express the true state of the case. The "people" who exercise the power are not always the same people with those over whom it is exercised; and the "self-government" spoken of is not the government of (65) each by himself, but of each by all the rest. The will of the people, moreover, practically means the will of the most numerous or the most active *part* of the people; the majority, or those who succeed in making themselves accepted as the majority; the (70) people, consequently, *may* desire to oppress a part of their number; and precautions are as much needed against this as against any other abuse of power. The limitation, therefore, of the power of government over individuals loses none of its (75) importance when the holders of power are regularly accountable to the community, that is, to the strongest party therein. This view of things, recommending itself equally to the intelligence of thinkers and to the inclination of those important (80) classes in European society to whose real or supposed interests democracy is adverse, has had no difficulty in establishing itself; and in political speculations "the tyranny of the majority" is now generally included among the evils against which (85) society requires to be on its guard.

Like other tyrannies, the tyranny of the majority was at first, and is still vulgarly, held in dread, chiefly as operating through the acts of the public authorities. But reflecting persons perceived that (90) when society is itself the tyrant—society collectively, over the separate individuals who compose it—its means of tyrannizing are not restricted to the acts which it may do by the hands of its political functionaries. Society can and does

(95) execute its own mandates: and if it issues wrong
mandates instead of right, or any mandates at all
in things with which it ought not to meddle, it
practices a social tyranny more formidable than
many kinds of political oppression, since, though
(100) not usually upheld by such extreme penalties, it
leaves fewer means of escape, penetrating much
more deeply into the details of life, and enslaving
itself. Protection, therefore, against the tyranny of
the magistrate is not enough: there needs to be
(105) protection also against the tyranny of the
prevailing opinion and feelings; against the
tendency of society to impose, by other means
than civil penalties, its own ideas and practices as
rules of conduct on those whose dissent from
(110) them; to fetter development, and, if possible,
prevent the formation, of any individuality not in
harmony with its ways, and compel all characters
to fashion themselves upon the model of its own.

27. C

In this question we are being asked to consider a word,
"popular" whose meaning has changed over the centuries.
Popular vote is the vote of the people, similar to the idea of
the word "populous." It has nothing to do with having or
not having a lot of friends as the word is today.

28. A

Occasionally you have to identify just what mode or
manner of writing the writer is using in a passage.
Exposition generally means explanation. It is the best
response for this question. (B), narration, is telling a story,
and this passage is not really an argument, (C); nor is it
comparison and contrast, (D), nor cause and effect, (E).

29. B

Paragraph one has numerous descriptions of the enemy as
animal, especially a predator. He does not, however, refer
to the enemy as the marauding hordes.

30. D

The author's fundamental belief is that the governing One
cannot have total, unrestrained control over anyone. That
would be tyranny. The author believes that liberty can be
won only by eliminating the tyranny of the One as well as
monitoring governance by the majority.

31. E

"Axiomatic" means that something is self evident. You may
have heard the term axiom—it is an idea or a belief that is
evident, something that can be relied upon as universally
true.

32. B

One irony that this author seems to want to stress is that
government by the people may be misleading. Sometimes
those who are in charge of governing manage to be
outside the government that they establish. True
government by the people would include everyone—the
governed and the governors.

33. C

This entire passage has to do with the governed and the
governing of the governed. The writer tries to explain how
best to achieve a reasonable balance that will give man the
most freedom without encroaching upon others' freedoms.

34. C

If you recall from Key Terminology, and allusion is an
historic or mythological reference that is brought into
something else for comparison purposes. Harpies are from
mythology—they were a type of witch. In fact, the witches
in Macbeth are referred to as three harpies.

35. E

The words "part" and "may" are italicized for emphasis. The
writer wants you to pay attention to the distinction he is
making. He is also being very critical about so-called self-
government, and he is emphasizing that there is often a
discrepancy within such a set up.

36. D

The antecedent for the pronoun "it" is the word society.

37. D

Go back to paragraph two; you will see that it deals with
the emergence of government by the populace and the
inherent problems even such a long-dreamt-of government
can hold. Control by the majority must not be allowed
without certain restrictions upon those who rule.

38. E

What the narrator seems most concerned about is the fact that even in a government by the people, those who exercise the power sometimes manage not to be those over whom the power is exercised. Sometimes these people in power can take unfair advantage of this situation.

39. A

In line with the last two questions, this narrator concludes that we must always be watchful, even in the world of government by the people checks and balances must be established, for the governors are also in need of being governed.

Moths that fly by day are not properly to be called moths; they do not excite that pleasant sense of dark autumn nights and ivy-blossom which the
Line commonest yellow-underwing asleep in the
(5) shadow of the curtain never fails to rouse in us. They are hybrid creatures, neither gay like butterflies nor sombre like their own species. Nevertheless the present specimen, with his narrow hay-coloured wings, fringed with a tassel
(10) of the same colour, seemed to be content with life. It was a pleasant morning, mid-September, mild, benignant, yet with a keener breath than that of the summer months. The plough was already scoring the field opposite the window, and where
(15) the share had been, the earth was pressed flat and gleamed with moisture. Such vigour came rolling in from the fields and the down beyond that it was difficult to keep the eyes strictly turned upon the book. The rooks too were keeping one of their
(20) annual festivities; soaring round the tree tops until it looked as if a vast net with thousands of black knots in it had been cast up into the air; which, after a few moments sank slowly down upon the trees until every twig seemed to have a knot at the
(25) end of it. Then, suddenly, the net would be thrown into the air again in a wider circle this time, with the utmost clamour and vociferation, as though to be thrown into the air and settle slowly down upon the tree tops were a tremendously exciting
(30) experience.

The same energy which inspired the rooks, the ploughmen, the horses, and even, it seemed, the

lean bare-backed downs, sent the moth fluttering from side to side of his square of the window-pane.
(35) One could not help watching him. One was, indeed, conscious of a queer feeling of pity for him. The possibilities of pleasure seemed that morning so enormous and so various that to have only a moth's part in life, and a day moth's at that,
(40) appeared a hard fate, and his zest in enjoying his meagre opportunities to the full, pathetic. He flew vigorously to one corner of his compartment, and, after waiting there a second, flew across to the other. What remained for him but to fly to a third
(45) corner and then to a fourth? That was all he could do, in spite of the size of the downs, the width of the sky, the far-off smoke of houses, and the romantic voice, now and then, of a steamer out at sea. What he could do he did. Watching him, it
(50) seemed as if a fibre, very thin but pure, of the enormous energy of the world had been thrust into his frail and diminutive body. As often as he crossed the pane, I could fancy that a thread of vital light became visible. He was little or nothing but
(55) life.

Yet, because he was so small, and so simple a form of the energy that was rolling in at the open window and driving its way through so many narrow and intricate corridors in my own brain
(60) and in those of other human beings, there was something marvellous as well as pathetic about him. It was as if someone had taken a tiny bead of pure life and decking it as lightly as possible with down and feathers, had set it dancing and
(65) zigzagging to show us the true nature of life. Thus displayed one could not get over the strangeness of it. One is apt to forget all about life, seeing it humped and bossed and garnished and cumbered so that it has to move with the greatest circum-
(70) spection and dignity. Again, the thought of all that life might have been had he been born in any other shape caused one to view his simple activities with a kind of pity.

After a time, tired by his dancing apparently, he
(75) settled on the window ledge in the sun, and, the queer spectacle being at an end, I forgot about him. Then, looking up, my eye was caught by him. He was trying to resume his dancing, but seemed

either so stiff or so awkward that he could only
(80) flutter to the bottom of the window-pane; and
when he tried to fly across it he failed. Being intent
on other matters I watched these futile attempts
for a time without thinking, unconsciously waiting
for him to resume his flight, as one waits for a
(85) machine, that has stopped momentarily, to start
again without considering the reason of its failure.
After perhaps a seventh attempt he slipped from
the wooden ledge and fell, fluttering his wings, on
to his back on the window sill. The helplessness of
(90) his attitude roused me. It flashed upon me that he
was in difficulties; he could no longer raise
himself; his legs struggled vainly. But, as I stretched
out a pencil, meaning to help him to right himself,
it came over me that the failure and awkwardness
(95) were the approach of death. I laid the pencil down
again.

The legs agitated themselves once more. I looked
as if for the enemy against which he struggled. I
looked out of doors. What had happened there?
(100) Presumably it was midday, and work in the fields
had stopped. Stillness and quiet had replaced the
previous animation. The birds had taken
themselves off to feed in the brooks. The horses
stood still. Yet the power was there all the same,
(105) massed outside indifferent, impersonal, not
attending to anything in particular. Somehow it
was opposed to the little hay-coloured moth. It
was useless to try to do anything. One could only
watch the extraordinary efforts made by those tiny
(110) legs against an oncoming doom which could, had
it chosen, have submerged an entire city, not
merely a city, but masses of human beings;
nothing, I knew, had any chance against death.
Nevertheless after a pause of exhaustion the legs
(115) fluttered again. It was superb this last protest, and
so frantic that he succeeded at last in righting
himself. One's sympathies, of course, were all on
the side of life. Also, when there was nobody to
care or to know, this gigantic effort on the part of
(120) an insignificant little moth, against a power of
such magnitude, to retain what no one else valued
or desired to keep, moved one strangely. Again,
somehow, one saw life, a pure bead. I lifted the
pencil again, useless though I knew it to be. But

(125) even as I did so, the unmistakable tokens of death
showed themselves. The body relaxed, and
instantly grew stiff. The struggle was over. The
insignificant little creature now knew death. As I
looked at the dead moth, this minute wayside
(130) triumph of so great a force over so mean an
antagonist filled me with wonder. Just as life had
been strange a few minutes before, so death was
now as strange. The moth having righted himself
now lay most decently and uncomplainingly
(135) composed. O yes, he seemed to say, death is
stronger than I am.

40. D

The first two sentences of this passage establish the fact
that daytime moths are not like those who haunt the
darkness, nor are they a part of the butterfly world of
daylight.

41. B

In line with question 40, the narrator calls the daytime
moths hybrid—having characteristics of the nighttime moth
and the daytime butterfly, but not belonging to either of
these species.

42. B

Personal reflection, or personal observation is the best
descriptor for this passage. It is not an argument, (A), nor a
definition, (C). It seems to be description, but there is also
an element of the narrator's own musings in this passage
as well, and that removes it from the mode of pure
description. This passage lacks any real scientific
information about moths, just personal observations, so it
cannot be classified as technical writing, (E).

43. D

Ripe pumpkins are not mentioned in this passage
anywhere. Even though pumpkins in their prime connote
the fall season, only the other characteristics of fall are
included, not ripe pumpkins.

44. C

These lines reiterate the idea of life several times: "a thread of *vital* light became visible. He was little or nothing but life . . . as if someone had taken a tiny bead of pure life . . . to show us the true nature of life."

45. C

An analogy is a comparison of one thing to another for clarification, often used in enhancing a descriptive passage. Metaphors and similes are simple analogies. In this passage, however, the vision of the rooks to the net is extended as the rooks rise and fall as if lifted by the edge, raised and lowered once again into the trees.

46. E

These lines read: "One was, indeed, conscious of a queer feeling of pity for him. The possibilities of pleasure seemed that morning so enormous and so various that to have only a moth's part in life, and a day moth's at that, appeared a hard fate, and his zest in enjoying his meagre opportunities to the full, pathetic. He flew vigorously to one corner of his compartment, and, after waiting there a second, flew across to the other." It is easy to hear the alliteration (of p, m, c), and the open vowel sounds (w<u>a</u>s, <u>c</u>onscious, p<u>o</u>ssible, m<u>o</u>rning, etc.) repeat, giving the lines strong assonance as well.

47. B

This question takes us to the second sentence of paragraph 3. "It was as if someone had taken a tiny bead of pure life and decking it as lightly as possible with down and feathers, had set it dancing and zigzagging to show us the true nature of life."

48. C

If you check the Key Terminology words, you will find that asyndeton is a series of words or phrases connected without the use of conjunctions. It is neither a periodic sentence nor run on, (A) and (B). Anaphora is the repetition of opening words of phrases or clauses in a series, (D). And there is no parallelism, (E).

49. D

Without referring to the fourth paragraph, it seems as if any one of these responses might be the possible correct answer. However, the paragraph concludes with these words: "as I stretched out a pencil, meaning to help him to right himself, it came over me that the failure and awkwardness were the approach of death. I laid the pencil down again."

50. E

Understanding tone is sometimes difficult to do. One must first get a feeling for the passage, a feeling for the message of the passage, and a feeling for the feelings of the narrator. In this case, the narrator is truly regretful for the brief heroic life of the little moth, and she has imbued this creature with a sense that it represents something far greater than what it seems at a glance, thus making (E) the correct response.

51. B

Unfortunately, despite the great awe the narrator feels for the valiant day moth, it is easy also to understand that she recognizes that it is just one piece of a much greater whole.

52. E

These last questions are making you delve into the narrator's point of view. She feels regret that such a stalwart figthter has such a brief life; she is also impressed that this creature seems to have the courage to make the most of its brief hours.

Essay Question I: Sandy Kempner letter

Analysis of Essay Question I

This charming, but heart-wrenching letter from Vietnam is a poignant anti-war testimonial. Students need to pay particular attention to Sandy's word choice, for connotations of many of his words carry a very strong message.

Like many young men in that war, he wasn't too sure exactly what he was doing or how he even got where he was. Nevertheless, he "soldiers" on with his duties. One of these more pleasant duties is writing to his beloved family. His subtle criticism is well hidden within an impressive presentation of descriptive images. You have a lot to look at in this short correspondence, but should find it accessible. Most of you will have at least something to say about it.

Scoring Guide for Question I

9 Essays meet all of the criteria for 8 papers, and in addition, are especially full or apt in their analysis or demonstrate particularly impressive composition skills.

8 Essays successfully analyze the rhetorical and stylistic strategies the letter employs to convey the writer's attitude about the Vietnam War and Sandy's part in it. They refer to the passage directly or indirectly and explain convincingly how specific strategies such as imagery, tone and figurative language contribute to an understanding of the writer's attitude. Their prose controls a wide range of effective writing but is not flawless.

7 Essays fit the description of 6 essays but employ more complete analysis or demonstrate a more mature prose style.

6 Essays adequately analyze the stylistic devices the letter employs to reveal the writer's attitude about the war in Vietnam and his part in the action. They refer to the passage directly or indirectly, and they recognize the narrator's attitude and how he conveys it by utilizing strategies such as choice of detail, tone, figurative language. A few lapses in diction or syntax may be present, but generally the prose of 6 essays is clear.

5 Essays analyze Sandy's rhetorical techniques, but the development of how these techniques work, or the understanding of Sandy's attitude is limited or too simplistic. These essays may treat techniques superficially or develop ideas about the narrator's attitude inconsistently. A few lapses in diction or syntax may appear, but the prose in these essays usually conveys the writers' ideas adequately.

4 Essays inadequately respond to the task of the prompt. They may misrepresent the writer's attitude or analyze rhetorical strategies inaccurately or with little understanding of how strategies reveal his attitude toward the war. Often the prose of these essays suggests immature control over organization, diction, or syntax.

3 Essays meet the criteria for the score of 4 but are less perceptive about how rhetorical strategies convey attitude or are less consistent in controlling the elements of writing.

2   Essays are unsuccessful in analyzing how stylistic strategies convey the writer's attitude about the War in Vietnam and his part in the war. These essays tend to pay little or cursory attention to the specific features, and they may generalize, or simplify attitude and tone. They may simply paraphrase or comment on the passage without analyzing technique. The prose of 2 papers often reveals consistent weaknesses in writing, such as a lack of development or organization, grammatical problems, or a lack of control.

1   Essays earning a score of 1 meet the criteria for the score of 2 but are especially simplistic in their discussion or weak in controlling elements of language

Robert's Response

In class this year we read <u>The Things They Carried</u> by Tim O'Brien, which led to an exploration of a lot of different so-called war-related literature. Overall, I found most of it to be subtle and not so subtle war protest literature. This letter by Sandy, describing his numerous experiences in Vietnam is no exception. He conveys a cynical and resentful attitude towards the situation he is in. He utilizes humor, vivid imagery, sarcasm and other rhetorical devoices to tell his family, and subsequently the rest of us, about the true nature of war.

People have been writing about war for centuries—the early Greeks and Romans spoke of war. War is present in many of Shakespeare's historical plays and he mentions it also in <u>Hamlet</u> and <u>Macbeth.</u> Many poets have written about war as well. A famous war poem that made a big impression on me is "Dulce Et Decorum Est" (World War I think). The powerful imagery in that poem sure stirred my anti-war feelings. In the last century or so anti-war books such as <u>Johnny Got His Gun</u> and <u>On the Beach</u> and <u>Hiroshima</u> have made powerful anti-war statements. Of course the movie industry has done its part as well with classics such as Failsafe and MASH. Sandy's letter from Vietnam fits right in with all of these classics. With not-so subtle imagery and undeniable sarcasm, this letter exposes us once again to the travesty of war.

In his greeting Sandy reveals that he is homesick and has much affection for his family—using their pet names. When he begins his letter, he tries to keep things light—possibly not wanting to worry his family. However, by mentioning the recent maneuvers as an "abortion" we are quickly apprised of Sandy's bitterness over the futility of what they are doing. As he relays his recent adventures, we quickly see that this was definitely no "walk in the sun." In fact, his tone is angry, with only a few details, we are quickly able to understand the grueling nature of his missions. The abundant use of negatives emphasizes even more pessimistic feelings about what he is doing, (and likewise) what America is doing. "No word," "no chow" and "no heels" expresses how ineffectual they are being. I can almost hear him add "no sense" as well. The reader is sucked into his frustration as he talks about blisters torn clothing, jungle rot and forced marches. How can we not empathize with him?

He tries to lighten things with a bit of comic relief about meals of peanut butter and coffee, but soon we realize that a daily diet of this is as bad as blisters and forced marches. Soon, however, even this attempt at humor is replaced by more frustration when he talks about his squadron's inability to effectively do much against the VC's. In fact, he implies that Charley seems not to have a care in the world until he sees the Americans. An inconsequential firefight settles nothing. The power of his description—the ridiculous battle with the snipers, expending $50,000 to no effect; throwing everything but the Missouri at the enemy—shows just how hopeless his situation is. All their efforts seem to have accomplished he says, almost as an aside, was to wake up a sleeping Marine sentry. (Perhaps if he had not been sleeping, there would have been no cause for a battle?)

By the end of the letter, Sandy may have realized that he has revealed too much of his emotion, frustration and even fear. He attempts a lighter mood by comparing the squadron to Indian Scouts. Instead of well-trained soldiers, however, it sounds like he's with a group of inept Cub Scouts who don't know what they are doing or even why they are doing it. Instead they manage to kill innocent bystanders and torch (innocent) houses. By now anyone reading this letter wants to scream and shout against such absurdity. The driving rain seems to be a metaphor for the driving futility of it all. Through his attempted humor, raw emotion, incredible imagery, clever sarcasm and total frustration, Sandy's short letter to his family is an outstanding example of anti-war sentiment. His last words are the most poignant, "I'm afraid" are his last words. The ultimate futility of it all, however, is my knowing that barely two months later, this sensitive, young man, just trying to do his duty, was killed. Dulce Et Decorum Est Pro Patria Mori. What a travesty.

Christina's Response

Sandy Kempner uses several stylistic and rhetorical techniques in this letter to his family. His tone is sarcastic and angry, and he uses humor, understatement, self-pity and incredibly strong imagery to make his anti-war statement.

At first this seems like a simple letter to his family. The nicknames he uses imply a strong affection for them. Soon, however, he becomes more serious, telling them about an "abortion" known as Operation Jackson. This is a well-chosen word, for what they were doing in Vietnam seemed to be all for nothing. He lists a number of sensations that show the severity of his mission. Sandy includes a number of negatives to emphasize the ineffectiveness of all their attempts. His diction is simple, but he makes it clear how bad things are as he talks about things like blisters and jungle rot.

He tries to use ironic humor as he tells his family about Marine Corps cuisine. Of course, cuisine is hardly an appropriate word for peanut butter and coffee. This just emphasizes his disgust with the whole operation. His squad has no luck with the VCs—it seems like he's telling a story, though, and he talks about the confrontation with the snipers as if he were describing some video game. In 1966, it would have been something like Pac Man. Even $50,000 dollars worth of ammunition, and everything but the kitchen sink (or the Missouri), the soldiers were unable to accomplish anything.

Finally he refers to his squadron as Indian Scouts—an apt metaphor. They seemed as ineffective as children running around in the dark not knowing what to do. He uses understatement when he mentions that they were "very successful"—of course success was killing innocents people and burning a few shacks—not much to brag about, that's for sure.

Sandy's letter is more than just a correspondence to his family. It is truly a statement that relates the horrors of war and his hopeless situation and the futility of their situation in Vietnam.

Commentary on Robert's Response

This student has obviously done some reading, and apparently has found at least a mild interest in war-related literature. In this instance, his additional interest and knowledge has aided his response. However, successful responses by students are often written by students who would not have had such a convenient reading background.

The prompt asks the student to analyze stylistic and rhetorical devices that are present in this letter from Vietnam, and how these devices reveal the writer's attitude toward his situation. In addition, the student must consider the value of this letter as a passage of anti-war sentiment. Looking at the scoring guide, this student has written an 8 essay. In fact, it may also garner some 9's from readers. Although some may criticize it as lacking extensive analysis, the total understanding of the letter and the techniques the writer has used are clearly evident. In addition, he has integrated this letter within the realm of war literature. He has done this so successfully, that there is no need for closer stylistic analysis.

The student's voice is very present in this response—a characteristic of very successful responses. No doubt other literature has also moved this student, and the way he as applied other literature to this piece makes this an exceptional response. The final Latin phrase, which is actually the title of the poem this student particularly liked reading, says it all—how sweet it is to give one's life to one's country—the ultimate irony of the original poem as well as of this letter from Vietnam.

Commentary on Christina's Response

Christina's response is adequate, but not as successful as Robert's. She covers the basics and addresses many of the stylistic devices that are found in this letter. She understands how the irony and dark humor help to make this writing far more than just a letter home.

She refers to the strategies both explicitly and implicitly, but her explanation of specifics is limited. The references she makes to specifics in the letter are appropriate but not extensive. This response tends to move through the letter, step by step, without a more global view. This response would probably garner a 6 from AP readers. It is more than a 5, for it is neither inconsistent nor uneven. Nor is it particularly weak in composition skills. This is truly an adequate response.

Essay Question II: Skin

Analysis of Essay Question II

Double passage questions are not unusual on the English Language and Composition exam. Many have been presented to students over the years. These have included two passages about the Oklahoma plains by Scott Momaday and D. Brown; two marriage proposals, one from Jane Austen, the other from Charles Dickens; two on the launching of the Sputnik satellite; two on the Galapagos Islands, one by Melville, the other by Darwin, and more recently, two descriptions of the Okeefenokee Swamp in Florida.

These questions require you to analyze the prose of each passage, paying particular attention to the techniques and stylistic devices each of the writers uses. In addition, you may be asked about the effect of each piece, the respective attitude of each author, the purpose of the pieces, etc.

The two passages on skin are similar to others that have appeared on the exam. The first passage, by Richard Selzer, a physician and writer, is poetic: he celebrates the skin he discusses. The second passage is more clinical and much more objective. Such passages are not difficult to understand or to analyze, but you must be able to answer the entire prompt—in this case analyze stylistic differences as well as discuss the purpose of each passage. Balancing these is sometimes tricky, and it is the expression of these ideas that separate OK writing from very good writing.

Scoring Guide for Question II

9   Essays meet all the criteria for 8 papers and in addition are especially full or apt in their analysis or demonstrate particularly impressive insight and/or stylistic control.

8   Essays effectively analyze how the differing styles of the two descriptions reveal each writer's purpose. They refer to the texts, directly or indirectly, assessing how selection and organization of detail, tone, point of view, syntax, and diction convey each writer's aim. Their prose demonstrates an ability to control a wide range of the elements of effective writing, but need not be flawless.

7   Essays fit the description of 6 essays but provide more complex analysis or demonstrate more mature prose style.

6   Essays clearly show the relationship between stylistic choice and purpose and adequately analyze that relationship. Referring to the texts, directly or indirectly, these essays compare the writers' use of specific stylistic elements in revealing purpose. A few lapses in diction or syntax may be present, but generally the prose of 6 essays demonstrates control of ideas and writing.

5   Essays analyze stylistic techniques, but their discussion of varying styles and purposes in the two passages is limited. They may treat techniques of style in a superficial way or develop ideas about purpose inconsistently. A few lapses in diction or syntax may be present, but usually the prose in 5 essays conveys the writers' ideas.

4   Essays inadequately respond to the question's tasks. They may misrepresent or merely touch on purpose, analyze stylistic elements inaccurately, or identify techniques without much development or understanding. The prose of 4 essays may convey the writers' ideas but may suggest immature control over organization, diction, or syntax.

3   Essays meet the criteria for the score of 4 but are less perceptive about how the techniques of style convey varying purposes, or are less consistent in controlling elements of writing.

2   Essays demonstrate little success in analyzing the stylistic elements that convey varying purposes in the two passages. They may lack development or substitute simpler tasks by summarizing passages or simply listing stylistic elements. They may misunderstand or ignore purpose. The prose of 2 papers often reveals consistent weaknesses in writing, such as a lack of development or organization, grammatical problems, or a lack of control.

1   Essays meet the criteria for the score of 2 but in addition are especially simplistic in their ideas or weak in their control of language.

Janah's Response

The skin on our bodies is an incredible and complex organ that has inspired extensive research and esthetic admiration from a wide range of people. The writers of these two passages on skin were both impressed with this organ; however, their purposes in writing about human skin were quite different. By analyzing the literary devices that each writer employs, we can see that the writer of the first passage intended to entertain his/her audience and celebrate the skin's amazing capacity while the author of the second passage meant to inform his audience in a straightforward manner.

The first line of Passage 1 reveals a great deal about the author's purpose in writing the selection. By using a simile "layered fine as baklava (comparing it to a delectable dessert), and a metaphor, "the scabbard upon which we are thrilled," in the introduction to the passage, the author indicated that his essay will be an ode to the skin, not an informative, scientific report.

The second paragraph of the first passage also provides evidence that the author's intent is to stir the reader's emotions. The entire paragraph is a rhetorical question, and it is filled with emotionally charged words such as "sensitive," and "flushes, pales and pains" that show the author's intense feelings for the skin. It is a reflection of who we are.

Although Passage I is chiefly a celebration of the skin, it is also informative. It does provide details about the skin, which are found in paragraphs 3 and 4. While describing the construction and life-cycles of the skin, however, the writer manages to present this information in an eloquent, graceful manner. He/she uses great imagery throughout, but it is particularly striking in the description of how the skin repairs itself—"the brigade breaks into a charge, fanning out laterally across the wound, racing to seal off the defect." Such an entrancing description captures the reader's imagination. The author manages to present information in an eloquent, graceful manner, and he even has a humorous tone when in line 40 he says, "Hurrah for stratified squamous epithelium." I say hurrah to this great writer.

While the author of passage I clearly intended for his/her essay to entertain and inspire, the author of passage 2 had a different purpose: to inform. This becomes apparent in the first paragraph of the selection in which the author supplies copious facts and figures pertaining to the skin. This is information more typical of a technical piece of writing.

Further proof that the writer of Passage 2's paramount goal was to inform is supplied by the author's style throughout the essay. By using straightforward, unornamented sentence construction, the author's tone in this passage is clinical and objective. It is clear from sentences such as those in paragraphs three and four that are devoted strictly to description and explanation of the skin's constructional and behavior that the writer's intent was entirely to inform the audience of the nature of the human skin.

In conclusion, both passages are very well written and stylized, but each is very different in presentation and effect upon the reader. It is clear that the author of Passage I intended to entertain as well as inform, while Passage 2's writer sought only to inform, and cared very little whether or not the reader was entertained or not.

Liz's Response

Who knew that two passages on skin could be so different? Passage 1 is amusing and poetic, and its purpose is to entertain, and as a second thought, educate. Passage 2, however, is just about education. These two passages reaveal their overall purposes with the use of language, rhetorical devices and style.

The language used in passage 1 is very poetic and descriptive, with some medical jargon thrown in. This is shown in the exclamation, "Hurrah for stratified squamous epithelium!" Passage 2, on the other hand, uses mostly simple language or straight medical terminology. The reader of passage one is to be entertained and maybe learn something. The reader of passage two is to be educated.

Passage 2 also uses no literary devices, a fact that contributes to its cold, clinical tone. In sharp contrast, Passage 1 uses similes, imagry and personification to illustrate the skin's importance and the biological processes it undergoes,.

Perhaps the biggest difference between the two passages is the style. Passage 1 is very poetic and makes the skin seem like a very beautiful thing, and the skin cells seem very heroic. Passage 2 is reminiscent of a biology textbook, and just delivers the facts in a cold, monotonous way. When I imagine these passages being read out loud, the first passage is accompanied by an interpretive dance and music, and is performed on stage. Passage is being read by a boring teacher in front of a sleepy class. Through the use of language, literary devices and style, both passages achieve their very different purposes in very different ways. "Hurrah for stratified squamus epithelium!" It sure beats "Each square centimeter has 6 million cells, 5,000 sensory points, 100 sweat glands and 15 sebaceous glands." Ick.

Abbot's response

Essays get written through the perspective of the author. Although this is no surprise, what is amazing is that so many essays can be written about the same thing. In these two essays about skin, you can see two very different ways of talking about the same thing. Passage 2 is your run of the mill scientific essay. Passage 1, however, manages to take the same topic, skin, and romanticize it in an almost poetic essay.

Passage 2 serves to inform and educate. This is evident from the beginning with all the details—"20% of the body weight, 100 sweat glands, 5000 sensory points and 15 sebaceous glands." There's nothing romantic there; this author gets right to the point.

Passage 1 speaks almost fondly of the skin. The diction in this passage is full of emotion, and the author sounds almost enthusiastic as he writes. Lots of imagery is used and even a bible allusion. This is truly a more poetic presentation than the straightforward (boring) passage 2.

Overall, the possibilities for an essay are endless. It's all up to the author. These two passages show how 2 people can write very differently on the very same topic. Passage one almost inspires the reader while passage two educates (or puts the reader to sleep).

Commentary on Janah's Response

Janah has responded to the double passage in block format. That is, she discusses one passage and then discusses the other passage. Overall, she is successful with her response. She does not discuss all the stylistic devices that make the first passage sing, she has focused on those that seem to have impressed her the most, using examples from the text and more than a touch of her own voice as well. The mention of baklava and the skin as delectable as a dessert is a nice touch. Also, her personal aside about "Hurrah to the writer" might be considered by some as too much, but she seems to be celebrating the writer (Richard Selzer) as much as the writer celebrates skin.

Just as the second passage slows down and is more objective, so too is Janah's response. She correctly discusses the informative, objective nature of the second passage in her own, informative, objective manner. Perhaps inadvertently Janah's own writing parallels the shift between the two passages.

Readers would have no trouble awarding this response with a 7 and I am sure that many would also vote for a score of 8. This would not be an 8 almost a 9, but an 8 just a bit better than a 7. Remember, each number of the scoring guide can have within it a great number of responses that garner the same score. Think of the difference between a B- and a B+. One score is a squeak above a C while the other score is just shy of an A. In either case, 7 or 8, Janah has done a more than adequate job of responding to the prompt and the two passages.

Commentary on Liz's Response

This response is a 5. There's no doubt about it. Liz understands the passage. She says all the right things. It's just that she *says* too much but doesn't *show* us enough. Her identification of some of the stylistic devices is accurate, it's just that she does not do enough with what she says.

It is the last paragraph of Liz's response that makes this a 5 and not a 4. There is just enough personal reaction here to give us a real sense of Liz's understanding of the passages and their intent. This is a student response that readers wish the student could rewrite for a higher grade. The potential is evident, but the essay does not have enough depth to reach beyond a score of a 5.

Commentary on Abbot's Response

At first you might think that this is a 4 response. Reread the description of a 4 paper, then read the description for a 3. This paper has some 4 characteristics, but is truly less perceptive. It seems that Abbot understands the most obvious differences between the impact of the two passages, but there is uncertainty in what he says. He uses the qualifier "almost" as if he's just taking a stab at a response rather than being sure of what he wants to say.

Abbot's response to this question would be scored a 3.

Essay Question III: Quindlen

Analysis of Essay Question III

You may have seen Anna Quindlen's face in *Newsweek*, where she is a regular contributor. In 1999 Anna Quindlen was the keynote speaker at the commencement exercises at Mt. Holyoke College. Doubtlessly, some of her listeners were a bit surprised by what they heard. They had just spent four years working toward achieving what some of them would consider the perfect life. Now this speaker is spoiling it all by telling them to stop being perfect. Who invited her to speak, anyway?

This message to those graduates in 1999 could easily be repeated in 2006. Nevertheless, it is a startling concept for many to grasp. Moreover, this passage presents a challenge as well. You must first understand just what it is she is saying. Then you have to move outside of your 16 or 17 year-old self and try to grasp the message from her perspective. This is truly a challenge. For years we have been striving to be the best, just look, we're AP students studying extra hard to get that 5 score, aren't we? How dare anyone tell us that we've got it all wrong. You will have to reserve your frustration as you read through her message and try to decipher the bigger picture.

You will see by the student responses that follow, that both of these students have made an attempt to do what the prompt asks of them. Neither is brilliant, but each has the right idea—sort of. Take a look at the following scoring guide and responses and judge for yourself.

Scoring Guide for Question III

9   Essays meet all of the criteria for 8 papers, and in addition, are especially full or apt in their analysis or demonstrate particularly impressive composition skills.

8   Essays successfully analyze the rhetorical and stylistic strategies that Quindlen employs to convey her attitude and message to graduates about the importance of their not being perfect. They refer to the passage directly or indirectly and explain convincingly how specific strategies such as imagery, tone and figurative language contribute to an understanding of the writer's attitude. Their prose controls a wide range of effective writing, but is not flawless.

7   Essays fit the description of 6 essays but employ more complete analysis or demonstrate a more mature prose style.

6   Essays adequately analyze how the stylistic devices the speech employs to reveal the speaker's attitude and her message to the graduates about not being perfect. They refer to the passage directly or indirectly, and they recognize the narrator's attitude and how she conveys it by utilizing strategies such as choice of detail, tone, and figurative language. A few lapses in diction or syntax may be present, but generally the prose of 6 essays is clear.

5   Essays analyze Quindlen's rhetorical techniques, but the explanation of how those techniques lead to understanding Quindlen's attitude is limited or too simplistic. These essays may treat techniques superficially or develop ideas about the narrator's attitude inconsistently. A few lapses in diction or syntax may appear, but the prose in these essays usually conveys the writers' ideas adequately.

4   Essays inadequately respond to the task of the prompt. They may misrepresent the writer's attitude or analyze rhetorical strategies inaccurately or with little understanding of how strategies reveal his attitude toward the war. Often the prose of these essays suggests immature control over organization, diction, or syntax.

3   Essays meet the criteria for the score of 4 but are less perceptive about how rhetorical strategies convey attitude or are less consistent in controlling the elements of writing.

2   Essays are unsuccessful in analyzing how stylistic strategies convey the speaker's message to the graduates. These essays tend to pay little or cursory attention the specific features, and they may generalize, or simplify attitude and tone. They may simply paraphrase or comment on the passage without analyzing technique. The prose of 2 papers often reveals consistent weaknesses in writing, such as a lack of development or organization, grammatical problems, or a lack of control.

1   Essays meet the criteria for the score of 2 but are especially simplistic in their discussion or weak in controlling elements of language

Tran's Response

> Quindlen instructs the graduates to look at their finger tips. Just as each one has its own unique design, different from all others, so too should each of us have our own unique design, not one that we have copied from someone else. This is the main point of Quindlen's speech. As Polonius instructed his son Laertes in Hamlet, "To thine own self be true." I am sure that Ms Quindlen would agree.

Quindlen utilizes a no-fail opening—she identifies with the students; she uses the phrase "for people like us." That is a sure way to get her audience to pay attention to her. On top of that, she compliments her audience (as well as herself) by telling them they are "smart and ambitious and interested in the world and in its good opinion." Who would not be taken in by such flattery? However, she complicates things by using the word "perfect." Upon consideration, the reader/listener realizes that she is not referring to a "perfect" size 6 nor a "perfect" quarterback, nor a "perfect" GPA. What she is talking about is being the "perfect" imitator.

The footnote informs us that "zeitgeist" means the general spirit or characteristic of the times. Quindlen alludes to these characteristics shifting and altering, but the "perfect" person is tuned in for the latest change in trend and even anticipates some of these changes. This, she assures her listeners, may make you "perfect," but it also makes you totally not you.

She instructs us in the opening of paragraph 3 that the hardest work is to stop being perfect and to work instead to be yourself. I agree with her that this is more complicated, for there is no template for us to follow except the one that is inside each of us. We must look within ourselves, and not be swayed by the "easier" path to just follow the dictates of culture. Thoreau insisted that we march to our own drummer; Anna Quindlen warns us that this is a terrifying task to accomplish. If, we listen to that drummer (or to inner "music of our heart"), however, Quindlen assures us we will hear a "symphony," unlike the "jingles" of our culture.

American culture certainly is full of jingles, and it's way too easy for us to sing along with them instead of singing acapella. Anna Quindlen is correct, we must be brave, work hard (the hardest ever, according to her) and not be lead by the tinny music of cultural pied pipers. Instead, although it may sometimes be "unfashionable" we must dance to our own music, even if, sometimes, it's occasionally off-key. At least it will be our very own. By manipulating the listener with her opening, and pointing out some harsh but true realities in life, but never talking down to her audience, Ms Quindlen very effectively has, perhaps, given these about to graduate college students the toughest lesson they may ever learn.

Kyle's Response

Anna Quindlen seems to be telling the graduates at Holyoke College, and, I suppose, all of us, that being "perfect" is not being ourselves. We need to not follow the cultural tendencies, and take off all of our social masks and be our own person.

It is true that many people are caught up in wanting to be like everyone else. Why else do we see so many Brittany Spears wannabe's walking the halls of American middle and high schools. If we want to be popular and accepted, we often have to dress and act like others in order to find that acceptance. For some people, unfortunately, this "fitting in" controls their lives.

On the other hand, it is important sometimes to "fit in" in order to get ahead. If you want to become a partner in a law firm, then you have to wear certain clothes, attend certain parties and work far more billable hours than is possible. That is part of the American success story. Of course, this too can be a problem, as seen in "Death of a Salesman" when Willy Lowman tries to do all the right things, or, as Quindlen would say, to "be perfect" but it doesn't work. Eventually this failure causes his suicide.

Some of the trends that Quindlen seems to object to, "where khakis, pierce your navel, bare your soul" are simply part of growing up. As a person passes through stages in their life, they also go through phases. Most of them they grow out of. Some of them they just adapt as their own. According to Quindlen, this adaptation is part of "being perfect." She encourages us to NOT be perfect but to find ourselves. Overall this is a good philosophy, but if a person finds that certain "tinny music" or an occasional "mask" or even a "traditional notion" doesn't clash with his or her beliefs, then what harm can there be in it?

Overall Anna Quindlen has a good message for these graduates. Maybe it's easier for her to make these statements since she is, apparently older than her audience, and has experienced more in her life. I commend her for her philosophy, but perhaps, she needs to remember that one size does not fit all.

Commentary on Tran's response

Revisit the prompt. It tells you to write an essay in which you define the central argument of the passage and evaluate the validity of Quindlen's argument. Tran has done just that.

First he talks about Quindlen's clever manipulation of her audience by identifying with them as well as flattering them—a clever and probably successful approach on Quindlen's part. Tran goes on to qualify exactly what he sees—her message is about being perfect.

Zeitgeist is discussed as an essential element for "perfect" people, and why not having a plan or direction is the hardest thing about not being perfect. He goes on to discuss the analogy of music—symphonies and jingles and the need for us to sing our own tune. Although there is not specific mention of metaphor, simile, imagery, etc., Tran has certainly covered these stylistic devices within the speech. Finally, he concludes with a strong statement about the effectiveness of this passage.

Tran's response falls between a 6 and an 8. It is better than simply adequate. He covers everything the prompt requires of him, but there is neither flash nor particularly clever insight nor even a very extensive discussion about the "how" of her speech. Most of his essay is about the "what" of the speech. Reviewing the scoring guide, you will find that a score of 7 says that these essays fit the description of 6 essays but employ more complete analysis or demonstrate a more mature prose style. His answer is more than adequate, but doesn't quite make it into the 8 category. It is a very strong 7 response.

Commentary on Kyle's Response

Kyle has written a classic 5 essay. It has flashes of really good points, and then it reverts to the commonplace. His writing is good, but not as consistent as Tran's.

Kyle does what so many students do. He has latched on to the most obvious detail of the passage— the idea of fitting in, and that becomes the focus of his essay. Anna Quindlen's speech really was not about students wearing just the right Abercrombie and Fitch shirt. There's much more to it than that. That is only a small piece of a much bigger and more important message.

There is nothing wrong with disagreeing with the ideas of an author. In fact the prompt tells you to identify the main idea and comment on the validity of the argument. Nevertheless, Kyle's objections seem a bit shallow. He says that a certain amount of this need to fit in is part of growing up, phases people go through. Anna Quindlen is not denying that. What she is telling the graduates is that now it is time to put away these childish phases and become your own person.

Rather than presenting a good defense for his point of view, Kyle tends to rely on a less mature approach—of course she's older, she would feel that way, and so on. In addition, his composition skills are not strong enough to warrant an upper-half score. Although an occasional spelling error is not held against a student, it is important that you spell as correctly as you can, and if you are using a direct quotation you should attempt to get all the words you are copying spelled correctly ("where khakis"). Reviewing the description of a 5 response you will see that is the appropriate score for Kyle's essay.

Practice Test 2 Answer Grid

Before taking this practice test, find a quiet place where you can work uninterrupted for about three hours. Make sure you have a comfortable desk, several No. 2 pencils, and a few ballpoint pens.

The practice test includes a multiple-choice section and a free-response question. Use the answer grid to record your multiple-choice answers. Write the essays on the pages provided; use additional sheets if needed.

Once you start the test, don't stop until you've finished, except for a 10-minute break between the multiple-choice and essay sections. The answer key and explanations follow the test.

Good luck!

1. Ⓐ Ⓑ Ⓒ Ⓓ Ⓔ
2. Ⓐ Ⓑ Ⓒ Ⓓ Ⓔ
3. Ⓐ Ⓑ Ⓒ Ⓓ Ⓔ
4. Ⓐ Ⓑ Ⓒ Ⓓ Ⓔ
5. Ⓐ Ⓑ Ⓒ Ⓓ Ⓔ
6. Ⓐ Ⓑ Ⓒ Ⓓ Ⓔ
7. Ⓐ Ⓑ Ⓒ Ⓓ Ⓔ
8. Ⓐ Ⓑ Ⓒ Ⓓ Ⓔ
9. Ⓐ Ⓑ Ⓒ Ⓓ Ⓔ
10. Ⓐ Ⓑ Ⓒ Ⓓ Ⓔ
11. Ⓐ Ⓑ Ⓒ Ⓓ Ⓔ
12. Ⓐ Ⓑ Ⓒ Ⓓ Ⓔ
13. Ⓐ Ⓑ Ⓒ Ⓓ Ⓔ
14. Ⓐ Ⓑ Ⓒ Ⓓ Ⓔ
15. Ⓐ Ⓑ Ⓒ Ⓓ Ⓔ
16. Ⓐ Ⓑ Ⓒ Ⓓ Ⓔ
17. Ⓐ Ⓑ Ⓒ Ⓓ Ⓔ
18. Ⓐ Ⓑ Ⓒ Ⓓ Ⓔ

19. Ⓐ Ⓑ Ⓒ Ⓓ Ⓔ
20. Ⓐ Ⓑ Ⓒ Ⓓ Ⓔ
21. Ⓐ Ⓑ Ⓒ Ⓓ Ⓔ
22. Ⓐ Ⓑ Ⓒ Ⓓ Ⓔ
23. Ⓐ Ⓑ Ⓒ Ⓓ Ⓔ
24. Ⓐ Ⓑ Ⓒ Ⓓ Ⓔ
25. Ⓐ Ⓑ Ⓒ Ⓓ Ⓔ
26. Ⓐ Ⓑ Ⓒ Ⓓ Ⓔ
27. Ⓐ Ⓑ Ⓒ Ⓓ Ⓔ
28. Ⓐ Ⓑ Ⓒ Ⓓ Ⓔ
29. Ⓐ Ⓑ Ⓒ Ⓓ Ⓔ
30. Ⓐ Ⓑ Ⓒ Ⓓ Ⓔ
31. Ⓐ Ⓑ Ⓒ Ⓓ Ⓔ
32. Ⓐ Ⓑ Ⓒ Ⓓ Ⓔ
33. Ⓐ Ⓑ Ⓒ Ⓓ Ⓔ
34. Ⓐ Ⓑ Ⓒ Ⓓ Ⓔ
35. Ⓐ Ⓑ Ⓒ Ⓓ Ⓔ
36. Ⓐ Ⓑ Ⓒ Ⓓ Ⓔ

37. Ⓐ Ⓑ Ⓒ Ⓓ Ⓔ
38. Ⓐ Ⓑ Ⓒ Ⓓ Ⓔ
39. Ⓐ Ⓑ Ⓒ Ⓓ Ⓔ
40. Ⓐ Ⓑ Ⓒ Ⓓ Ⓔ
41. Ⓐ Ⓑ Ⓒ Ⓓ Ⓔ
42. Ⓐ Ⓑ Ⓒ Ⓓ Ⓔ
43. Ⓐ Ⓑ Ⓒ Ⓓ Ⓔ
44. Ⓐ Ⓑ Ⓒ Ⓓ Ⓔ
45. Ⓐ Ⓑ Ⓒ Ⓓ Ⓔ
46. Ⓐ Ⓑ Ⓒ Ⓓ Ⓔ
47. Ⓐ Ⓑ Ⓒ Ⓓ Ⓔ
48. Ⓐ Ⓑ Ⓒ Ⓓ Ⓔ
49. Ⓐ Ⓑ Ⓒ Ⓓ Ⓔ
50. Ⓐ Ⓑ Ⓒ Ⓓ Ⓔ
51. Ⓐ Ⓑ Ⓒ Ⓓ Ⓔ
52. Ⓐ Ⓑ Ⓒ Ⓓ Ⓔ
53. Ⓐ Ⓑ Ⓒ Ⓓ Ⓔ
54. Ⓐ Ⓑ Ⓒ Ⓓ Ⓔ

Practice Test 2

Section I: Multiple-Choice Questions

Time: 1 hour
Number of questions: 54
Percent of total grade: 45%

<u>Directions:</u> This section contains selections from prose works with questions on their content, style, form, structure, and purpose. Read each selection. Then read each question, choosing the best of the five responses that follow. Fill in each oval with the correct answer, checking to be sure the number of the question corresponds to the number on the answer sheet.

Questions 1–14. Read the following essay carefully before responding to the questions.

Since the afternoon in 1967 when I first saw Hoover Dam, its image has never been entirely absent from my inner eye. I will be driving down
Line Sunset Boulevard, or about to enter a freeway, and
(5) abruptly those power transmission towers will appear before me, canted vertiginously over the tailrace. Sometimes I am confronted by the intakes and sometimes by the shadow of the heavy cable that spans the canyon and sometimes by the
(10) ominous outlets to unused spillways, black in the lunar clarity of the desert light. Quite often I hear the turbines. Frequently I wonder what is happening at the dam this instant, at this precise intersection of time and space, how much water is
(15) being released to fill downstream orders and what lights are flashing and which generators are in full use and which just spinning free.

I used to wonder what it was about the dam that made me think of it at times and in places where I
(20) once thought of the Mindanao Trench, or of the stars wheeling in their courses, or of the words *As it was in the beginning, is now and ever shall be, world without end, amen.* Dams, after all, are commonplace: we have all seen one. This
(25) particular dam had existed as an idea in the work's mind for almost forty years before I saw it. Hoover Dam, showpiece of the Boulder Canyon project, the several million tons of concrete that made the Southwest plausible, the *fait accompli* that was to
(30) convey, in the innocent time of its construction, the notion that mankind's brightest promise lay in American engineering.

Of course the dam derives some of its emotional effect from precisely that aspect, that sense of
(35) being a monument to a faith since misplaced. "They died to make the desert bloom," reads a plaque dedicated to the ninety-six men who died building this first of the great high dams, and in context the worn phrase touches, suggests all of
(40) that trust in harnessing resources, the meliorative power of the dynamo, so central to the early Thirties. Boulder City, built in 1931 as the construction town for the dam, retains the

ambience of a model city, a new town, a toy
(45) triangular grid of green lawns and trim bungalows, all fanning out from the Reclamation building. The bronze sculptures at the dam itself evoke muscular citizen of tomorrow that never came, sheaves of wheat clutched heavenward,
(50) thunderbolts defied. Winged Victories guard the flagpole. The flag whips in the canyon wind. The empty Pepsi-Cola can clatters across the terrazzo. The place is perfectly frozen in time.

But history does not explain it all, does not
(55) entirely suggest what makes that dam so affecting. Nor, even, does energy, the massive involvement with power and pressure and the transparent sexual overtones to that involvement. Once when I revisited the dam I walked through it with a man
(60) from the Bureau of Reclamation. Once in a while he would explain something, usually in that recondite language having to do with "peaking power," with "outages" and "dewatering," but on the whole we spent the afternoon in a world so
(65) alien, so complete and so beautiful unto itself that it was scarcely necessary to speak at all. We saw almost no one. Cranes moved above us as if under their own volition. Generators roared. Transformers hummed. The gratings on which we stood
(70) vibrated. We watched a hundred-ton steel shaft plunging down to that place where the water was. And finally we got down to that place where the water was, where the water sucked out of Lake Mead roared through thirty-foot penstocks and
(75) then into thirteen-foot penstocks and finally into the turbines themselves.

There was something beyond all that, something beyond energy, beyond history, something I could not fix in my mind. When I came up from the dam
(80) that day the wind was blowing harder, through the canyon and all across the Mojave, but out at the dam there was no dust, only the rock and the dam and a little greasewood and a few garbage cans, their tops chained banging against a fence. I
(85) walked across the marble star map that traces a sidereal revolution of the equinox and fixes

GO ON TO THE NEXT PAGE ⟶

Test Prep and Admissions

forever, the Reclamation man had told me, for all time and for all people who can read the stars, the date the dam was dedicated. The star map was, he
(90) had said, for when we were all gone and the dam was left. I had not thought much of it when he said it, but I thought of it then, with the wind whining and the sun dropping behind a mesa with the finality of a sunset in space. Of course that was the
(95) image I had seen always seen it without quite realizing what I saw, a dynamo finally free of man, splendid at last in its absolute isolation, transmitting power and releasing water to a world where no one is.
(100)   From "At the Dam" by Joan Didion

1. The overall tone of this passage can best be described as

(A) regretfully reminiscent
(B) philosophically introspective
(C) whimsically lighthearted
(D) anxiously foreboding
(E) hesitantly guileful

2. The opening sentence serves the purpose of

   I. illustrating the topic of the essay
   II. demonstrating that the narrator's experience has remained with her
   III. comparing this experience to an earlier one the narrator has had

(A) I only
(B) II only
(C) II and III
(D) I and II
(E) I, II, and III

3. Paragraph two, lines 18–32, makes reference to all of the following EXCEPT

(A) a national symbol
(B) religious allusion
(C) foreign terminology
(D) regional hyperbole
(E) understated importance

4. Throughout this passage the narrator utilizes

(A) pathos
(B) deductive reasoning
(C) logic
(D) ethos
(E) definition

5. The narrator's view of the dam in contrast to her view of the world can best be described as

(A) mechanistic : human
(B) confined : spacious
(C) hopeful : damaged
(D) optimistic : pessimistic
(E) commonplace : significant

6. Lines 68–70 "Generators roared . . . vibrated" have all of the following EXCEPT

(A) imagery
(B) onomatopoeia
(C) parallel syntax
(D) nostalgic description
(E) simple sentences

7. The underlying purpose of this passage seems to be to

(A) explain the hypnotic spell the dam seems to have on the narrator
(B) express the importance and somewhat mystical beauty of the Hoover Dam
(C) describe the purpose of the dam and the work that went into its construction
(D) explain how the dam operates and its importance to the Southwest United States
(E) articulate the narrator's fascination with the dam as well as her reverence for its power

GO ON TO THE NEXT PAGE

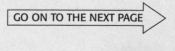

8. "The star map was, he said, for when we were all gone and the dam was left," lines 89–91, reinforces which of the following statements?

   (A) " . . . something beyond energy, beyond history . . ."

   (B) " . . . muscular citizens of tomorrow . . ."

   (C) "The place is frozen in time."

   (D) "We saw almost no one."

   (E) "This particular dam had existed as an idea in the world's mind for almost forty years. . . ."

9. In the context of this passage, the phrase "canted vertiginously," line 6, most closely means

   (A) aligned fearfully

   (B) presented awfully

   (C) angled dizzyingly

   (D) chanting comfortably

   (E) appearing disgustedly

10. The first sentence of the fifth paragraph, lines 77–79, contains the specific rhetorical device known as

   (A) anaphora

   (B) simile

   (C) connotation

   (D) personification

   (E) repetition

11. As the passage comes to a close it establishes a feeling that can best be described as

   (A) mystifying

   (B) surprised

   (C) baffled

   (D) celebratory

   (E) haunting

12. The sentence beginning "Nor, even, does energy, the massive involvement with power" (lines 56–58) can be identified as having or being all of the following EXCEPT

   (A) a sentence fragment

   (B) alliteration

   (C) apposition

   (D) a compound sentence

   (E) negation

13. The narrator most likely emphasizes the toy-like layout of the city in order to stress the idea that

   (A) the people of that time had little imagination

   (B) budget restraints kept the city simple in design

   (C) this was a planned city built for a pragmatic purpose

   (D) to minimalize the city in contrast to the greatness of the dam

   (E) the bronze sculptures and Winged Victory are more important than the town

14. Considering the passage, the narrator seems to be amazed by which of the following ideas?

   (A) Hoover Dam is truly one of the great wonders of the world.

   (B) What it took so many men to build no longer needs any human beings.

   (C) Hoover Dam has proven to be truly the salvation of the Southwest.

   (D) The Dam is able to convert the water from Lake Mead into energy and power.

   (E) Visitors to the Dam can learn history, politics, and physics all in one trip.

GO ON TO THE NEXT PAGE

Questions 15–27. Read the following essay carefully before responding to the questions.

He who lets the world, or his own portion of it, choose his plan of life for him, has no need of any other faculty than the ape-like one of imitation.
Line He who chooses his plan for himself, employs all
(5) his faculties. He must use observation to see, reason and judgment to foresee, activity to gather materials for decision, discrimination to decide, and when he has decided, firmness and self-control to hold to his deliberate decisions. And
(10) these qualities he requires and exercises exactly in proportion as the part of his conduct which he determines according to his judgment and feelings is a large one. It is possible that he might be guided in some good path, and kept out of harm's way,
(15) without any of these things. But what will be his comparative worth as a human being? It really is of importance, not only what men do, but also what manner of men they are that do it. Among the works of man, which human life is rightly
(20) employed in performing a beautifying, the first in importance surely is man himself. Supposing it were possible to get houses built, corn grown, battles fought, causes tried, and even churches erected and prayers said, by machinery—by
(25) automations in human form—it would be a considerable loss to exchange for these automatons even the men and women who at present inhabit the more civilized parts of the world, and who assuredly are but starved specimens of what nature
(30) can and will produce. Human nature is not a machine to be built after a model, and set to do exactly the work prescribed for it, but a tree, which requires to grow and develop itself on all sides, according to the tendency of the inward forces
(35) which make it a living thing.

It will probably be conceded that it is desirable people should exercise their understandings, and that an intelligent following of custom, or even occasionally an intelligent deviation from custom,
(40) is better than a blind and simply mechanical adhesion to it. To a certain extent it is admitted that our understanding should be our own: but there is not the same willingness to admit that our desires and impulses should be our own likewise;
(45) or that to possess impulses of our own, and of any strength, is anything but a peril and a snare. Yet desires and impulses are as much a part of a perfect human being as beliefs and restraints: and strong impulses are only perilous when not
(50) properly balanced; when one set of aims and inclinations is developed into strength, while others, which ought to co-exist with them, remain weak and inactive. It is not because men's desires are strong and they act ill: it is because their
(55) consciences are weak; there is no natural connection between strong impulses and a weak conscience; the natural connection is the other way. To say that one person's desires and feelings are stronger and more various than those of
(60) another, is merely to say that he has more of the raw material of human nature, and is therefore capable, perhaps of more evil, but certainly of more good. Strong impulses are but another name for energy. Energy may be termed to bad uses; but
(65) more good may always be made of an energetic nature, than of an indolent and impassive one.

Those who have most natural feeling are always those whose cultivated feelings may be made the strongest. The same strong susceptibilities which
(70) make the personal impulses vivid and powerful, are also the source from whence are generated the most passionate love of virtue, and the sternest self-control. It is through the cultivation of these that society both does its duty and protects its
(75) interests: not by rejecting the stuff by which heroes are made, because it knows not how to make them. A person whose desires and impulses are his own is said to have a character. One whose desires and impulses are not his own, has no character, no
(80) more than a steam engine has character. If, in addition to being his own, his impulses are strong, and are under the government of a strong will, he has an energetic character. Whoever thinks that individuality of desires and impulses should not be
(85) encouraged to unfold itself, must maintain that society has no need of strong natures—is not the

GO ON TO THE NEXT PAGE ⟩

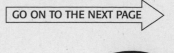

better for containing many persons who have much character—and that a high general average of energy is not desirable.

(90)   In some early states of society, these forces might be, and were, too much ahead of the power which society then possessed of disciplining and controlling them. There has been a time when the element of spontaneity and individuality was in

(95) excess, and the social principle had a hard struggle with it. The difficulty then was to induce men of strong bodies or minds to pay obedience to any rules which required them to control their impulses. To overcome this difficulty, law and

(100) discipline, like the Popes struggling against the Emperors, asserted a power over the whole man, claiming to control all his life in order to control his character—which society had not found any other sufficient means of binding. But society has

(105) now fairly got the better of individuality: and the danger which threatens human nature is not the excess, but the deficiency, of personal impulses and preferences. Things are vastly changed since the passion of those who were strong by station or by

(110) personal endowment were in a state of habitual rebelling against laws and ordinances, and required to be rigorously chained up to enable the persons within their reach to enjoy any particle of security. In our times, from the highest class of

(115) society down to the lowest, every one lives as under the eye of a hostile and dreaded censorship. Not only in what concerns others, but in what concerns only themselves, the individual or the family do not ask themselves—what do I prefer?

(120) Or, what would suit my character and disposition: or, what would allow the best and highest in me to have fair play and enable it to grow and thrive? They ask themselves, what is suitable to my position, what is usually done by persons of my

(125) station and pecuniary circumstances? Or (worse still) what is usually done by persons of a station and circumstances superior to mine? I do not mean that they choose what is customary in preference to what suits their own inclination. It

(130) does not occur to them to have any inclination

except for what is customary. Thus the mind itself is bowed to the yoke: they like in crowds; they exercise choice only among things commonly done: peculiarity of taste, eccentricity of conduct,

(135) are shunned equally with crimes: until by dint of not following their own nature they have no nature to follow: their human capacities are withered and starved: they become incapable of any strong wishes or native pleasures, and are

(140) generally without either opinions or feelings of home growth, or properly their own, Now this, or is it not, the desirable condition of human nature?

From *Of Individuality* by John S. Mill

15.   The main idea of this passage can best be summarized as which of the following?

(A) It is best to let the world choose our plan of life.

(B) If life chooses for us, it is possible that we may be guided in some good path.

(C) Automatons really could take care of all of our tasks.

(D) We must be nurtured and grow into our own person, not just copy others.

(E) We should exercise imitation and employ all our faculties in making decisions.

16.   "Human nature is not . . . living thing," lines 30–35, combines the following two stylistic devices?

(A) Metaphor and personification

(B) Simile and metaphor

(C) Personification and hyperbole

(D) Understatement and hyperbole

(E) Litote and metaphor

GO ON TO THE NEXT PAGE

KAPLAN
Test Prep and Admissions

17. Although the narrator encourages us to become ourselves and exercise personal understandings, he also cautions that

    (A) men's desires are often not very strong

    (B) strong impulses are dangerous because of their energy

    (C) individual energy can never be anything but good

    (D) strong impulses are really separate from individual conscience

    (E) energy must be carefully self-monitored to do good

18. The sentence "It is not because . . . the connection is the other way," lines 53–58, can be syntactically characterized as containing both a

    (A) run on sentence and parallelism

    (B) series of clauses and asyndeton

    (C) complex sentence and antithesis

    (D) compound sentence and parenthetical asides

    (E) compound-complex sentence and antithesis

19. In paragraphs two and three, the narrator makes all of the following points EXCEPT

    (A) strong impulses and a weak conscience have no natural connection

    (B) energy is a synonym for the concept "strong impulses"

    (C) despite his conscience, man's desires will cause him to act ill

    (D) one who has character is one whose desires and impulses are his own

    (E) society does not desire people with strong natures

20. In this passage, the writer compares society's struggle to "conquer" man's individuality with

    (A) man copying ape

    (B) an emperor fighting a pope

    (C) desire conquering conscience

    (D) impulse overriding logic

    (E) the Popes struggling against the Emperors

21. The stylistic discourse of the third paragraph, lines 67–89, can best be described as

    (A) hypothetical, idealistic speculation

    (B) personal reflection and observation

    (C) internal argumentation

    (D) emotional diatribe

    (E) theoretical query

22. The main point established by paragraph three can best be stated as which of the following?

    (A) Man must learn to control his impulses.

    (B) Censorship is the evil which man must avoid.

    (C) Society has overcome the best of man's personal impulses and preferences.

    (D) Society embraces the man who is able to think independently.

    (E) It is important for man not to have in libation contrary to what is customary

23. Paragraph four, lines 90–142, can best be described as

    (A) a diatribe against the power of the Pope

    (B) a celebration of man's independent spirit

    (C) a reaffirmation of the conformity of pleasure

    (D) an argument against man's instinct to please himself

    (E) a lament over the loss of personal impulses and preferences

GO ON TO THE NEXT PAGE

24. In the last sentence of paragraph three, lines 83–89, contains all of the following syntactical characteristics EXCEPT

    (A) series preceded by a colon

    (B) loose parallel structure

    (C) compound-complex structure

    (D) multiple use of verbs

    (E) a parenthetical insert

25. Within the context of the passage, lines 108–114, the sentence beginning "Things are vastly changed" can best be interpreted as meaning

    (A) people no longer have to fear for their personal security

    (B) habitual rebellions are no longer a problem in society

    (C) times have improved the prison situation

    (D) human nature has been tamed to submission

    (E) neither the poor nor the rich need worry about insurrection

26. The author of this essay would most likely agree with the following statements?

    I. Man must join the ranks of custom in order to get along.

    II. Man has succumbed to the dictates of society's norm.

    III. Society appreciates a man with a strong, energetic nature.

    IV. Indolent and impassive men are easier to manipulate than those with "energy."

    (A) I only

    (B) II and III

    (C) II and IV

    (D) I, III, and IV

    (E) I, II, and IV

27. In paragraph four, lines 90–142, the author is most concerned that

    (A) ultimately people will follow a path of behavior that best suits who they are

    (B) ultimately the Pope has the most power over the disciplining of man

    (C) upper class society people are more likely to "be themselves" than lower class people

    (D) social principal has a difficult time in overcoming man's natural tendency towards individuality and spontaneity

    (E) people will sacrifice what is best and natural for what is customary and appropriate

GO ON TO THE NEXT PAGE

Questions 28–40. Read the following passage carefully before responding to the questions.

Thomas Jefferson believed that to preserve the very foundations of our nation, we would need dramatic change from time to time. Well, my
Line fellow citizens, this is our time. Let us embrace it.
(5) Our democracy must be not only the envy of the world but the engine of our own renewal. There is nothing wrong with America that cannot be cured by what is right with America.

And so today, we pledge an end to the era of
(10) deadlock and drift—a new season of American renewal has begun.

To renew America, we must be bold.

We must do what no generation has had to do before. We must invest more in our own people, in
(15) their jobs, in their future, and at the same time cut our massive debt. And we must do so in a world in which we must compete for every opportunity.

It will not be easy; it will require sacrifice. But it can be done, and done fairly, not choosing sacrifice
(20) for its own sake, but for our own sake. We must provide for our nation the way a family provides for its children.

Our Founders saw themselves in the light of posterity. We can do no less. Anyone who has ever
(25) watched a child's eyes wander into sleep knows what posterity is. Posterity is the world to come—the world for whom we hold our ideals, from whom we have borrowed our planet, and to whom we bear sacred responsibility.
(30) We must do what America does best: offer more opportunity to all and demand responsibility from all.

It is time to break the bad habit of expecting something for nothing, from our government or
(35) from each other. Let us all take more responsibility, not only for ourselves and our families but for our communities and our country.

To renew America, we must revitalize our democracy.
(40) This beautiful capital, like every capital since the dawn of civilization, is often a place of intrigue and calculation. Powerful people maneuver for position and worry endlessly about who is in and

who is out, who is up and who is down, forgetting
(45) those people whose toil and sweat sends us here and pays our way.

Americans deserve better, and in this city today, there are people who want to do better. And so I say to all of us here, let us resolve to reform our
(50) politics, so that power and privilege no longer shout down the voice of the people. Let us put aside personal advantage so that we can feel the pain and see the promise of America.

Let us resolve to make our government a place
(55) for what Franklin Roosevelt called "bold, persistent experimentation," a government for our tomorrows, not our yesterdays.

Let us give this capital back to the people to whom it belongs.
(60) To renew America, we must meet challenges abroad as well at home. There is no longer division between what is foreign and what is domestic—the world economy, the world environment, the world AIDS crisis, the world arms race—they affect
(65) us all.

Today, as an old order passes, the new world is more free but less stable. Communism's collapse has called forth old animosities and new dangers. Clearly America must continue to lead the world
(70) we did so much to make.

While America rebuilds at home, we will not shrink from the challenges, nor fail to seize the opportunities, of this new world. Together with our friends and allies, we will work to shape
(75) change, lest it engulf us.

When our vital interests are challenged, or the will and conscience of the international community is defied, we will act—with peaceful diplomacy whenever possible, with force when
(80) necessary. The brave Americans serving our nation today in the Persian Gulf, in Somalia, and wherever else they stand are testament to our resolve.

But our greatest strength is the power of our
(85) ideas, which are still new in many lands. Across the world, we see them embraced—and we rejoice.

GO ON TO THE NEXT PAGE

Our hopes, our hearts, our hands, are with those on every continent who are building democracy and freedom. Their cause is America's cause.

(90)   The American people have summoned the change we celebrate today. You have raised your voices in an unmistakable chorus. You have cast your votes in historic numbers. And you have changed the face of Congress, the presidency and

(95) the political process itself. Yes, you, my fellow Americans have forced the spring. Now, we must do the work the season demands.

To that work I now turn, with all the authority of my office. I ask the Congress to join with me.

(100) But no president, no Congress, no government, can undertake this mission alone. My fellow Americans, you, too, must play your part in our renewal. I challenge a new generation of young Americans to a season of service—to act on your

(105) idealism by helping troubled children, keeping company with those in need, reconnecting our torn communities. There is so much to be done— enough indeed for millions of others who are still young in spirit to give of themselves in service, too.

(110)   In serving, we recognize a simple but powerful truth—we need each other. And we must care for one another. Today, we do more than celebrate America; we rededicate ourselves to the very idea of America.

(115)   An idea born in revolution and renewed through two centuries of challenge. An idea tempered by the knowledge that, but for fate, we— the fortunate and the unfortunate—might have been each other. An idea ennobled by the faith that

(120) our nation can summon from its myriad diversity the deepest measure of unity. An idea infused with the conviction that America's long heroic journey must go forever upward.

And so, my fellow Americans, at the edge of the

(125) twenty-first century, let us begin with energy and hope, with faith and discipline, and let us work until our work is done. The scripture says, "And let us not be weary in well-doing, for in due season, we shall reap, if we faint not."

(130)   From this joyful mountaintop of celebration, we hear a call to service in the valley. We have heard the trumpets. We have changed the guard. And now, each in our way, and with God's help, we must answer the call.

(135)   Thank you and God bless you all.
Inaugural address, William Clinton

28.   This inaugural speech opens using the stylistic technique of appealing to the audience's sense of

(A) intelligence

(B) humor

(C) patriotism

(D) sympathy

(E) empathy

29. "There is nothing wrong with America that cannot be cured by what is right with America," lines 6–8, sets up a contradiction that is known as

(A) paradox

(B) parallelism

(C) oxymoron

(D) absurdity

(E) allusion

30.   In lines 30–32, "We must do what America does best: offer more opportunity to all and demand responsibility from all," President Clinton utilizes the stylistic device known as

(A) apostrophe

(B) alliteration

(C) epistrophe

(D) anaphora

(E) allegory

GO ON TO THE NEXT PAGE ⟩

31. Paragraph 11 (lines 40–46) includes all of the following syntactical characteristics EXCEPT

    (A) a parenthetical statement
    (B) an independent clause series
    (C) a participial phrase
    (D) a compound verb
    (E) a compound sentence

32. The best interpretation of the phrase "a government for our tomorrows, not our yesterdays," lines 56–57, is that it refers to

    (A) looking to the past for guidance in government
    (B) a government that is based on tradition and values
    (C) looking to the future for inspiration in government
    (D) a government that is forward looking and adaptable
    (E) a government guided by the philosophy of strong leaders

33. The main stylistic characteristic of paragraph 12, lines 47–53, is

    (A) alliteration
    (B) assonance
    (C) asyndeton
    (D) parallel syntax
    (E) simple sentence structure

34. The phrase, "To renew America" is used throughout this passage as

    (A) a reminder to listeners
    (B) an exhortation and refrain
    (C) an opportunity to pause and think
    (D) a demonstration of the lack of speaker ingenuity
    (E) emphasis for a point

35. In lines 76–83, " . . . we will act—with peaceful diplomacy whenever possible, with force when necessary" is an example of the stylistic device known as

    (A) antithesis
    (B) oxymoron
    (C) hyperbole
    (D) zeugma
    (E) paradox

36. Considering the passage as a whole, the words "Yes, you, my fellow Americans have forced the spring" (lines 95–97) is best interpreted by which of the following?

    (A) Through force the American people have had their way.
    (B) America has retaliated in the best way they know how.
    (C) Through their vote, Americans have created a new season in government.
    (D) Spring is about to blossom in the Capital.
    (E) The government needs to have a spring like the city is experiencing.

37. Lines 84–89 contain all of the following EXCEPT

    (A) alliteration
    (B) assonance
    (C) anaphora
    (D) parallelism
    (E) ambiguity

GO ON TO THE NEXT PAGE

KAPLAN
Test Prep and Admissions

38. Within lines 98–109, "To that work I now turn, . . .
    to give of themselves in service, too," Clinton seems
    to be presenting what challenge?

    (A) Children in America need to become more
        informed about their government.

    (B) Troubled children in America must keep
        better company in their communities.

    (C) Everyone must take on part of the load of
        government by the people.

    (D) The new generation of Americans must reach
        out to children and adults in their
        community.

    (E) The new generation and those still young in
        spirit must do their share in their local
        communities.

39. Lines 115–123 contain all the following syntactical
    structures EXCEPT

    (A) fragmented sentences

    (B) parenthetical insertion

    (C) delayed subject

    (D) complex sentence structure

    (E) parallel structure

40. Clinton's overall tone within this speech is one of

    (A) optimism and encouragement

    (B) reference and hope

    (C) challenge and confrontation

    (D) supplication and pleading

    (E) patriotism and pandering

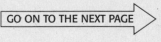
GO ON TO THE NEXT PAGE

Questions 41–54. Read the following essay carefully before responding to the questions.

Here was my soup. Dinner was being served in the great dining-hall. Far from being spring it was in fact an evening in October. Everybody was
Line assembled in the big dining-room. Dinner was
(5) ready. Here was the soup. It was a plain gravy soup. There was nothing to stir the fancy in that. One could have seen through the transparent liquid any pattern that there might have been on the plate itself. But there was no pattern. The plate was
(10) plain. Next came beef with its attendant greens and potatoes—a homely trinity, suggesting the rumps of cattle in a muddy market, and sprouts curled and yellowed at the edge, and bargaining and cheapening and women with string bags on
(15) Monday morning. There was no reason to complain of human nature's daily food, seeing that the supply was sufficient and coal-miners doubtless were sitting down to less. Prunes and custard followed. And if anyone complains that
(20) prunes, even when mitigated by custard, are an uncharitable vegetable (fruit they are not), stringy as a miser's heart and exuding a fluid such as might run in misers' veins who have denied themselves wine and warmth for eighty years and
(25) yet not given to the poor, he should reflect that there are people whose charity embraces even the prune. Biscuits and cheese came next, and here the water-jug was liberally passed round, for it is in the nature of biscuits to be dry, and these were biscuits
(30) to the core. That was all. The meal was over. Everybody scraped their chairs back; the swing-doors swung violently to and fro; soon the hall was emptied of every sign of food and made ready no doubt for breakfast next morning. Down corridors
(35) and up staircases the youth of England went banging and singing. And was it for a guest, a stranger, to say 'The dinner was not good,' or do say now that Mary and I are in her sitting room, 'Could we not have dined up here alone?' for if I
(40) had said anything of the kind I should have been prying and searching into the secret economies of a house which to the stranger wears so fine a front of gaiety and courage. No, one could say nothing

of the sort. Indeed, conversation for a moment
(45) flagged. The human frame being what it is, heart, body and brain all mixed together, and not contained in separate compartments as they will be no doubt in another million years, a good dinner is of great importance to good talk. One
(50) cannot think well, love well, sleep well, if one has not dined well. The lamp in the spine does not light on beef and prunes. We are all PROBABLY going to heaven, and Vandyck is, we HOPE, to meet us round the next corner—that is the
(55) dubious and qualifying state of mind that beef and prunes at the end of the day's work breed between them. Happily my friend, who taught science, had a cupboard where there was a squat bottle and little glasses—(but there should have been sole and
(60) partridge to begin with)—so that we were able to draw up to the fire and repair some of the damages of the day's living. In a minute or so we were slipping freely in and out among all those objects of curiosity and interest which form in the mind
(65) in the absence of a particular person, and are naturally to be discussed on coming together again—how somebody has married, another has not; one thinks this, another that; one has improved out of all knowledge, the other most
(70) amazingly gone to the bad—with all those speculations upon human nature and the character of the amazing world we live in which spring naturally from such beginnings. While these things were being said, however, I became
(75) shamefacedly aware of a current setting in of its own accord and carrying everything forward to an end of it own. The best course, unless the whole talk was to be distorted, was to expose what was in my mid to the air, when with good luck it would
(80) fade and crumble like the head of the dead king when they opened the coffin at Windsor. Briefly, then, I told Miss Seton about the masons who had been all those years on the roof of the chapel, and about the kings and queens and nobles bearing
(85) sacks of gold and silver on their shoulders, which they shoveled into the earth; and then how the

GO ON TO THE NEXT PAGE

great financial magnates of our own time came
and laid cheques and bonds, I suppose, where the
others had laid ingots and rough lumps of gold. All
(90) that lies beneath the colleges down there, I said;
but this college, where we are now sitting, what lies
beneath its gallant red brick and the wild unkempt
grasses of the garden? What force is behind that
plain china off which we dined, and (here it
(95) popped out of my mouth before I could stop it)
the beef, the custard and the prunes?

41. In the opening of the passage, the author best
reinforces the overall plainness of the meal by

(A) using simple words

(B) describing the undecorated plates

(C) utilizing a succession of simple sentences

(D) making the soup sound unappealing

(E) mentioning that her fancy was not stirred

42. The "homely trinity" and "muddy market," lines
11–12, are mentioned as

(A) an appeal to the common folk who might
read the passage

(B) an analogy for the beef, attendant greens, and
potatoes

(C) a simile for the meal being consumed

(D) an appeal to any reader who might be
religious

(E) a distraction for readers who find her
description too boring

43. The main point of the sentence about prunes, lines
19–27, is best stated in which of the following?

(A) Some people's charity is great enough even to
include prunes.

(B) Miser's hearts are often stringy.

(C) Wine and warmth cannot make up for
prunes.

(D) Misers do not have blood in their veins but
prune juice.

(E) If misers gave to the poor they would enjoy
warmth and wine.

44. The water jug was liberally passed around during
the meal because

(A) the prunes were stringy

(B) the beef was plain

(C) wine was not offered to drink

(D) the custard was gooey

(E) the biscuits were dry

45. "One cannot think well, love well, sleep well, if one
has not dined well," lines 49–51, utilizes a
syntactical structure (the opposite of anaphora)
known as

(A) juxtaposition

(B) epistrophe

(C) parallelism

(D) conditional contrast

(E) juxtaposition

46. As it is used in line 20, the word "mitigated" can
best be defined as

(A) moderated with

(B) lessened by

(C) replaced with

(D) accompanied by

(E) cancelled by

47. The use of capital letters in the sentence beginning
"We are all PROBABLY going to heaven," lines
52–57, might best be explained as signifying that

(A) the narrator is suffering a loss of faith

(B) the narrator is actually an agnostic

(C) we can never be sure who will also be in
heaven

(D) the narrator is always in a "dubious and
qualifying" state of mind

(E) beef and prunes can cause us to doubt
unnecessarily

GO ON TO THE NEXT PAGE

48. The attitude of the narrator towards the meal she experienced can best be described as one of

    (A) horror and revulsion
    (B) derision and amazement
    (C) disdain and annoyance
    (D) aloof superiority
    (E) disgusted surprise

49. The phrase " . . . so that we were able to draw up to the fire and repair some of the damages of the day's living," lines 60–62, can best be interpreted as which of the following?

    (A) We were able to build a fire and repair the logs that were disturbed in the fireplace.
    (B) We were able to draw conclusions as to what had gone wrong in our lives that day.
    (C) We were able to sit by the fireplace and rebuild the banked fire from the day before.
    (D) We were able to sit by the fire and undo the stress of our respective day.
    (E) We were able to sketch the fireplace and the damage done to the room that day.

50. In lines 52–62 the series of clauses connected by commas and semicolons rather than conjunctions demonstrates the syntactical structure of

    (A) polyphrasis
    (B) periodic sentence
    (C) simple sentence
    (D) anaphora
    (E) asyndeton

51. The best description of the tone in lines 77–81, the sentence beginning "The best course," would be

    (A) hesitant inquiry
    (B) modest curiosity
    (C) blatant bragging
    (D) subtle jibing
    (E) financial pedantry

52. The most likely purpose of the story about the masons at another school, line 81–89 to the end of the passage, is to

    (A) express empathy for the pathetic working environs of her friend
    (B) display historical background of this institute that she is visiting
    (C) explore the historical and financial basis of a nearby college
    (D) criticize her surroundings and let her friend know she's unhappy
    (E) retaliate for the terrible meal she has recently endured

53. The most probable overall purpose of this passage is to

    (A) complain about a bad meal eaten in a poor school.
    (B) make sure her friend knows that things are better elsewhere
    (C) console her friend for having to work under such conditions
    (D) lament the sad conditions of the school where her friend works
    (E) make a socio-political statement about the inequities within public education

54. The best description of the type of writing in this passage is

    (A) comparison and contrast
    (B) argumentation
    (C) personal reflection
    (D) political diatribe
    (E) whimsical narrative

IF YOU FINISH BEFORE TIME IS CALLED, YOU MAY CHECK YOUR WORK ON THIS SECTION ONLY. DO NOT TURN TO ANY OTHER SECTION IN THE TEST.

STOP

Section II

Total time—2 hours
Number of questions—3
Percent of total grade—55%

<u>**Directions:**</u> This section contains three essay questions. Answer all three questions, budgeting your time carefully. Each essay counts as one-third of your total essay score.

Question I
(Suggested time—40 minutes)

The following passage by Rick Reilly, humorous sports writer for Sports Illustrated, discusses the increasing incidence of sports on Sunday in lieu of religious worship. More specifically, he focuses on parents' involvement in their children's sports. In a well-written essay, analyze Reilly's concerns about children, and support, challenge, or qualify his conclusions.

Let Us ~~Pray~~ Play

Another Easter Sunday in the Cathedral. Hushed voices. Amens. People holding hands and praying. At the end, all of them rising as one and screaming, "My God, it's a miracle!" Church?

Line   No. Augusta National. It was Phil Mickelson's win at the Masters.

(5)   Sports has nearly swallowed Sunday whole. Every pro sport plays on Sunday. The big day in pro golf and tennis is Sunday. College football started playing bowl games on Sunday. Here's March Madness: 10 NCAA tournament games were played on Sunday. Now more and more youth sports teams are playing on Sunday, when the fields are easier to get and parents are available to drive.

(10)   It's that kind of stuff that has really torqued off Pope John Paul II lately. In March he decried the fact that Sundays are losing their "fundamental meaning" to "such things as entertainment and sport." It's not as if he's antijock. The pope was a goalkeeper, skier and kayaker in his day. Hey, he just blessed New England Patriots quarterback Tom Brady's right arm. He's just hacked at the way sport is crowding God right off the list of Sunday

(15) passions.

The first people he might want to crack down on are the Christians themselves. Think he knows that the Santa Clarita (Calif.) YMCA has youth hoops on Sundays? Think the pope would be down on Notre Dame if he knew its softball team will play more games on Sundays in May than on any other day of the week?

(20)   He's not the only one who's chapped about sports becoming this country's main religion. Priests and pastors across the country have noticed something lately: God is competing more and more with Sunday sports—and losing. Especially with youth sports.

"It's only happened the last two years," says Rich Cizik of the National Association of Evangelicals. "Coaches never used to schedule games on Sunday."

(25)   Says the Reverend Julie Yarborough of Summit (N.J.) Christ Church, "You see kids coming to Sunday school late and their parents coming early to get them for games—if they come at all. Sports is really eating into our time."

Her colleague at Christ Church, the Reverend Charles Rush, knew there was a problem the other day when his 12-year-old acolyte lit the candles at the front of the church

(30) wearing his soccer cleats.

I'll tell you exactly what's going on here: the upping of American youth sports.

For some reason overcaffeinated parents feel they have to *keep up* with the Joneses. They used to do it with their cars. Now they do it with their kids. Upping means putting little Justin into not one soccer league but three, not one soccer camp but four.

(35)   Upping also means *playing up,* forcing a kid to play one or even two levels above his age group, so that little Benjamin, age eight, can sit on the 10-year-olds' bench, play three minutes a game and whiff in his only at bat. But, hey, he *is* playing up!

And upping means *moving up*. The local team isn't high-profile, so little Amber has to switch to an elite team, usually in another town. That means extended drives to and from
(40) practice plus traveling three or four or six hours to play in tony *invitational* tournaments on weekends. This way parents from far-flung towns can flaunt the status symbol of spending beautiful warm weekends in a freezing ice rink watching 14 mind- and butt-numbing hockey games.

"I admit, we're guilty from time to time," John Burrill, head of the Massachusetts Youth
(45) Soccer Association, says of playing on Sundays. "We don't feel particularly good about it, but with today's busy schedules Sunday is the only time some of us have to do these things. And if you're going to travel two states away, it doesn't make sense to not play Sunday, too."

Well, religion bosses have decided that they're not going to take it anymore. Spiritual
(50) leaders in Summit got together recently and appealed for sports leagues to stop scheduling games before noon on Sunday. A meeting between them and area youth coaches is set for May. We'll see who kneels first.

Don't bet on coaches doing the right thing. If they could, they'd have your kids running stairs on Christmas morning. What has to happen is the parents have to start saying no.
(55) Not to their kids—to their kids' coaches. "I told my boy's coach he wouldn't be playing on Sundays," says Cizik, "and he looked shocked. I said, 'You act like nobody's ever said that to you before.' And he said, 'Honestly? They haven't.'"

I'm with the holy men. Not that I'm the Reverend Lovejoy, but I just feel sorry for these kids who get nothing but organized sports crammed down their gullets 24/7. My Lord,
(60) even God took a day off.

Kids might weep with joy to get a day off from sports. If they don't spend it at church, maybe they'll spend it getting to know their siblings' names again. Or swing in a hammock without a coach screaming, "Get your hips into it, Samantha!"

Hey, you do what you want. Just remember, when little Shaniqua has two free throws to
(65) win or lose a game on some Sunday morning, good luck finding somebody who'll answer your prayers.

April 26, 2004

Write Your Essay Here

Question II
(Suggested time—40 minutes)

In this narrative from *Incidents in the Life of a Slave Girl*, "Linda," whose name was actually Harriet Jacobs, comments on her experience teaching an old male slave (Uncle Fred) how to read and write. Read the passage carefully. Then write an essay in which you define the attitude the author has toward slavery and toward the double standard under which the white man lives.

There are thousands, who, like good Uncle Fred, are thirsting for the water of life; but the law forbids it, and the churches withhold it. They send the Bible to heathen abroad,
Line and neglect the heathen at home. I am glad that missionaries go out to the dark corners
(5) of the earth; but I ask them not to overlook the dark corners at home. Talk to American slaveholders as you talk to savages in Africa. Tell them it was wrong to traffic in men. Tell them it is sinful to sell their own children, and atrocious to violate their own daughters. Tell them that all men are brethren, and that man has no right to shut out the light of knowledge from his brother. Tell them they are answerable to God for sealing up the
(10) Fountain of Life from souls that are thirsting for it.

There are men who would gladly undertake such missionary work as this; but, alas! their number is small. They are hated by the south, and would be driven from its soil, or dragged to prison to die, as others have been before them. The field is ripe for the harvest, and awaits the reapers. Perhaps the great grandchildren of uncle Fred may have freely
(15) imparted to them the divine treasures, which he sought by stealth, at the risk of the prison and the scourge.

Are doctors of divinity blind, or are they hypocrites? I suppose some are the one, and some the other; but I think if they felt the interest in the poor and the lowly, that they ought to feel, they would not be so easily blinded. A clergyman who goes to the south, for
(20) the first time, has usually some feeling, however vague, that slavery is wrong. The slaveholder suspects this, and plays his game accordingly. He makes himself as agreeable as possible; talks on theology, and other kindred topics. The reverend gentleman is asked to invoke a blessing on a table loaded with luxuries. After dinner he walks round the premises, and sees the beautiful groves and flowering vines, and the comfortable huts of
(25) favored household slaves. The southerner invites him to talk with those slaves. He asks them if they want to be free, and they say, "O, no, massa." This is sufficient to satisfy him. He comes home to publish a "South Side View of Slavery," and to complain of the exaggerations of abolitionists. He assures people that he has been to the south, and seen slavery for himself; that it is a beautiful "patriarchal institution;" that the slaves don't want
(30) their freedom; that they have hallelujah meetings and other religious privileges.

What does he know of the half-starved wretches toiling from dawn till dark on the plantations? of mothers shrieking for their children, torn from their arms by slave traders? of young girls dragged down into moral filth? of pools of blood around the whipping post? of hounds trained to tear human flesh? of men screwed into cotton gins
(35) to die? The slaveholder showed him none of these things, and the slaves dared not tell of them if he had asked them.

There is a great difference between Christianity and religion at the south. If a man goes to the communion table, and pays money into the treasury of the church, no matter if it

be the price of blood, he is called religious. If a pastor has offspring by a woman not his
(40) wife, the church dismisses him, if she is a white woman; but if she is colored, it does not
hinder his continuing to be their good shepherd.

When I was told that Dr. Flint had joined the Episcopal church, I was much surprised. I
supposed that religion had a purifying effect on the character of men; but the worst
persecutions I endured from him were after he was a communicant. The conversation of
(45) the doctor, the day after he had been confirmed, certainly gave me no indication that he
had "renounced the devil and all his works." In answer to some of his usual talk, I
reminded him that he had just joined the church. "Yes, Linda," said he. "It was proper for
me to do so. I am getting on in years, and my position in society requires it, and it puts an
end to all the damed slang. You would do well to join the church, too, Linda."

(50) "There are sinners enough in it already," rejoined I. "If I could be allowed to live like a
Christian, I should be glad."

"You can do what I require; and if you are faithful to me, you will be as virtuous as my
wife," he replied.

I answered that the Bible didn't say so.

(55) His voice became hoarse with rage. "How dare you preach to me about your infernal
Bible!" he exclaimed. "What right have you, who are my negro, to talk to me about what
you would like and what you wouldn't like? I am your master, and you shall obey me."

No wonder the slaves sing—

"Ole Satan's church is here below;

(60) Up to God's free church I hope to go."

Write Your Essay Here

Question III
(Suggested time—40 minutes)

Read the following passages about friendship carefully. Then write an essay in which you analyze the specific stylistic and rhetorical devices of each passage and how these differences lend insight into the purpose of each passage and help to reveal each writer's attitude toward friends.

Passage 1

I awoke this morning with devout thanksgiving for my friends, the old and the new. Shall I not call God the Beautiful, who daily showeth himself so to
Line me in his gifts? I chide society, I embrace solitude,
(5) and yet I am not so ungrateful as not to see the wise, the lovely, and the noble-minded, as from time to time they pass my gate. Who hears me, who understands me, becomes mine—a possession for all time. Nor is nature so poor but she gives me this
(10) joy several times, and thus we weave social threads of our own, a new web of relations; and, as many thoughts in succession substantiate themselves, we shall by and by stand in a new world of our own creation, and no longer strangers and pilgrims in a
(15) traditional globe. My friends have come to me unsought. The great God gave them to me. By oldest right, by the divine affinity of virtue with itself, I find them, or rather not I, but the Deity in me and in them derides and cancels the thick walls
(20) of individual character, relation, age, sex, circumstance, at which he usually connives, and now makes many one. High thanks I owe you, excellent lovers, who carry out the world for me to new and noble depths, and enlarge the meaning of
(25) all my thoughts. These are new poetry of the first Bard—poetry without stop—hymn, ode, and epic, poetry still flowing, Apollo and the Muses chanting still. Will these, too, separate themselves from me again, or some of them? I know not, but I fear it
(30) not; for my relation to them is so pure, that we hold by simple affinity, and the Genius of my life being thus social, the same affinity will exert its energy on whomsoever is as noble as these men and women, wherever I may be.
(35)   I confess to an extreme tenderness of nature on this point. It is almost dangerous to me to "crush

Passage 2

Would that I could enrich this sketch with the names of all those who have ministered to my happiness! Some of them would be found written
Line in our literature and dear to the heats of many,
(5) while others would be wholly unknown to most of my readers. But their influence, though it escapes fame, shall live immortal in the lives that have been sweetened and ennobled by it. Those are red-letter days in our lives when we meet people who thrill
(10) us like a fine poem, people whose handshake is brimful of unspoken sympathy, and whose sweet, rich natures impart to our eager, impatient spirits a wonderful restfulness which, it its essence, is divine. The perplexities, irritations and worries
(15) that have absorbed us pass like unpleasant dreams, and we wake to see with new eyes and hear with new ears the beauty and harmony of God's real world. The solemn nothings that fill our everyday life blossom suddenly into bright possibilities. In a
(20) word, while such friends are near us we feel that all is well. Perhaps we never saw them before, and they may never cross our life's path again; but the influence of their calm, mellow natures is a libation poured upon our discontent, and we feel its
(25) healing touch, as the ocean feels the mountain stream freshening its brine.
    I have often been asked, "Do not people bore you?" I do not understand quite what that means. I suppose the calls of the stupid and curious,
(30) especially the newspaper reporters, are always inopportune. I also dislike people who try to talk down to my understanding. They are like people who when walking with you try to shorten their steps to suit yours; the hypocrisy in both cases is
(35) equally exasperating.
    The hands of those I meet are dumbly eloquent

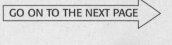

GO ON TO THE NEXT PAGE

the sweet poison of misused wine" of the
affections. A new person is to me a great event, and
hinders me from sleep. I have often had fine fancies
(40) about persons which have given me delicious
hours; but the joy ends in the day; it yields no fruit.
Thought is not born of it; my action is very little
modified. I must feel pride in my friend's
accomplishments as if they were mine,—and a
(45) property in his virtues. I feel as warmly when he is
praised, as the lover when he hears applause of his
engaged maiden. We over-estimate the conscience
of our friend. His goodness seems better than our
goodness, his nature finer, his temptations less.
(50) Every thing that is his—his name, his form, his
dress, books, and instruments—fancy enhances.
Our own thought sounds new and larger from his
mouth.

   Yet the systole and diastole of the heart are not
(55) without their analogy in the ebb and flow of love.
Friendship, like the immortality of the soul, is too
good to be believed.

to me. The touch of some hands is an
impertinence. I have met people so empty of joy,
that when I clasped their frosty finger-tips, it
(40) seemed as if I were shaking hands with a northeast
storm. Others there are whose hands have
sunbeams in them, so that their grasp warms my
heart. It may be only the clinging touch of a child's
hand; but there is as much potential sunshine in it
(45) for me as there is in a loving glance for others. A
hearty handshake or friendly letter gives me
genuine pleasure.

   I have many far-off friends whom I have never
seen. Indeed they are so many that I have often
(50) been unable to reply to their letters; but I wish to
say here that I am always grateful for their kind
words, however insufficiently I acknowledge them.

   I am too happy in this world to think much
about the future, except to remember that I have
(55) cherished friends awaiting there in God's beautiful
Somewhere. In spite of the lapse of years, they
seem so close to me that I should not think it
strange if at any moment they should clasp my
hand and speak words of endearment as they used
(60) to before they went away.

GO ON TO THE NEXT PAGE

Write Your Essay Here

Practice Test 2: **Answer Key**

PASSAGE 1	PASSAGE 2	PASSAGE 3	PASSAGE 4
1. B	15. D	28. C	41. C
2. D	16. A	29. A	42. B
3. E	17. E	30. C	43. A
4. A	18. B	31. E	44. E
5. A	19. C	32. D	45. B
6. D	20. E	33. A	46. A
7. E	21. A	34. B	47. E
8. C	22. C	35. D	48. C
9. C	23. E	36. C	49. D
10. A	24. A	37. E	50. E
11. E	25. D	38. E	51. A
12. D	26. C	39. D	52. A
13. C	27. E	40. A	53. E
14. B			54. C

ANSWERS AND EXPLANATIONS

Section I: Multiple Choice

Since the afternoon in 1967 when I first saw
Hoover Dam, its image has never been entirely
absent from my inner eye. I will be driving down
Line Sunset Boulevard, or about to enter a freeway, and
(5) abruptly those power transmission towers will
appear before me, canted vertiginously over the
tailrace. Sometimes I am confronted by the intakes
and sometimes by the shadow of the heavy cable
that spans the canyon and sometimes by the
(10) ominous outlets to unused spillways, black in the
lunar clarity of the desert light. Quite often I hear
the turbines. Frequently I wonder what is
happening at the dam this instant, at this precise
intersection of time and space, how much water is
(15) being released to fill downstream orders and what
lights are flashing and which generators are in full
use and which just spinning free.

I used to wonder what it was about the dam that
made me think of it at times and in places where I
(20) once thought of the Mindanao Trench, or of the
stars wheeling in their courses, or of the words *As
it was in the beginning, is now and ever shall be,
world without end, amen.* Dams, after all, are
commonplace: we have all seen one. This
(25) particular dam had existed as an idea in the work's
mind for almost forty years before I saw it. Hoover
Dam, showpiece of the Boulder Canyon project,
the several million tons of concrete that made the
Southwest plausible, the *fait accompli* that was to
(30) convey, in the innocent time of its construction,
the notion that mankind's brightest promise lay in
American engineering.

Of course the dam derives some of its emotional
effect from precisely that aspect, that sense of
(35) being a monument to a faith since misplaced.
"They died to make the desert bloom," reads a
plaque dedicated to the ninety-six men who died
building this first of the great high dams, and in
context the worn phrase touches, suggests all of
(40) that trust in harnessing resources, the meliorative
power of the dynamo, so central to the early
Thirties. Boulder City, built in 1931 as the
construction town for the dam, retains the

ambience of a model city, a new town, a toy
(45) triangular grid of green lawns and trim
bungalows, all fanning out from the Reclamation
building. The bronze sculptures at the dam itself
evoke muscular citizen of tomorrow that never
came, sheaves of wheat clutched heavenward,
(50) thunderbolts defied. Winged Victories guard the
flagpole. The flag whips in the canyon wind. The
empty Pepsi-Cola can clatters across the terrazzo.
The place is perfectly frozen in time.

But history does not explain it all, does not
(55) entirely suggest what makes that dam so affecting.
Nor, even, does energy, the massive involvement
with power and pressure and the transparent
sexual overtones to that involvement. Once when I
revisited the dam I walked through it with a man
(60) from the Bureau of Reclamation. Once in a while
he would explain something, usually in that
recondite language having to do with "peaking
power," with "outages" and "dewatering," but on
the whole we spent the afternoon in a world so
(65) alien, so complete and so beautiful unto itself that
it was scarcely necessary to speak at all. We saw
almost no one. Cranes moved above us as if under
their own volition. Generators roared. Transformers hummed. The gratings on which we stood
(70) vibrated. We watched a hundred-ton steel shaft
plunging down to that place where the water was.
And finally we got down to that place where the
water was, where the water sucked out of Lake
Mead roared through thirty-foot penstocks and
(75) then into thirteen-foot penstocks and finally into
the turbines themselves.

There was something beyond all that, something
beyond energy, beyond history, something I could
not fix in my mind. When I came up from the dam
(80) that day the wind was blowing harder, through the
canyon and all across the Mojave, but out at the
dam there was no dust, only the rock and the dam
and a little greasewood and a few garbage cans,
their tops chained banging against a fence. I
(85) walked across the marble star map that traces a
sidereal revolution of the equinox and fixes
forever, the Reclamation man had told me, for all
time and for all people who can read the stars, the
date the dam was dedicated. The star map was, he
(90) had said, for when we were all gone and the dam

was left. I had not thought much of it when he said it, but I thought of it then, with the wind whining and the sun dropping behind a mesa with the finality of a sunset in space. Of course that was the
(95) image I had seen always seen it without quite realizing what I saw, a dynamo finally free of man, splendid at last in its absolute isolation, transmitting power and releasing water to a world where no one is.

From "At the Dam" by Joan Didion

1. B

Although there is a sense of mysticism to this passage, there is not a true anxiety or foreboding (D). It is somewhat reminiscent, but not regretful (A); it's definitely not lighthearted nor whimsical (C). You could never classify it as guileful, although a bit of the description might be deemed hesitant or at least unsure (E).

2. D

This is one of those dreaded Roman numeral questions. What you have to do is to consider all the choices—which of them is true? Then, consider the combinations that you are offered as response possibilities and choose your answer accordingly. In this case, the opening sentence not only introduces the topic of the passage, but also expresses the strange haunting the narrator has experienced by the dam. It does not, however, do any comparing or contrasting with any other experience.

3. E

The only thing this paragraph does not contain is any sort of understatement. All of the other choices—national symbol is self explanatory, religious allusion (see words in italics), foreign terminology is *fait accompli,* and the Southwest would exist without the dam, it just would not exist as it does now, making that statement an exaggeration or hyperbole.

4. A

The key word in this question is the word "throughout." Although there is some logic, and she does call on the "expert's" opinion at the dam, providing some ethos, the reality is that throughout the passage she is working with emotion, or pathos.

5. A

This question asks for a comparison, or in this case, a contrast between the world and the dam. The world is made of and for people. The dam might have been created by people, but now that it has been built, the narrator depicts it as a mechanical wonder working by itself, perhaps eternally, free of human interference.

6. D

This is a rather easy question. These lines contain imagery, the sound device of onomatopoeia, parallel structure and simple sentences. However, there is nothing nostalgic about the description.

7. E

Although you might be tempted to answer choose (A), this is a good case for looking at *all* responses before deciding. Choice (E) most accurately describes the underlying purpose of the passage.

8. C

These lines best reinforces the idea that the entire dam is frozen in time. The main fascination for Didion in this passage is the eternality of the dam.

9. C

Occasionally the AP test will throw a basic vocabulary question at you. Canted means angled; vertiginously means dizzyingly. In her minds eye, home in California, she sees the dam, causing her mind to experience instability or unsteadiness. The dam itself is a monstrous structure shored up by an amazing array of oddly angled supports. Just looking at their size and angles would make any observer dizzy.

10. A

These lines in the fifth paragraph repeat the word "something" as the first word of several phrases in succession. While this is definitely a form of repetition (E), it is most specifically a type of repetition known as anaphora. You will find this and definitions in the *Key Terminology* section of this book.

11. E

The passage closes with "There was something beyond all that, something beyond energy, beyond history, something I could not fix in my mind. . . what I saw, a dynamo finally free of man, splendid at last in its absolute isolation, transmitting power and releasing water to a world where no one is." Joan Didion's closing comments have an eerie and haunting tone about them.

12. D

This is NOT a sentence at all, so (D) is not possible. Also, the characteristics mentioned by the other choices are present in this fragment.

13. C

These lines are, "Boulder City, built in 1931, as the construction town for the dam, retains the ambience of a model city, a new town, a toy triangular grid of green lawns and trim bungalows, all fanning out from the Reclamation building." Just as a child might lay out a city with toy houses and cars, so too did the planners of Boulder Dam lay out the city for the workers who would build this mighty structure. The workers are long gone, but the city has been maintained. Its emptiness reminds the viewer of a toy city, meticulously constructed and left abandoned by its child architect in search of more compelling activities.

14. B

Didion is amazed by this structure. In her passage she relates the great energy and manpower it took to build this powerhouse of the Southwest. However, what amazes her most is the "feeling" she has that this dam is so perfectly constructed that there may come a time that man may no longer be around, but the dam, in its self-sufficiency will continue "transmitting power and releasing water to a world where no one is."

He who lets the world, or his own portion of it, choose his plan of life for him, has no need of any other faculty than the ape-like one of imitation. *Line* He who chooses his plan for himself, employs all (5) his faculties. He must use observation to see, reason and judgment to foresee, activity to gather materials for decision, discrimination to decide, and when he has decided, firmness and self-control to hold to his deliberate decisions. And (10) these qualities he requires and exercises exactly in proportion as the part of his conduct which he determines according to his judgment and feelings is a large one. It is possible that he might be guided in some good path, and kept out of harm's way, (15) without any of these things. But what will be his comparative worth as a human being? It really is of importance, not only what men do, but also what manner of men they are that do it. Among the works of man, which human life is rightly (20) employed in performing a beautifying, the first in importance surely is man himself. Supposing it were possible to get houses built, corn grown, battles fought, causes tried, and even churches erected and prayers said, by machinery—by (25) automations in human form—it would be a considerable loss to exchange for these automatons even the men and women who at present inhabit the more civilized parts of the world, and who assuredly are but starved specimens of what nature (30) can and will produce. Human nature is not a machine to be built after a model, and set to do exactly the work prescribed for it, but a tree, which requires to grow and develop itself on all sides, according to the tendency of the inward forces (35) which make it a living thing.

It will probably be conceded that it is desirable people should exercise their understandings, and that an intelligent following of custom, or even occasionally an intelligent deviation from custom, (40) is better than a blind and simply mechanical adhesion to it. To a certain extent it is admitted that our understanding should be our own: but there is not the same willingness to admit that our desires and impulses should be our own likewise; (45) or that to possess impulses of our own, and of any strength, is anything but a peril and a snare. Yet desires and impulses are as much a part of a perfect human being as beliefs and restraints: and strong impulses are only perilous when not (50) properly balanced; when one set of aims and inclinations is developed into strength, while others, which ought to co-exist with them, remain weak and inactive. It is not because men's desires are strong and they act ill: it is because their (55) consciences are weak; there is no natural connection between strong impulses and a weak conscience; the natural connection is the other way. To say that one person's desires and feelings

are stronger and more various than those of
(60) another, is merely to say that he has more of the
raw material of human nature, and is therefore
capable, perhaps of more evil, but certainly of
more good. Strong impulses are but another name
for energy. Energy may be termed to bad uses; but
(65) more good may always be made of an energetic
nature, than of an indolent and impassive one.

Those who have most natural feeling are always
those whose cultivated feelings may be made the
strongest. The same strong susceptibilities which
(70) make the personal impulses vivid and powerful,
are also the source from whence are generated the
most passionate love of virtue, and the sternest
self-control. It is through the cultivation of these
that society both does its duty and protects its
(75) interests: not by rejecting the stuff by which heroes
are made, because it knows not how to make them.
A person whose desires and impulses are his own
is said to have a character. One whose desires and
impulses are not his own, has no character, no
(80) more than a steam engine has character. If, in
addition to being his own, his impulses are strong,
and are under the government of a strong will, he
has an energetic character. Whoever thinks that
individuality of desires and impulses should not be
(85) encouraged to unfold itself, must maintain that
society has no need of strong natures—is not the
better for containing many persons who have
much character—and that a high general average
of energy is not desirable.

(90)   In some early states of society, these forces might
be, and were, too much ahead of the power which
society then possessed of disciplining and
controlling them. There has been a time when the
element of spontaneity and individuality was in
(95) excess, and the social principle had a hard struggle
with it. The difficulty then was to induce men of
strong bodies or minds to pay obedience to any
rules which required them to control their
impulses. To overcome this difficulty, law and
(100) discipline, like the Popes struggling against the
Emperors, asserted a power over the whole man,
claiming to control all his life in order to control
his character—which society had not found any
other sufficient means of binding. But society has
(105) now fairly got the better of individuality: and the
danger which threatens human nature is not the

excess, but the deficiency, of personal impulses and
preferences. Things are vastly changed since the
passion of those who were strong by station or by
(110) personal endowment were in a state of habitual
rebelling against laws and ordinances, and
required to be rigorously chained up to enable the
persons within their reach to enjoy any particle of
security. In our times, from the highest class of
(115) society down to the lowest, every one lives as
under the eye of a hostile and dreaded censorship.
Not only in what concerns others, but in what
concerns only themselves, the individual or the
family do not ask themselves—what do I prefer?
(120) Or, what would suit my character and disposition:
or, what would allow the best and highest in me to
have fair play and enable it to grow and thrive?
They ask themselves, what is suitable to my
position, what is usually done by persons of my
(125) station and pecuniary circumstances? Or (worse
still) what is usually done by persons of a station
and circumstances superior to mine? I do not
mean that they choose what is customary in
preference to what suits their own inclination. It
(130) does not occur to them to have any inclination
except for what is customary. Thus the mind itself
is bowed to the yoke: they like in crowds; they
exercise choice only among things commonly
done: peculiarity if taste, eccentricity of conduct,
(135) are shunned equally with crimes: until by dint of
not following their own nature they have no
nature to follow: their human capacities are
withered and starved: they become incapable of
any strong wishes or native pleasures, and are
(140) generally without either opinions or feelings of
home growth, or properly their own, Now this, or
is it not, the desirable condition of human nature?
From *Of Individuality* by John S. Mill

15. D

The main message of this passage can be borrowed from
Hamlet: "To thine own self be true." Mill's message, again
and again, is that we must develop as our own person, not
copy others or go along with the crowd just because it's an
easier route.

16. A

"Human nature is not a machine to be built after a model, and set to do exactly the work prescribed for it, but a tree, which requires to grow and develop itself on all sides according to the tendency of the inward forces which make it a living thing." This question may send you back to the Key Terminology chapter of this book. Refresh your understanding of simile, metaphor, personification, etc. Sometimes we think we know what something means, but when confronted with it within any sort of literature, we often become a bit shaky in our identification.

17. E

To answer this question, you need to look again at paragraph two of the passage. You will not have enough time while taking the multiple-choice part of the AP exam to reread the passage closely, but you should have gleaned two main ideas from the passage. The narrator wants us to become our own person, not copies of something else, no matter how convenient or conventional. The second point, however, is that in developing into our own person, we must maintain our conscience. As a barometer of our actions, we must remain conscious of what we are doing, and we must always be in control of those "energies" that once unloosed, can lead us into danger.

18. B

Again, you may want to consult the Key Terminology. What we have here is a series of clauses *without* conjunctions (therefore asyndeton in contrast to polysyndeton).

19. C

In actuality, the narrator tells us that if a person listens to his conscience, then he will *not* act ill but will act appropriately, even when he or she is following his or her own individuality.

20. E

In the fourth paragraph, the narrator tells us "The difficulty then was to induce men of strong bodies or minds to pay obedience to any rules which required them to control their impulses. To overcome this difficulty, law and discipline, like the Popes struggling against the Emperors, asserted a power over the whole man, claiming to control all his life in order to control his character—which society had not found any other sufficient means of minding."

21. A

This question asks you to consider the particular mode of discourse of one paragraph, paragraph three. You have to admit that there is something speculative and wishful about this passage. What the narrator suggests is not necessarily what might happen immediately. Therefore, he is both hypothetical—anticipating what might be—and speculative—anticipating the best case scenario based upon the moment.

22. C

Again you are drawn back to paragraph three. The main point of this paragraph is that man's innately "wild" energies must succumb to the concept of decorum. Despite the struggle for individuality, society, at least in the narrator's views, has overcome and even squashed any attempts for man to step forward as his own person.

23. E

Several of these responses might possibly work. For the most part this paragraph celebrates man and his tenacity to remain an individual.

24. A

The last sentence of paragraph three says, "Whoever thinks that individuality of desires and impulses should not be encouraged to unfold itself, must maintain that society has no need of strong natures—is not the better for containing many persons who have much character—and that a high general average of energy is not desirable." It is not difficult to identify this sentence as containing both a series and a colon preceding the series.

25. D

"Things are vastly changed since the passion of those who were strong by station or by personal endowment were in a state of habitual rebelling against laws and ordinances, and required to be rigorously chained up to enable the persons within their reach to enjoy any particle of security." The narrator is lamenting the fact that we have all been tamed into submission. No longer does our inner self speak out against being sucked in by the majority.

26. C

Basically, this narrator has just about given up on mankind. We have "gone to the dark side." Men no longer think for themselves and make their own decisions. Instead, man goes with the flow of society and chooses to be indolent rather than harnessing his energy to become himself.

27. E

In the final paragraph, the author is afraid that man will sacrifice everything that makes him an individual, independent person in order to go along with society's mores. Whatever is customary and appropriate is easiest to pursue.

Thomas Jefferson believed that to preserve the very foundations of our nation, we would need dramatic change from time to time. Well, my
Line fellow citizens, this is our time. Let us embrace it.
(5) Our democracy must be not only the envy of the world but the engine of our own renewal. There is nothing wrong with America that cannot be cured by what is right with America.

And so today, we pledge an end to the era of
(10) deadlock and drift—a new season of American renewal has begun.

To renew America, we must be bold.

We must do what no generation has had to do before. We must invest more in our own people, in
(15) their jobs, in their future, and at the same time cut our massive debt. And we must do so in a world in which we must compete for every opportunity.

It will not be easy; it will require sacrifice. But it can be done, and done fairly, not choosing sacrifice
(20) for its own sake, but for our own sake. We must provide for our nation the way a family provides for its children.

Our Founders saw themselves in the light of posterity. We can do no less. Anyone who has ever
(25) watched a child's eyes wander into sleep knows what posterity is. Posterity is the world to come— the world for whom we hold our ideals, from whom we have borrowed our planet, and to whom we bear sacred responsibility.
(30) We must do what America does best: offer more opportunity to all and demand responsibility from all.

It is time to break the bad habit of expecting something for nothing, from our government or
(35) from each other. Let us all take more responsibility, not only for ourselves and our families but for our communities and our country.

To renew America, we must revitalize our democracy.
(40) This beautiful capital, like every capital since the dawn of civilization, is often a place of intrigue and calculation. Powerful people maneuver for position and worry endlessly about who is in and who is out, who is up and who is down, forgetting
(45) those people whose toil and sweat sends us here and pays our way.

Americans deserve better, and in this city today, there are people who want to do better. And so I say to all of us here, let us resolve to reform our
(50) politics, so that power and privilege no longer shout down the voice of the people. Let us put aside personal advantage so that we can feel the pain and see the promise of America.

Let us resolve to make our government a place
(55) for what Franklin Roosevelt called "bold, persistent experimentation," a government for our tomorrows, not our yesterdays.

Let us give this capital back to the people to whom it belongs.
(60) To renew America, we must meet challenges abroad as well at home. There is no longer division between what is foreign and what is domestic—the world economy, the world environment, the world AIDS crisis, the world arms race—they affect
(65) us all.

Today, as an old order passes, the new world is more free but less stable. Communism's collapse has called forth old animosities and new dangers. Clearly America must continue to lead the world
(70) we did so much to make.

While America rebuilds at home, we will not shrink from the challenges, nor fail to seize the opportunities, of this new world. Together with our friends and allies, we will work to shape
(75) change, lest it engulf us.

When our vital interests are challenged, or the will and conscience of the international community is defied, we will act—with peaceful diplomacy whenever possible, with force when

(80) necessary. The brave Americans serving our nation today in the Persian Gulf, in Somalia, and wherever else they stand are testament to our resolve.

But our greatest strength is the power of our
(85) ideas, which are still new in many lands. Across the world, we see them embraced—and we rejoice. Our hopes, our hearts, our hands, are with those on every continent who are building democracy and freedom. Their cause is America's cause.
(90) The American people have summoned the change we celebrate today. You have raised your voices in an unmistakable chorus. You have cast your votes in historic numbers. And you have changed the face of Congress, the presidency and
(95) the political process itself. Yes, you, my fellow Americans have forced the spring. Now, we must do the work the season demands.

To that work I now turn, with all the authority of my office. I ask the Congress to join with me.
(100) But no president, no Congress, no government, can undertake this mission alone. My fellow Americans, you, too, must play your part in our renewal. I challenge a new generation of young Americans to a season of service—to act on your
(105) idealism by helping troubled children, keeping company with those in need, reconnecting our torn communities. There is so much to be done— enough indeed for millions of others who are still young in spirit to give of themselves in service, too.
(110) In serving, we recognize a simple but powerful truth—we need each other. And we must care for one another. Today, we do more than celebrate America; we rededicate ourselves to the very idea of America.
(115) An idea born in revolution and renewed through two centuries of challenge. An idea tempered by the knowledge that, but for fate, we— the fortunate and the unfortunate—might have been each other. An idea ennobled by the faith that
(120) our nation can summon from its myriad diversity the deepest measure of unity. An idea infused with the conviction that America's long heroic journey must go forever upward.

And so, my fellow Americans, at the edge of the
(125) twenty-first century, let us begin with energy and hope, with faith and discipline, and let us work

until our work is done. The scripture says, "And let us not be weary in well-doing, for in due season, we shall reap, if we faint not."
(130) From this joyful mountaintop of celebration, we hear a call to service in the valley. We have heard the trumpets. We have changed the guard. And now, each in our way, and with God's help, we must answer the call.
(135) Thank you and God bless you all.
Inaugural address, William Clinton

28. C

"Thomas Jefferson believed that to preserve the very foundations of our nation, we would need dramatic change from time to time. Well, my fellow citizens, this is our tie. Let us embrace it." This opening paragraph is expecting some empathy (E) from the audience, but overall the appeal is to the audience's patriotism (C).

29. A

"Nothing wrong that cannot be cured by what is right" is enough to make you scratch your head for a minute. What we have here is a seeming contradiction that really does make sense, therefore a paradox.

30. C

Epistrophe is the repetition of a word or words at the end of two or more successive verses, clauses or sentences; "offer more opportunity to all and demand responsibility from all" demonstrates this syntactic device.

31. E

This rather short paragraph contains a parenthetical statement ("like every capital since the dawn of civilization"), independent clauses in a series ("who is in and who is out, who is up and who is down"), participial phrase ("*forgetting* those people who toil") and a compound verb ("maneuver" and "worry"). What this paragraph does not contain is a compound sentence.

32. D

"A government for our tomorrows, not our yesterdays" is a government that cannot and does not rest on prior accomplishments and laurels but one that is forward thinking and is ready to take on new challenges.

33. A

Take a look at these lines. To borrow from *Sesame Street*, this paragraph is brought to you by the letter "P."

34. B

When a particular line is repeated throughout a poem or piece of prose, it has a stylistic purpose. Often in poetry it is the main message of the poem. Such a repetition is a *refrain* (in music the chorus). In a speech such as this one, Clinton is strongly emphasizing the idea of renewal. This is known as a refrain.

35. D

A zeugma is a linkage of one subject with two or more verbs, or in this speech, a verb with two or more objects or descriptors. " . . . we will act—with peaceful diplomacy . . . with force . . ." Both peaceful diplomacy and force go back to the verb act.

36. C

When you force a flower, you cause it to bloom (change) early, before its normal season. Since it was not spring yet in the capital, when Clinton gave this speech, he says the people (their vote) have forced the spring. In other words, through their vote change has happened and things are going to grow, albeit a bit early in the season.

37. E

If you are unsure of any of the terms offered as choices for this question, go back to Key Terminology and check definitions and examples. Alliteration is repetition of consonants; assonance is repetition of vowel sounds; anaphora is repetition of phrase, clause, or sentence openings; parallelism is recurrent structure. All of these are present except ambiguity. There is nothing in these lines wherein multiple connotations are offered, often to confuse or obfuscate meaning.

38. E

Typical of many political speeches of this nature, Clinton is challenging the public—especially the younger generation or those young in spirit—to do their share in the effort to make America a stronger nation.

39. D

You may say that the jumble of sentences (and fragments) found in these lines is truly complex. But here you must ask yourself: Does this sentence represent *complex sentence structure*? No, it does not. A complex sentence is one that has at least one independent clause and one dependent clause. These lines do not represent such a structure.

40. A

This one you should have been able to figure out almost without reading the passage (not a recommended tactic, however). As with most inaugural addresses, Clinton offers encouragement, and he is, of course, optimistic about the future of the United States under his leadership.

> Here was my soup. Dinner was being served in
> the great dining-hall. Far from being spring it was
> in fact an evening in October. Everybody was
Line assembled in the big dining-room. Dinner was
> (5) ready. Here was the soup. It was a plain gravy soup.
> There was nothing to stir the fancy in that. One
> could have seen through the transparent liquid any
> pattern that there might have been on the plate
> itself. But there was no pattern. The plate was
> (10) plain. Next came beef with its attendant greens
> and potatoes—a homely trinity, suggesting the
> rumps of cattle in a muddy market, and sprouts
> curled and yellowed at the edge, and bargaining
> and cheapening and women with string bags on
> (15) Monday morning. There was no reason to
> complain of human nature's daily food, seeing that
> the supply was sufficient and coal-miners
> doubtless were sitting down to less. Prunes and
> custard followed. And if anyone complains that
> (20) prunes, even when mitigated by custard, are an
> uncharitable vegetable (fruit they are not), stringy
> as a miser's heart and exuding a fluid such as
> might run in misers' veins who have denied
> themselves wine and warmth for eighty years and
> (25) yet not given to the poor, he should reflect that
> there are people whose charity embraces even the
> prune. Biscuits and cheese came next, and here the
> water-jug was liberally passed round, for it is in the
> nature of biscuits to be dry, and these were biscuits
> (30) to the core. That was all. The meal was over.

Everybody scraped their chairs back; the swing-doors swung violently to and fro; soon the hall was emptied of every sign of food and made ready no
(35) doubt for breakfast next morning. Down corridors and up staircases the youth of England went banging and singing. And was it for a guest, a stranger, to say 'The dinner was not good,' or do say now that Mary and I are in her sitting room,
(40) 'Could we not have dined up here alone?' for if I had said anything of the kind I should have been prying and searching into the secret economies of a house which to the stranger wears so fine a front of gaiety and courage. No, one could say nothing
(45) of the sort. Indeed, conversation for a moment flagged. The human frame being what it is, heart, body and brain all mixed together, and not contained in separate compartments as they will be no doubt in another million years, a good
(50) dinner is of great importance to good talk. One cannot think well, love well, sleep well, if one has not dined well. The lamp in the spine does not light on beef and prunes. We are all PROBABLY going to heaven, and Vandyck is, we HOPE, to
(55) meet us round the next corner—that is the dubious and qualifying state of mind that beef and prunes at the end of the day's work breed between them. Happily my friend, who taught science, had a cupboard where there was a squat bottle and
(60) little glasses—(but there should have been sole and partridge to begin with)—so that we were able to draw up to the fire and repair some of the damages of the day's living. In a minute or so we were slipping freely in and out among all those objects
(65) of curiosity and interest which form in the mind in the absence of a particular person, and are naturally to be discussed on coming together again—how somebody has married, another has not; one thinks this, another that; one has
(70) improved out of all knowledge, the other most amazingly gone to the bad—with all those speculations upon human nature and the character of the amazing world we live in which spring naturally from such beginnings. While these
(75) things were being said, however, I became shamefacedly aware of a current setting in of its own accord and carrying everything forward to an end of it own. The best course, unless the whole

talk was to be distorted, was to expose what was in
(80) my mid to the air, when with good luck it would fade and crumble like the head of the dead king when they opened the coffin at Windsor. Briefly, then, I told Miss Seton about the masons who had been all those years on the roof of the chapel, and
(85) about the kings and queens and nobles bearing sacks of gold and silver on their shoulders, which they shoveled into the earth; and then how the great financial magnates of our own time came and laid cheques and bonds, I suppose, where the
(90) others had laid ingots and rough lumps of gold. All that lies beneath the colleges down there, I said; but this college, where we are now sitting, what lies beneath its gallant red brick and the wild unkempt grasses of the garden? What force is behind that
(95) plain china off which we dined, and (here it popped out of my mouth before I could stop it) the beef, the custard and the prunes?

41. C

All these responses seem to reinforce the plainness of this dreadful meal (described by Virginia Woolf), don't they? However, the most forceful is the syntax of the first ten sentences, which are as dreadfully plain as the meal sounds. If you are not sure, read them aloud and listen to the short, choppy cadence. The plainness of her sentences reflect the plainness of the meal.

42. B

Perhaps you can see the religious overtones with the word trinity, but it is not enough to call this any sort of religious allusion. Basically, what we have here is a simple analogy—another way of describing the three elements that make up the meal: beef, greens, and potatoes. However, the imagery Woolf chooses to use does not dress up the plainness of this fare, but only makes it sound worse.

43. A

"And if anyone complains that prunes, even which mitigated by custard are an uncharitable vegetable . . . there are people whose charity embraces even the prune". These lines indicate that some people are actually charitable enough to embrace prunes. The narrator is obviously not among these charitable folk.

44. E

It sounds like the best thing for this meal would be to drown in all in water. However, Woolf says that "it is in the nature of biscuits to be dry, and these were biscuits to the core." No wonder the water jug had to be passed around so much!

45. B

Epistrophe is the repetition of a word or words at the end of two or more successive verses, clauses, sentences or phrases. The repetition of the word "well" within these lines identifies it as an epistrophe.

46. A

Here the narrator is talking again about prunes. ". . . even when mitigated with custard." Apparently even custard could neither disguise nor improve upon the prunes.

47. E

It is not unusual for writers to use capital letters, italics, or underlining to add emphasis to a passage. Punctuation can also used to express tone or show emotion within a passage, especially in poetry. In this case, the capital letters emphasize how negatively this meal has affected her. She is no longer sure about things she used to know for certain. "We are all PROBABLY going to heaven, and Vandyck is, we HOPE, to meet us round the next corner—that is the dubious and qualifying state of mind that beef and prunes . . . breed between them." Although you might be tempted to choose (D), (E) is the more exact explanation.

48. C

By this point there can be no doubt—the narrator not only feels disdain for this poor excuse for a meal, but she is also annoyed. After all, she is a guest, and, apparently, used to being treated to better fare.

49. D

This sentence must be taken figuratively, not literally. Now the narrator can be alone with her friend. They can sit near ("draw up") to the fire and unwind ("repair damages") from their stressful days as well as the terrible meal they just endured.

50. E

Asyndeton is the practice of omitting conjunctions between words, phrases, or clauses. (In contrast, polysyndeton is when a conjunction is used between each part of the series). These terms are a good example of how prefixes can give you clues as to the meaning of a word. The prefix "a" means without; "poly" means many.

51. A

In this case, the narrator is not too sure how to broach a subject. She seems concerned that her friend must work and live under such dire circumstances, but she does not want to hurt her comrade's feelings nor, it seems, does she want to sound like she is superior to her in any way. A person who did not hesitate to speak unkindly of her (free) meal, at least shows she is sensitive to the feelings of another person.

52. A

This question goes along with question 51. Again the narrator is concerned about her friend's rather meager working and living conditions. She is attempting to draw comparisons, perhaps to lure her friend into changing to a more pleasant environment.

53. E

Although you might think that this passage is simply a diatribe against prunes, there is a greater purpose. Woolf is concerned about the gross inequities among institutes of public education. Actually, she was most appalled at the unconscionable conditions inherent in the schooling of young women, in contrast to the luxuries inherent in the educating males, in the early 1900's. Nevertheless, as with most essays, writers often have far more than one agenda for us to unearth within their words.

54. C

This is a question concerning mode or identifying what type of writing best describes this essay. "Personal reflection" is the best response among the choices offered. You might think that there is more to this essay than simple reflection, but remember that your response is limited to the choices you are offered.

Essay Question I: Rick Reilly's "Let Us ~~Pray~~ Play"

Analysis of Essay Question I

Rick Reilly has been a writer for *Sports Illustrated* for some time. He has also been voted National Sportswriter of the Year nine times. He often uses humor in discussing various sports issues, many of them controversial in nature.

This passage has two aspects to it. At first it seems that it will be a discussion on religion vs. sports. He takes a few good jabs at how sports is now a 24/7 thing, often leaving little time for religion. With a few jabs at Notre Dame and the YMCA, he gets his point across. Nevertheless, he implies that balance and moderation are really key to the issue.

His main concern, however, is found in the statement: "I'll tell you exactly what's going on here: the upping of American youth sports." This is the crux of his argument.

It starts with the Sunday concern—practices and even games on what used to be considered a day of rest. From there, however, he widens his complaint to include the intensity of kids and sports and pressure and parents and even coaches. He does not go into great detail, however, his message is clear. Sundays or any days—kids need time to be kids. Parents need to back off and pull back on the pressure they are putting on youngsters to perform—whatever day of the week it is.

This argument is one that you should have a lot to say about. If you have not experienced what Reilly is referring to personally, you are certainly aware of it through your friends and classmates.

Scoring Guide Essay Question I

9 Essays meet all of the criteria for 8 papers, and in addition, are especially full or apt in their analysis or demonstrate particularly impressive composition skills.

8 Essays successfully analyze the writer's attitude about Sunday sports and parents and their children's sports. They refer to the passage directly or indirectly and clarify convincingly Reilly's attitude about parents and how they are interfering with their children's sports. Their own arguments are effective while demonstrating a wide range of writing skills, though they may not be flawless.

7 Essays fit the description of 6 essays but employ more complete analysis or demonstrate a more mature prose style.

6 Essays adequately analyze Reilly's attitude about sports on Sundays and sports and children. They refer to the passage directly or indirectly, and effectively explain Reilly's concerns and subsequently respond with their own opinion. Their prose may demonstrate minor lapses in diction or syntax, but the 6 response usually conveys the writers' ideas adequately.

5 Essays analyze how the writer's attitude about sports on Sunday and parents and sports. They refer to the passage directly or indirectly, and they recognize the narrator's position and respond accordingly. However they may analyze superficially or respond to the narrator's position inconsistently. A few lapses in diction or syntax may appear, but the prose in these essays conveys the writers' ideas satisfactorily.

4 Essays inadequately respond to the task of the prompt. They may misrepresent the writer's attitude or analyze his position inaccurately, or they may generalize or simplify Reilly's attitude. Their own response to Reilly's stance may often suggest immature control over organization, diction, or syntax.

3 Essays meet the criteria for the score of 4 but are less perceptive about the narrator's attitude or respond to the argument with less consistent control of the elements of writing. They may respond to only part of Reilly's message.

2 Essays are unsuccessful in analyzing Reilly's attitude about Sunday sports and parents and their children's sports. These pay little or cursory attention to the specifics of Reilly's concerns, and they may over generalize, or oversimplify his attitude. They may simply paraphrase or comment on the passage without developing their own response. The prose of 2 papers often reveals consistent weaknesses in writing, such as a lack of development or organization, grammatical problems, or a lack of control.

1 Essays meet the criteria for the score of 2 but are especially simplistic in their discussion or weak in controlling elements of language.

Cameron's Response

Rick Reilly is a well-known sports writer. Often his pieces are cleverly presented arguments in favor or against one thing or another. This passage is no exception. At first he seems to be talking about sports versus religion. He makes some very good points, and he catches the reader's attention with his clever comments about the Pope and Notre Dame, YMCA (church affiliated) Sunday sports and so on. Some of what he says is certainly true, and he uses a humorous tone rather than coming across as super critical. The truth is, however, that today we have more sports than ever, and more people are involved in organized sports—both children as well as adults. There are only so many baseball fields, basketball courts and hockey rinks to play on. In the US we are committed to a 5-day workweek, and in the winter, in many states it is dark way too early to do much after school. Consequently, someone has to do some playing or practicing on Sundays. It's a matter of common sense. Even before organized sports were so popular, I imagine that many neighborhood pick-up games took place on Sunday afternoons. As long as everyone is given time to attend religious services, and accommodations are made for those who must miss practices, compromise can be the solution.

However, this is not the main point of Reilly's piece. It just provided the clever title and attention getter. What he seems most concerned about is the way that over-ambitious parents are ruining sports for their children. Having been a little league player myself as well as an assistant T-ball coach, I know what Reilly is saying.

Almost every year the news carries a story about an irate father punching out a coach or an over-zealous mother attacking another mother at junior's soccer game. When I coached T-ball I actually felt sorry for some of the kids. They never had an unorganized day just to be a kid. It seems that many children are so super-scheduled; they don't even know how to entertain themselves. I remember one 8 year old, Tommy, who told me that Friday night was the only night he did not have to play a sport or take a lesson of some kind. He said Fridays were when he went to his big brother's high school football games in the fall and basketball games in the winter. What kind of life is that for a child?

Way too much pressure is put on some kids way too soon. Some teams require players to try out. Parents are so intent on their little all-star making the team, they fail to see what damage they are doing. What ought to be an enjoyable, learning experience becomes a life-or-death situation. For instance, my T-ball team had a little girl named Karla. When she was practicing with her teammates and her parents weren't around, she was a great player for a 6-year-old. Whenever we had a game, however, her father was constantly screaming at her to do this or that, to hold the bat a certain way, to keep her eye on the ball, etc. Every time he was there, her performance was terrible. He squashed all her talent and enjoyment. Often she would be in tears by the end of a game, which made her father even more upset with her.

This is parent pressure is not just with little kids, either. I've seen it among the parents of many guys I have played sports with. The saddest thing was a buddy of mine, a few years ahead of me, on the football team. He was a great player, and was offered a terrific scholarship at a big 10 university. His dad was ecstatic. Bill chose to put off college and joined the Army, instead. You'd think his father would be proud to have a patriot son. No, his father just about disowned him. Bill had visions of doing his patriotic duty; his father had visions of a million dollar pro contract down the line.

Maybe Rick Reilly should not cross out "Pray" in the title of his article. I think we need a bit of prayer to help parents see what they are doing to their kids. Instead of learning the basics of sportsmanship, getting exercise and having a good time, children are being driven. As Reilly says, even God took a day off. Maybe it's time for parents to do the same thing and give the kids a break.

Tomas's Response

Sunday afternoon football is as American as Mom and apple pie. Rick Reilly points out perhaps sports may be superceding religion. More specifically, for some people sports <u>is</u> their religion. There's nothing wrong with sports any day of the week as long as people keep it in perspective.

The movie, Chariots of Fire demonstrates the sports and religion controversy. Although I cannot remember much of the film (our track coach showed it to us), I remember that one of the runners would not participate in competition if it fell on Saturday, the Jewish Sabbath. Although he might have been a world-class runner, religion was more important than sports. Others are able to find a happy medium. They may attend service very early on Sunday, or very late or even on Saturday evening. There's nothing wrong with sports on Sunday as long as everything is kept in perspective. Wearing soccer cleats to serve Mass, however, is a bit much.

Even the SAT exam has alternate testing day to accommodate religious beliefs. Most people can find a compromise. The important thing is that if Sundays have to be used for practice, that the times are later in the day, and personal religious beliefs and restrictions would never hurt a player who might have to miss sports on that day.

Reilly says a similar balance must be found by parents of future all-stars. They have ruined sports for their kids by pushing them too soon and making everything way more serious than it ought to be. Instead of playing through their children, maybe these parents need to get off their duffs in the sidelines and find a sports activity of their own before they turn off their children towards sports forever.

Have you ever walked by a Little League field in the summer time? What do you hear? Not the cheering of the crowd or the laughter and excitement of the young players, what you hear are parents screaming at their kids to do better, to run faster, to throw more accurately and disputing calls made by umpires and referees against their child, and complaining to coaches that their child isn't getting enough playing time. This is the focus of the passage by Rick Reilly, writer for "Sports Illustrated."

Niki's Response

Rick Reilly is right; we are putting sports before God and we will be sorry.

What has happened to the concept of a day of rest? It used to be that Sundays (or other days for other religions) were for church and family. Now church and family are taking a second place to sports.

Instead of coming home from services and having a nice dinner with the family, dads come home from church and sit down with the TV remote. In the meantime junior is off to practice some sport or another.

Places like Notre Dame and the YMCA should know better than to have practice or games on Sundays. After all, these are religious places. If a catholic college can't even keep Sunday's for God, what sort of example does that present to everyone else?

Parents need to take a stronger stand about this situation. They need to just say "no" when practices or games are scheduled for Sundays. If coaches can't work around God, then maybe kids should be finding something else to do. Some parents are so wrapped up in their kids' sports that they are the ones who ought to be playing. Maybe the kid would rather stay home and read a book, or even go to Sunday school.

Although Mr Reilly tries to impart a bit of humor into his argument, he has made some strong points. Unfortunately, the people and parents who ought to pay attention are probably too busy driving their kids to practice to even read what Reilly has written.

KAPLAN
Test Prep and Admissions

Commentary on Cameron's Response

Obviously this student understands the implications of Rick Reilly's passage. He shows good perception and understanding of the double messages in the piece. First he discusses the issue of sports on Sundays. As he says, accommodation and compromise have to be the solution. Then he tackles the main issue.

Cameron uses examples from his own experiences for his essay. First he discusses situations with little children and the pressures parents sometime place on them. He follows this with the story about an older friend of his whose father wanted a player, not a patriot.

This essay is well executed and effectively responds to all elements of the prompt. The student refers to the passage both directly and indirectly, as he efficiently explains Reilly's messages and intentions. This student has a strong control of prose, and his writing is interesting and effective. Cameron weaves personal observations into his analysis well, which lends veracity to the Reilly piece while enhancing the reader's interest in the student's composition.

This is a successful response, deserving an 8 score. Although the essay is not without a few weak spots, this student has been very successful in responding to the tasks of the prompt, understanding the dual nature of Reilly's original passage, and communicating those ideas well.

Commentary on Tomas's Response

This sample scored a 5; it adequately responds to the prompt. It clearly identifies what the student sees as Reilly's message, but it doesn't look closely enough at Reilly's passage. This student puts too much emphasis on the idea of Sunday sports, and much less on the issue of parents and children and sports. Although both ideas are mentioned, they are done inconsistently, and that is what makes this paper a 5 instead of a 6.

The issues about sports on days of religious importance are well covered. However, when he gets to the second issue, Tomas does more summarizing than analyzing. There is a lecturing tone at the end of the third paragraph, but he doesn't go very far with his ideas. The final paragraph demonstrates some originality and reveals more of the voice of the student writer, but again, he doesn't do enough with it.

As the scoring guide for a 5 paper states: "They may analyze superficially or develop ideas about the narrator's attitude inconsistently"—precisely what this paper has done.

Commentary on Niki's Response

This student has fallen into a dangerous trap with her response—she is lecturing, not analyzing. Not only is she lecturing, but she is speaking in broad generalizations, waving around banners, beliefs, and placards while substantiating little of what she says.

No matter how strongly you feel about a topic, keep the rules of rhetorical argument in the forefront of your mind as you respond. Don't point fingers and make accusations. Develop an argument and support your ideas with details and evidence, not just with knee-jerk reactions.

This essay is also incomplete. Nowhere does this student discuss the other aspect of Rick's complaint—children, parents, and sports. Because this essay is unsuccessful in analyzing the strategies Reilly uses to display his attitude towards Sunday sports, and fails to address parents and children and organized sports, this essay has earned the score of 2. Some might vote for a 3 because the writing itself is OK, but the thinking is shallow. The essay pays only cursory attention to all the features, and she tends to generalize and over simplify Reilly's attitude.

Essay Question II: "Linda's" Narrative

Analysis of Essay Question II

You should have little trouble in responding to this prompt and passage. By now you have studied several similar passages in high school literature and history classes. It is reminiscent of Frederick Douglass or George Washington Carver. What is unique about this passage, however, is not just what Linda says about slavery, but her discussion of the hypocrisy of the Slave owners themselves and the so-called Christians of that time.

The passage opens with Linda's frustrations over the fact that so many slaves are thirsting for knowledge, longing to learn to read and write, but they are forbidden to. Immediately she presents her argument: white missionaries will go to darkest Africa to spread the Word and to distribute bibles—bibles the slaves in the South are forbidden to read. She begs these missionaries to look to the dark corners of home to "save their brethren."

Briefly she concedes that a few brave souls have tried to help the slaves, but only at great risk. She hopes that perhaps Uncle Fred's great grandchildren will have the right to these treasures that he has been denied.

In paragraph four, Linda's diatribe really begins. Her challenge is straightforward: "Are doctors of divinity blind, or are they hypocrites?" That is the crux of her argument. From there she cites many instances of the double standard of the South. She describes the false front that many slave owners present to the outside world, and she reveals the horrors that are barely hidden behind "benevolent patriarchy."

Finally she concludes that Christianity and religion are two very different things in the South. When she refuses to join the church because her master directs her to, he loses his temper. She responds with the powerful lines:

"Ole Satan's church is here below;
Up to God's free church I hope to go."

Scoring Guide for Question II

9 Essays meet all of the criteria for 8 papers, and in addition, are especially full or apt in their analysis or demonstrate particularly impressive composition skills.

8 Essays successfully analyze stylistic strategies the passage employs to convey the writer's attitude under which the White man lived during the time of Southern slavery. They refer to the passage directly or indirectly and define convincingly the attitude the author has towards slavery and her attitude toward the slave owner's double standard. Their prose controls a wide range of effective writing but is not flawless.

7 Essays fit the description of 6 essays but employ more complete analysis or demonstrate a more mature prose style.

6 Essays adequately analyze how the writer's attitude towards slavery and the double standard under which the slave owners lived. They refer to the passage directly or indirectly, and they recognize the narrator's attitude and how she conveys it through her language. A few lapses in diction or syntax may be present, but generally the prose of 6 essays is clear.

5 Essays adequately analyze how the writer's attitude about the double standard of the Southern White slave owners. They refer to the passage directly or indirectly, and they recognize the narrator's attitude. These essays may convey their thoughts superficially, or develops ideas about the narrator's attitude inconsistently. A few lapses in diction or syntax may appear, but the prose in these essays usually conveys the writers' ideas adequately.

4 Essays inadequately respond to the task of the prompt. They may misrepresent the writer's attitude or analyze rhetorical strategies inaccurately or with little understanding of how strategies reveal his attitude toward the double standard. Often the prose of these essays suggests immature control over organization, diction, or syntax.

3 Essays meet the criteria for the score of 4 but are less perceptive about how rhetorical strategies convey attitude or are less consistent in controlling the elements of writing.

2 Essays are unsuccessful in analyzing how stylistic strategies convey the writer's attitude about the double standard under which Southern White slave owners lived. These essays tend to pay little or cursory attention the specific features, and they may generalize, or simplify attitude and tone. They may simply paraphrase or comment on the passage without analyzing technique. The prose of 2 papers often reveals consistent weaknesses in writing, such as a lack of development or organization, grammatical problems, or a lack of control.

1 Essays meet the criteria for the score of 2 but are especially simplistic in their discussion or weak in controlling elements of language.

Charlotte's Response

> We have learned about the horrors of slavery from several fine writers such as Fredrick Douglas, Sojourner Truth and Harriet Tubman. This essay, from "Incidents in the Life of a Slave Girl" gives us more background, and maybe more information than we'd like to read about. But I think there's more to her passage than just relating her experiences as a slave. What she is really talking about in this passage is man's incredible capacity for hypocrisy.

Hypocrisy is a term from the Greeks, originating with Hippocrates. Over the centuries, however, it has developed into the skill of human beings to say one thing and to do another. Literature is full of famous hypocrites—Brutus in Julius Caesar, Holden Caulfield in Catcher in the Rye are just two. Former President Clinton is another, as are many politicians, either because of their personal and public lives. Some would say that Michael Jackson is another—he claimed he loved children, but (allegedly) he was molesting them.

I think about the man in the church parking lot after services on Sunday who becomes irate because some little old lady cuts in front of him. Wasn't he just professing love and Christianity? In our neighborhood a respectable lawyer and town councilman was recently arrested and convicted of beating his wife and abusing his children. The entire Catholic priest scandal is another sign of hypocrisy as well. In fact, within religion we could probably find a number of hypocrites. Personally, I think people who blow up abortion clinics, and often hurt and even kill those inside, because they are pro-life are hypocrites as well.

The slave owner in Linda's world presented a loving, caring "patriarchal" front to the world, while behind the scenes horrors were taking place that we cringe to read about. The slaves will not, dare not, speak up for they or their loved ones would be punished.

Linda's main point is the contrast between Southern religion vs. Southern Christianity. Her slave owner joined the church because it was the appropriate thing to do. It was good for his standing in the community, and he "pays money into the treasury of the church." After services, however, he might go home and punish a slave who is hiding a book, even the Bible. Negro slaves in the south counted for nothing. No one cared if a white man took a slave girl to bed. Even if that man was an important person in the community, everyone just looked the other way. In fact, slaves were considered less important than the "heathens" in the jungle where the church sends missionaries and bibles. How twisted is that? Where did those white people think their slaves came from?

Hypocrisy is all around us, and if we are not careful, we may also get caught in its trap—either as victim or (let's hope not) victimizer. Perhaps Linda is right: "Ole Satan's church _is_ here below."

Britta's Response

This narrator is a very angry young woman who seems to have every right to be angry. In a combination of personal narration and reflection, she eloquently reveals her very strong feelings toward the double standard under which the Southern white man lives.

She opens calmly enough—she relates her efforts to teach an old negro slave known as Uncle Fred, to read. Immediately, however, she shows the dichotomy in thinking—it's against the law for slaves to learn to read or write. On the other hand, missionaries from churches in the South go to deepest Africa carrying the words of religion and providing Bibles for the natives to read. What she says they ought to be preaching is that it is wrong to traffic in slavery, that everyone should have the right to learn and they will answer to God for not treating everyone the same. Immediately the narrator sets up her central idea of the ultimate paradox of the double standard.

She concedes that there are some who might take up the "at home" missionary work (paragraph 2) but those people are few and often do so at risk of their lives. She hopes that some day this will be possible, but it is not to be now.

Commentary on Charlotte's Response

This is an interesting essay. It is truly an upper-half response, a 7; let's take a look at what Charlotte has done.

This student has internalized the inherent message of the original passage. In the introduction, this essay mentions other writers, not unlike Linda, such as Frederick Douglass or Harriet Tubman. This is a good comparison. She draws on these other writers who were former slaves to tell us that the experiences of slavery have been discussed (and obviously studied) before. Then Charlotte moves to her main point: "man's incredible capacity for hypocrisy."

She does not return to the original passage until the second-to-last paragraph. In the meantime, however, Charlotte talks about mankind's propensity for hypocrisy. How many people live lives of duplicitous thinking—whether it be in a church parking lot or in the White house. This student obviously understands the frustrations that Linda is trying to express. What we see on the surface is not necessarily what is really going on.

She returns to the original passage with the discussion of Southern religion versus Southern Christianity. Charlotte's points are well made, but the outrage expressed by the two rhetorical questions should have been expressed in well supported statements rather than questions flung into the air. Rhetorical questions are not a recommended presentation of information. Sometimes they are effective early in an essay if they are eventually answered. Then they become the focus point of the composition. Placed near the end, however, they weaken this response. Therefore what might have been an 8 response would more likely receive a 7.

Charlotte has more than adequately answered this question. Her composition skills are strong. Probably if she had more time to analyze the composition, she would recognize that her own anger was interfering with the most successful presentation of her ideas.

Commentary on Britta's Response

This response is clearly a lower-half response. Although this writer shows that she can write, there is little analysis and the tasks of the prompt have not all been addressed.

Unfortunately, sometimes students run out of time when they are responding to AP questions. It is imperative that you get used to writing within a 40 minute time period for each response. If you take a few minutes more on one response, you have a few minutes less on the next.

It is unfortunate for Britta that she did not take more time to develop this response. She clearly understands the passage and the tasks of the prompt. However, her response is abbreviated. Her main points are compacted into the short middle paragraph. She touches on the narrator's anger and even refers to the "dichotomy" of thinking in the South. She tells us everything hurriedly with no analysis or attempt at support from specific evidence. This is an unfortunate. Her thoughts and her understanding of the passage seem adequate, but the presentation of these views is less than adequate. Due to the lack of development, this is more of a 3 response than even a 4.

Essay Question III: Emerson and Keller

Analysis of Essay Question III

We have a double passage. This prompt asks you to analyze specific stylistic and rhetorical devices that each of these authors has employed in his or her writing. You must consider how these differences lend insight into the purpose of each passage and help to reveal each writer's attitude toward friends.

The first passage is by Ralph Waldo Emerson, the second by Helen Keller. You will quickly notice that the student responses to this question vary greatly. The first passage is depicts an unusual outlook towards friendship—he is not against friendship, but he doesn't seem prone to seek it out. In fact, he seems to imply a reluctance regarding friendship. It is not that he doesn't appreciate friends when they come along, but he admits, "My friends have come to me unsought." In addition, he mentions friends that are not human—they are the poet and the bard who live within their works. Human or not, this narrator is thankful to God for whatever friends are sent his way.

In the second passage, Helen Keller is overwhelmed by friendship. She refers to those whom she knows as well as those she does not. She cannot comprehend the idea of people (friends) ever boring her. She does not look to the future, but enjoys what she has in the present. Yes there are some who are cold, distant, and possibly even demeaning towards her. Overall, however, she rejoices in the sunbeams she finds in most people.

The names of these writers have purposely not been provided. Sometimes it is best for students not to have any preconceived notions about the authors of a passage or what to expect from a particular writer.

Scoring Guide for Question III

9 Essays meet all the criteria for 8 papers and in addition are especially full or apt in their analysis or demonstrate particularly impressive insight and/or stylistic control.

8 Essays effectively analyze how the differing styles of the two descriptions reveal each writer's style and purpose. They refer to the texts, directly or indirectly, assessing how selection and organization of detail, tone, point of view, syntax, and diction convey each writer's aim and reveal his or her style and purpose. In addition, these essays discuss the authors' attitude toward friends with appropriate support from the passages. Their prose demonstrates an ability to control a wide range of the elements of effective writing, but need not be flawless.

7 Essays fit the description of 6 essays but provide more complex analysis or demonstrate more mature prose style.

6 Essays clearly show the relationship between stylistic choice and purpose and adequately analyze that relationship. Referring to the texts, directly or indirectly, these essays compare the writers' use of specific stylistic elements in revealing their style and purpose as well as interpret the attitude of the author towards friends. A few lapses in diction or syntax may be present, but generally the prose of 6 essays demonstrates control of ideas and writing.

5 Essays analyze stylistic techniques, but their discussion of varying styles and purposes in the two passages is limited. They may treat techniques of style in a superficial way or develop ideas about purpose inconsistently. They may fail to discuss the authors' attitudes toward friendship. A few lapses in diction or syntax may be present, but usually the prose in 5 essays conveys the writer's ideas.

4 Essays inadequately respond to the question's tasks. They may misrepresent or merely touch on purpose, analyze stylistic elements inaccurately, or identify techniques of the passages without demonstrating, understanding of stylistic devices and how these help to present each author's attitude towards friends. The prose of 4 essays may convey the writers' ideas but may suggest immature control over organization, diction, or syntax.

3 Essays meet the criteria for the score of 4 but are less perceptive about how the techniques of style convey varying purposes or less consistent in controlling elements of writing.

2 Essays demonstrate little success in analyzing the elements that convey the style and purpose of each passage. They may lack development or substitute simpler tasks by summarizing passages or simply listing stylistic elements. They may misunderstand or ignore purpose and/or attitude of the narrator. The prose of 2 papers often reveals consistent weaknesses in writing, such as a lack of development or organization, grammatical problems, or a lack of control.

1 Essays meet the criteria for the score of 2 but are especially simplistic in their ideas or weak in their control of language.

Alex's Response

As these essays bring to light, the value of friendship can be a very controversial issue. One may believe, as does the first author, that the disadvantages of friendship will inevitably outweigh the advantages, or, one can choose to believe that friendship "enriches" life and provides a constant source of happiness and fulfillment. While both passages utilize numerous rhetorical devices, the differences among those devices accentuate the difference in opinions found in the two essays.

In the first passage, structure, syntax, allusions and tone all allow the reader insight into the purpose of the passage. Through formulated structure, literary allusions, formal syntax, and an insistent tone, the author presents what appears to be an educated argument protesting the idea of friendship being all "goodness . . . and beauty." Instead, the author maintains that friendship is in fact "too good to be believed." Although love is found in friendship, it "ebbs and flows"—similar to the "systole and diastole of the heart." The author's well-planned structure first sings the praise of friendship—leading the reader to believe that the author is in favor of loving companionship—only to perform a complete reversal at the end of the passage by stating that true friendship doesn't exist. This revelation is foreshadowed throughout the passage by the author's clear focus on the future: "eternity . . . for a thousand years . . . for all time . . . immortality." By focusing his or her sights on the future, the author indirectly makes the point that friendship cannot conceivably last for "all time" or "eternity," and therefore, it must be flawed and unachievable. An insistent tone continues to emphasize the author's point. By acknowledging the benefits of friendship, but then insistently contradicting them, the author placed doubt in the reader's mind that results in the reader questioning the true value of friendship. The author continues to gain credibility throughout a formal structure and literary allusions. These tools provide the passage with a sense of superior intellect that the reader would be negligent in not heeding. With the utilization of structure, syntax, allusions, and tone, the passage successfully conveys the author's negative attitude toward friendship.

Although the second passage also employs multiple rhetorical devices, those found—figurative language, similes, personification, sensory details, and tone—sharply contrast those of the first passage. The second passage is written in a joyful, stream-of-conscious tone that celebrates life and the role friendship plays in i. The second author's purpose—manifested through numerous similes and personifications—is to declare that with friendship in one's life, "all is well." The gift of a friend is "like a fine poem," or a "handshake brimful" of joy, "irritations . . . pass like unpleasant dreams," and friends' hands have "sunbeams in them." Other devices such as sensory details and descriptive language continue to expound on the beauty and joy of life. The tone also lends believability to the essay because it is so genuine; one cannot help but agree that friendship can be the light of one's world. The figurative language and genuinely joyful tone throughout the passage expertly illustrates the author's positive outlook on friendship.

Just as the rhetorical devices in each respective passage gives perspective to the essay's purpose, the difference between the two passages also provide insight into their purposes. The most obvious and significant difference between the passages is their negative and positive attitudes on friendship. They also differ in their temporal focus; the first author is focused on the future, while the second author prefers to live in the present: "I am too happy in this world to think much about the future." This fact is important because it helps to clarify the two authors' reasoning methods; while the first looks into the future to see all the possible negative outcomes of a friendship, the second simply enjoys what he/she has right now. Another difference between the two is that the first passage is highly analytical while the second is a fluid, emotion-based analysis of friendship. The final variation between them is their conclusions. A somewhat depressing and hopeless ending can be attributed to the first passage; phrases such as friendship is "too good to be believed," love only "ebbs and flows," and all "the joy ends" convey a negative attitude. The second passage thought, recognizes sadness but continues on positively—hoping for the best in the future where he or she can "clasp hands" with "cherished friends" and listen to "words of endearment." Each passage's conclusion, along with the other differences between the essays, reinforces each author's attitude and persuasive purpose.

As these passages show, even what appears to be a simple issue—friendship—can have many arguable sides. Both authors have credible arguments concerning friendship, and both utilize multiple rhetorical devices to illustrate their beliefs. Structure, syntax, allusions and tone aid in the first passage's persuasiveness, while figurative and descriptive language and tone create mood in the second passage. Differences between the essays further strengthen each author's argument; neither essay could be complete or as persuasive without rhetorical devices and stylistic differences.

Rachel's Response

In these two passages, the reader is given insight into two very profound perspectives on the matters of friends and friendship. Both authors proclaim the same idea regarding the idea of such a companion: a friend is something to cherish and friendship makes a person happy. Both authors put extreme emphasis on the importance of friendship and what friends mean to people, seeing as friends are deemed as great gifts to love and to treasure. However, though their messages are similar, the authors' ideas on what friendship actually is appear to be somewhat at odds, as one is romantic, and the other more analytical and objective. Each writer presents a unique delivery of the message through either a poetic and elegant writing style such as the first passage, or a simple and straightforward explanation as is used in the second. Their use of diction and differing tones paint two pictures of camaraderie and sow how each of the writers views this important concept.

In the first passage, the reader can immediately recognize the excitement and joy of the author regarding the happiness one finds in friendship through his figurative speech and poetic images. The first five lines of the passage speak of nothing but the glamorous effect that friendship has on people. "What is so pleasant as these jets of affection which make a young world for me again? What so delicious as a just firm encounter of two . . . How beautiful . . ." The focus of the passage is nearly lost in all of the imagery and romantic thoughts about how wonderful friendship is. The great amount of detail and use of extreme imagery portray such bliss that the message could not be anymore intensified or exaggerated. The writer obviously desires to convey an ecstasy that is found only in true companions, perhaps even from personal experience. Such a writer would definitely support the argument that faithful companions are not cheap treasures. The writing style illustrates friends as being priceless and once-in-a-lifetime finds that people should be eternally grateful for. "My friends have come to me unsought. The Great God gave them to me . . . I find them." Though the exaggeration could probably be interpreted as coming from a standpoint of one who is overly passionate in his or her happiness, the message is not lost or misinterpreted.

The second passage, on the other hand, though it conveys a clear portrayal of friendship and its importance, does not use the same passion or extravagance in illustrating friendship and its meaning. The author writes in such a way that compares the different kinds of friends and what encounters with each are like, using a logical perspective rather than an all-is-right-with-the-world standpoint. "In a word, while such friends are near to us we feel that all is well. Perhaps we never saw them before, and they many never cross our life's path again; but the influence of their calm, mellow natures is a libation poured upon our discontent." Although this interpretation is less invigorating, it gives friendship a face that is easy to understand and a simple means of obtaining happiness. The writing, even though it is done in first person, analyzes friendship from more of a third-person perspective.

However, that is not to say that the author does not find happiness in having friends. The first seventeen lines (in contrast to the other passage's first 5 lines) express deep gratitude and cheerfulness in having friends to call his or her own. The first sentence says, "Would that I could enrich this sketch with the names of all those who have ministered on my happiness!" There should be no misunderstanding when evaluating each author's respect for their friends, as they obviously convey similar attitudes toward his or her own friends.

In conclusion, each author has a deep respect and gratitude for friendship. Both see it as a happy influence in their lives and their friends as treasures that make all the difference in the world to them. Though one is extremely passionate where the other is straight-forward, their message remains strong throughout both passages, emphasizing the importance of friends and how important such relationships are. Their difference in word choice and viewpoints convey camaraderie in two ways, but at the same time they are equally appreciative of the gift of friendship. These two portrayals show how each author regards friendship and its significance in people's lives.

Lori's Response

Friendship holds a heartening place for everyone. It is a place unto which only the beholder can access. In this way, one's perception of friendship differs greatly. As these two passages support, through past experiences and encounters, one develops an attitude—either optimistic, or pessimistic—on the subject of friendship. Due to the first author's figurative language, religious allusions, and optimistic tone, one can clearly understand his or her positive outlook on the concept of friendship; however, as a result of a bittersweet tone and icy imagery, it is apparent that the second author does not possess the same warmhearted trustworthiness towards friends.

With a purpose of sharing his encouraging encounters in the past, the first author drips with inspiration. Through an optimistic tone, the author relays a message to appreciate old friends as well as experience the joy of meeting new ones. "I awoke this morning with devout thanksgiving for my friends, the old and the new. . . . A new person is to me a great event, and hinders me from sleep." The author radiates love for one's neighbor and proves how contagious kindness can be. "I must feel pride in my friend's accomplishments as if they were mine." The selflessness this author reveals through his positive tone is admirable. He also explains his adoration of friendship with religious allusions proclaiming that God gave his friends to him. "Shall I not call God the Beautiful, who daily showeth himself so to me in his gifts? // nor in nature so poor but she gives me this joy several times . . ." The author also credits his peaceful and non-judgmental relationships to the Creator. "By oldest right, by the divine affinity of virtue with itself, I find them, or rather not I, but the Deity in me and in them derides and cancels the thick walls of individual character, relation, age, sex, circumstance, at which he usually connives, and now makes many one." Looking past the "thick walls" of outward appearances is an accomplishment worth boasting. This author does so through religious allusions. He also reveals his purpose and attitude toward friendship through figurative language. "I feel as warmly when he is praised as the lover when he hears applause of his engaged maiden." This metaphor compares his relationship to his friend ad soon-to-be-husband admiring his fiancée. This comparison conveys the depth of his loyalty toward his comrades. He further states, "Friendship, like the immortality of the soul, is too good to be believed." Here, the author closes his passage with a statement comparing the greatness of friendship to the greatness of one's soul's immortality. The simile depicts his simplistic adoration for companionship.

In contrast, the second author relays a more picky attitude towards accomplices. Speaking from what seems like a celebrity's point of view, one can understand her bitter-sweet tone and icy imagery. Although she does express a sense of appreciation for friendship such as in her opening paragraph : "In a word, while such friends are near us we feel that all is well," and her heartening reference to her many "far-off friends whom [she] has never seen" (her fans?), the author goes on in a rather less adoring tone. "The hands of those I meet are dumbly eloquent to me. The touch of some hands is an impertinence." The author also states her dislike of media personalities and "empty joy" through imagery. "I have met people so empty of joy, that when I clasped their frosty finger-tips, it seemed as if I were shaking hands with a northeast storm" The author's words can easily be pictured through her descriptive imagery. She continues describing the judgmental features of the media. "I also dislike people who try to talk down to my understanding. They are like people who when walking with you try to shorten their steps." This speaker has a bittersweet attitude towards trust and friendship. However, through her imagery and tone, illustrating positive longing to be among her appreciative friends, the author relays her purpose of the writing: hold on to those whom you love and trust.

In conclusion, the two passages proclaim the joys of friendship; however, both express the negative aspect of loyalty in different ways. In the first passage, merely positive experiences are recalled and portray a purpose to spread optimism through descriptive figurative language, penetrating religious allusions and a positive tone. Contrastingly, the second passage possessed a darker side as the author spoke of the negative effects of the media through sensory imagery and a bittersweet tone conveying a message of hostility towards blind trust. The two passages possess contrasting qualities that show the multidimensional aspects of friendship.

Commentary on Alex's Response

It may not be without flaws, but this is an outstanding essay, worthy of a 9. The introduction is strong and straightforward. As with most successful introductions to timed writings, this student states her intentions and is ready to get on with her explanations.

Alex very successfully combines the block approach to comparison and contrast with the part-by-part approach. First she analyzes passage one, then passage two. The fourth paragraph tackles both of the passages—discussing rhetorical devices and then, in the next paragraph, the overall concept of friendship. Note Alex's comfortable use of transitions: "In the first passage," "Although the second passage," "Just as the rhetorical devices in each respective passage gives perspective to the essay's purpose, the difference between the two passages also proved," "As these passages show." It is readily apparent that this student has strong composition skills. Her writing flows easily, and she tells us a lot in a very comfortable manner. She demonstrates her understanding of these passages as well as of crafting a comparison and contrast response.

Finally, she pulls everything together in her first-rate conclusion. If you look at the scoring guide for the 8–9 paper, the "successful" papers effectively analyze how the differing styles of the two passages reveal each writer's style and purpose. Alex has certainly accomplished this. In addition, a successful response refers to the texts directly or indirectly, assessing how selections and organization of detail and other rhetorical features convey each writer's aim and reveal his or her style and purpose. All of these qualities are present in Alex's essay. She responds to the tasks of the prompt, demonstrates fine composition skills, and reveals insight and comprehension of both of the passages. Her essay is extremely well developed and she shows strong language control.

Commentary on Rachel's Response

Rachel's response would most likely earn a 7. It is definitely a more-than-adequate upper-half response, but does not quite meet the requirements for an 8. She identifies stylistic differences between the two friendship passages and clearly analyzes that relationship. She comprehends the style of each piece and seems to grasp the purposes of each.

What is important for you, the student, to notice about this response is that it is not in full agreement with Alex's essay. Rachel sees the two passages and their writer's attitudes differently. Rarely is there one right interpretation of any passage. AP readers do NOT have preconceived notions of "right" or "wrong" responses. What they are looking for are well-articulated arguments that demonstrate ample support and explanation for their positions.

That is exactly what Rachel has accomplished. The mantra of AP readers is: "Reward them for what they do well." Students are not "punished" for a response that might not be in accord with the reader's interpretation. However you "see" a passage needs to be clearly explained; your analysis has to be well developed and supported with textual proof as well as observations of your own.

In her response, Rachel has demonstrated more than adequate interpretation, analysis and composition skills. She has responded well to the tasks of the prompt, has analyzed each passage carefully, supported her positions and has written a very commendable response.

Commentary on Lori's Response

Lori has written an inconsistent response. In fact, her writing is stronger, perhaps than some of her analysis.

She lauds the sentiments presented by the first writer and is somewhat critical of the second. Although she has ample support and evidence for the first passage, she seems to have much less to support her analysis of the second.

The biggest "fault" of Lori's essay is that it is more summary and paraphrase than analysis. Just when she seems to be analyzing one of the passages, you realize that she is mostly just retelling what has already been written by the author of the original passage. If you review the characteristics of a 5 score, it says: " their discussion of varying styles and purposes in the two passages is limited. They may treat techniques of style in a superficial way or develop ideas about purpose inconsistently. They may fail to discuss the authors' attitudes toward friendship. A few lapses in diction or syntax may be present, but usually the prose in 5 essays conveys the writer's ideas." That is exactly what Lori has done in her essay.

Overall Lori's response is almost there. She has written one of those compositions that AP readers just want so much to push a bit higher. No doubt, with a rewrite this essay could soar well into the upper-half range.

Although you want to think in terms of scores of 6 and 7, the score of a 5 is not a disaster. In fact, if you take a look at the conversion chart for AP scores, you will quickly see that a 5 is a very salvageable score. With two other adequate scores and reasonable success on the multiple-choice questions, you can earn a 3 or even a 4 as your final AP score.

Grammar Reference Guide

SENTENCE STRUCTURE

Be sure to know this basic material.

Run-On Sentences

When a sentence consists of more than one clause (a group of words that contains a subject and a verb), those clauses must be joined properly. It is never acceptable to hook two clauses together with a comma, as the "sentence" below does. That's called a **run-on sentence**.

Wrong: Nietzsche moved to Basel in 1869, he planned to teach classical philology.

There are a number of acceptable ways to fix a run-on.

Correct: Nietzsche moved to Basel in 1869; he planned to teach classical philology.
Also Correct: Nietzsche planned to teach classical philology; therefore, he moved to Basel in 1869.
Also Correct: Nietzsche moved to Basel in 1869, and he planned to teach classical philology. (The word *and*, like *or*, *for*, *but*, *nor*, and *yet*, is what's called a *coordinating conjunction*.)
Also Correct: Because Nietzsche planned to teach classical philology, he moved to Basel in 1869. (The word *because*, like *although*, *if*, *though*, etc., is what's called a *subordinating conjunction*.)
Also Correct: Nietzsche, who planned to teach classical philology, moved to Basel in 1869. (The word *who*, like *which*, *where*, *whom*, *that*, and *whose*, is what's called a *relative pronoun*.)

Sentence Fragments

Every sentence must contain at least one complete independent clause. If there is no independent clause at all, or if what's supposed to be the independent clause is incomplete, you've got a **sentence fragment**.

Wrong :   While most people, who have worked hard for many years, have not managed to save any money, although they are trying to be more frugal now.

This sentence fragment consists of nothing but subordinate clauses. One of the subordinate clauses must be made into an independent clause.

Correct:	Most people, who have worked hard for many years, have not managed to save any money, although they are trying to be more frugal now.
Also Correct:	While most people, who have worked hard for many years, have not managed to save any money, they are trying to be more frugal now.

SUBJECT-VERB AGREEMENT

Remember, in English, a subject and its verb must **agree** in number and person. **Number** refers to whether a subject (or a verb) is singular or plural. **Person** refers to first person (*I*, *we*), second person (*you*), and third person (*he*, *she*, *it*, *one*, *they*).

Intervening Phrases

When the subject of a sentence is followed by a phrase (a group of words that does not have a subject and verb) or relative clause, the words are not part of the subject. They simply add information about that subject.

Learn to recognize groups of words that can come between the subject and verb!

1. **Relative clauses**, which contain important information about the subject of another clause, are very often placed in between a subject and verb. (The previous sentence contains a relative clause.)

Wrong:	John Clare, *who during the mid-nineteenth century wrote many fine poems on rural themes*, were confined for decades to an insane asylum.

The subject is *John Clare*, which is singular, but the verb is *were*, which is plural. The fact that the relative clause ends with a plural noun (*themes*) is supposed to distract you from the fact that the subject and verb don't agree.

Correct:	John Clare, who during the mid-nineteenth century wrote many fine poems on rural themes, *was* confined for decades to an insane asylum.

2. **Appositives** often come between a subject and a verb. Appositives are nouns, pronouns, or noun phrases that are placed next to nouns to describe them further.

Wrong:	John Smith, *the man who led British expeditions to several American sites*, have left several written accounts of dramatic events there.
Correct:	John Smith, the man who led British expeditions to several American sites, *has* left several written accounts of dramatic events there.

Relative clauses and appositives are sometimes set off from the rest of the sentence by commas. When this is the case, it's a dead giveaway that those words are not part of the subject. That makes checking for subject-verb agreement much easier; just ignore the words set off by commas and concentrate on the subject and the verb.

3. The **prepositional phrase** is an all-time favorite.

Wrong:	Wild animals *in jungles all over the world* is endangered.
Correct:	Wild animals in jungles all over the world *are* endangered.

Prepositional phrases, and some relative clauses and appositives, are not set off by commas. It's harder to recognize intervening phrases and clauses when they're not set off by commas, but if you remember to check each sentence carefully for such things, you'll be able to pick them out anyway.

Compound Subjects

When two nouns or groups of nouns are joined by *and*, they're called a **compound subject** and are therefore plural.

Correct: *Ontario and Quebec* contain about two thirds of the population of Canada.

There are some connecting phrases that may look as though they should make a group of words into a compound subject—but they don't result in a compound subject.

Wrong: George Bernard Shaw, as well as Mahatma Gandhi and River Phoenix, were vegetarians.

And is the only connecting word that results in a compound and plural subject. The following words and phrases do not create compound subjects:

along with	*as well as*
together with	*besides*
in addition to	

Correct: *George Bernard Shaw*, as well as Mahatma Gandhi and River Phoenix, *was* a vegetarian.

Wrong: Neither Thomas Jefferson nor Alexander Hamilton were supportive of Aaron Burr's political ambitions.

When words in the subject position are connected by *either . . . or* or *neither . . . nor*, the verb agrees with the last word in the pair. If the last word is singular, the verb must be singular. If the last word is plural, the verb must be plural.

Correct: Neither Thomas Jefferson nor *Alexander Hamilton was* supportive of Aaron Burr's political ambitions.

Correct: Neither Thomas Jefferson nor *the Federalists were* supportive of Aaron Burr's political ambitions.

Both . . . and is the only pair that always results in a plural subject.

Correct: *Both* Thomas Jefferson *and* Alexander Hamilton *were* unsupportive of Aaron Burr's political ambitions.

Unusual Sentence Patterns

When you're checking for subject-verb disagreement, remember that the subject doesn't always appear before the verb.

Wrong: Dominating the New York skyline is the Empire State Building and the Chrysler Building.

The subject of this sentence is a compound subject, *the Empire State Building and the Chrysler Building*. The verb should be plural.

Correct: Dominating the New York skyline *are* the Empire State Building and the Chrysler Building.

Subjects That Are Not Nouns or Pronouns

An entire clause can serve as the subject of a sentence. When used as subject, a clause always takes a singular verb.

>Whether the economy will improve in the near future *is* a matter of great concern.

Infinitives and gerunds can be used as subjects. Remember that they're singular subjects.

>*To err* is human.

>*Rollerblading* is dangerous.

See the section on verbs for more on infinitives and gerunds.

MODIFICATION

Adjectives and adverbs aren't the only sentence elements whose job it is to modify. Phrases and even relative clauses can act as modifiers in a sentence. The following sentence contains several types of modifiers:

>Waiting to regain enough strength to eat, a cheetah, which expends most of its energy in the chase, must rest beside its prey.

Waiting to regain enough strength to eat is a phrase that describes the cheetah, as does the relative clause *which expends most of its energy in the chase*. The phrase *beside its prey* modifies the verb *rest*.

English depends heavily on word order to establish modifying relationships. In other words, most modifiers attach themselves to the first things they can get their hands on in the sentence, even if it's the wrong thing.

Introductory Modifiers

Wrong: Sifting the sand of a river bed, gold was discovered by prospectors in California in 1848.

A modifying phrase that begins a sentence refers to the noun or pronoun immediately following the phrase. But if we apply that rule here, the sentence says that the *gold was sifting sand*. See the problem? The author apparently meant to say that the prospectors were sifting sand. There are several ways to correct the sentence so that it expresses the intended meaning.

Correct: Sifting the sand in a river bed, prospectors discovered gold in California in 1848.

Also Correct: Prospectors, sifting the sand in a river bed, discovered gold in California in 1848.

Also Correct: Gold was discovered by prospectors, who were sifting the sand in a river bed, in California in 1848.

In all three cases the phrase or clause directly precedes or follows the noun it describes.

Dangling Modifiers

A modifying phrase or clause should clearly refer to a particular word in the sentence. A modifying phrase or clause that does not sensibly refer to any word in the sentence is called a **dangling modifier**. The most common sort of dangler is an introductory modifying phrase that's followed by a word it can't logically refer to.

Wrong: Desiring to free his readers from superstition, the theories of Epicurus are expounded in Lucretius's poem *De rerum natura*.

The problem with this sentence is that the phrase that begins the sentence seems to modify the noun following it: *theories*. In fact, there is really nowhere the modifier can be put to make it work properly, and no noun to which it can reasonably refer (*Lucretius's*, the possessive, is functioning as an adjective modifying *poem*). Get rid of dangling constructions by clarifying the modification relationship or by making the dangler into a subordinate clause.

Correct: Desiring to free his readers from superstition, Lucretius expounded the theories of Epicurus in his poem *De rerum natura*.

Now the phrase *desiring to free his readers from superstition* clearly refers to the proper noun *Lucretius*.

Other Modifiers

In correcting some of those misplaced introductory modifiers, we move the modifier to a position inside the sentence rather than at the beginning. This is perfectly acceptable, but just remember that modifying phrases inside a sentence can also be misplaced.

Wrong: That night they sat discussing when the cow might calve in the kitchen.

The problem here is the phrase *in the kitchen*, which seems to refer to where the cow might have her calf. What the author probably meant to say is the following correct sentence:

Correct: That night they sat in the kitchen discussing when the cow might calve.

This sentence is correct because the phrase comes directly after the word it modifies: the verb *sat*.

Wrong: As a young man, the French novelist Gustave Flaubert traveled in Egypt, which was a fascinating experience.

It's not that *Egypt* itself was a fascinating experience, but that traveling there was fascinating.

Correct: Traveling in Egypt as a young man was a fascinating experience for the French novelist Gustave Flaubert.

PRONOUNS

Always try to locate the antecedent of a pronoun (that is, the word to which the pronoun refers). Most of the pronoun problems you'll encounter result from a problem in the relationship of the pronoun and its antecedent.

Pronoun Reference

A pronoun must refer clearly to one and only one antecedent.

1. Watch out for sentences in which pronouns refer to indefinite antecedents, paying particular attention to the pronoun *they*. (Avoid references to some vague *they*.)

Wrong: They serve meals on many of the buses that run from Santiago to Antofagasta. (Who are *they*?)

Better: Meals are served on many of the buses that run from Santiago to Antofagasta.

Note: It's quite all right to use *it* like this:

It seldom rains in Death Valley.

2. Sometimes a sentence is structured so that a pronoun can refer to more than one thing, and as a result the reader doesn't know what the author intended.

Wrong: Pennsylvania Governor William Keith encouraged the young Benjamin Franklin to open his own printing shop because he perceived that the quality of printing in Philadelphia was poor. (*Which* man perceived that the quality of printing in Philadelphia was poor?)

Pronouns are assumed to refer to the nearest reasonable antecedent. Nonetheless, it is best to avoid structural ambiguity of the sort that occurs in this sentence.

Better: Because *he* perceived that the quality of printing in Philadelphia was poor, Pennsylvania Governor *William Keith* encouraged the young Benjamin Franklin to open his own printing shop. (*Keith* perceived that the quality of printing was poor.)

Better: Because the young *Benjamin Franklin* perceived that the quality of printing in Philadelphia was poor, Pennsylvania Governor William Keith encouraged *him* to open *his* own printing shop. (In this version, *Franklin* is the one who perceived that the printing was poor.)

3. Sometimes it's easy to see what the author meant to use for the antecedent, but when you examine the sentence more closely that antecedent is nowhere to be found. Correct the problem either by replacing the pronoun with a noun or by providing a clear antecedent.

Poor: The proslavery writer A. C. C. Thompson questioned Frederick Douglass's authorship of *The Narrative*, claiming that he was too uneducated to have written such an eloquent book.

What's the antecedent of *he*? It should be the noun *Frederick Douglass*, but the sentence contains only the possessive form *Douglass's*. As a rule, avoid using a possessive form as the antecedent of a personal pronoun.

Better: The proslavery writer A. C. C. Thompson questioned whether Frederick Douglass actually wrote *The Narrative*, claiming that *he* was too uneducated to have written such an eloquent book.

Oddball Problems

Here are two oddball pronoun reference problems to watch out for:

DO SO

Wrong: It is common for a native New Yorker who has never driven a car to move to another part of the country and have to learn to do it.

Better: It is common for a native New Yorker who has never driven a car to move to another part of the country and have to learn to *do so*.

ONE AND *YOU*

When we give advice to others or make general statements, we often use the pronouns *one* and *you*. "You should brush your teeth every day." "One never knows what to do in a situation like that."

It is never acceptable to mix *one* and *you*, or *one* and *yours*, or *you* and *one's* in a sentence together.

Wrong:	One shouldn't eat a high-fat diet and avoid exercise, and then be surprised when you gain weight.
Correct:	*One* shouldn't eat a high-fat diet and avoid exercise, and then be surprised when one gains weight.
Also Correct:	*You* shouldn't eat a high-fat diet and avoid exercise, and then be surprised when *you* gain weight.

Also, never use *one* or *one's* to refer to any antecedent except *one*.

Wrong:	A person should leave a light on in an empty house if one wants to give the impression that someone is at home.
Correct:	A *person* should leave a light on in an empty house if *he or she* wants to give the impression that someone is at home.
Also Correct:	*One* should leave a light on in an empty house if *one* wants to give the impression that someone is at home.
Also Correct:	*One* should leave a light on in an empty house if *he or she* wants to give the impression that someone is at home.

Pronoun Agreement

Always use singular pronouns to refer to singular entities and plural pronouns to refer to plural entities. First, identify the antecedent of a given pronoun, and don't allow yourself to be distracted by a phrase that comes between the two.

Wrong:	A cactus will flower in spite of the fact that they receive little water.
Correct:	A *cactus* will flower in spite of the fact that *it* receives little water.
Wrong:	The number of people with college degrees is many times what they were last summer.
Correct:	The *number* of people with college degrees is many times what *it* was last summer.

Note: *The number* is always singular. (The number of cookies he ate *was* impressive.) *A number* is always plural. (A number of turkeys *were* gathered outside the shed.)

Pronoun Case

One type of pronoun problem you can't catch by looking at the relationship between a pronoun and its antecedent is wrong case.

	Subjective Case	Objective Case
First Person:	*I, we*	*me, us*
Second Person:	*you*	*you*
Third Person:	*he, she, it, they, one*	*him, her, it, them, one*
Relative Pronouns:	*who, that, which*	*whom, that, which*

When to Use Subjective Case Pronouns

1. Use the subjective case for the subject of a sentence.
   She is falling asleep.

2. Use the subjective case after forms of *to be*.
   It is *I*.

3. Use the subjective case in comparisons between the subjects of understood verbs.
   Gary is taller than *I* (am).

When to Use Objective Case Pronouns

1. Use the objective case for the object of a verb.
   I called *him*.

2. Use the objective case for the object of a preposition.
   I laughed at *her*.

3. Use the objective case after infinitives and gerunds.
   Asking *him* to go was a big mistake.

4. Use the objective case in comparisons between objects of understood verbs.
   She calls you more than (she calls) *me*.

There probably won't be many times when you are in doubt as to which case of a pronoun is correct. However, the following hints may prove helpful:

When two or more nouns or pronouns are functioning the same way in a sentence, determine the correct case of any pronoun by considering it separately:

Beatrice and (*I* or *me*) are going home early.

Without *Beatrice*, should the sentence read: *Me am going home early* or *I am going home early*? *I am going*, of course, so *Beatrice and I are going home early*.

A common mistake in the use of RELATIVE PRONOUNS is using *who* (subject case) when *whom* (object case) is needed, or vice versa. If you tend to confuse the two, try the following system.

Scholars have disagreed over (*who* or *whom*) is most likely to have written *A Yorkshire Tragedy*, but some early sources attribute it to Shakespeare.

1. Isolate the relative pronoun in its own clause: *whom is most likely to have written* A Yorkshire Tragedy.

2. Ask yourself the question: Who or whom wrote *A Yorkshire Tragedy*?

3. Answer with an ordinary personal pronoun: *He* did. (If you are a native speaker of English, your ear undoubtedly tells you that *him did* is wrong.)

4. Since *he* is in the subjective case, we need the subjective case relative pronoun: *who*. Therefore this sentence should read:

    > Scholars have disagreed over *who* is most likely to have written *A Yorkshire Tragedy*, but some early sources attribute it to Shakespeare.

VERBS

Here are some important terms and concepts to review before you read this section:

Verb: A word that expresses an action or a state of being.

Verbal: A word that is formed from a verb but is not functioning as a verb. There are three kinds of verbals: *participles*, *gerunds*, and *infinitives*.

It is important to realize that a verbal is not a verb, because a sentence must contain a verb, and a verbal won't do. A group of words containing a verbal but lacking a verb is not a sentence.

Participle: Usually ends in *-ing* or *-ed*. It is used as an adjective in a sentence.

> Let *sleeping* dogs lie.
>
> It is difficult to calm a *frightened* child.
>
> *Peering* into his microscope, Robert Koch saw the tuberculosis bacilli.

Gerund: Always ends in *-ing*. It is used in a sentence as a noun.

> *Skiing* can be dangerous.
>
> *Raising* a family is a serious task.
>
> I was surprised at his *acting* like such a coward.

Note from the third sentence that a noun or pronoun that comes before a gerund is in the possessive form: *his*, not *him*.

Infinitive: The basic form of a verb, generally preceded by *to*. It is usually used as a noun, but may be used as an adjective or an adverb.

> Winston Churchill liked *to paint*. (Infinitive used as a noun.)
>
> The will *to conquer* is crucial. (Infinitive used as an adjective—modifies the *will*.)
>
> Students in imperial China studied the Confucian classics *to excel* on civil service exams. (Infinitive used as an adverb—modifies *studied*.)

Verb Tense

You need to be familiar with both the way each tense is used individually and the ways the tenses are used together.

Present Tense

Use the present tense to describe a state or action occurring in the present time.

> Congress *is* debating about health policy this session.

Use the present tense to describe habitual action.

> Many Americans *jog* every day.

Use the present tense to describe "general truths"—things that are always true.

> The earth *is* round and *rotates* on its axis.

Past Tense

Use the simple past tense to describe an event or state that took place at a specific time in the past, and is now over and done with.

> Hundreds of people *died* when the Titanic sank.

> Few people *bought* new cars last year.

There are two other ways to express past action:

> Bread *used to* cost a few cents per loaf.

> George Bush *did promise* not to raise taxes.

Future Tense

Use the future tense for intended actions or actions expected in the future.

> The twenty-second century *will begin* in the year 2101.

We often express future actions with the expression *to be going to*:

> I *am going to move* to another apartment as soon as possible.

The simple present tense is also used to speak of future events. This is called the **anticipatory future**. We often use the anticipatory future with verbs of motion such as *come*, *go*, *arrive*, *depart*, and *leave*:

> The senator *is leaving* for Europe tomorrow.

We also use the anticipatory future in two-clause sentences when one verb is in the regular future tense:

> The disputants will announce the new truce as soon as they *agree* on its terms.

Present Perfect Tense

Use the present perfect tense for actions and states that started in the past and continue up to and into the present time.

> Hawaii *has been* a state since 1959.

Use the present perfect for actions and states that happen a number of times in the past and may happen again in the future.

> Italy *has had* many changes in government since World War II.

Use the present perfect for something that happened at an unspecified time in the past. Notice the difference in meaning between the following two sample sentences:

Present Perfect: Susan Sontag *has written* a critical essay about Leni Riefenstahl. (We have no idea when—we just know she wrote it.)

Simple Past: Susan Sontag *wrote* a critical essay about Leni Riefenstahl in 1974. (We use the simple past because we're specifying when Sontag wrote the essay.)

Past Perfect Tense

The past perfect tense is used to represent past actions or states that were completed before other past states or actions. The more recent past event is expressed in the simple past, and the earlier past event is expressed in the past perfect.

> After he came to America, Vladimir Nabokov translated novels that *he had* written in Russian while he was living in Europe.

Note the difference in meaning between these two sentences:

> The Civil War *had ended* when Lincoln was shot. = *The war was over by the time of Lincoln's death.*
>
> The Civil War *ended* when Lincoln was shot. = *The war ended when Lincoln died.*

Future Perfect Tense

Use the future perfect tense for a future state or event that will take place before another future event.

> By the time the next election is held, the candidates *will have debated* at least once. (Note that the present tense form [anticipatory future] is used in the first clause.)

Sequence of Tenses

When a sentence has two or more verbs in it, you should always check to see whether the tenses of those verbs correctly indicate the order in which things happened. As a general rule, if two things happened at the same time, the verbs should be in the same tense.

Wrong: Just as the sun rose, the rooster crows.

Rose is past tense and *crows* is present tense, but the words *just as* indicate that both things happened at the same time. The verbs should be in the same tense.

Correct: Just as the sun *rose*, the rooster *crowed*.

Also Correct: Just as the sun *rises*, the rooster *crows*.

When we're talking about the past or the future, we often want to indicate that one thing happened or will happen before another. That's where the past perfect and the future perfect come in.

Use the past perfect for the earlier of two past events, and the simple past for the later event.

Wrong: Mozart finished about two thirds of the Requiem when he died.

Putting both verbs of the sentence in the simple past tense makes it sound as if Mozart wrote two thirds of the Requiem after dying. If we put the first verb into the past perfect, though, the sentence makes much more sense.

Correct: Mozart *had finished* about two thirds of the Requiem when he *died*.

Use the future perfect for the earlier of two future events.

Wrong: By the time I write to Leo he will probably move.

The point the author is trying to get across is not that Leo will move when he gets the letter, but that by the time the letter arrives he'll be living somewhere else.

Correct: By the time I write to Leo, he *will* probably *have moved*.

When you use a participial phrase in a sentence, the action or the situation that phrase describes is assumed to take place at the same time as the action or state described by the verb of the sentence.

Wrong: *Being* a French colony, Senegal is a Francophone nation.

This implies that Senegal is still a French colony. We can make the information in the participial phrase refer to an earlier time than does the verb by changing the regular participle to what's called a **perfect participle**. The way to do it is to use *having + the past participle*.

Correct: *Having been a French colony*, Senegal is a Francophone nation.

You can do the same thing with infinitives by replacing the regular infinitive with *to have + the past participle*.

I'm glad *to meet you*. (I'm glad to be in the process of meeting you right now.)

I'm glad *to have* met you. (I'm glad now that I met you earlier today, last week, or whenever.)

Subjunctive Mood

Subjunctive verb forms are used in two ways.

The subjunctive form *were* is used in statements that express a wish or situations that are contrary to fact.

I wish I *were* a rich man. (But I'm not.)

If I *were* you, I wouldn't do that. (But I'm not you.)

The **subjunctive of requirement** is used after verbs such as *ask*, *demand*, *insist*, and *suggest*—or after expressions of requirement, suggestion, or demand. A subjunctive verb of requirement is in the base form of the verb: the infinitive without *to*.

Airlines insist that each passenger *pass* through a metal detector.

It's extremely important that silicon chips *be made* in a dust-free environment.

Conditional Sentences

Conditional sentences are if-then statements.

If you go, *then* I'll go, too.

We use conditional sentences when we want to speculate about the results of a particular situation. There are three types of conditional sentences.

Statements of Fact: There is a real possibility that the situation described in the *if* clause really happened, or is happening, or will happen.

If Vladimir Putin resigns, there will be unrest in Russia.

If John Milton met Galileo, they probably discussed astronomy.

Contrary to Fact: The situation in the *if* clause never happened, so what is said in the *then* clause is pure speculation.

> Blaise Pascal wrote that if Cleopatra's nose had been shorter, the face of the world would have changed.

> Alexander the Great said, "If I were not Alexander, I would want to be Diogenes."

Future Speculation: Some conditional sentences speculate about the future, but with the idea that the situation in the *if* clause is extremely unlikely to happen.

> If Shakespeare's manuscripts were to be discovered, the texts of some of his plays would be less uncertain.

PARALLELISM

Remember, when you express a number of ideas of equal importance and function in the same sentence, you should always be careful to make them all the same grammatical form (that is, all nouns, all adjectives, all gerunds, all clauses, or whatever). That's called **parallel structure** or **parallelism**.

Coordinate Ideas

Coordinate ideas occur in pairs or in series, and they are linked by conjunctions such as *and*, *but*, *or*, and *nor*, or, in certain instances, by linking verbs such as *is*.

Wrong:	To earn credits, an American college student can take up folk dancing, ballet, or study belly dancing.
Correct:	To earn credits, an American college student can take up *folk dancing*, *ballet*, or *belly dancing*.

Note that once you begin repeating a word in a series like the following, you must follow through:

Wrong:	A wage earner might invest her money in stocks, in bonds, or real estate.
Correct:	A wage earner might invest her money *in* stocks, *in* bonds, or *in* real estate.
Also Correct:	A wage earner might invest her money *in* stocks, bonds, or real estate.

This principle applies equally to prepositions (*in*, *on*, *by*, *with*, etc.), articles (*the*, *a*, *an*), helping verbs (*had*, *has*, *would*, etc.), and possessive pronouns (*his*, *her*, etc.). You must either repeat the preposition, helping verb, or whatever, in front of each element in the series, or include it only in front of the first item in the series.

Correlative Constructions

There is a group of words in English which are called **correlative conjunctions**. They are used to relate two ideas in some way. Here's a list of them:

> *both . . . and*
>
> *either . . . or*
>
> *neither . . . nor*
>
> *not only . . . but (also)*

You should always be careful to place correlative conjunctions immediately before the terms they're coordinating.

Wrong: Isaac Newton not only studied physics but also theology.

The problem here is that the author intends to coordinate the two nouns *physics* and *theology*, but makes the mistake of putting the verb of the sentence (*studied*) after the first element of the construction (*not only*), and in so doing destroys the parallelism. Note that the solution to an error like this is usually to move one of the conjunctions.

Correct: Isaac Newton studied not only *physics* but also *theology*.

Compared or Contrasted Ideas

Frequently two or more ideas are compared or contrasted within the same sentence. Compared or contrasted ideas should be presented in the same grammatical form.

Certain phrases should clue you in that the sentence contains ideas that should be presented in parallel form. These phrases include *as . . . as* and *more (or less)* x *than* y.

Wrong: Skiing is as strenuous as to run.
Correct: *Skiing* is as strenuous as *running*.
Wrong: Skiing is less dangerous than to rappel down a cliff.
Correct: *To ski* is less dangerous than *to rappel* down a cliff.

TO BE

In certain cases, sentences with forms of *to be* must be expressed in parallel form.

Wrong: To drive while intoxicated is risking grave injury and criminal charges.

When an infinitive is the subject of *to be*, don't use a gerund after the verb, and vice versa. Pair infinitives with infinitives and gerunds with gerunds.

Correct: *To drive* while intoxicated is *to risk* grave injury and criminal charges.

Note that we wouldn't change both words to gerunds in this sentence because it wouldn't sound idiomatic.

COMPARISONS

A sentence that makes a comparison must do two things: It must be clear about what is being compared, and it must compare things that logically can be compared. A sentence that makes an unclear or illogical comparison is grammatically unacceptable. When you see a comparative expression such as *like*, *as*, *more than*, *unlike*, *less than*, *similar to*, or *different from*, it should remind you to ask yourself two questions about the comparison in the sentence: Is it clear? Is it logical?

Unclear Comparisons

Sometimes it isn't clear what the author is trying to compare.

Wrong: Byron admired Dryden more than Wordsworth.

There are two ways to interpret this sentence: that Dryden meant more to Byron than Wordsworth did, or that Byron thought more highly of Dryden than Wordsworth did. Whichever meaning you choose, the problem can be cleared up by adding more words to the sentence.

Correct: Byron admired Dryden more than *he did* Wordsworth.

Also Correct: Byron admired Dryden more than *Wordsworth did*.

Illogical Comparisons

Sometimes what the author meant to say is clear enough, but what the author meant to say is not what he or she ended up saying.

Wrong: The peaches here are riper than any other fruitstand.

This sentence is comparing *peaches* to *fruitstands*, even though that's clearly not the intention of the author. We can correct it so that we're comparing peaches to peaches by inserting the phrase *those at*.

Correct: The peaches here are riper than *those at* any other fruitstand.

Now the pronoun *those* is standing in for *peaches*, so the sentence is accurately comparing things that can be reasonably compared: the peaches here and some other peaches.

Incomplete comparisons like this one are normally corrected by inserting a phrase like *those of, those in, those at, that of, that in,* and *that at*.

Incomplete comparisons can also be corrected by use of the possessive.

Wrong: Many critics considered Enrico Caruso's voice better than any other tenor. (This is comparing a voice to a person.)

Correct: Many critics considered Enrico Caruso's voice better than *any other tenor's*. (Note that this is a shortened version of: *Many critics considered Enrico Caruso's voice better than any other tenor's voice*.)

The second sort of incomplete comparison occurs when one thing is being compared to a group it is a part of. This error is corrected by inserting either the word *other* or the word *else*.

Wrong: Astaire danced better than any man in the world.

This is wrong because he couldn't have danced better than himself.

Correct: Astaire danced better than any *other* man in the world.

Comparative Forms

The comparative form is used when comparing only two members of a class, and the superlative for three or more.

   Loretta's grass grows *more vigorously* than Jim's.

   Loretta's grass grows the *most vigorously* of any in the neighborhood.

   Of Buchanan and Lincoln, the *latter* was *taller*.

   Of McKinley, Roosevelt, and Taft, the *last* was *heaviest*.

Idiom

Sometimes the right way to say something isn't a matter of grammar but is a matter of **idiom**: an accepted, set phrase or usage that's right for no other reason than that's just the way we say it.

Most of what we call "idioms" are pairs of words that are used together to convey a particular meaning, and many "idiom errors" result from substituting an unacceptable word—usually a preposition—for a word that is always part of the idiom.

Wrong: Brigitte Bardot has joined an organization that is concerned in preventing cruelty to animals.

The adjective *concerned* is followed by either *about* or *with*, either of which would be idiomatic here. But the expression *concerned in* simply isn't idiomatic—we just don't say it that way.

Correct: Brigitte Bardot has joined an organization that is *concerned with* preventing cruelty to animals.

Also Correct: Brigitte Bardot has joined an organization that is *concerned about* preventing cruelty to animals.

There are so many possible idiom errors of this kind that we can't list them all.

ELLIPSIS

An **ellipsis** is the omission from a sentence of words that are clearly understood. Ellipsis is perfectly acceptable as long as it's done properly—in fact, we do it all the time. Not many people would make a statement like:

I've seen more movies this year than you have seen movies this year.

Instead, we would automatically shorten the statement to the much more concise and natural sounding:

I've seen more movies this year than you have.

In the following sentence, ellipsis is properly used:

The Spectator was written by Addison and Steele.

This is a shorter way of saying:

The Spectator was written by Addison and by Steele.

It's all right to leave the second *by* out of the sentence because the same preposition appears before *Addison* and before *Steele*, so you need to use it only once.

Now watch what happens when ellipsis is improperly used.

Wrong: Ezra Pound was interested but not very knowledgeable about economics.

This is wrong because the preposition that's needed after the word *interested* (*in*) is not the same as the preposition that follows the word *knowledgeable* (*about*).

Correct: Ezra Pound was *interested in* but not very *knowledgeable about* economics.

Wrong: London always has and always will be the capital of the United Kingdom.

This is wrong because the verb form that's needed after *has* is not the same as the one that's needed after *will*, so both must be included.

Correct: London *always has been* and *always will be* the capital of the United Kingdom.

Negatives

You will probably run across at least one item that tests your ability to recognize the difference between idiomatic and unidiomatic ways to express negative ideas. You already know that a double negative is a no-no in standard written English. You wouldn't have any trouble realizing that a sentence such as "I don't want no help" is unacceptable. But the incorrect negatives you will probably see on the exam won't be quite that obvious.

The obviously negative words are *neither, nobody, nor, nowhere, never, none, not, no one,* and *nothing.* But don't forget that *barely, rarely, without, hardly, seldom,* and *scarcely* are also grammatically negative.

You'll find problems with these words where sentences connect two or three negative ideas. Read through the following example sentences carefully.

> There were *neither* threats *nor* bombing campaigns.
>
> There were *no* threats *or* bombing campaigns.
>
> There were *no* threats *and no* bombing campaigns.
>
> There were *no* threats, *nor* were there bombing campaigns.

These are the most common idiomatic ways to join two negative ideas. If you can remember these patterns, you can probably eliminate many wrong answers, because they in some way violate these idiomatic patterns.

Wrong: When Walt Whitman's family moved to Brooklyn, there were no bridges nor tunnels across the East River.

The phrase *no bridges nor tunnels* is just not idiomatic—it contains a double negative. The sentence can be rewritten to correct the problem in several ways.

Correct: There were *no bridges or tunnels* across the East River.

Also Correct: There were *neither bridges nor tunnels* across the East River.

Also Correct: There were *no bridges and no tunnels* across the East River.

Another situation in which negatives can cause problems is in a series. Words like *no*, *not*, and *without* must follow the same rules as prepositions, articles, helping verbs, etc.

Wrong: After the floods in the Midwest, many farmers were left without homes, businesses, and huge bills to replace all they had lost.

When a preposition, such as *without* in this sentence, is used in front of only the first member of a series, it's taken to refer to all three members of the series. Here, that causes the sentence to say that the farmers were left without homes, without businesses, and without huge bills to replace what they had lost, which makes no sense. There are several ways to rewrite the sentence so that it makes sense.

Correct: After the floods in the Midwest, many farmers were left *without* homes, *without* businesses, and *with* huge bills to replace all they had lost.

Also Correct: After the floods in the Midwest, many farmers were left *with no* homes, *with no* businesses, and *with* huge bills to replace all they had lost.

Also Correct: After the floods in the Midwest, many farmers were left *with no* homes, *no* businesses, and huge bills to replace all they had lost.

Guide to Usage and Style

To write an effective essay, there are three things you need to do:

- Be concise.
- Be forceful.
- Be correct.

An effective essay is concise: It wastes no words. An effective essay is forceful: It makes its point. And an effective essay is correct: It conforms to the generally accepted rules of grammar and form.

The following pages break down the three broad objectives of concision, forcefulness, and correctness into 16 specific principles. Don't panic! Many of them will already be familiar to you. And, besides, you will have many chances to practice in the exercises we provide.

Principles 1 through 4 aim primarily at the first objective: concise writing; Principles 5 through 10 aim primarily at the second objective: forceful writing; and Principles 11 through 16 aim primarily at the third objective: grammatically correct writing. For a thorough understanding of the third of these objectives, though, you should consult the Grammar Reference Guide.

The principles of concise and forceful writing are generally not as rigid as the principles of grammatically correct writing. Concision and forcefulness are matters of art and personal style as well as common sense and tradition. But if you are going to disregard a principle, we hope you will do so out of educated choice.

BE CONCISE

The first four principles of good writing relate to the goal of expressing your points clearly in as few words as possible. Each principle represents a specific way to tighten up your writing.

Principle 1: Avoid Wordiness

Do not use several words when one will do. Wordy phrases are like junk food: They add only fat, not muscle. Many people make the mistake of writing phrases such as *at the present time* or *at this point in time* instead of the simpler *now*, or *take into consideration* instead of simply *consider*, in an attempt to make their prose seem more scholarly or more formal. It does not work. Instead, their prose ends up seeming inflated and pretentious. Don't waste your words or your time.

Wordy:	I am of the opinion that the aforementioned managers should be advised that they will be evaluated with regard to the utilization of responsive organizational software for the purpose of devising a responsive network of customers.
Concise:	We should tell the managers that we will evaluate their use of flexible computerized databases to develop a customer network.

Exercise 1: Wordy Phrases

Improve the following sentences by omitting or replacing wordy phrases.

1. In view of the fact that John has prepared with much care for this presentation, it would be a good idea to award him with the project.

   _____

2. The airline has a problem with always having arrivals that come at least an hour late, despite the fact that the leaders of the airline promise that promptness is a goal which has a high priority for all the employees involved.

   _____

3. In spite of the fact that she only has a little bit of experience in photography right now, she will probably do well in the future because she has a great deal of motivation to succeed in her chosen profession.

   _____

4. Accuracy is a subject that has great importance to English teachers and company presidents alike.

   _____

5. The reason why humans kill each other is that they experience fear of those whom they do not understand.

   _____

Principle 2: Don't Be Redundant

Redundancy means that the writer needlessly repeats an idea. It's redundant to speak of "a beginner lacking experience." The word *beginner* implies lack of experience by itself. You can eliminate redundant words or phrases without changing the meaning of the sentence. Watch out for words that add nothing to the sense of the sentence.

Here are some common redundancies:

Redundant	Concise
refer back	*refer*
few in number	*few*
small-sized	*small*
grouped together	*grouped*
end result	*result*

Redundancy often results from carelessness, but you can easily eliminate redundant elements when proofreading.

Exercise 2: Redundancy

Repair the following sentences by crossing out redundant elements.

1. All these problems have combined together to create a serious crisis.

2. A staff that large in size needs an effective supervisor who can get the job done.

3. He knows how to follow directions and he knows how to do what he is told.

4. The recently observed trend of spending on credit has created a middle class that is poorer and more impoverished than ever before.

5. Those who can follow directions are few in number.

Principle 3: Avoid Needless Qualification

Since the object of your essay is to convince your reader, you will want to adopt a reasonable tone. There will likely be no single, clear-cut "answer" to the essay topic, so don't overstate your case. Occasional use of such qualifiers as *fairly*, *rather*, *somewhat*, and *relatively*, and of such expressions as *seems to be*, *a little*, and *a certain amount of* will let the reader know you are reasonable, but overusing such modifiers weakens your argument. Excessive qualification makes you sound hesitant. Like wordy phrases, qualifiers can add bulk without adding substance.

Wordy: This rather serious breach of etiquette may possibly shake the very foundations of the corporate world.

Concise: This serious breach of etiquette may shake the foundations of the corporate world.

Just as bad is the overuse of the word *very*. Some writers use this intensifying adverb before almost every adjective in an attempt to be more forceful. If you need to add emphasis, look for a stronger adjective (or verb).

Weak: Novak is a very good pianist.

Strong: Novak is a virtuoso pianist.

          or

          Novak plays beautifully.

And don't try to qualify words that are already absolute.

Wrong	Correct
more unique	*unique*
the very worst	*the worst*
completely full	*full*

Exercise 3: Excessive Qualification

Practice achieving concision by eliminating needless qualification in the sentences below.

1. She is a fairly excellent teacher.

2. Ferrara seems to be sort of a slow worker.

3. You yourself are the very best person to decide what you should do for a living.

4. Needless to say, children should be taught to cooperate at home and in school.

5. The travel agent does not recommend the trip to Tripoli, since it is possible that one may be hurt.

Principle 4: Do Not Write Sentences Just to Fill Up Space

This principle suggests several things:

- Don't write a sentence that gets you nowhere.
- Don't ask a question only to answer it.
- Don't merely copy the essay's directions.
- Don't write a whole sentence only to announce that you're changing the subject.

If you have something to say, say it without preamble. If you need to smooth over a change of subject, do so with a transitional word or phrase, rather than with a meaningless sentence. If your proofreading reveals unintentional wasted sentences, neatly cross them out.

Wordy: Which idea of the author's is more in line with what I believe? This is a very interesting . . .

Concise: The author's beliefs are similar to mine.

The author of the wordy example above is just wasting words and time. Get to the point quickly and stay there. Simplicity and clarity win points.

Exercise 4: Unnecessary Sentences

Rewrite each of these multiple-sentence statements as one concise sentence.

1. What's the purpose of getting rid of the chemical pollutants in water? People cannot safely consume water that contains chemical pollutants.

    _____

2. I do not believe those who argue that some of Shakespeare's plays were written by others. There is no evidence that other people had a hand in writing Shakespeare's plays.

    _____

3. Which point of view is closest to my own? This is a good question. I agree with those who say that the United States should send soldiers to areas of conflict.

    _____

4. Frank Lloyd Wright was a famous architect. He was renowned for his ability to design buildings that blend into their surroundings.

    _____

5. A lot of people find math a difficult subject to master. They have trouble with math because it requires very precise thinking skills.

    _____

BE FORCEFUL

The next group of principles aim at the goal of producing forceful writing. If you follow these principles, your writing will be much more convincing to the reader.

Principle 5: Avoid Needless Self-Reference

Avoid such unnecessary phrases as "I believe," "I feel," and "in my opinion." There is no need to remind your reader that what you are writing is your opinion.

Weak: I am of the opinion that air pollution is a more serious problem than the government has led us to believe.

Forceful: Air pollution is a more serious problem than the government has led us to believe.

Self-reference is another form of qualifying what you say—a very obvious form. One or two self-references in an essay might be appropriate, just as the use of qualifiers like *probably* and *perhaps* can be effective if you practice using them *sparingly*. Practice is the only sure way to improve your writing.

Exercise 5: Needless Self-Reference

Eliminate needless self-references in these sentences.

1. I do not think this argument can be generalized to most business owners.

    _____

2. My own experience shows me that food is the best social lubricant.

    _____

3. Although I am no expert, I do not think privacy should be valued more than social concerns.

    _____

4. My guess is that most people want to do good work, but many are bored or frustrated with their jobs.

    _____

5. I must emphasize that I am not saying the author does not have a point.

    _____

Principle 6: Use the Active Voice

Using the passive voice is a way to avoid accountability. Put verbs in the active voice whenever possible. In the active voice, the subject performs the action (e.g., we write essays). In the passive voice, the subject is the receiver of the action and the performer of the action is often only implied (e.g., essays are written).

You should avoid the passive voice EXCEPT in the following cases:

- When you do not know who performed the action: *The letter was opened before I received it.* (For example, see the last sentence of the above paragraph.)
- When you prefer not to refer directly to the person who performs the action: *An error has been made in computing this data.*

Passive: The estimate of this year's tax revenues was prepared by the General Accounting Office.

Active: The General Accounting Office prepared the estimate of this year's tax revenues.

Exercise 6: Undesirable Passives

Replace passive voice with active wherever possible.

1. The politician's standing in the polls has been hurt by recent allegations of corruption.

    _____

2. The bill was passed in time, but it was not signed by the president until the time for action had passed.

    _____

3. Advice is usually requested by those who need it least; it is not sought out by the truly lost and ignorant.

    _____

4. The minutes of the City Council meeting should be taken by the city clerk.

    _____

5. The report was compiled by a number of field anthropologists and marriage experts.

   _____

Principle 7: Avoid Weak Openings

Try not to begin a sentence with *there is*, *there are*, or *it is*. These roundabout expressions usually indicate that you are trying to distance yourself from the position you are taking.

Exercise 7: Weak Openings

Rewrite these sentences to eliminate weak openings.

1. It would be unwise for businesses to ignore the illiteracy problem.

   _____

2. It would be of no use to fight a drug war without waging a battle against the demand for illicit substances.

   _____

3. There are many strong points in the candidate's favor; intelligence, unfortunately, is not among them.

   _____

4. It has been decided that we, as a society, can tolerate homelessness.

   _____

5. There seems to be little doubt that Americans like watching television better than conversing.

   _____

Principle 8: Avoid Needlessly Vague Language

Don't just ramble on when you're writing. Choose specific, descriptive words. Vague language weakens your writing because it forces the reader to guess what you mean instead of concentrating fully on your ideas and style. The essay topics you're given aren't going to be obscure. You will be able to come up with specific examples and concrete information about the topics. Your argument will be more forceful if you stick to this information.

Weak: Brown is highly educated.
Forceful: Brown has a master's degree in business administration.

Weak: She is a great communicator.
Forceful: She speaks persuasively.

Notice that sometimes, to be more specific and concrete, you will have to use more words than you might with vague language. This principle is not in conflict with the general objective of concision. Being concise may mean eliminating unnecessary words. Avoiding vagueness may mean adding necessary words.

Exercise 8: Needlessly Vague Language

Rewrite these sentences to replace vague language with specific, concrete language.

1. Water is transformed into steam when the former is heated up to 100° C.

    _____

2. The diplomat was required to execute an agreement that stipulated that he would live in whatever country the federal government thought necessary.

    _____

3. The principal told John that he should not even think about coming back to school until he changed his ways.

    _____

4. The police detective had to seek the permission of the lawyer to question the suspect.

    _____

5. Thousands of species of animals were destroyed when the last ice age occurred.

    _____

Principle 9: Avoid Clichés

Clichés are overused expressions, expressions that may once have seemed colorful and powerful but are now dull and worn out. Time pressure and anxiety may make you lose focus; that's when clichés may slip into your writing. A reliance on clichés will suggest you are a lazy thinker. Keep them out of your essay.

Weak: Performance in a crisis is the acid test for a leader.

Forceful: Performance in a crisis is the best indicator of a leader's abilities.

Putting a cliché in quotation marks in order to indicate your distance from the cliché does not strengthen the sentence. If anything, it just makes weak writing more noticeable. Notice whether or not you use clichés. If you do, ask yourself if you could substitute more specific language for the cliché.

Exercise 9: Clichés

Make the following sentences more forceful by replacing clichés.

1. Beyond the shadow of a doubt Jefferson was a great leader.

    _____

2. Trying to find the employee responsible for this embarrassing information leak is like trying to find a needle in a haystack.

   _____

3. The military is putting all its eggs in one basket by relying so heavily on nuclear missiles for the nation's defense.

   _____

4. Older doctors should be required to update their techniques, but you can't teach an old dog new tricks.

   _____

5. A ballpark estimate of the number of fans in the stadium would be 120,000.

   _____

Principle 10: Avoid Jargon

Jargon includes two categories of words that you should avoid. First is the specialized vocabulary of a group, such as that used by doctors, lawyers, or baseball coaches. Second is the overly inflated and complex language that burdens many students' essays. You will not impress anyone with big words that do not fit the tone or context of your essay, especially if you misuse them.

If you are not certain of a word's meaning or appropriateness, leave it out. An appropriate word, even a simple one, will add impact to your argument. As you come across words you are unsure of, ask yourself "Would a reader in a different field be able to understand exactly what I mean from the words I've chosen?" "Is there any way I can say the same thing more simply?"

Weak: The international banks are cognizant of the new law's significance.

Forceful: The international banks are aware of the new law's significance.

Wrong: The new law would negatively impact each of the nations involved.

Correct: The new law would hurt each of the nations involved. (*Impact* is also used to mean *affect* or *benefit*.)

The following are commonly used jargon words:

prioritize	*parameter*
optimize	*time frame*
utilize	*input/output*
finalize	*maximize*
designate	*facilitate*
bottom line	

Exercise 10: Jargon

Replace the jargon in the following sentences with more appropriate language.

1. We anticipate utilizing hundreds of paper clips in the foreseeable future.

    _____

2. Education-wise, our schoolchildren have been neglected.

    _____

3. Foreign diplomats should always interface with local leaders.

    _____

4. There is considerable evidentiary support for the assertion that Vienna sausages are good for you.

    _____

5. In the case of the recent railway disaster, it is clear that governmental regulatory agencies obfuscated in the preparation of materials for release to the public through both the electronic and print media.

    _____

BE CORRECT

Correctness is perhaps the most difficult objective for writers to achieve. The complex rules of standard English usage can leave you feeling unsure of your writing and more than a bit confused. But remember, the most important lesson you can take from this section is how to organize your thoughts into a strong, well-supported argument. Style and grammar are important but secondary concerns. Your readers will *not* mark you down for occasional errors common to first-draft writing. So just think of this section, together with the Grammar Reference Guide, as helping you to improve the details of good writing. If it begins to overwhelm you, stop and take a break. You need time to absorb this information.

Do the exercises and then compare your answers to ours. Make sure you understand what the error was in each sentence. Use what you learn in this section to help you proofread your practice essays; later, return to your practice essays and edit them. Better yet, ask a friend to edit them, paying special attention to correctness.

Principle 11: Avoid Slang and Colloquialisms

Slang terms and colloquialisms can be confusing to the reader, since these expressions are not universally understood. Even worse, such informal writing may give readers the impression that you are poorly educated or arrogant.

Inappropriate: He is really into gardening.
Correct: He enjoys gardening.

Inappropriate:	She plays a wicked game of tennis.
Correct:	She excels in tennis.

Inappropriate:	Myra has got to go to Memphis for a week.
Correct:	Myra must go to Memphis for a week.

Inappropriate:	Joan has been doing science for eight years now.
Correct:	Joan has been a scientist for eight years now.

With a little thought you will find the right word. Using informal language is risky. Play it safe by sticking to standard usage.

Exercise 11: Slang and Colloquialisms

Replace the informal elements of the following sentences with more appropriate terms.

1. Cynthia Larson sure knows her stuff.

   _____

2. Normal human beings can't cope with repeated humiliation.

   _____

3. If you want a good cheesecake, you must make a top-notch crust.

   _____

4. International organizations should try and cooperate on global issues like hunger.

   _____

5. The environmentalists aren't in it for the prestige; they really care about protecting the yellow-throated hornswoggler.

   _____

Principle 12: Use Commas Correctly

When using the comma, follow these rules:

A. Use commas to separate items in a series. If more than two items are listed in a series, they should be separated by commas; the final comma—the one that precedes the word *and*—is optional. Never use a comma AFTER the word *and*.

Correct:	My recipe for buttermilk biscuits contains flour, baking soda, salt, shortening, and buttermilk.
Correct:	My recipe for chocolate cake contains flour, baking soda, sugar, eggs, milk and chocolate.

B. Do not place commas before the first element of a series or after the last element.

Wrong: My investment adviser recommended that I construct a portfolio of, stocks, bonds, commodities futures, and precious metals.

Wrong: The elephants, tigers, and dancing bears, were the highlights of the circus.

C. Use commas to separate two or more adjectives before a noun; do not use a comma after the last adjective in the series.

Wrong: I can't believe you sat through that long, dull, uninspired, movie three times.

Correct: I can't believe you sat through that long, dull, uninspired movie three times.

D. Use commas to set off parenthetical clauses and phrases. (A parenthetical expression is one that is not necessary to the main idea of the sentence.)

Correct: Gordon, who is a writer by profession, bakes an excellent cheesecake.

The main idea is that Gordon bakes an excellent cheesecake. The intervening clause merely serves to identify Gordon; thus it should be set off with commas.

Correct: The newspaper that has the most insipid editorials is the *Daily Times*.

Correct: The newspaper, which has the most insipid editorials of any I have read, won numerous awards last week.

In the first of these examples the clause beginning with *that* defines which paper the author is discussing. In the second example, the main point is that the newspaper won numerous awards, and the intervening clause beginning with *which* identifies the paper.

E. Use commas after introductory participial or prepositional phrases.

Correct: Having watered his petunias every day during the drought, Harold was very disappointed when his garden was destroyed by insects.

Correct: After the banquet, Harold and Martha went dancing.

F. Use commas to separate independent clauses (clauses which could stand alone as complete sentences) connected by coordinate conjunctions such as *and*, *but*, *not*, *yet*, etc.

Correct: Susan's old car has been belching blue smoke from the tailpipe for two weeks, but it has not broken down yet.

Note: Make sure the comma separates two *independent* clauses, joined by a conjunction. It is incorrect to use a comma to separate the two parts of a compound verb.

Wrong: Barbara went to the grocery store, and bought two quarts of milk.

Exercise 12: Commas

Correct the punctuation errors in the following sentences.

1. It takes a friendly energetic person to be a successful salesman.

2. I was shocked to discover that a large, modern, glass-sheathed, office building had replaced my old school.

3. The country club, a cluster of ivy-covered whitewashed buildings was the site of the president's first speech.

4. Pushing through the panicked crowd the security guards frantically searched for the suspect.

5. Despite careful analysis of the advantages and disadvantages of each proposal Harry found it hard to reach a decision.

Principle 13: Use Semicolons Correctly

When using a semicolon, follow these rules:

A. Use a semicolon *instead of* a coordinate conjunction such as *and*, *or*, or *but* to link two closely related independent clauses.

Wrong:	Whooping cranes are an endangered species; and they are unlikely to survive if we continue to pollute.
Correct:	Whooping cranes are an endangered species; there are only fifty whooping cranes in New Jersey today.
Correct:	Whooping cranes are an endangered species, and they are unlikely to survive if we continue to pollute.

B. Use a semicolon between independent clauses connected by words like *therefore*, *nevertheless*, and *moreover*.

Correct:	Farm prices have been falling rapidly for two years; nevertheless, the traditional American farm is not in danger of disappearing.

Exercise 13: Semicolons

Correct the punctuation errors in the following sentences.

1. Morgan has five years' experience in karate; but Thompson has even more.

   _____

2. Very few students wanted to take the class in physics, only the professor's kindness kept it from being canceled.

   _____

3. You should always be prepared when you go on a camping trip, however you must avoid carrying unnecessary weight.

   _____

Principle 14: Use Colons Correctly

When using a colon, follow these rules:

A. In formal writing the colon is used only as a means of signaling that what follows is a list, definition, explanation, or concise summary of what has gone before. The colon usually follows an independent clause, and it will frequently be accompanied by a reinforcing expression like *the following*, *as follows*, or *namely*, or by an explicit demonstrative like *this*.

Correct: Your instructions are as follows: read the passage carefully, answer the questions on the last page, and turn over your answer sheet.

Correct: This is what I found in the refrigerator: a moldy lime, half a bottle of stale soda, and a jar of peanut butter.

Correct: The biggest problem with America today is apathy: the corrosive element that will destroy our democracy.

B. Be careful not to put a colon between a verb and its direct object.

Wrong: I want: a slice of pizza and a small green salad.

Correct: This is what I want: a slice of pizza and a small green salad. (The colon serves to announce that a list is forthcoming.)

Correct: I don't want much for lunch: just a slice of pizza and a small green salad. (Here what follows the colon defines what "don't want much" means.)

C. Context will occasionally make clear that a second independent clause is closely linked to its predecessor, even without an explicit expression like those used above. Here, too, a colon is appropriate, although a period will always be correct also.

Correct: We were aghast: the "charming country inn" that had been advertised in such glowing terms proved to be a leaking cabin full of mosquitoes.

Correct: We were aghast. The "charming country inn" that had been advertised in such glowing terms proved to be a leaking cabin full of mosquitoes.

Exercise 14: Colons

Edit these sentences so they use colons correctly.

1. I am sick and tired of: your whining, your complaining, your nagging, your teasing, and, most of all, your barbed comments.

    _____

2. The chef has created a masterpiece, the pasta is delicate yet firm, the mustard greens are fresh, and the medallions of veal are melting in my mouth.

    _____

3. In order to write a good essay, you must: practice, get plenty of sleep, and eat a good breakfast.

    _____

Principle 15: Use Hyphens and Dashes Correctly

When using a hyphen or a dash, follow these rules:

A. Use the hyphen with the compound numbers twenty-one through ninety-nine, and with fractions used as adjectives.

Correct:	Sixty-five students constituted a majority.
Correct:	A two-thirds vote was necessary to carry the measure.
Wrong:	Only two-thirds of the students passed the final exam.

B. Use the hyphen with the prefixes *ex*, *all*, and *self* and with the suffix *elect*.

Correct:	The constitution protects against self-incrimination.
Correct:	The president-elect was invited to chair the meeting.

C. Use the hyphen with a compound adjective when it comes before the word it modifies, but not when it comes after the word it modifies.

Correct:	The no-holds-barred argument continued into the night.
Correct:	The argument continued with no holds barred.

D. Use the hyphen with any prefix used before a proper noun or adjective.

Correct:	They believed that his activities were un-American.

E. Use a hyphen to separate component parts of a word in order to avoid confusion with other words or to avoid the use of a double vowel.

Correct:	The sculptor was able to re-form the clay after the dog knocked over the bust.
Correct:	They had to be re-introduced, since it had been so long since they last met.

F. Use the dash to indicate an abrupt change of thought. In general, however, formal writing is best when you think out what you want to say in advance and avoid abrupt changes of thought.

Correct:	To get a high score—and who doesn't want to get a high score?—you need to devote yourself to prolonged and concentrated study.

Exercise 15: Hyphens and Dashes

Edit these sentences so they use hyphens and dashes correctly.

1. The child was able to count from one to ninety nine.

2. The adults only movie was banned from commercial TV.

3. It was the first time she had seen a movie that was for adults-only.

4. A two thirds majority would be needed to pass the budget reforms.

5. The house, and it was the most dilapidated house that I had ever seen was a bargain because the land was so valuable.

Principle 16: Use the Apostrophe Correctly

When using an apostrophe, follow these rules:

A. Use the apostrophe with contracted forms of verbs to indicate that one or more letters have been eliminated in writing.

Full Forms:

you are	*it is*	*you have*	*the boy is*
Harry has	*we would*	*was not*	

Contracted:

you're	*it's*	*you've*	*the boy's*
Harry's	*we'd*	*wasn't*	

One of the most common errors involving use of the apostrophe is using it in the contraction *you're* or *it's* to indicate the possessive form of *you* or *it*. When you write *you're*, ask yourself whether you mean *you are*. If not, the correct word is *your*. Similarly, are you sure you mean *it is*? If not, use the possessive form *its*. You spell *his* or *hers* without an apostrophe, so you should spell *its* without an apostrophe.

Incorrect: You're chest of drawers is ugly.

Incorrect: The dog hurt it's paw.

Correct: Your chest of drawers is ugly.

Correct: The dog hurt its paw.

B. Use the apostrophe to indicate the possessive form of a noun.

Not Possessive:

the boy	*Harry*	*the children*	*the boys*

Possessive Form:

the boy's	*Harry's*	*the children's*	*the boys'*

Correct: Ms. Fox's office is on the first floor. (One person possesses the office.)

Correct: The Foxes' apartment has a wonderful view. (There are several people named Fox living in the same apartment. First you must form the plural, then add the apostrophe to indicate possession.)

C. The apostrophe is used to indicate possession only with nouns; in the case of pronouns there are separate possessives for each person and number.

my, mine	*our, ours*
your, yours	*your, yours*
his, his	*their, theirs*
her, hers	
its its	

The exception is the neutral "one," which forms its possessive by adding an apostrophe and an *s*.

Exercise 16: Apostrophes

Edit these sentences so they use apostrophes correctly.

1. The presidents limousine had a flat tire.
2. You're tickets for the show will be at the box office.
3. The opportunity to change ones lifestyle does not come often.
4. The desks' surface was immaculate, but it's drawers were messy.
5. The cat on the bed is hers'.

Answers to Exercises

Answers to Exercise 1: Wordy Phrases

1. Since John has prepared for this presentation so carefully, we should award him the project.
2. Flights are always at least an hour late on this airline, though its leaders promise that promptness is a high priority for all its employees.
3. Although she is inexperienced in photography, she will probably succeed because she is motivated.
4. Accuracy is important to English teachers and company presidents alike.
5. Humans kill each other because they fear those whom they do not understand.

Answers to Exercise 2: Redundancy

1. All these problems have combined to create a crisis.
2. A staff that large needs an effective supervisor.
3. He knows how to follow directions.
4. The recent trend of spending on credit has created a poorer middle class.
5. Few people can follow directions.

Answers to Exercise 3: Excessive Qualification

1. She is a good teacher.
2. Ferrara is a slow worker.
3. You are the best person to decide what you should do for a living.
4. Children should be taught to cooperate at home and in school. (If there's no need to say it, don't!)
5. The travel agent said not to go to Tripoli, since one may be hurt. (Saying *it is possible that one may be hurt* is an example of redundant qualification, since both *possible* and *may* indicate uncertainty.)

Answers to Exercise 4: Unnecessary Sentences

1. People cannot safely consume water that contains chemical pollutants.
2. No present evidence suggests that Shakespeare's plays were written by others.
3. The United States should send soldiers to areas of conflict.
4. The architect Frank Lloyd Wright was famous for his ability to design buildings that blend into their surroundings.
5. A lot of people find math a difficult subject because it requires very precise thinking skills.

Answers to Exercise 5: Needless Self-Reference

1. This argument cannot be generalized to most business owners.
2. Food is the best social lubricant.
3. Privacy should not be valued more than social concerns.
4. Most people want to do good work, but many are bored or frustrated with their jobs.
5. The author has a point.

Answers to Exercise 6: Undesirable Passives

1. Recent allegations of corruption have hurt the politician's standing in the polls.
2. Congress passed the bill in time, but the president did not sign it until the time for action had passed.
3. Those who need advice least usually request it; the truly lost and ignorant do not seek it.
4. The city clerk should take the minutes of the City Council meeting.
5. A number of field anthropologists and marriage experts compiled the report.

Answers to Exercise 7: Weak Openings

1. Businesses ignore the illiteracy problem at their own peril.
2. The government cannot fight a drug war effectively without waging a battle against demand for illicit substances.
3. The candidate has many strong points; intelligence, unfortunately, is not among them.
4. We, as a society, have decided to tolerate homelessness.
5. Americans must like watching television better than conversing.

Answers to Exercise 8: Needlessly Vague Language

1. When water is heated to 100° C, it turns into steam.
2. The diplomat had to agree to live wherever the government sent him.
3. The principal told John not to return to school until he was ready to behave.
4. The police detective had to ask the lawyer for permission to question the suspect.
5. The last ice age destroyed thousands of animal species.

Answers to Exercise 9: Clichés

1. Jefferson was a great leader.
2. Trying to find the employee responsible for this embarrassing information leak may be impossible.
3. The military should diversify its defense rather than rely so heavily on nuclear missiles.
4. Older doctors should be required to update their techniques, but many seem resistant to changes in technology.
5. I estimate that 120,000 fans were in the stadium. (Even when a cliché is used in its original context, it sounds old.)

Answers to Exercise 10: Jargon

1. We expect to use hundreds of paper clips in the next two months.
2. Our schoolchildren's education has been neglected.
3. Foreign diplomats should always talk to local leaders.
4. Recent studies suggest that Vienna sausages are good for you.
5. Government regulatory agencies lied in their press releases about the recent railway accident.

Answers to Exercise 11: Slang and Colloquialisms

1. Cynthia Larson is an expert.
2. Normal human beings cannot tolerate repeated humiliation.
3. If you want a good cheesecake, you must make a superb crust.
4. International organizations should try to cooperate on global issues like hunger.
5. The environmentalists are not involved in the project for prestige; they truly care about protecting the yellow-throated hornswoggler.

Answers for Exercise 12: Commas

1. It takes a friendly, energetic person to be a successful salesman.
2. I was shocked to discover that a large, modern, glass-sheathed office building had replaced my old school.
3. The country club, a cluster of ivy-covered whitewashed buildings, was the site of the president's first speech.
4. Pushing through the panicked crowd, the security guards frantically searched for the suspect.
5. Despite careful analysis of the advantages and disadvantages of each proposal, Harry found it hard to reach a decision.

Answers for Exercise 13: Semicolons

1. Morgan has five years' experience in karate; Thompson has even more.
2. Very few students wanted to take the class in physics; only the professor's kindness kept it from being canceled.
3. You should always be prepared when you go on a camping trip; however, you must avoid carrying unnecessary weight.

Answers to Exercise 14: Colons

1. I am sick and tired of your whining, your complaining, your nagging, your teasing, and, most of all, your barbed comments.
2. The chef has created a masterpiece: the pasta is delicate yet firm, the mustard greens are fresh, and the medallions of veal are melting in my mouth.
3. In order to write a good essay, you must do the following: practice, get plenty of sleep, and eat a good breakfast.

Answers to Exercise 15: Hyphens and Dashes

1. The child was able to count from one to ninety-nine.
2. The adults-only movie was banned from commercial TV.
3. It was the first time she had seen a movie that was for adults only.
4. A two-thirds majority would be needed to pass the budget reforms.
5. The house—and it was the most dilapidated house that I had ever seen—was a bargain because the land was so valuable.

Answers to Exercise 16: Apostrophes

1. The president's limousine had a flat tire.
2. Your tickets for the show will be at the box office.
3. The opportunity to change one's lifestyle does not come often.
4. The desk's surface was immaculate, but its drawers were messy.
5. The cat on the bed is hers.